Dear Friends—

Thanks for sharing your decade with me!

Larry Knight

the best of
Larry
King

The
Greatest
Interviews

Live

Turner Publishing, Inc.

ATLANTA

Library of Congress Cataloging-in-Publication Data
King, Larry, 1933–
The best of Larry King live: the greatest interviews/selected by Larry King.
—1st ed.
p. cm.
ISBN 1-57036-208-4
1. Celebrities—Interviews. 2. Biography—20th century.
I. Title.
CT120.K56   1995
920'.0609'04—dc20   95-22
                                 CIP

Editor's Note:
While the printed page lends permanence to the spoken word, no book can hope to capture all of the emotional intensity of great conversation. However, the editor of this volume has tried to do just that: to convey the immediacy, emotion, and intellectual acuity of truly revealing talk. Accordingly, the interviews that follow are presented in a form that resembles dramatic dialogue more than verbatim, courtroom-style transcription, and editorial comment, emendation, and condensation, while exercised when absolutely necessary for clarity, have been kept to a minimum.

Published by Turner Publishing, Inc.
A Subsidiary of Turner Broadcasting System, Inc.
1050 Techwood Drive, N.W.
Atlanta, Georgia 30318

Distributed by Andrews and McMeel
A Universal Press Syndicate Company
4900 Main Street
Kansas City, Missouri 64112

First Edition
10 9 8 7 6 5 4 3 2 1

Printed in the U.S.A.

contents

foreword

I have to say that this kid from Brooklyn is very proud of this book. Over the past ten years, as host of Larry King Live, I have interviewed some of the most fascinating and noteworthy personalities of this century. From political leaders Richard Nixon, Barbara Bush, Ross Perot, Mikhail Gorbachev, Yasir Arafat, and Bill Clinton, to entertainment and sports legends Frank Sinatra, Arthur Ashe, Barbra Streisand, Mike Tyson, and Marlon Brando, *Larry King Live* has a lot of great interviews to celebrate! What a decade it has been! Every year I say to myself, "That's it, kid! It can't get any better than this!" and then ... surprise! I get a call from Al Gore wanting to debate Ross Perot on NAFTA, and then the next thing I know, Marlon Brando is kissing me on worldwide television! It never stops. It's great fun! I must have the best job in the world.

If I had to pinpoint exactly when *Larry King Live* started to turn millions of heads and make major headlines, it would have to be during the dizzying 1992 presidential campaign. It was in February of '92 on *Larry King Live* that Ross Perot launched his insurgent candidacy, incumbent President George Bush agreed to become the first chief executive since 1977 to field live viewer calls, and Vice President Dan Quayle made headlines when he told me he'd support his daughter's hypothetical decision to have an abortion. News was breaking into my microphone like you wouldn't believe, and the viewers were gathering around their sets in droves, the calls just pouring in. It was a snowball effect. The hotter the race got, the hotter the show became. Voters were screaming to play a bigger role in the 1992 election process, and many were tuning into *Larry King Live* to get unfiltered access to the candidates and the issues. Not only did we present an unmatched troika of live ninety-minute specials with Bill Clinton, Ross Perot, and George Bush, we had open lines to America and the world for voters to call in with their questions and concerns. I really felt like our show was helping people make better-informed decisions on election day. I felt smack in the middle of history in the making, and, boy, was it a great feeling!

One of my most memorable nights over the past ten years was in November 1993. The historic NAFTA debate on *Larry King Live* was by far one of the year's most discussed political events. Until this event, no elected official of the Vice President's stature had ever engaged a private citizen in such a televised debate on a question of public policy. Vice President Al Gore and Ross Perot's classic repartee and heated exchanges not only rendered the nation spellbound, but set record ratings in the cable industry. Eleven million Americans tuned in to watch, plus untold numbers around the world: 2.2 million callers attempted to dial in. What a night!

As significant as the *Larry King Live* NAFTA debate was, it was but one of many exclusive television events that unfolded live on our show, some of which are a part of this book. The week preceding the debate, for example, featured such gripping exclusives as the first-ever interview with Michael Durant, the young helicopter pilot held hostage in Somalia; a one-hour special with Hillary Clinton on the Whitewater controversy; a live remote with Michael Jordan from his Chicago restaurant; Margaret Thatcher live from our Washington studios; and a full hour with Mikhail Gorbachev on the demise of communist regimes. Gorbachev! Live on my set! Sometimes I just have to pinch myself.

As *Larry King Live* celebrates its tenth anniversary, I promise to continue offering our viewers the most direct and exclusive access to the nation's most important policy debates, intriguing celebrities, and political leaders. Whether it's Clinton, Oprah, Brando, Tyson, or Streisand, I guarantee you it's never dull!

Every day is a little miracle for me. And there are a thousand people I could thank for this, starting with Ted Turner, who created the network that had the foresight to hire me in the first place. (Just kidding!) Tom Johnson, president of CNN—the best people person I've ever worked for! My incredibly talented senior executive producer and close friend Wendy Walker Whitworth, and her very competent and wonderful staff: Mary Gregory, Peter Tedeschi, Ellen Beard, Korey Dorsey, Katie Thomson, Linda Wolf, Lisa Durham, Kyle Kaino, Brit Kahn, Tom Mazzarelli, and Tom Hanes. A special thanks to Carrie Stevenson, who acted as special producer for my tenth anniversary, and last, but not least, to my great public relations director, Maggie Simpson.

But most importantly, I want to thank all of you—my viewers—for faithfully tuning in every night. Whether you are a long-time viewer or have just recently discovered my show, I must say that the one hour I spend with you every evening is the hour I look forward to most. At 9 PM eastern standard time, I sit down on my set, I hook my microphone onto my suspenders, and I am happy. I am home. Thank you for being there every night. I can only hope that you're having as much fun as I am!

Yours faithfully,
The Kid from Brooklyn

the best of Larry King Live

Bob Hope

Leslie Townes Hope, one of the funniest men in America, was born in England on May 23, 1903, the fifth of seven children in a struggling stonemason's family. After the family moved to America, Hope changed his name to Bob, went to Douglas Fairbanks movies, and plunged into vaudeville. In 1938 he was given his own radio show, which rocketed to number-one within a year.

Following the attack on Pearl Harbor, Hope launched tours to entertain troops all over the world. He did the same during the Korean and Vietnam wars, and during the Cold War years.

Hope's genial rivalry with Bing Crosby resulted in a series of "Road Pictures," which proved to be box office successes. Although his popularity faded somewhat during the liberal 1960s, Hope has endured as a master of the one-liner and as a cultural icon.

"Laughs.

Laughs.

That's all

I want."

LARRY KING: Our first guest tonight is an American legend in his own time, author of one of the hottest books on the bestseller list today, *Confessions of a Hooker*, from Doubleday. He is the one and only Bob Hope. The subtitle is: *My Lifelong Love Affair with Golf*. Is this your best seller ever?

BOB HOPE: No. I had two of them. I had one called *I Never Left Home* in 1944. Then I had another one about 1960, *I Owe Russia $1200*. This is my third one.

LK: But *this* one looks like it's gonna be bigger than both of them.

BH: Yeah, I hope so. I hope so.

LK: I remember both of those books, but *this* one keeps climbing. . . . Did you title it?

BH: Yeah. Yeah, I titled it. Sure. We've been playing with that thing for years, you know—that title, 'cause I remember telling . . . doing the joke about the guy that went to Vegas and met this beautiful gal and had a few drinks and got married the same afternoon. Woke up in the morning and said, "Honey, I have a little surprise for you. You won't see me much of the day because I'm a golfer. I play golf all day." And she said, "Well, I have a little surprise for you. I'm a hooker." And he said, "Well, that's nothin'. You just take your right hand, and you put it over a little bit, like that." [*He adjusts his hands on an imaginary golf club.*]

LK: [*laughs*] So funny! . . . Do you like that aspect, writing books?

BH: I think so. If I had *time*. But Doubleday has been after me for seven or eight *years* to do this book, and I never found time to do it. And I finally got ahold of Duane Netland with *Golf Life*, and we ran around with each other for a year—all over the place. Every place I'd be with a personal appearance—he'd fly in, and we'd work for a few hours and tape and—so on and so on and so on and so—and then play a little golf, and then he'd meet me again in St. Louis for two or three days when I was there. We finally got it together.

LK: Not many men could get a former president to write a foreword for their book. Gerald Ford writes the foreword for this. . . . Is he as bad a golfer as you kid him to be?

BH: He's the best golfer among the presidents. Really.

LK: Is that, uh—does that say a *lot* or a little?

BH: Well, it says a lot, but he has his moments like all of us do, you know. We would all be great if we could hit every shot like we like, but every once in a while he loses concentration and sails one into the gallery and thins out the gallery a little bit, you know?

LK: We have talked a lot, but never in this vein. What is your—and it's in the title *My Lifelong Love Affair*—what is your fascination for a game in which guys go out and girls go out, and they take little sticks, and they hit a little white ball that falls in the lake or falls on the sand? What is it? What is that?

BH: I'll tell you what it is—it's a *challenge*. Outside of the health aspect of it, it's the challenge of it, because you're playing yourself. You're the dummy. You're the dummy or the champ, and you get a kick out of it. You go out and play a pretty good round like— I was a four handicap when I was at my *best*, and see, now today I'm an eighteen, you know? And I'm still out there fighting, trying to knock a score out around the high eighties or the low eighties. If I, if I shoot a low eighty, I order like that [*he snaps his fingers*]—California champagne.

LK: [*laughs*] Well, what's the difference, say, between golf and shooting pool? I mean, why golf? Why is that so *consuming* a game?

BH: Well, it's just the game that is, is *played*. You know, it's *hard* to play baseball. You have to get a group together. But you can go over and practice a little while and meet a guy at the club and say, "Hey, wanna play a few holes?" You know?

LK: Jackie Gleason, who you write about a lot in this, says that it's also the great leveler. I mean, if you have an ego, golf will reduce it.

BH: Oh boy! That'll do it. That'll do it. And Jack is something. You know, he putts with a swizzle stick, so he, uh, he—[*both laugh*] I played a lot of golf with Jack.

LK: Tell me about the eyes. I know you're very involved in eye research, and in—lots of people involved with this problem that you had, which seems to me to look terrific now. You look great, by the way.

BH: Well, I was very lucky. You know I had four operations on my *left* eye, which I lost a little sight in, and then I had trouble just about two years ago, and I thought maybe I'd have to have another operation on my right eye, but *luckily* I went to the New York Hospital, and they ducked that. So, I was very grateful, and I got to be very careful with it now. That's another thing about it, you know? Golf *cools* you out. When you get out there, you forget about all your troubles—you're just playin' that little ball. . . .

LK: You're raising money now for eye research. . . . Did you ever fear losing your sight?

BH: Oh boy, did I! I should say so. I was very—semi-hysterical when I was in there in New York Hospital, because if I had lost sight in my right eye, I wouldn't have been able to *read*, you know? And, uh, that was quite a problem.

LK: You're gonna be what? Eighty-two?

BH: Yup. Uh, I *am* eighty-two.

LK: You are the *picture* of health. I mean, someone would turn on the camera right now and look close at you. . . . You look in your—late sixties. You look—somewhere—sixty-five, sixty-six—

BH: Well, you know, it's in my make-up, you know. And I stop at Earl Scheib and—

LK: [*laughs*] You get painted?

BH: —and stop over to Forest Lawn, get my cheeks stuffed, you know. I do a lot of tricks.

LK: Have you ever had a face lift?

BH: [*laughs*] God no! Are you kidding? If I had a face lift, would I be stuck with this? [*turns profile*]

LK: [*laughs*] Were you a health nut? How do you account for longevity?

BH: Exercise and careful with your diet, and I walk every night—walk a mile and a half, two miles every night.

LK: Yeah, but you fly a lot, you work a lot . . . You continue to work, and you never—

BH: And I enjoy it. I enjoy it. I wouldn't be doing *this* if I didn't enjoy it.

LK: So it's no strain, then.

BH: That's right! No strain. No stomach problem. This is my *third* show today, you know, and it's a pleasure. You do it. That's my racket.

LK: What about longevity in the family? Did your father live a long time?

BH: My grandfather lived until one month short of a hundred—my grandfather in England.

LK: Do you have a goal—a life-living goal?

BH: Yeah. I want to live within a week of it. I want to top him a little bit.

LK: Go past it. [*laughs*] You never think about quitting, do you?

BH: No way! No way. Not when I feel good. My god!

LK: Is there something in the air here? We've got you. We've got George Burns—way past you. You're a kid compared to Burns.

BH: Burns is eighty-nine years old.

LK: And how do you explain him?

BH: Because he enjoys it. We have a lot of talks about it. He's one of my *dear* friends, because I was in a picture with him in 1938 and knew him in vaudeville long before that. But he didn't make another picture from '38 till '78. He won the Oscar for *Sunshine Boys*, and he's been *steaming* ever since. And I watch him walk out—I've done many of his shows—he walks out and does a monologue, and after two laughs, he grows a foot, you know?

LK: But he smokes a lot of cigars.

BH: Doesn't inhale. That's a prop. That cigar is a prop.

LK: Okay. Is he like you? Does he exercise? Does he walk?

BH: He is very careful. He takes a two-hour nap every afternoon. Gets up in the morning, then he takes a two-hour nap in the afternoon. That's pretty good, you know. It keeps you safe.

LK: And both of you do a lot. I mean, you do commercials. You do benefits. You do shows. George does record albums.

BH: [*laughs*] He does anything. He had me over to the house last year. He had me— trying to interest me in doing a country song. You see, he knew two guys in Nashville that needed to come see me. He said, "Yeah I can get you a couple of country songs, you know? . . ." I said, "George, I don't need it. I got enough stuff to do."

LK: Why don't you work together? That'd be great.

BH: I want to do a road picture with him, but we could never get a script. *His timing is beautiful.* I love him. . . . We've worked together. He's been on my show many times, and I've worked his show many times.

LK: How many specials do you do a year now?

BH: I do six. . . . This is my thirty-sixth year I'm going into now.

LK: Now, you asked me, just while the commercial was on, how old I am, and I told you I was fifty-one, and you said, "Boy." Like, I'm a *boy* to you?

BH: Yeah. You're a boy. You gotta get some clubs. I'd like to sell you some golf clubs. I've got some old Tony Peña specials I could whip you over. . . .

LK: Do you resent when people write about how rich you are?

BH: No. Not at all. Because, you know, half of it is *garbage.* . . . They, uh, they come out—*Forbes*—I had a big, big fight with *Forbes* about coming out and saying how old—how rich I was, because they didn't know. And they sent a man out. They took me off the list, you know. I was one of the fifteen most wealthy men—or something, and—in the country. And I said, "Come out and look at that. How *dare* you put that in?" Do you know that when I was in Vietnam in 1970 or something, they—*Time* magazine came out and said I was worth *five hundred million dollars?* . . . You know how they found that out? They asked a guy backstage at NBC who sort of a— just got—knocked off a bottle of wine or something. They said, "What do you think Hope is worth?" He said, "Oh, about half a billion dollars." And they put it in the magazine—*Time* magazine! You wouldn't think that would happen with *Time* magazine. . . . So I wired the editor. I said, "If you can find it, I'll split it with you."

LK: The *Wall Street Journal* said you were the richest show business person. As a person who's been salaried and employed all your life, you're the richest.

BH: [*frowns*] Yeah.

LK: Why do you get angry? Why bother with it? Why call *Time?* Why call *Forbes?*

BH: Well, you can't. Because the next, you know, Greyhound Bus pulls up to the house with nineteen relatives. They eat the hedges. They try to get in the house, you know. And I beat 'em back.

LK: Money was never your driving force, you told me once, though.

BH: No, not really. Not really. . . . No. Laughs. Laughs. That's all I want.

LK: Is it still? Is it like a need, Bob? . . . I mean, do you have a—? All right, you don't have a *need* for money. Do you still have a need to make people laugh?

BH: Sure. Sure I do. I like to entertain. Sure I do. That's my business, you know? As long as I *feel* good, I want to do that, because it makes *me* feel good.

LK: Right. So you're doing it for you?

BH: That's right.

LK: Is going on stage just another night to you?

BH: No.

LK: Sinatra told me recently that it's still a kick to walk on stage, take a microphone and entertain people.

BH: Oh sure! Sure he does. And George Burns. I told you. It's the same way. Anybody that's been in the business that long, they appreciate, you know. And try to better yourself. I've been working all week because I'm starting a tour now, Friday, and I just . . . I just want to *change* my whole act because I'm going back to a lot of places, and I want to get all the new stuff, you know, about Reagan's operation and the different things—and Rambo and Madonna.

LK: It's gotta be current. You're always current. . . . How many writers do you use?

BH: Well. When I'm off season, I have like three writers. In season, I have about six or seven.

LK: And they come to you with material, right? And you're the selection process.

BH: That's right. That's right.

LK: Any of it your own?

BH: Oh sure. You use it. Sure. And, you know, things fall naturally that you ad lib.

LK: What are you gonna do? You're gonna work one week at one city, one week in another. You gonna do the whole thing?

BH: No. No. No. I'm working, you know, one-nighters. I start in Ohio and go to Mansfield and Cincinnati. Then I go up to play in Sammy Davis's thing and do his show the next day, and then I go to New York and do a show. Then I come out, jump out to Denver and do another show. And then I jump back to Louisville and do another show.

LK: [*Puts his hands up, as though shocked.*] Why?! I mean, I know you like it, but most eighty-two-year-old guys, despite . . . Eighty-two-year-old lawyers aren't going into court every day.

BH: That's right. That's right. Well, I don't blame 'em. . . . But if they got laughs, they might go in.

LK: It's a love affair with the laugh.

BH: Let me give you just a hint. I don't want to drag that thing out, but I feel better when I walk *off* the stage than I did when I walked on. Why is that? It's because it starts all your mechanism working, your brain and everything, your blood and everything. And I . . . I know people that way. I saw Jack Benny when, oh about ten years ago at the Ziegfeld theater. Did a show there, you know. And I tell you, he came out there, and he *knocked* that audience out. And I went backstage. I said, "You love that, don't you?" [*Smiles and winks*] He said, "You know it!" You know it!

LK: Do you know it's funny before you say it?

BH: Well, you got a better idea than anybody else.

LK: It made *you* laugh.

BH: Yeah. Because you know from experience. You know what's pretty funny. . . . I mean, that's the whole thing. If you don't know what's funny, you better not be in the business.

LK: Can it be that what works in Toledo might not work in New York?

BH: No. No. It works everywhere. Everywhere they have television. Everywhere they know about the news. It plays everywhere. . . . It's a mass audience. . . . There used to be hick towns where they didn't have anything. Today, they all see the same thing. They all see the same news. They all know what's going on. They all know Rambo. They know so and so. They know Madonna with her nude pictures. They know so and so and so and so. And every happening. They know what's going on—the tax thing, the tax reform, the da-ta-dum . . . I don't care whether it's Toledo or Podunk or anywhere. That's the audience today.

LK: What edge does Bob Hope have because he's Bob Hope?

BH: Well, it's just familiarity—

LK: Am I gonna laugh because I know it's you?

BH: No. But they know your record and familiarity. And they laugh when you walk on. It used to be, when you played vaudeville, acts could go twenty-five years. Jack Benny did the same act. George Burns and Allen did "lamb chops" for *twenty-five* years without changing a line on the Orpheum circuit. And when they would come, people would say "Let's go and see them." They loved them. And they'd just sit there. Knowing the act! And to watch them do it, and laugh at every . . . every line. You know? That's . . . That's the secret of it. Because they liked those people for what they did.

LK: How about public figures? . . . How many presidents have you known?

BH: Oh, about nine. Crosby said I knew Lincoln, but you know how he lied.

LK: [*laughs*] Reagan. Have you known him pretty well? Did you know him out here? [meaning in Los Angeles, before he became president]

BH: Oh sure. . . . I've known him from the time he was governor. . . .

LK: Are you surprised at his strength out of this thing?

BH: No. I'm just amazed at his showmanship and everything else—the way he's developed. I think that this man has shown something to the political scene that's unbelievable—the showmanship that he's used, you know, and the way he's handled things. It's just marvelous that the economy, for the first term, the way he turned it around, you know?

LK: You're a big supporter.

BH: Well. I think I'm like any other American. Look at the *landslide* he had.

LK: But you have to stay friends with *all* presidents. For example, if you'd supported Reagan—and people generally knew you did—and Mondale had won, you're still going to be at the White House. You're going to be entertaining. You managed to keep friends on both sides of the aisle.

BH: Yeah. Yeah. Because I don't . . . I try to level when I do a monologue. I never try to be one-sided about it. I'll pick on the president more than I'll pick on anybody else.

LK: You can make a joke of the cancer thing, too? [This is a reference to President Reagan's recent skin cancer operation.]

BH: Ah ha ha. Pretty tough . . . pretty tough. . . . But you *can* talk about him being in there, you know?

LK: Do hospital stuff.

BH: And about how Bush, you know, acted as president for quite a while. He took a nap.

LK: Now, what do you do? [*snaps fingers*] Give me a Rambo line.

BH: Rambo? Well. Did you see him? In the picture?

LK: Stallone.

BH: Clint Eastwood—he made him look like a nun.

LK: [*laughs*] That's good stuff. You're gonna get laughs. This is gonna be a big tour for you. Couple of other things I want to cover—we got about three minutes left. Were you angry—I sensed you were—during the time of the Vietnam War when people rapped you for going there and doing television shows?

BH: No. I wasn't angry. I was just as angry at the way some of the people were handling it, you know? You see, the media . . . the media has to be provocative. You know that. . . . They *have* to be. They *have* to be provocative. They can't report all sweet news and everything. And they were saying in the front pages . . . they were saying "Get out of Vietnam. Get out of Vietnam." You know? On the front pages! Kids were going, and they were defecting to Canada. You know? And you noticed that they pardoned all those kids afterwards. When it finally got around to the thing . . . If the politicians had stayed out of that thing . . . if they had given that to the military, we would have saved three million lives. . . . Three *million* lives! And about fifty thousand of our kids and, maybe, another two hundred thousand casualties.

LK: Do you feel better now that the Vietnam veteran is getting a better deal?

BH: Oh yeah. You have to, Larry. You have to because nobody . . . You know, they went over there because they were . . . They were sent over there. You know? And that was a dirty . . . that was a dirty war.

LK: Have you been to the Memorial?

BH: Yeah. It's really something.

LK: How did you feel about [being honored at the] Kennedy Center?

BH: I like it. I like it. It's a nice thing.

LK: [*laughs*] Nice thing?

BH: Breaks up the year.

LK: [*laughs*] You've gotten everything a country can give you.

BH: Well, I've been pretty lucky.

LK: You were born in Great Britain, though. . . . Is there ever that tinge of loyalty to the Crown—the place of your birth?

BH: Yeah. Yeah. Sure. Sure. Sure.

LK: I mean, sometimes you think it. You are a Britisher.

BH: My first command performance was to leave.

LK: [*laughs*] You're glad you didn't grow up there?

BH: [*chuckles*] That's right.

LK: A couple of other quick things. How good a boxer would you have been if you'd stayed with boxing?

BH: I was known as Rembrandt Hope. I was on the canvas so much! . . . And I would have won the last fight, but the referee stepped on my hand.

LK: [*laughs*] Were you good? No, seriously. Were you good?

BH: Fair. Fair. Fair. In my last fight, a guy hit me so hard I bounced right into dancing school. . . . Didn't miss a beat.

LK: Your big start was Broadway, right? . . . You did a show, and that brought you out here [to Los Angeles and Hollywood]. Did you ever go back and do theater again?

BH: No! No. I have been asked to do theater quite a bit.

LK: Why not? When you worked so . . . Why not . . . ?

BH: Because why? Why? When you're doing television and you're doing . . . out here you're doing the things you want to do? What for? You know? I mean, my god, we get a chance to do different things all the time. And I *love* theater. I love the stage. But they've asked me to do a lot of different shows, and I've said, "No way." I wouldn't be interested.

LK: You're totally at ease with yourself, aren't you?

BH: I guess. When I'm awake.

LK: [*laughs and stomps his foot*] You're happy, though. You're a happy person.

BH: Well . . . well . . . well, what else?

LK: "When I'm awake!" Fame—one other thing—last question. Everybody knows you. Not many people can say that, that they can walk down the street, and *everybody* knows that face.

BH: Yeah. It doesn't help you. . . . Especially when you're coming out of a motel. [*laughs*]

LK: [*laughs*] Have you gotten now so accustomed to it that you . . . it's just part of your . . .

BH: Oh yeah. I've had my face hanging out a long time, you know. I've done so many pictures and so many television shows . . .

LK: So you step on an airplane, and you know everybody's looking at you.

BH: That's right. That's right. . . . What can you do about it?

LK: Well, like Presley. He got removed from it. He couldn't handle it.

BH: Who's that?

LK: Elvis.

BH: Oh, Elvis. Well, you know. You get . . . It was some hysterical people. And, you know, they probably climbed all over him, and . . .

LK: You never had women jumping over you?

BH: No, not lately. . . . Not since last night. [*grins broadly*]

LK: Robert!

BH: Larry.

Stephen King

Born September 21, 1949 in Portland, Maine, Stephen Edwin King was a lonely child whose father had abandoned the family and whose mother worked day and night to keep her children fed and sheltered. He began to write short stories after graduating from the University of Maine and haltingly wrote a first novel, which he discarded. His wife fished the manuscript out of the trash and urged King to finish it. The book was called Carrie *and sold 4,000,000 copies.*

Most of King's novels have been made into popular movies or TV programs. King has also written five novels under the name Richard Bachman. This interview probes the lively mind of the master of the horror thriller.

"I don't say,

'Is there

something

wrong?'

I say,

'How bad

is it?

Is anybody

dead?'"

LARRY KING: For a long time he has been the master of the horror thriller, scaring millions of Americans— and very profitably, I might add. How did this all start?

STEPHEN KING: Well I think it started when I was a child. Before we went on we were talking about radio programs that we listened to as a kid, and I can remember creeping to the door of our bedroom to listen to *Lights Out* and then trying to crawl into bed with my brother afterwards.

LK: Well, we all did that, but not many of us then started to write.

SK: No, no, but I think that if you have a warp in a certain direction, or a predilection to a certain kind of thing— maybe I'm the sort of person that's always been a little bit frightened. I'm the kind of guy where, if somebody comes to my house, and they look a little bit down-hearted, I don't say, "Is there something wrong?" I say, "How bad is it? Is anybody dead?" It's just the way that I'm built, I guess.

LK: Did you start writing in school?

SK: I began writing when I was about six or seven years old, yeah.

LK: In other words, you were afraid of the bogeyman.

SK: I was afraid of the bogeyman.

LK: The lights were on when you went to sleep.

SK: Well as a kid, that was always something that was a little bit hard to ask for. I used to tell my mother that I had to "see to go to sleep," that that was "very important to me." There has to be a light somewhere because, if there's a light then you're safe. It's like bogeyman kryptonite.

LK: Where'd you grow up?

SK: I grew up in Maine.

LK: Where you still live, right?

SK: Yeah. I've lived there my whole life.

LK: You're a Maineian.

SK: Maine*iac*—

LK: What was the first hit book?

SK: Well, I guess that the first real hit book was the second one, *Salem's Lot*, which went to number one in paperback. *Carrie* was bought for paperback for a lot of money. It was published in hardcover and was well received by members of my family and some friends. First printing of the book was 2,500 copies, but it did extremely well in paperback. One of the nice things about my career, I think, is that my audience has grown up with me. That's one of the reasons, I think, that probably the hardcovers do well now. It also helps that I come from an anxious generation. We've grown up with a lot of anxiety. People have got to have some kind of a basket to put all those fears in.

LK: Then you took off. Everything you write now sells, doesn't it?

SK: It has, but I like to think it's because I've written the right things. You know, you read critics who say, "He could publish his laundry list," but I don't think it'd be a bestseller. Nobody would want to read about how many shorts and how many shirts need starch.

LK: When you write this style, do you enjoy frightening people?

SK: Okay, let me put it to you this way: I write for an audience of one, and that's me. One of the things that you have to think about when you're a success on a large level is, if you write for yourself, if you write for that audience of one, you must have some kind of a mind to write right in the middle of everything. And you must be like Mr. Average, at the bottom. I enjoy writing things that either scare me, or, if they don't scare me, I know they're going to scare the audience. I know that's it's gonna get you. And there's something about that that's intensely pleasing to me.

LK: It's a fine line though between good writing and manipulative writing. Is it always a thin line?

SK: No. If you're good enough, you don't have to feel bad about manipulating people, about manipulating their emotions. Isn't that one of the things that art's supposed to do? We're talking about radio or TV, that sort of thing. We can go over programs on TV, on the old *Alfred Hitchcock* series, that sort of thing, where you manipulate people, where you set them up. That sort of thing. The important thing to remember is that you can't manipulate anybody that doesn't want to be manipulated. Reading something and really getting into it is like being hypnotized. You can't hypnotize somebody that doesn't want to be hypnotized. And my attitude in my writing is that I want to be your friend. And I want to come up to you and say—[*moves forward in chair, speaks in low, enticing tones*]—"Come here, I've got a story, I want to tell you something. You're going to like it, you're going to *like* this story." And I put my arm around your shoulder, and I say, "It's around the corner here. It's a little bit dark, but you'll be able to see." And then I lead this guy around the corner. And when he can't get away, when I've got him totally hooked—then I put it to him. . . . That sounds really sadistic!

LK: It does. Are the stories all formulated, Stephen? Do the characters surprise you?

SK: Yeah, they do from time to time. And it's funny how these things come out. I've been working on something where I knew there was a character who was going to commit suicide, a Vietnam vet, and I was positive that this guy was going to go into the bathroom and shoot himself. It turned out that, instead of doing that, he took a hammer and a nail and, you know, pounded the nail into his head. And I knew that it was right when I wrote it, but I had no idea that that guy was going to do that. He did it on his own.

LK: Have you had characters that were supposed to die who didn't?

SK: Yes.

LK: And vice-versa?

SK: Yes. Everybody was supposed to die at the end of *Salem's Lot*. Everybody was supposed to die at the end of *The Shining*. But the thing about good horror fiction is that there can't be any horror without a little love. There can't be any darkness without light. Unless you give people a contrast, it's all—it's useless. It's like the *Friday the 13th* movies, where you have, you know, X number of young teenagers who are just there to be killed. So you're waiting to see each new and exciting murder. At least it must be exciting to some people; that whole genre disturbs me a lot. But if you fall in love with the people that you're working with, uh, and a lot of times they surprise me by their toughness and strength, so that they survive.

LK: Let's cover some things specific. You just finished a new movie. It won't be out until July. Mr. King is here tonight, not to promote that film, but just because he likes being on our show.

SK: That's right, but it *will* be at a theater near you!

LK: In July. *Maximum Overdrive*. That's based on the book, a short story, right?

SK: Based on a short story called "Trucks," yeah. It was always my favorite short story in that collection, which is, I guess, why when Dino DeLaurentis asked me would I write the screenplay, I finally gave in. And when he asked me would I direct it, I talked with my wife about it. I had the chance before. But I'm more than a writer, I do have a wife, I have a family, and I'm committed to all those things. She said "Go ahead. If it's time, it's time. Do it. Get it out of your system. . . ." It's about machines out of control.

LK: Machines take over, you mean?

SK: Well, most of my stories— You were asking if I'm a formula writer. I'm not, but I *am* sort of a "situational writer." It's sort of like black situation comedy, you know? In a way, *The Shining* is sort of like *I Love Lucy* gone bad. In a resort hotel—[*adopts a Desi Arnaz accent*] "Loo—cee, I'm home!!!" You know, that sort of thing. So, you know, it's basically a hammock. You have a situation where I said, "Well, suppose that the earth passed into the tail of a comet, and this comet was actually the tool of some alien species who used technological societies to wipe themselves out so they could have their planets." But what I was *really* interested in was, what would people do in any situation that's totally inexplicable, where their own hair dryers turn against them, where their trucks and cars start to run them down? There's a woman who, uh, has a rather nasty problem with an electric knife. That sort of thing.

LK: It sounds like it could be a big hit.

SK: It would be nice. You know, the reason that I [directed] it was because for years, people have said that the movies don't carry the spirit of the books. And it's a very difficult thing to define, because you take a writer like Elmore Leonard, I like his work a lot, he's a great writer. You take it sentence by sentence—they're sentences—but the man has got a spirit, he's got a personality, he's got a quirky sense of humor that exists somewhere between those lines. He wrote the screenplay for *Stick*, a book that I like a lot, that Burt Reynolds directed, and I didn't feel that Elmore Leonard was there in that movie. And I felt that way about some of mine, so I thought, if I do it one time, now it may come out, and the critics may say "Guess what, Stephen King can't do Stephen King either!"

LK: Why don't you take the tack that Erskine Caldwell takes? He told me once that when a book of his is made into a film, he regards it as apples and oranges. He doesn't treat it as his book. If he watches the film, he doesn't say, "That's my book." It's a story, I got paid for it, I will not write the screenplay, I will not be present one day of the shooting, etc.

SK: That's the attitude that I always have taken in the past. I've done screenplays a few times because people have asked me to, but in most cases that's been exactly my attitude. It's like sending a kid off to college. You hope they're going to do well, you hope they're not going to get into trouble, you hope they're going to graduate summa cum laude, you hope they're not going to get hooked on drugs or get into any kind of trouble—but you realize at the same time, this really isn't yours anymore. It's going to belong to somebody else. There was a grad student who came to talk to James M. Cain near the end of his life—he wrote *The Postman Always Rings Twice* that's been made two or three times; *Double Indemnity*, with Fred MacMurray; *Mildred Pierce*, with Joan Crawford—and the grad student was moaning about how the movies had butchered his books. They'd totally destroyed his books. Cain turned around and said, "Don't look to me like they did, sonny. Look, they're all right up there on the shelf!" And that's the way that it is. A movie is a very perishable commodity. It's in the theaters, and then it's gone.

LK: Are you particularly difficult to translate to film?

SK: I don't know. I *like* a lot of the movies that have been made out of my stuff.

LK: Let's see, we had *The Dead Zone*. I like that a lot.

SK: That was a good one.

LK: *Carrie*. That was the biggest hit, right?

SK: Yep.

LK: *The Shining* you didn't like.

SK: No. I thought that the real problem with *The Shining* was that [director Stanley] Kubrick didn't have a real background in the genre. He *wanted* to make a horror film, it was the stated idea to make the scariest horror film of all time. He's a fantastic director, and I thought, "Okay, they're going to have ambulances out in front of every theater in America, because they're going to bring people out to cardiac units!" It's a tremendously interesting film, but at the same time it seems to me like a great big luxury car with no motor in it.

LK: Our guest is Stephen King. He's got another book coming out this fall. Are you surprised? You shouldn't be. Mr. King writes a book and a half a year. He even used a pseudonym for a major bestseller called *Thinner*, and he used the name

Richard Bachman, who had earlier written books as well. We'll also talk about his new book called *The It*, and there'll be *another* movie coming from the mind of Stephen King, based on his short story "The Body." That one directed by Carl Reiner. In July we'll see *Maximum Overdrive*, based on his short story "Trucks." You've written a lot of short stories. You like that?

SK: Yeah. I got to correct you, it's *Rob* Reiner.

LK: Oh, Rob, the son of Carl Reiner. And his new book will be *The It*. Before we take our first call, why did you write under a pseudonym? Why Richard Bachman?

SK: I had these books that were piling up. I had written at the rate of about a book and a half a year, and in 1979 I had a book that was almost published before *Carrie*, and it was called *Getting It On*. We later retitled it *Rage* and published it as a paperback original. It was well reviewed by my relatives and friends, who were in the know. And over the course of years I did three more under that name. They were all done by my paperback publisher, and then they branched out. They had a hardcover house, and I did have this one novel, *Thinner*, that was sort of like a Stephen King novel, but had sat in my drawer for a long time. I really liked the story, I liked the concept of the idea of the guy who is cursed and who starts to lose weight. We all want to lose weight and, again, it's that situation comedy aspect, where you create a hammock and you just say, "Okay, lets put it here and then start to tighten it and see where it stands."

LK: Who tipped us that it was you?

SK: Actually it was a guy named Larry Brown, who works in a bookstore, and he works in the Library of Congress, and he's also an attorney. He read all of the books, and he suspected a similarity, and he went back to the Library of Congress and the first one was the smoking gun, that one had been registered for copyright under my name. But the thing started to collapse with *Thinner*. It was like trying to carry home a grocery bag in the rain, where the bottom starts to fall out.

LK: It's interesting that once it was announced it was you, the book automatically went crazy.

Let's take some calls for Stephen King, and we begin with Buffalo, New York.

CALLER: [*Buffalo, New York*] Hi. When a person reads a scary book and then goes to bed that night and has nightmares, and then gets up the very next day and reads that book again, does that come from reading a book by a good novelist, or is that just some people need fear in their lives?

SK: I think it comes from having read something that really impressed you a lot. I really do believe that. If you're going to carry it over in your dreams with you, then it's something that just won't fall out of your circuits. In a way I don't mean to cause anybody nightmares, but I like to think that, if you're reading the book, you're having your nightmare awake.

LK: For Stephen King, San Francisco. Hello?

CALLER: [*San Francisco*] I'd like to know why you have a tendency to have young kids as victims in your books. For example, in *Firestarter* and *The Shining*?

SK: Well, I'm interested in young kids, because I've had young kids since I was twenty-two years old. So I've always wanted to investigate children and the minds of children, and to try to make some kind of connection between the kid that I was and the grown-up that I am and the children that my kids are, and what that whole relationship is. With *The Shining* in particular, I think one of the things that startled me about becoming a parent was to discover after a diet of

Father Knows Best and *The Donna Reed Show*—all these wonderful textbook fathers—that it was also possible to sometimes feel extremely angry with your children. Sometimes I'd feel that way. It wasn't as though I ever, you know, child abuse or anything, but the feelings were enough to be disturbing. So I wrote the book about the father who was torn by these awful feelings, and as I said before, I have a tendency to write my own worst nightmares. I was trying to get rid of that, or maybe just trying to understand it.

LK:　Concord, California, for Stephen King. Hello?

CALLER:　[*Concord, California*] Yes, I was wondering, when you write a screenplay, either an original or an adaptation of one of your novels, how come you tend to use more graphic violence than in the old Hitchcock style of suggested violence?

SK:　Well, keep in mind that Hitchcock was the guy who showed in *Frenzy* this mad killer chopping off all this woman's fingers and also strangling her with a necktie. Things change with the times. Hitchcock always had a tendency to let your mind finish the job for you, and I've always felt that way, too. There has to be a place where you draw away and let you imagination take over. It's like in *The Birds*, where you see them pecking at the woman, and then the next thing you see is that it's happened, and she's just totally lost. You don't have to see it all happening, but I do think you have to see *some* of it happen. I think Hitchcock would agree with that. The idea has always been, if you give them a good wallop at the beginning they'll believe that you'll do anything.

LK:　Where are you calling from?

CALLER:　[*Chapel Hill, North Carolina*] Chapel Hill, North Carolina. Stephen King was in his own movie, *Creepshow*, and I really thought you were pretty funny in that. I just wondered if you were going to maybe act in any more of your movies or anybody else's?

SK:　I directed a picture called *Maximum Overdrive* down in North Carolina, in Wilmington, and the funny thing about it was—we were talking about Hitchcock— I did a little Hitchcock turn at the beginning of that. So if you look fast, you'll see me in that. I got two lines.

LK:　What did you do in *Creepshow*?

SK:　In *Creepshow* I turned into a human weed. [*long pause*] I know this sounds crazy, but it's the way these things work out.

LK:　Sacramento, California, hello?

CALLER:　[*Sacramento, California*] It's truly an honor and a privilege to speak to two Kings at once. I want to find out who the picture on the jacket of *Thinner*—supposedly of Richard Bachman—really is? And also, will *The Stand* ever be a movie?

SK:　[*laughs*] I get the question about *The Stand* a lot. Let me answer the other one first. The picture on the jacket. We knew when we did the book it was sort of a horror and more in Stephen King territory, and we might have some problems. And so the picture is actually— My agent used to be an Allstate Insurance agent in a Sears store in Minneapolis, and the picture is a picture of a man named Richard Manuel, who was his boss. That's who Richard Bachman was. A good-looking guy, too.

LK:　There'll be no more Bachman books, will there?

SK:　I think he died of cancer of the pseudonym. As far as *The Stand* becoming a movie, there's a script there. I've worked harder on that screenplay than I have anything in my life. It's now a picture that could be made as a theatrical picture. It's a little long, but it's not an epic like *Ben Hur* or anything. The real problem, I think, with *The Stand*, is that studios tend to shy away from the end of the world. Simple as that.

LK: Fort Rucker, Alabama, hello?

CALLER: [*Fort Rucker, Alabama*] Hello. Recently I read *The Trap* by your wife, Tabitha, and I enjoyed that very much. Is she going to be coming out with any new books soon?

SK: She's working on a book now. She's written three. There's a book called *Small World*, a book called *Caretakers*, and *The Trap*, and she's working on a novel now. The funny thing was, she came to me one day, and she said "I don't know how to tell you this—" and I said, "*Tell* me. What is it?" You know, I didn't know what she was going to say: Cancer? Divorce? What is this going to be? She said, "I'm writing a novel." Well, I knew that she could write. One of the reasons that I was attracted to her in the beginning—we met in a library, we met again at a poetry seminar—it's obvious she can write, but I thought, "My God, what am I going to say if this book is bad, or if I think this book is bad?" So the book was *Small World*, and I didn't think it was bad. I thought it was great! And I'm glad she called and said that. Tabby will be happy, too. They are good books.

LK: She, then, now is a full-time writer, too?

SK: And a full-time mother, and I'm a full-time writer and a full-time father.

LK: How many kids?

SK: We have three kids, so that we alternate between our fantasy world and PTA and little league and all the rest of it.

LK: South Miami, Florida, for Stephen King.

CALLER: [*South Miami, Florida*] A while back I read in *Broadcasting* magazine that you were going to do a radio show or something like that. So whatever happened to that?

SK: The only thing that I really know of is that there was a radio program broadcast called *The Mist*. It was broadcast on a lot of Public Radio stations; it was like the old radio programs in that it had all the sound effects and that sort of thing. And this is not a plug, because if I get a royalty at all, it's a very small one. The cassette is actually available. You can buy it. And if you listen to it with earphones, it's got a startling stereo quality.

LK: Someone said that you do five-minute spots called "Lists That Matter." Is that radio?

SK: Yeah. I have a radio station in Bangor, which is where I live. It's a little AM rock 'n' roll station and—

LK: You *own* a radio station? . . . What's the call letters?

SK: It's WZON, that's The Rock Zone in Bangor, Maine.

LK: And on that show, on that station, you go on with five-minute shows called "Lists That Matter"? Lists of what?

SK: Well, let's say, "The 10 Best Lines in Movies," you know. "Do you feel lucky, punk?" Stuff like that. Or "The 10 Worst Things You Can Put in Your Mouth." Like okra. Things that people should never eat. Whatever.

LK: Have you ever thought of leaving your genre?

SK: I don't think about leaving it or staying in it. I have ideas, and a lot of times they end up being in the genre. The Bachman books, three of the four, well, let's say

LK: if there are five Bachman books total, three of them are just straight novels. I dunno, in a way, there are a couple of the novels that are published under my own name that a lot of people would argue aren't really classic horror novels.

LK: How do you react to critics when you see yourself—even though you're a major bestseller, enormously successful, the bestselling author, probably, in this genre that we have ever produced in this country—when you see yourself rapped? How do you react?

LK: It's somebody else. That's somebody that gets made up. I mean, you get pigeon-holed after a while. You are a horror writer. You become that person. It's like that American Express ad I did, where they put you in an old dark house, you know, so that you become almost like a brand name yourself. But it doesn't have anything to do with who you are. That's not a real person—that persona, or that thing. For instance, if I do an autographing, I always feel disappointed going in, because I feel like I can't do what they want me to do. I can't come in in a sweeping black cloak and then suddenly disappear at the end of it.

LK: So you don't mind it if you're rapped in print?

SK: It's like when we were talking about the movies before. You see it on the screen, you know. That's a movie. It isn't your book. And when I see that sort of stereo-typing, whatever, I just think, "Well, that's fine."

LK: What would annoy me though is when you read the one that goes "poorly writ-ten, cliché-ridden, can't-put-it-down book." Or "page-turner." Why do they like it, then?

SK: I think that a lot of times with critical reaction there's a critical mindset that sug-gests that if a lot of people like it, it can't be good, because most people aren't that bright. In fact, we live in a time when an awful lot of people are bright and well-read.

LK: We go to Tacoma, Washington. Hello?

CALLER: [*Tacoma, Washington*] There's a lot of talk these days about violence on tele-vision and how it affects especially children. Considering your genre, what are your feelings on violence on television?

SK: I think that the whole problem of violence on television, or the whole question of violence on television, is terribly overrated, and I think there's been an awful overreaction to the whole thing. Maybe the best case-in-point is a TV movie called *The Day After*, which was a thing about terminal nuclear war. For weeks beforehand there were things about "How are children going to react to this?" and how you should have a group seminar with your kids afterwards about all this stuff—as though it weren't really there. In most cases, we tend to forget that chil-dren are raised on a diet of fear, because they know about fear almost before they know about any other reaction—except for the love of their parents and the warmth of their family. They're the ones that fall down and scrape their knees, who fall down the stairs and bump their heads. They're the ones who are afraid of the dark. I can remember a friend of mine, as a kid, who was terrified of a crea-ture in the closet. I wrote a couple of stories about this, but he'd heard his father talking about this creature, and he was sure that it lived in his closet. The crea-ture was called a "twi-nite doubleheader." He knew this creature was in his closet. It was this awful thing that wore a baseball uniform and had two heads. It's because kids believe everything, and they see everything. But that doesn't mean that they can't cope with it. We get this idea that children aren't tough, that they can't deal with violence, but the most important thing is, we have this failure to recognize that children can't grasp the difference between reality and fantasy. That's only true if they grow up in an environment where those discriminations are not made.

LK: Azuza, California, hello.

CALLER: [*Azuza, California*] I was wondering if you get any manuscripts from potential novelists, or any strange gifts from fans, and do you have any favorites?

SK: I get manuscripts from fans or aspiring novelists, and most times I send them back unread. Because I think if I made a practice of reading them all, what eventually would happen is I wouldn't do anything but read manuscripts.

LK: Do fans send you gifts?

SK: Yeah. I got two ounces of pot from a lady one time. "This is what makes me creative. Maybe it'll make you creative." I didn't smoke it.

LK: North Platte, Nebraska, hello.

CALLER: [*North Platte, Nebraska*] I noticed that for his next movie, *Maximum Overdrive*, that AC/DC is doing the soundtrack. Why did you pick them? Is it the intensity of the music? I think it's an excellent choice.

SK: I picked them because they're loud! And because it's sort of violent, head-long music. They're sort of stereotyped, heavy-metal rockers. They've got what I think is an ill-deserved reputation for Satanism and all sorts of things but—I like them because they're a heavy-metal group that actually can play. I think that Angus Wilson is a very talented guitarist, and they're able to stretch in a lot of different directions, and they did one heck of a soundtrack for us.

LK: Savannah, Georgia, hello.

CALLER: [*Savannah, Georgia*] Could you tell me if George Romero is making *Pet Semetary* and what's it like to work with him?

SK: George is going to make *Pet Semetary*, I think, probably next year. He'll make it up in Maine, where I've written all sorts of novels—where they've been set, but one's never been made there. And working with him is great. He's laid back, he's easy to deal with, he grasps the reality of the situation, and because he's not an autocrat, the situation is always fairly loose. And he's always open to innovation and new ideas.

LK: How did you get the idea for *Pet Semetary*?

SK: The thing was, we lived in a house that was on a busy road, and my daughter had a cat that she was crazy about, and there was actually a pet cemetery behind the house, and it was spelled the way that the title of the book is spelled, because children had put up this sign. And there were markers for parakeets and guinea pigs and rabbits, but mostly for dogs and cats that had been greased in that road by, you know, heavy-industry trucks. So we ended up burying my daughter's cat in the pet cemetery. She seemed fine and everything, and I was sitting in the living room a little while later, and I hear this thumping coming from the garage, and she's out there jumping up and down on the floor, screaming, "I want my cat back! God can't have my cat! Let God have his own cat!" And then she cried. I thought, "Okay, this is her first experience. It's just a cat. It isn't Grammy. It isn't Grampa." But it's a valid grief experience, and it was her first real one, and it made me think about how we react to those losses, and so I started to write the book, and it got very tough to finish, but eventually I did.

LK: Stephen King. He'll be with us an hour and twenty minutes from now, on the radio, and we'll get lots of phone calls in there, if you tune in. And Stephen and I are going to drive over to the network together. I feel kind of weird, being with Stephen alone in a car—

SK: [*in low, evil tones*] I can sit in the back seat.

LK: Stephen will sit in—the back—seat.

SK: Yes. In the dark—

LK: In the dark.

SK: In the night—

LK: In the night.

Frank Sinatra

Francis Albert Sinatra, the son of a fireman, was born on December 12, 1917, in Hoboken, New Jersey. Teaming up with three other young men as the Hoboken Four, he won first prize on radio's Major Bowes' Original Amateur Hour, *which led to a tour, a $15-a-week gig at the Rustic Cabin roadhouse, and, ultimately, contracts with Harry James and Tommy Dorsey. By 1943, Sinatra was the idol of swooning bobbie soxers, and after a slump complicated by throat trouble, he made a spectacular comeback as an actor in 1953's* From Here to Eternity.

Sinatra built a reputation for a quick temper and disdain for the media. This Larry King interview is a rarity.

"The first four or five seconds, I tremble every time I . . . walk out of the wing onto the stage, because I wonder if it will be there when I go for the first sounds I have to make. Will it be there?"

LARRY KING: Our special guest this evening—if you don't know by now you ain't gonna know it—is Francis Albert Sinatra. Frank is here for a big dinner tomorrow night honoring his wife at the Friars' Club. He's Abbot of the New York Friars. And last night, of course, he entertained for the Irving Berlin gala. Why are you here? Why did you come to this program? I mean, I'm glad you came—

FRANK SINATRA: No, because you asked me to come, and I haven't seen you in a long time. To begin with, I thought we ought to get together and chat. . . . Talk about—yeah, just talk about a lot of things. But, we came to town, obviously, for the Irving Berlin thing—which, by the way, was a big thrill and was fun to do. He was a great man. I knew him for years.

LK: Why don't you do more interviews?

FS: Nobody invites me. [*pause*] I'm serious. I'm *quite* serious. We don't get many calls for me to sit down and chat and do interviews.

LK: Do you think it's because they think you won't come?

FS: Maybe. It's possible, you know. In some cases, I probably *wouldn't* do it, either because of the person himself, or herself, or their attitude about things would maybe rub me the wrong way. So I just stay away from that. But I like doing them. I think they're interesting, and it gives people a chance around the country, if they're interested at all, to find out what I'm doing, where I'm at, what I'm gonna do.

LK: And you also learn a lot about yourself, don't you?

FS: Ah, of course, too, of course. Because a good question can open up doors in my mind that I would never think of discussing with anybody. And, ah, it's important, actually, that the interviewer does homework and gets going, instead of [asking] dull [questions like:] Where were you born? And so on and so forth. And, how tall's your old man?

LK: But you also have to have an element of trust, don't you?

FS: I think so.

LK: A feeling that the person is sincerely interested?

FS: Yeah, I think so. I don't mind a question that borders on the difficult to answer, because I try to fight my way out of it, if I can. If I can't, then I say, I don't think I can answer your question.

LK: There's so many things to talk about with you.

FS: Shoot.

LK: Okay, let's start with, when we spoke on the phone last week, you were hysterical. You know, sometimes you don't know how funny you are, but you said—it's okay to tell them, right?

FS: Sure.

LK: You said, "Larry, on your show can we say the words, *pimps* and *whores*?" And since I just said it, it's obviously okay. What were we referring to?

FS: Well, I did an interview not long ago about what I'm doing—my work and so on and so forth. And we got around to discussing people who are writing kiss-and-tell books. That's really what started the whole thing. And I said, those kiss-and-tell books, I have another name for people who write those kinds of books, and they're pimps and whores. Because they can't write their own name to earn a living properly. They got to lean on somebody else. And they know nothing about the person about whom they've written—*really* don't know. They just read newspaper clips, and they write a story. And fortunately, and unfortunately—but more fortunately—we have the right to say whatever we want in our country, which I agree with. And I just feel that there's that element, which brought about the title, *pimps* and *whores*.

LK: You told me once that people who make a living off other peoples' fortunes or misfortunes are parasites, in a sense. Why don't you respond to them sooner? When a book was written about you, why didn't you come out? Because when the personality written about doesn't come out, isn't there an assumption?

FS: Oh, I agree that there's probably a large assumption. But with advice from family members and an attorney—I mean, we didn't take a vote, but if we had, answering that would have lost. . . . I mean, I wouldn't have answered it anyway, because we would have agreed, *No, don't answer it, just be quiet about it.* I hope that she [Kitty Kelly, author of *His Way: An Unauthorized Biography of Frank Sinatra*] had a lot of fun with the money she made by writing a lot of crap that she wrote about, which most of it was, anyway.

LK: All right, how about the pain, though?

FS: It wasn't too bad.

LK: Didn't harm you?

FS: Nah, it didn't really sting me that much. I've been whacked around before and came through pretty good.

LK: How about your kids?

FS: The kids—I worried about my family a lot. They never said a word. They never mentioned it, we never discussed it, my friends never discussed it. They were angry, you know. They said: That so-and-so. But I said, forget about it. In six months' time, nobody will ever remember what she wrote about, and she can never do it again. She'll never do it again.

LK: Was it a mistake to try to stop it, by the way?

FS: It would have been a mistake. I think you cause more notoriety if you try to stop it. Don't you agree to that?

LK: Yeah. That was a mistake you made, right?

FS: Yeah. Well, we didn't try to stop it. What we wanted to do was to have something to say about it. I don't remember now what my people were saying to her people, because that's a long time ago.

LK: But the whole reaction to this on your part is, you think—are you extending that to Donald Regan's book about Nancy Reagan and Larry Speakes?

FS: That's correct. I'm saying that those are the pimps and the whores. They're the ones who write the books about people with whom they had a kind of a privy association and believed in them, and they believed in the other guy, and suddenly they're out making a buck because they got a pigeon.

LK: What is, Frank, do you think, our right to know? Do we have a right to know, as a people, whether Nancy Reagan reads horoscopes? Is that our right to know?

FS: I don't want to know. I mean, it's a if-you-don't-like-Nancy question. I don't want to know about a lot of people, about a lot of things that they do. I really don't want to know. I think there's a— Listen, we could talk for the next week about how badly we feel when we read things about people, but we're never gonna stop it because it's gonna go on and on and on—

LK: Human nature.

FS: Absolutely. Particularly if it's a hot subject. Particularly a hot subject. You talk about the first lady in this case—she's a famous lady. They're gonna take shots at her. Listen, they take shots at the president. Everybody takes it. That's the American way. Everybody takes it.

LK: You know Don Regan, don't you?

FS: Yeah, sure.

LK: Are you surprised by this?

FS: I was surprised, yes.

LK: You know Nancy very well.

FS: Very well, yes.

LK: And you know her intimately. I mean, you're a close associate.

FS: That's right: long time, long time.

LK: So, give us the other side. We haven't heard that, yet. There's some thinking that this family's a little kooky.

FS: I don't think that's the proper word, do you? I don't know how they sit around their table and discuss their problems. But I do know that Nancy Reagan is a straightforward, very honest, strong lady—very strong lady. And she's bright, too. She's not in any sense in the dark about too many things, I would have to guess. I don't know about how much power she may hold over the president or how often they may discuss his problems. I don't know that. None of us knows that. But I would say she is a great help to the president.

I'd have to go on and make a statement like that. I've never been present when they've had a kind of a private conversation, but I have to believe that she's a big help.

LK: You've known them both a long time.

FS: Long time.

LK: And almost—I don't want to paraphrase you, but last time we were together on radio you said part of the reason you were for them was because you liked them so much. Because you're a lifelong Democrat.

FS: That's correct. I like them as people, you know? And then ah—I got a little cold about my team there for a while. It wasn't pleasing me. I didn't like the way they were doing things when they got elected. And I began to move around a bit. And it's a wonderful thing to be able to do—to switch from one party to another. We have the right to do that. But, I believe in the president very much. He's a straight-ahead guy, he's a clear-thinking man—

LK: Are you going to support George Bush?

FS: Yes.

LK: Campaign?

FS: I don't know whether I will or not—yet—but I will support him.

LK: You think it matters? Do you think we're affected if Frank Sinatra supports someone?

FS: I don't know. I don't think so. I mean, we have a right to do that, don't we?

LK: I mean, do you think you sway people?

FS: Oh, I don't know if I sway. I may sway my family or my kids or somebody, but maybe not, because the kids are all grown now, and they have their own opinions, too. For instance, my son Frank and I, we often discuss politics, he's a bright kid, he wants to know what's happening. And they're proud of the fact I happen to know people who are in office, and they ask me questions about them: What is he like? And, what do you talk about? And so on and so forth. But I have to guess that a great many people in America resent the fact that we in public life take sides like that. I think they resent it.

LK: Saying like: Who are they?

FS: That's right. Why should they be trying to sway other people to vote the way they vote?

LK: So you think it can work in reverse? Like, Warren Beatty endorses—

FS: —Absolutely. Absolutely. I've had mail through the years with people saying, *Would you butt out and shut your mouth!* We'll *choose a candidate.*

LK: Because you're always an activist. You go back to Al Smith.

FS: All the way back to Al Smith. My mother was always in politics, so I learned everything from her.

LK: You still get a lot of fan mail?

FS: Oh, yes.

LK: You ever read any?

FS: My gal saves the interesting ones for me. The ones that just say *Please send a photograph,* fine, or *You stink, and I don't know why you're still singing; I like the other guy better.* We get all kinds of mail, which is fun. We get fan mail from foreign countries. A lot of mail from countries like Norway, Albania—places you'd never dream. With tapes and recordings and whatever they have—the films—they see everything we see.

LK: The kid from Hoboken is internationally known. Does that flip you? Do you ever pinch yourself?

FS: Oh, sure. I'm delighted. If we go, if Barbara and I are going on vacation—let's say we go to France—and if we go shopping and people stop, and in their own language they end up talking about me. And we turn around, and we smile, and they smile, and they timidly want to shake hands, and we shake hands. And it's a kick. It really is a marvelous feeling. It's wonderful. Really, quite wonderful.

LK: Is there still a lot of that little boy in you?

FS: Yeah, sure. You never lose that. I think if I lost it, it would be all over.

[*Commercial break*]

LK: Frank just asked an interesting question: Do we have to pay ASCAP if you hum?

FS: If I do more than eight bars, I guess we'd have to pay a fee.

LK: By the way, why do you hum? You hum a lot.

FS: I hum a lot when I vocalize, because it moves up everything in the mask. Comes forward like that. And I found that out from Pavoratti and a couple of other opera singers who said, hum once in a while, and it's good for the mask. I said to Mr. Pavoratti once—who I've gotten to know now very well, he's a marvelous man, and a great artist—I said to him, I said, "Maestro, I'm having trouble closing out a note so that it sounds as though it's almost as thin as a butter knife—finish it out quietly, like that." I said, "I have trouble doing that. What do you think I should do?" He said, "Just close up-a you mouth." That's all he said, and I fell on the floor. *That* was the answer. I thought he was going to give me a dissertation on how to let the breath run out just normally—which is very difficult to do, by the way—if you want a diminuendo, in other words. They do it beautifully. They have great control. He said, "You just close up-a you mouth."

LK: And he's right.

FS: He's right. Just close your mouth. But he did it with his teeth. He went like *that*.

LK: Why, this opens up a wonderful area. Why do you still sing? We're raised in a culture that thinks about retirement: work hard all your life, get the home, move somewhere. You don't have to sing for money. You don't need the concert money.

FS: I don't have to work, no. But I feel that— First of all, I enjoy what I do. If I didn't, then I wouldn't be doing it. I enjoy it because it's a challenge for me also. I'm considered an over-the-hill performer at my age. There's no doubt about it. I think in the industry, I'm considered an over-the-hill performer. But I do it because I do the best I can when I work, and I don't work that much. I'd rather do benefits and have more fun doing that. If I work, I work in Vegas or Atlantic City. That's where I work. The only places. I go to—

LK: You don't do concerts, too?

FS: Well, occasionally. I do Carnegie Hall, but that's rare.

LK: You think you're over-the-hill? You classify yourself that way?

FS: Oh sure, sure. Because, if you think about what's selling today, who are the people who are known by millions of people? The younger people. Not any of us anymore. They know who we were, and they know who we are by people discussing us. So maybe if I did a concert somewhere, and a family took their eighteen-year-old daughter or son to hear you, then they get to hear you. But it depends on what they're looking at. They're looking at the guys up there with the guitars and all the noise. So that's not what we have, you know.

LK: You're a legend, though. I mean—you *do* know that, right?

FS: I don't know about legend. I mean, everybody's a legend. If everybody's a legend, there would be no normal people in the world. I mean, everybody would be a legend.

LK: Yeah but, you've gone beyond. You're in another ballpark.

FS: Yeah, I agree with that. And there's a good chance I probably should have gotten out by now. But I enjoy it.

LK: You did quit. You had a formal announcement—

FS: Well, I took a hiatus is what I did. I took a year and a half, and I just took it easy. I was tired. My throat was tired, I was tired, and I wasn't thinking clearly enough about what I was doing. And I thought: *I think I need a lot of fresh air.*

LK: Is it still a kick when the man says, "And now, ladies and gentlemen"? They don't even say it anymore, I guess. You just walk out, right?

FS: No, they make an announcement. It's a kick. . . . Absolutely. And the first—I swear on my mother's soul—the first four or five seconds, I tremble every time I take the step and I walk out of the wing onto the stage, because I wonder if it will be there when I go for the first sounds I have to make. Will it be there? I was talking about it just the other night at Carnegie Hall, at the Irving Berlin thing. I said, even just going out and looking at the audience, I was terrified for about the first four seconds. Then it goes away.

LK: How do you explain that?

FS: I don't know. I can't explain.

LK: You've always had it? Harry James—when you stood up to sing to Harry James?

FS: Every—always had it. All the time. "Will you remember the lyrics? Is your tie right? Will you use your hands right? Will you look pleasant at the audience?"

LK: So this dumb "Frank doesn't care" or "He's beyond this—"?

FS: No, that's not true. If anybody describes me that way, it's the way they see me. It's not what I am. It's not what I'm doing.

LK: In fact, you're a performer's performer.

FS: You've got to be on the ball. From the minute you step into that spotlight, you've got to know exactly what you're doing every second on that stage. Otherwise the act goes right into the bathroom. It's all good night.

LK: You had surgery.

FS: I had a lot of surgery. They had to cut up my tummy pretty badly. I looked like a road map.

LK: What was wrong?

FS: Ah, it was an intestinal infection that began to spread throughout my entire stomach and bowel and so on and so forth. It was a very serious operation.

LK: Were you close to buying it?

FS: Close to buying it. If I hadn't come back from the trip that I was on, I would have bought it. They'd've had flowers and a big band behind the casket. [*laughs*] I'm serious.

LK: Not Frank Sinatra. [*laughs*]

FS: I nearly bought it.

LK: Pain bad?

FS: Terrible. Really terrible. I was bent over, trying to sing songs. We were in Spain, finishing a tour, and everybody kept saying to me, including my wife, why don't you—why don't we go home? Let's go to London, or go to a hospital here. I said, no way am I going to go here. We're gonna go home, if I'm gonna do this. So I did. I went back. I cut the tour short. I went back, and they allowed me one day while I was home to prep me for the thing. And I came out of it and, thank God, not a problem. Not one single problem.

LK: Were you scared?

FS: Of course. Of course I was frightened. I said to our physician, the surgeon, "How serious is it?" He said, "It's serious, Frank. I'm not gonna tell you we're gonna remove a tooth out of your mouth," he said. "We have to put you together very carefully when we finish this." And it was a seven-and-a-half-hour operation, and when I came out of it, they were all smiles. Everybody was smiling, and I said, "I guess we won." And he said, "We sure did." He said, "You're in great shape. You'll never have another problem."

LK: And working again must have been a great kick, I guess.

FS: Oh, of course. Because I was having trouble breathing before I had the surgery done. My usual manner of breathing—which is deep, lots of breaths when I need it, you know, which of course is a trademark, it has been in my singing, the long phraseology—I couldn't do that with the pain.

LK: We have more to come. I want to talk about *The Manchurian Candidate*, which has become one of the great cult films in America. This is Larry King, and we're in New York for this appearance tonight.

FS: The Big Apple.

LK: The place where I was raised. And Frank was raised, like across the river. In the slums.

FS: Yeah, but as soon as I could get out of there, I came over here. [*laughs*]

LK: When you're here, when you're in this city—we're at 34th—we're four blocks, eight blocks from the Paramount. Eight blocks! Do you think about that?

FS: Sure, when I drive by there. I remember the marquee and all that other jazz.

LK: "Frank Sinatra"—and they lined up, nine in the morning.

FS: And they went down to Eighth Avenue, and all the way around the back, and up to Broadway again.

LK: And you did how many a day?

FS: Ah, one time, one Saturday, I did eleven shows. We started at 8:10 in the morning, and I finished at 2:30 the next Sunday morning. We did eleven shows.

LK: Does it give you an affinity for this city?

FS: Oh, absolutely. Always. Oh, yes. First time I left to come here to be in New York City, I was maybe sixteen, seventeen years old, just to look around. I was here with my parents when I was younger. They'd take me to Macy's, to the Christmas thing. Then maybe when I was ten or eleven years old. Then when I started jumping the ferry boat. It cost four cents. And sometimes you didn't pay four cents. When they used to pull out, then you jumped on the boat.

LK: You snuck over on the ferry.

FS: Yeah, you got on the ferry boat. They'd take the chain, put the chain across so you could jump on the boat. But I fell in love with this city, I guess. I don't even remember when it was.

LK: It shows when you sing that song, you know?

FS: It's alive. It's got so much to it.

LK: Still true? You make it here, you make it anywhere?

FS: That's right: anywhere. You make it here, you're a hit wherever you go. I don't care where you are. "Direct from New York," so and so, here he comes. And you know you're a hit.

LK: Francis Albert, what an incredible career. What an incredible *screen* career—

[*Commercial break*]

LK: A long time ago, twenty years ago, Richard Conden wrote a book called *The Manchurian Candidate*. It was a hit book. It turned into a terrific film. Richard Conden guested on my radio show a couple years ago, and I said, where is that film? And Richard Conden said, Frank Sinatra controls that film. I hope he lets it out, but he has not let it out. And now it is out. It has become one of the major cult films in America. In July, it will be released on home video. Why did you hold onto that film?

FS: I don't know. I really don't know. I didn't even know we had the right to do that until it happened. I didn't know. I swear to God.

LK: You didn't know you owned the rights?

FS: I didn't know we owned the rights outright. . . . I didn't know. Whoever it was who was working for me made a pretty good deal, apparently, and I never knew about that, that we really owned the film.

LK: So when you made that, you had no idea. So when Richard Conden told me on the radio you owned the film, you didn't know.

FS: I didn't know. I didn't deal much with my business people. I rarely spend time with them. They bawl me out for spending too much money every time we talk.

LK: Did you ever wonder: Why is *The Manchurian Candidate* never on TV?

FS: Yeah, I wondered. But I never looked into it. I never asked questions.

LK: In retrospect: How good a film is this?

FS: I think it's a damn good film. A fine film, too. The screenplay was wonderful. Working with Larry [Laurence Harvey], who was a consummate actor, you had to, he *made* you work up to him. He demanded it. His attitude about performing: He was a powerful actor. He really was. Had great inner strength. It all began, if you're interested at all, I got a phone call. I was in New York—no, I was in Miami—and I had a phone call from George Axelrod and John Frankenheimer.

LK: The director.

FS: Yeah, and they said: "Did you ever read a book called *The Manchurian Candidate*?" And I said, I sure did. And they said, "Would you like to make a movie of it? Would you like to play in it?" And I said, "When do we start?" Because that was one of the most interesting things I had ever read. And that's how we came about, and we became partners, and I found out later that most of it belonged to me, so my people must've said, we want this, and—

LK: So you didn't know you had that kind of deal. It was a hell of a movie. You know now it's amazing. Video comes out in July, right?

FS: Yes. It will be interesting to see what happens. The kids who have never seen it can watch it at home.

LK: Do you enjoy film work as much?

FS: Oh yes. I like films.

LK: You are a natural, aren't you?

FS: I think so. I never studied, no. I never went to any of the schools. I just felt that if you learned your words, like you know your name, and, first of all, when you've taken the job you honestly believe in what you're about to do, and then learn the words properly, you're a cinch. If you have any brains at all, you should be able to do it very well.

LK: Why?

FS: I don't know. I thought that acting was play-acting, like we did when we were kids. But suddenly you've grown up, and it's real, and you become immersed in what you're playing. I made myself think that I was really that guy—in anything—in comedy or whatever it might have been.

LK: So when you did *The Detective*, or *First Deadly Sin*, you felt like a cop?

FS: Absolutely.

LK: Tried to think like a cop?

FS: I tried to think like a cop every day, carried a badge in my pocket whether I had to show it or not. I had the gun on my hip all the time. I *was* a cop, through the whole picture, all the time. And at the time when Johnny Broderick was alive, at the time when I did that, a famous detective here in New York, an old friend of mine, wonderful man, I used to chat with him about little idiosyncrasies that they have. "I don't know," he said. "I never noticed anything." I said, "What are—what did you do if you were waiting around?" He said, "That was the toughest part of the job, waiting. Waiting to nail somebody." And I tried to put all those things that he told me about, I tried to put it all together. And I don't know if I did.

LK: But you began to feel like—

FS: —I *was* a cop. I *was* a cop.

LK: And when you do that well of course, *I* believe you're a cop.

FS: I think so. That's my point. I want you to believe that I'm thinking I'm a cop.

LK: And it's fun being someone else.

FS: Of course, it's fun. Because you can do things that you can't do if you're yourself. You know what I mean? Playing a cop with a badge, and the authority, and yet . . . I was always trying to keep a little tenderness in it somewhere, so that it was not a hangman.

LK: Yeah, you were very conscious of that. In singing, too.

[*Commercial break*]

LK: Are you going to be doing a movie again?

FS: I hope so. I keep waiting for somebody to give me something to read. I'd like to do— I love making films.

LK: You don't get parts to read?

FS: No. Not many.

LK: I'm having trouble conceiving this. You don't get parts to read?

FS: No. No, I don't. My daughter Tina, who now is actually working for me and with me, is a bright little girl, and she is now hunting for things for me to do. She's reading everything she can get her hands on, and if she comes up with something, we'll even finance the movie ourselves if we have to.

LK: How about her story about you?

FS: Well, she's on that. That's going to take some time. That'll be a serial, actually. I don't know if she can do that in one time. I think she's going have to do that in sections. It's an awful lot to be done.

LK: Who would play you?

FS: I don't know, but I think we should put on a wonderful, well thought-of hunt for a youngster of seventeen or eighteen and then move him up—use several actors and move him up. We know that we're not going to get the same face, but I think if we do it gently the audience will buy it: that here he is seventeen years old, and he's starting out with a dance band, and so on and so forth, and then with [Harry] James and then Tommy [Dorsey] and then on my own and at the Paramount and all that stuff. That's a lot of work, a lot of work on that thing. It's gonna be a tough job for her to put together. It's a good team she'll need.

LK: Is it kind of weird to be alive and see that happening?

FS: Yeah, I think so. I think it'll be interesting. And also I think it'll help a lot with my being around, just to be consulted. If we were on a set watching them shoot with the actor, I could very conceivably say to you, "I think that's wrong, what they're doing with this thing. . . ." And I would say to the director, "Can I see you a minute. Let's talk about this thing a little bit."

LK: There's a standing offer from publishers in New York—the amount is incredible—for you to write *your* book.

FS: I don't—I don't think so.

LK: You don't think there's an offer?

FS: Yeah, but I don't think I want to do that.

LK: Why not?

FS: I don't know. I just never thought about it in a positive way. Every time somebody talks to me about it, I think of the negative side. I don't want to write a book. But someday, who knows? Someday I might say, let's sit down and go to work.

LK: But you do agree that there's a great book there?

FS: I think there's an interesting book there. But also, there's the wonderful opportunity to straighten out a lot of *junk* that's been said—

LK: That's right. From you.

FS: Coming right from me. From the horse's mouth, so to speak.

LK: Don't you want to do that?

FS: Yeah, I'd like to do that. I think that even for my family's sake and my friends and all the people I've known for years, I think that they would be happy with it, too. It could conceivably happen. It wouldn't take long to do it. It would take a couple months. We could do that book like that—

LK: Yeah, if you do it intensely, yeah. By the way, concerning that, do you get angry at the people who talk to the people who write the books?

FS: I get disappointed. I don't get angry because I figure why waste my energy if they want to make fools of themselves. I'm disappointed, but fortunately, I don't think that's happened in my case too many times—unless I don't know and I'm ignorant, completely ignorant of it.

LK: Did you read that book about you, by the way?

FS: Yes. Yes. And so much of it is such, it's so far out of what—of the actuality—that it's scary—

LK: Because it's all second hand.

FS: Yes, and third hand, you know, and things like that. But then you stop for a minute—I mean, I do—and I say, well, somebody wanted to make a buck and so they decided they're gonna write a book. So they write a book . . . so what you gonna do?

LK: It had no effect on your career, did it?

FS: No.

LK: Audiences didn't drop off?

FS: No, no. My mail was marvelous mail.

LK: Oh, yeah? What'd you get?

FS: I got thousands of letters saying, please don't pay any attention to it. We read it, and if you haven't read it, don't read it, and so on and so forth. It'll hurt you, hurt your feelings, and so on. It was wonderful mail, great mail. And we answered everybody—thanked them for writing, and I promised them in each letter that I would not read the book, and I *didn't*. I really didn't read the book. I just skimmed through it—things that my secretary turned the dog ears down. And I read the things that she thought I should read, and I said, that's nothing, the same thing all over again.

LK: How about when gossip columnists write, "Your marriage is in trouble," these kinds of things? Normal people don't read about these kinds of things.

FS: Aw, what are you going to say about gossip columnists—?

LK: You've lived with them all your life?

FS: All my life. Ever since they started to even know my name, ever since that time.

LK: So you've had that all your life. Is it just a question of being used to it now?

FS: I think so. I don't see much about it—

LK: That means you don't read Liz Smith every day?

FS: No, no, no, no. I don't read those kinds of things. If it's something that my girl thinks is important enough for me to see, she'll clip it and put it in my mail—in case we want to do something about it, either refute it or, say, get her on the phone, and I'll tell her what the actual fact was, which I've done many times—called and said, *Listen, thanks for so and so, but that was wrong: this is what really happened*, and then they did it. And instead of making enemies, I've made friends by doing that, you know.

[*Commercial break*]

LK: Fame. Let's say we're in Washington, you and I, and we go into Duke Zeever's restaurant, popular restaurant. You're aware when you walk in that place at lunch—let's say—*everybody* recognizes you, everybody knows you, everybody's looking at you. What's that like, to feel that? Very few people have felt that in their lives.

FS: Well, I think it's an honor.

LK: Are you very aware of it?

FS: I'm aware of it, yeah, but I just—I have imaginary blinders in a sense, you know. I mean, I look around and if somebody smiles at me, I smile—hello, how are you, or whatever—but it's not unlike anybody else that we both know in our world. They walk in a restaurant or theater. The only time that I felt, you know, like I was causing a problem was if I go to the theater in New York, and, as you come down to go to your seat, people get up and they look around, and they buzz—it's sweet, it's wonderful, but, you know, you want to run and hide a little bit. And between acts you go out and get a smoke or get a drink next door at the bar, and it happens again, and you got to walk down there again, is what takes place. But it's a nice thing, though. The recognition is really quite nice.

LK: Unless Frank Jr. gets married or adopts or something—

FS: Oh, yeah, let's talk about that—

LK: —we're not going to see the continuation of the name Sinatra.

FS: That's correct, yeah. He's had some lovely little ladies that he's brought home for dinner from time to time, and I keep saying to him, "You've got to have a boy. If you don't have a boy, the family name *dies* right, right now." He says, "Dad, there's plenty of time." I say, "What do you mean? You're getting old. What do you mean, plenty of time?" And I said, "Be sure you marry a lady who's young enough to have a baby when you do get married."

LK: It is very important to you?

FS: Very important. Most important to me. Don't you think it's worthwhile that we do try to continue the family name? I would think so. And the girls, of course, they can't help it, they're going to take another man's name. And Frankie, he's a loner, he's pretty much a loner. He's had nice little ladies that I've met with him, went to dinner, or when Nancy Sr. cooked, and we all gathered at the house. And of course, sitting around the table, it's hysterical because it might be a pretty little girl, and we're saying *maybe this is the one, maybe this is the one*. And the poor kid is getting hustled all the time.

LK: [*laughs*] Well, we're out of time, Francis.

FS: We're out already?

LK: Thank you so much.

FS: Well, I had a good time. I enjoyed it. [*Sinatra and King shake hands*] Anytime. Just call me, and I come running. Ask me what time. What do I wear?

LK: Our guest has been Francis Albert Sinatra.

FS: All three of them.

LK: Arrivedérci.

FS: Ta-ta.

In 1903, George Burns formed the Peewee Quartet, which performed throughout the Lower East Side of Manhattan. By the time Burns was fourteen, he quit school and earned his living as an entertainer, working first as a trick roller skater and then as a comic singer and dancer. Next, he teamed up with an unemployed seventeen-year-old actress named Gracie Allen. Burns and Allen married and, in 1929, appeared in movies, next playing on radio and then on television as the most popular husband and wife team in show business.

In 1958, Gracie retired because of ill-health and six years later died of a heart attack. Burns continued doing television and concerts, and starred in The Sunshine Boys *(1975), which earned him an Oscar. Then came* Oh, God *(1977), with Burns in the title role.*

The publication of All My Best Friends, *a memoir, occasioned this interview.*

"I had seven sisters and five brothers— twelve in the family. We were very poor. We ate one of my sisters."

LARRY KING: Our special guest is George Burns, the world's youngest ninety-three-year-old man. The secret to his long life? Smoking cigars, drinking martinis, making people laugh. And for more than *eighty* years, George Burns has been a star in vaudeville, radio, television, and the movies. Burns has been honored as the king of comedy, chosen as one of *Playgirl*'s "ten sexiest men," and now he has just completed his eighth book for Putnam. It's called *All My Best Friends*. There you see it's cover. Most of his books have been major best-sellers, and this one is a nostalgic trip into show business. Why do you write books?

GEORGE BURNS: They pay me. . . . I get paid, and I enjoy doing it. I enjoy— Look, I enjoy working. Here I am, ninety-three years old, and I'm working. Nice to get out of bed when you're ninety-three.

LK: [*laughs*] Yeah! Nice to do anything.

GB: You can't make any money in bed.

LK: Really? But, back to the aspect, the aspect—

GB: [*chuckles*] Really. [*chuckles*]

LK: —to the aspect of books, George. I mean, the first idea. Do they come to you and say let's—

GB: No. I don't write a book. I talk a book. Like, David Fischer thought of the Gracie book, and then he spoke to Putnam, and Putnam introduced me to David Fischer, and we talked, and from that came a Gracie book.

LK: And so, you sit down with a writer—

GB: We sit and talk—just talk. Like we're talking now.

LK: And then he puts it all together—

GB: He puts it all together, and he makes it sound like I'm writing it. I can't spell. I only went to the fourth grade in school. When I was eight years old, I was in show business. I was singing with the Peewee Quartet. I—

LK: How could you get out of school in the fourth grade?

GB: Played hooky.

LK: I mean, didn't they come get you? Didn't they want—?

GB: No. They were glad I left school. See, I read in the paper that Caruso used to eat a lot of garlic. It made his voice sing. I ate garlic, so when I played hooky from school, my teacher wrote a letter of thanks to my mother.

LK: [*laughs*] This was right here in New York?

GB: Yeah. P.S. 22 on Sheriff Street. I was born on Pitt Street. Right here.

LK: Lower East Side?

GB: Lower East Side.

LK: Were your parents from Russia?

GB: I had seven sisters and five brothers—twelve in the family. We were very poor. We ate one of my sisters. . . . We had to use ketchup, though.

LK: That's large for a Jewish—

GB: No. Let me tell you, everybody had big families in that neighborhood. That doesn't mean that Jews were great lovers. It meant that it was freezing down there.

LK: [*laughs*] Oh, we're doing all the schtick here, George. Oh, so the book is done in galley form, and you read it, right?

GB: Yeah.

LK: You *do* read it before I read it?

GB: Yeah. Well, they pay me to write it. They don't pay me to read it.

LK: So you don't even read the galley?

GB: I don't even read it.

LK: [*laughs*] This book is out, and you don't even know what's in it?

GB: [*laughs*] No, no, no. I know what's in it. I know. It's a good book.

LK: Now, the idea of this book was to trace you and your friends back through radio, right?

GB: Practically, they're all gone, though—all of them, all my friends. You're the only one I know that's alive.

LK: [*laughs*] What's that like, by the way, to face the fact that all of your contemporaries—*all* of them, except Berle, right? . . . And he's a kid to you.

GB: Yeah. Berle and Danny Thomas, both kids. They'll make it in show business.

LK: But, isn't it kind of strange—that kind of feeling? I mean, there's nothin' you can do about it.

GB: Well, I'm not going to die again. I died in Altoona. I don't believe in doing things that have been done. Dying has been kicked.

LK: All right. Obviously, we'll move to longevity first, then we'll get to books. Do you, uh—

GB: The *reason* I'm around—

LK: You've done this a hundred times. Let's not do it like it's a hundred times—

GB: No! [*Punches out at Larry and slaps the table.*]

LK: [*Holds up his hands and laughs.*] I respect my elders.

GB: Okay. The reason I'm around for a long time— I love what I do for a living, and that's terribly important. Fall in love with what you're gonna do for a living. Very important. Keep you around a long time.

LK: So, in other words, you still like standing backstage when the man says, "And now, ladies and gentlemen, our special star is—" You like that?

GB: I love it. I walk out. The people stand up. They applaud. *How is he like that? He walks!*

LK: All right. So the kick can't be financial.

GB: No, no. But I still get paid.

LK: And do you save money like—?

GB: No, no. I don't. I give my— I don't. I came from a very poor family, but money is not the answer to me, you know. I'd like to, you know, get money, so I can give some money away.

LK: That's a joy you get? . . . Giving away. All right. You write a lot about radio. There was a review in the *New York Times* last Sunday that really praised the book. . . . It had one criticism—if that could be called a criticism—that George Burns doesn't much like to get into himself. He gives credit to Gracie, he talks about all the other friends in show business. He tells stories, but he doesn't want to get into *him*. . . . How did you react to that?

GB: Well, maybe they think so, but I don't mind talking about myself. But I—my life was that way when I started. From eight until twenty-seven, I did all kinds of lousy acts. I worked with a seal. I worked with a dog. I worked with two girls. I worked with another fellow. All bad acts. But in those days, there were theaters you could be bad in. There's no place to be bad today. The kids have to go to the Comedy Store or to *The Johnny Carson Show* or your show, you know? There's no place—

LK: No place to fail.

GB: No place. See, there were theaters that were worse than I was. So in those theaters, I was good. Then when I'd play a good theater, I was bad. But I loved what I was doing. I was sorry for the audience that didn't like me.

LK: [*laughs*] So you loved it even when you were bombing?

GB: Yes, sir. Because I had pictures of myself. I had music in my key. I had cards printed. But no job.

LK: [*laughs*] The singing: were you always a singer?

GB: I love to sing.

LK: I used to listen to your radio show. I used to love the singing parts.

GB: I loved to sing.

LK: Those are my favorite parts of your show.

GB: Well, I used to make syrup for a candy store—in the basement. Chocolate and vanilla and strawberry. You put it in a vat, and you cook it, and you put it in bottles. And three kids were singing and making syrup. And there was a letter carrier. His name was Lou Farley, from the East Side, and he wanted the whole world to sing harmony. He came down. He saw four kids. He taught us how to sing harmony. So I was singing. I was singing pretty good. One day, I look up—this was in the basement—look up. There's about eight or ten people standing up there.

They threw a couple of pennies. We stopped making syrup. We went into show business. We sang in yards, on ferry boats, on street corners, passed around the hat. Sometimes they put something in our hat. Sometimes they took our hats.

LK: [*laughs*] Did you give the group a name?

GB: Yeah, the Peewee Quartet. We called ourselves the Peewee Quartet.

LK: And what part of the four-part harmony were you?

GB: I was the tenor.

LK: Somebody told me today that you can still sing, that your country-and-western album—I'm not an *aficionado* on this—that your—

GB: It was a hit.

LK: —was a hit.

GB: How that happened is, they wrote a song called "I Wish I Was Eighteen Again," and they wanted the oldest man around to sing it. And Moses happened to be booked. So I gave up sky diving and became a country singer.

LK: So you were first a singer?

GB: Yeah. Sang all kinds of songs—harmony songs.

[*Commercial break*]

LK: The cigar—how many cigars do you smoke a day?

GB: I smoke between ten and twenty cigars a day.

LK: That's a big swing.

GB: Well, at my age I gotta hold onto something. . . . And I also drink three or four martinis a day.

LK: That's the truth?

GB: Yeah, and I don't eat spinach.

LK: Oh.

GB: There you are!

LK: Health.

GB: That's what keeps me alive.

LK: And you told me this is a domestic cigar.

GB: Yeah. These are three for a dollar: *El Productos*. See, a good cigar is well-packed. If I paid three or four dollars for a cigar, first I'd sleep with it. *Then* I'd smoke it.

LK: But you can afford it, George. We're going to get to girls.

GB: But let me tell you something about a good cigar. A good cigar is well-packed, and I—

LK: So I notice the ash falls.

GB: I smoke on the stage, and if you don't have a well-packed cigar—the cigar, it goes out—and if the cigar goes out three or four times on the stage, the audience goes out, too. And this doesn't go out. It stays lit.

LK: So you, so this is both a prop and a—

GB: A prop. When they laugh, I smoke. When they stop laughing, I talk. Are they laughing now?

LK: [*chuckles*] Yes.

GB: Then I'll smoke. [*He pointedly takes a drag on the cigar.*]

LK: [*laughs*] Okay, back to the candy store. George is a singer now. You're gonna be a singer. . . . Were you always a funny kid, though? Did you make the other kids laugh?

GB: Well, I have a sense of humor. My mother, my mother was very funny. Seven sisters. I came home when she was having breakfast. I was the bread-winner of the family. And my mother said, she says—she called me Natty, so my name is Nathan—she says, "You know, Natty, you come from a nice family." I said, "I do, huh?" We're having breakfast. She said, "All your seven sisters were married virgins." I said, "Mama, the reason they were married virgins, they weren't very pretty." My mother said, "Pass the salt."

LK: [*laughs*] She was funny.

GB: Oh, my mother was something fine! I brought home a girl once, Gerta Defor. . . . I was fourteen years old. She was sixteen. And she wore lipstick. In those days if you wore lipstick, you were a prostitute. She not only had on lipstick, she had on a beauty mark here, too. Made it even worse.

LK: A *shonda*.

GB: A *shonda*. So I brought her home, and I said to my mother, "I want you to meet my sweetheart, Gerta Defor." My mother said to Gerta, "Are you Jewish, Gerta?" And Gerta says, "No." She says, "Do you understand Jewish?" And Gerta says, "No." And, in Jewish, my mother turned around to me. She says, "Geh men rehl," which means "Go to hell." And she turned around to Gerta and says, "I just told my son what a charming girl you are." Good?

LK: Good. Were you a ladies' man early?

GB: No. I was never a great—even when I married Gracie—I was never a great lover.

LK: You were not?

GB: No.

LK: Well, how did this image come then?

GB: I—I made Gracie laugh. I made Gracie laugh. I had a sense of humor. Well, after you're married twenty-five years, and you get in bed with your wife, it's easy to make her laugh, and I made Gracie laugh.

LK: In other words, you were—this image of George Burns—sexy—you were never—

GB: No, no.

LK: You are admitting here that—

GB: No. I didn't need any women when I was young. Could do it myself. [*pause*] I was very careful. I wore gloves.

LK: [*laughs*] You know, when you're gonna be ninety-four, you can say anything. What are we gonna do to you?

GB: You can say: Well, now [*puts the palm of his hand on his waistline*], from here up, I'm fine. From here down, I need makeup. [*pause*] Very little makeup.

LK: [*laughs*] But you dated some—you date some beautiful women.

GB: Well, I—I was a good dancer. . . . I was a very good dancer. I was a Peabody dancer. You ever hear of that dance—Peabody?

LK: There was the Peabody. That's an *old* dance.

GB: Yeah. A police captain, Captain Peabody, he started that dance.

LK: It's kind of like a two-step and—

GB: Yeah. It's a fast dance. And my mother—I came home late. I used to go to the dances. My mother thought I'd turn out to be a gangster. And there was the Strolling Arm Squad on the East Side. Sneidecker was the head of the strongmen, so my mother went to him and says, "I'm worried about my son. He comes home three, four o'clock in the morning." He said, "Who? What's his name?" "He calls himself Nat Burns." At that time I wasn't George. He said, "Don't worry about him. He loves to dance too much. Nothing will happen to him." I danced.

LK: And that was the attraction for a woman? Women were attracted to that?

GB: Yeah. I was a very good dancer. I was a very good dancer.

LK: How did you meet Gracie?

GB: Gracie was living with Mary Kelly and Rina Arnold—three Catholic girls—and Rina Arnold was playing a vaudeville theater in Union Hill. I was working with Billy Lorraine—a lousy act—and we were gonna split up Wednesday, Wednesday night. And Rina Arnold knew that. And Gracie came to visit us. Gracie was an Irish dramatic actress at that time. She was not a comedienne. And Rina Arnold said to Gracie, "These two guys are splitting up. Why don't you go out front and take a look at them? Maybe you'd like to work with one of these guys." And she went out front, and she did—liked me. Two weeks later—

LK: She liked you right away?

GB: Two weeks later we did an act together, and I was the comedian in that act. I wrote it, you know—but the audience didn't laugh.

LK: Did you like her right away?

GB: Yes—no—well—oh— When I heard the audience, when she got all those laughs, I started to like her. [*pause*] Had to make a living.

LK: No. But, I mean, how 'bout the love part?

GB: Well, Gracie wasn't gonna marry me. Gracie was gonna marry Benny Ryan, who was a very, very good writer, a very good, uh, a very good actor—was a star— Ryan and Lee. But Mary Kelly liked *me*. And if it wasn't for Mary Kelly, Gracie would have married Benny Ryan. Mary Kelly *made* Gracie marry me.

LK: Because she wanted a challenge?

GB: She figured I'd be a better husband. And I was. I *was* a good husband. I was. I was a— We had a wonderful marriage, Gracie and I.

[*Commercial break*]

LK: . . . Al Jolson. First, was he— There's a biography out on him recently in which the writer—who had never seen him work, but based on all that had been written—said that he was the best—

GB: He was.

LK: —entertainer ever—

GB: He was.

LK: —that you would never want to go on stage following him.

GB: He was, he was.

LK: What did he *do*? I mean how—?

GB: Well, I'll tell you what he did. Al Jolson came from a Jewish family. His father was a cantor. There's a guy that went out on the stage, blackened up, and sang "I got a mammy in Alabamy" and made the people cry. *He's* got a mammy in Alabamy?

LK: [*chuckles*] You seem offended, George.

GB: No. No, I mean, that's how great he was. He convinced that audience that he had a mammy in Alabamy. Gracie and I were playing in Denver, and we were on number three. We were a little man-and-woman act. We weren't doing—we were playing the big time, but a small act. And Jolson was playing in *Bon-Bon* in Denver. We got two tickets. We ran over to see Jolson and never took off our makeup. We got there about 9:10, ten minutes after nine, and no Jolson. Nine-thirty—no Jolson. A quarter to ten, there are people applauding. Finally, Jolson walked on the stage, full of snow. It was snowing in Denver. He told the audience he went to a party, got carried away, he was talking, and he's sorry that he's late.

He said, "Do you mind if I put on my makeup here?"—instead of going back. He stripped from his waist up, put on blackface, did about twenty minutes of the show, and then he said, "Wait a minute. You know what happens: the horse wins the race. The fellow gets the girl. You want to see that? Or do you want me to entertain you?" They all said, "Entertain us!" He brought all the girls out on the stage. He said, "You girls that have dates, go about your business." Three or four girls left. He said, "The rest of you, sit down on the floor." He entertained the audience until one o'clock in the morning. Gave out candy, too. At one o'clock in the morning, he says, "I'm gonna take off my makeup, and I'm going next door to the restaurant. There's a piano in there. I'll bring along my piano player, sing you a few songs." Everybody ran out of the theater and ran to the restaurant. He was— There was nobody like him.

LK: Wow! Was he a bad guy?

GB: Not to me.

LK: Because he's had a bad reputation.

GB: Well—Jolson was a tough guy. He always had the water running in his dressing room. He never wanted to hear another act be a hit. You know, it don't always help.

LK: [*laughs*] That's true?

GB: Yeah, true. True.

LK: So he shouldn't hear applause or laughter?

GB: He never heard applause or laughter or anything. The water ran. Then he walked on the stage. And I used to meet him at the club, and I told him, I said: "Jolie," I says, "I seen everybody. You're the greatest entertainer I've ever seen in my life." And I complimented him. And he says to me, "George," he says, "you know they don't allow sturgeon in California. Do you like sturgeon?" I said, "I love sturgeon." He said, "I send for $200 worth of sturgeon every month from Barney Greengrass. You want some sturgeon for lunch?" I said, "Sure." Well, I had sturgeon like two or three times a week. I kept complimenting Jolson. [*pause*] I got so I liked sturgeon better than I did Jolson.

LK: [*laughs*] He—the transition to radio—he never had a big radio show.

GB: No, no. You had to *see* Jolson.

LK: You had to see him.

GB: You had to *see* him, had to see him, had to see him. It was—nobody like him. He wasn't the greatest *talent* in the world.

LK: He wasn't a good actor.

GB: He could only do two things. He was a great comedian, a great light comedian, but nobody appreciated that, because his singing was so great that you forgot that he got all those laughs. He was— There was nobody like him. Nobody.

LK: Did he always do blackface, though? Did he *have* to do that?

GB: Yeah. And everybody else did blackface when *he* did blackface. Cantor did blackface. Cantor went to the Ziegfeld Roof after seeing Jolson. He blackened up and did blackface.

LK: Cantor was not a great talent, was he? He was exuberant more than—

GB: He was—oh—had a lot of vitality. But Cantor wasn't in Jolson's class. When Cantor—Cantor was managed by Max Hays—When Cantor went up to the Ziegfeld Roof, it was a big hit. He was in blackface. Max Hays blackened up everybody: Buddy Doyle, his secretary—everybody.

LK:　[*laughs*] Cantor also had a hit television show—I think you write—for one week, and then he had to follow it a second week and didn't have anything more to do.

GB:　Well, he had a hit radio show—*Chase and Sanborne Show*. As a matter of fact, Gracie and I—

LK:　[*sings*] "I love to spend each—"

GB:　What?

LK:　That theme song.

GB:　[*sings*] "I love the—to spend this hour with you—" Yeah, exactly. It's like that.

LK:　[*sings*] "—and like a friend, I'm sorry it's through—"

GB:　[*sings along*] "—I'm sorry—"

LK:　Yeah, I remember that.

GB:　You sing pretty good. I remember [*leans forward*]. Sing this. [*sings rapidly*] "For she can carry a gun as good as any mother's son—"

LK:　[*sings*] "For she can carry a gun as good as any mother's son—"

GB:　Sing it again.

LK:　[*sings*] "For she can carry a gun as good as any mother's son."

GB:　[*sings simultaneously with King*] "For she can carry a gun as good as any mother's son." [*Burns slaps the table.*] You're singing my part! . . . Peewee Quartet—and Cantor. The first radio we did—television show—radio!—was on the Cantor show. We were playing the Palace Theater with Cantor and Georgie Jessel, and Cantor said, "How about going on my show just now?" We said, "Love to." He said, "Not you. Just Gracie." I said, "Sure, providing you do our material. How long do you want Gracie to do?" He says, "Five minutes." He says, "Write it out, and we'll do it." I said, "You don't have to write it out. You just walk on the show and say to Gracie, 'How is your brother?' and she'll talk for five minutes." Then the next week we got a job on the Rudy Vallee show, then on the Guy Lombardo show, then all of show business.

LK:　Gracie was a great light comedienne, was she not? It was—

GB:　Well, Gracie was a great actress.

LK:　That was what it was.

GB:　Gracie was—Gracie— The whole world thought that Gracie was dumb, but not Gracie. Gracie thought she was smart. When Gracie said these strange things, you didn't understand her. She felt sorry for you. And Gracie never *told* a joke. She *explained* it to you. Like—I came home. I says, "What are we having for dinner?" She says, "Roast beef. I just put two roasts in the oven, a big one and little one." I says, "Why two?" She said, "Why? Because when the little one burns that means the big one is done!"

LK:　[*laughs*]

GB:　Gracie was great. Without Gracie, I wouldn't—you wouldn't be interviewing me.

LK:　You really believe that?

GB:　Gracie made it all possible. Look, from seven—from eight to twenty-seven, I was a failure. Then I met Gracie, and things happened.

LK:　You had a great gimmick on your show. It's done now. Gary Shandling does it. It's *called* modern. Jackie Mason does it.

GB:　Talking to the audience.

LK:　Talk to the audience. Now your television show *always* talked to the audience. Your radio show talked to the audience.

GB:　I made it up.

LK: You took out a skit and talked to the audience.

GB: That's right.

LK: Was that a device? I mean to—

GB: My talent was off the stage. I was able to think of the things, and Gracie was able to do them. That's what made us a good combination.

LK: And then you would tell us what's happening. . . . You walked out of the living room. The scene was—

GB: I also had a television set upstairs in the library. When Gracie was planning things to do to me, I used to watch her on television. And our sponsor said, "You can't do that. It's not a reality." I said, "I'm going to do it." And he said, "Then you're gonna have to get a new sponsor." I said, "Well, then, we'll get one." But they kept us, and the television gimmick was a riot.

LK: The idea of talking to the audience was yours?

GB: Yeah.

LK: Is that what you did in vaudeville a lot? You would step out of frame?

GB: Stepped out of frame and stuff? In vaudeville, you could be canceled after the first show. I was always canceled. I played the Folly Theater in Brooklyn. I was doing a single then. I was rehearsing my music at ten o'clock in the morning. The manager heard me rehearse and canceled me. [*pause*] I'm the only act in show business that was canceled before he opened.

LK: [*laughs*] Why did you take the name *George*?

GB: Because my brother, they called my brother George, and we were five brothers, and we all loved my brother George, so we all called ourselves George. We had five Georges.

LK: [*laughs*] It was admiration, then?

GB: Yeah. We loved him.

[*Commercial break*]

LK: . . . True or false—that you could say "hello," and Jack Benny fell down laughing? That you had the ability to make him—

GB: Well, I'll tell you. If you told Jack Benny a joke, he wouldn't laugh, 'cause he dealt in that. But if you told Jack Benny something on the spur of the moment, if something happened, *that* would make him laugh. Like—he came in the club. I said, "Hello, Jack." He said, "I didn't sleep last night." That's no answer to hello, but that's what he said. "I didn't sleep last night." I said, "How did you sleep the night before?" He said, "The night before, I slept great." I said, "Sleep every other night." [*pause*] And that, you know, you won't believe this, but this is true. I went to Jack Benny's house. There was about two hundred people at a party, and Jack Benny called me aside. He says, "George, the party isn't moving." I says, "The party's moving fine. Everybody's drinking. Everybody's talking." And he got very angry. He said, "Hey, look. I'm in show business, too. I know when a party moves. This party isn't moving!" So, to have a little fun, I thought I'd play a—I said, "Look, why don't you go upstairs, and take off your pants, and come down in your shorts with Mary's hat on and play the violin?" And he said, "Do you think that will make it move?" I said, "Of course." So he went upstairs, and I told everybody, "Jack is coming down in his shorts with Mary's hat on playing the violin. Don't pay attention to him." Down came Jack with the violin. Nobody looked at him. He fell on the floor, started to laugh, and said, "George, now the party's moving."

LK: [*laughs*] That's great. How, how close were you? Were you *best*-best friends?

GB: Oh we were—we— Yeah, my closest friend. He was my closest friend. And the things that make that—for instance: . . . We were sitting and talking once, and he starts to laugh. I said, "What are you laughing at? I'm not saying anything." And he said, "But you're *not* saying it on purpose." [*pause*] That I couldn't understand.

LK: He had the best—what?—*timing* of all, right?

GB: Yeah.

LK: The longest jokes and—right?

GB: Quiet. A quiet riot. Jack Benny.

LK: All right. He understood pace.

GB: That's right. . . . And pauses, pauses, pauses.

LK: And you write that he transitioned radio to television. . . . Very easily. Not many did. . . . *He* did. Why? Because you would think pauses would be much more effective on radio. . . . I mean, we could imagine what—

GB: Well, yeah, yeah. Jack was a very strong personality on the stage. He didn't look it. He looked like you wanted to take him home and adopt him. . . . But he was a powerhouse. Like when the Coldmunds lived next door—this was on radio. You heard a sound effect. You heard one, two, three, four—coming down eight steps, walking on the pavement. Oh, he went over to borrow a cup of sugar. He had a little tin can. Walking on the pavement, then you heard somebody drop a dime into the tin cup, and Jack said, "Thank you."

LK: [*laughs*]

GB: And kept walking to the Coldmunds' door. Nobody would do that in radio! Nobody would hold that pause. You'd lose your audience. But not Jack.

LK: Was he very ill? Was his a sudden death?

GB: It was sudden for me, yeah. I was there the night he died. And Mary came down, and she says, "Jack just died." I said, "I'm going up to see him." She says, "You can't go up. The doctor says that nobody can come up." I said, "Mary, I've known Jack Benny longer than the doctor. I'm going up." And I went up. And there was Jack Benny with his hands this way and his head on the side. [*Burns folds his hands over his chest and turns his head.*] He looked like he'd just told a joke, and he's timing a laugh. And he was gone. He was gone, he was gone, he was gone, he was gone.

LK: Do you still go to Gracie's grave? Is that true?

GB: Every month I go to see Gracie.

LK: And you talk to her?

GB: I talk to her. I'll tell her that I've done a show with you. I tell her we got something. Sometimes I tell her a joke. She doesn't laugh. She heard 'em before.

LK: Do you just go out— People go out with you, and they leave you alone—

GB: No. I go alone. Sometimes. Sometimes I take my son. Sometimes, my daughter. But I go every month. And I know—I don't know whether Gracie hears me or not, but I feel her when I come away from Forest Lawn. She was—Gracie was special, you know. *You* just got married, didn't you?

LK: Yeah. Four weeks.

GB: How many weeks?

LK: Four weeks.

GB: Hmm. You're able to cheat now.

LK: Would you—

GB: You can only cheat when you're married.

LK: [*chuckles*] Would you remarry?

GB: No.

LK: Never.

GB: Never.

LK: No chance.

GB: No.

LK: Did anyone come close to getting you?

GB: Yeah, yeah. I went around with a little girl, uh, Kathy Coward in Dallas, and she wanted to get married, but I was fifty years older than she was. So I told *her* to get married.

LK: [*chuckles*] But not to you.

GB: I couldn't take care—I couldn't do— No. I was married before, you know.

LK: Before Gracie?

GB: I was married for twenty-six weeks. I was married to a— I did a dancing act, a ballroom dancing act, and I was booked for twenty-six weeks on the small time. And this girl was a very Orthodox Jewish girl, and we had twenty-six weeks booked. She was about seventeen years old. I was about twenty-one. And her mother and father wouldn't let me take her on the road unless I married her. Well, I wasn't going to cancel twenty-six weeks, so I married her. And we played to twenty-six weeks. But I never slept with her. We slept with a sheet in between in the room. Just two of us. Cheaper than taking two rooms. And she went around with another fellow, Al Klein, that she later on married, and he used to come to visit us, because Al Klein went with her.

LK: A weird set-up. So you were kind of ahead of your time. . . . This was almost like a *ménage à trois*, then?

GB: Yeah. And so when Klein would come up, he'd take my place in bed, and I'd take his room.

LK: [*chuckles*] Did you get legally divorced, then?

GB: Oh, after the twenty-six weeks, we were divorced. I played twenty-six weeks. I loved show business more than I loved the girl.

[*Commercial break*]

LK: . . . Durante. Great act?

GB: Great.

LK: Why? What did he have?

GB: Because, well, religion. They loved him! . . . There was something about purity, religion—a religious man, nicely married, no scandal about him, and everybody loved him.

LK: He had that wonderful voice.

GB: Yeah. He'd evoke—and sang great, and—

LK: He *did* sing great.

GB: The "Inky-Dinky-Doo," you know, and I saw him before they were Clayton, Jackson, and Durante.

LK: Before that? They were—

GB: A little band. He had a little band. . . . 125th Street. Used to play in a rathskeller. Down there. . . . And then Clayton, Jackson, and Durante got together. And Lou Clayton was a good businessman. Clayton, Jackson, and Durante were playing some cafe in New York, and they were getting $7,000 a week. But they didn't do business for two weeks. So when they went to pay him—and gangsters owned this cafe—they gave him ten, they gave Clayton $10,000 instead of $14,000. And Clayton said, "No, no, no. We got a contract for $14,000. I don't want $10,000." So the guy picked up the money and hit Clayton in the face and says, "Take the $10,000 and go." And Clayton picked up the money and hit him back in the face again and said, "I want $14,000." And this murderer looked at Clayton, who'd hit him back and given him a sore face. He not only gave him the $14,000, he bought Clayton a Cadillac car.

LK: The moral is?

GB: The moral is: always hit a gangster in the face with $10,000.

LK: [*laughs*] Frank Faye. The legendary Frank Faye.

GB: Frank Faye was a great, great comedian, but he was a tough guy. When he got divorced from Barbara Stanwyck—when they got him on the stand, they said, "What do you do for a living?" He says, "I'm the world's greatest comedian." So somebody at the club said, "Frank, did you say you were the world's greatest comedian?" He says, "I had to. I was under oath."

LK: [*laughs*]

GB: And Frank Faye didn't like the Jews and didn't like the blacks, but he was very religious. And I used to sit in the Brown Derby with him. And when his food—just before his food came, I used to go over and mention about eight or nine people that are dead. And every time you'd mention somebody dead, he'd bless himself or say a little prayer. I'd say, "Tom Fitzpatrick died." He'd say some prayers. "And Joe Phillips died." When his food got cold, I'd leave.

LK: [*laughs*] Berle.

GB: Great comedian.

LK: Now Milton Berle was *not* a hit in radio. . . . His radio show—even though I used to like his radio show with his brother Frank. It was funny, but it was never a hit.

GB: Yeah. Well, who knows? I, I can't answer that.

LK: How do you explain his success on television?

GB: Well, because he came in when it was brand new. In that time . . . there was nobody in television at the time.

LK: So he was on *versus* a test pattern.

GB: Everybody was in the first ten years. There was only eight acts.

LK: [*laughs*] But, he was a great visual comic.

GB: And then he could thank his mother for being a hit.

LK: Why?

GB: Well, his mother used to sit in the audience and applaud and stand up and do all kinds of things and make him a smash. And his mother was a very attractive lady. She's sitting in the audience next to some man, and the guy's making a play for her—playing with her knee. But she didn't pay any attention because Milton was on. And she applauded. She stood up. And she laughed in the right spots. When she got through, she slapped the man in the face. [*pause*] But not while Milton was on. She never made a relationship.

LK: You were always, though— My image of George Burns is you were above it. You were always kind of cool. You were removed from that crowd. I mean, I know you hung around with that crowd, but you had a special place—you and Gracie. Were you aware of that? You were different. You weren't a schtick kind of comic.

GB: No, I—

LK: You weren't a schtick kind of comic.

GB: No, no, no. I like, uh— Let me tell you something—about right now on the stage. When I go out on the stage, I don't do anything that isn't my age. I allow myself to get old. It's very important. Sophie Tucker used to sing "Poppa Goes Where Mama Goes or Poppa Doesn't Go Out Tonight" when she was twenty years old. But she had nice things—very sexy. [*He gestures to suggest a large bosom.*] And the sex kept 'em home. When she was forty-five, she still sang the same song: "Poppa Goes Where Mama Goes or Poppa Doesn't . . . ," but she held a gun in her hand. The *gun* kept them home! Now Blossom Sealy didn't allow herself to get old. You know that Blossom Sealy was a tremendous talent? You know that Blossom Sealy got down on one knee and sang a song before Jolson?

LK: I did not know that.

GB: Yeah. When she sang "Toddling the Totalo." She went from the Weber and Field Show to the Wintergarden show, and Jolson was there. And "Toddling the Totalo"—for the encore—she got down and sang on one knee. And Jolson came out and sang with her. And she got up, and he didn't.

LK: When you say, "allow yourself to get old"— meaning?

GB: Meaning Sophie Tucker allowed herself to get old. Blossom Sealy was booked on the *Ed Sullivan Show*. She was eighty-two years old, and she sang "Toddling the Totalo." You can't "toddle the totalo" when you're eighty-two. [*pause*] You can only toddle until you're about twenty-one. Then you walk very slowly. You start slowing up. But she never got old.

LK: The Hillcrest Country Club and you? Are you like, uh, are you the founder? Are you the president? Are you the—

GB: No, no, no, no. I'm just a member. I've been a member about fifty-five years. I used to sit at the same table with Jolson and Eddie Cantor and—

LK: You go there every day?

GB: Yeah. I go there every day, play a little bridge, and then I go home around three o'clock and—

LK: And then what?

GB: Take off my hair, put it on the block.

LK: And you, uh—

GB: —go to bed and get up at five-thirty and have a double martini. . . .

LK: Five-thirty. Then what happens?

GB: When I go out I have a martini, a couple of martinis.

LK: Do you go out a lot?

GB: Not too much.

LK: You're not a man about town, are you?

GB: No, no, no, no, no. I go. Yeah, I go. Sometimes once or twice a week. I go out. . . . I've a very nice house. I've got a very nice cook—nice husband and wife. They've been with me for years. *Everybody's* been with me for years.

LK: [*chuckles*] That's right. Everybody who's been with you has been with you for—

GB: Yeah. For years. For years. Years and years and years. My secretary has been with me for twenty-five years.

LK: These are all like baby times to you, right? . . . Your frame of reference. You've got a— I mean, when— You're the *century*, George. Do you realize this? You're older than our century. I mean, in the sense that we're not at 1990 yet. You were born, what? 1890, what?

GB: 1896. Well, if you think I'm old now, I'm booked to play the Palladium Theater when I'm 100 years old. . . . I'm booked there for two weeks. And if I don't like my dressing room, I won't show up.

[*Commercial break*]

LK: . . . You danced with Fred Astaire? *With* him?

GB: With him. Gracie and I did *Damsel in Distress.* You see, I'm a right-legged dancer.

LK: A what?

GB: A right-legged dancer.

LK: No, I don't know that.

GB: I can tap with my right foot. My left foot wants me to go into some other business. [*pause*] And the audience agreed with my left foot. . . . So when you get to dance with Fred Astaire, before they sign the contract, Fred Astaire has to see you dance. And I knew, once Fred Astaire takes a look at my left leg, we won't sign the contract. So there was an act in vaudeville, they did the whisk-broom dance—two guys—and it was a big hit. So I sent for one of the guys—they were out of vaudeville then. I said, "Teach Gracie and myself the whisk-broom dance." And he taught it to us. And we went to see Fred Astaire. I brought my piano player, and we showed Fred Astaire the whisk-broom dance, and he loved it. I says, "If you want it for your movie, you can have it." He says, "Are you kidding? I'd love it." And that was that. So he never saw my left leg.

LK: Why? . . . It is a one-legged dance?

GB: No. The whisk broom— You use the whisk broom instead of taps. The whisk broom does all the brushing off: brush notes.

LK: Oh. Weren't you a little nervous, dancing for Fred Astaire?

GB: [*Shakes his head no.*]

LK: Do you ever get nervous?

GB: No. To get nervous, you gotta have talent. Gracie got nervous. [*chuckles*]

LK: [*laughs*] That's funny.

GB: Jack Benny got nervous.

LK: You really don't think you have talent. Why do you put yourself down?

GB: No, no, no. Yeah, I've got—

LK: First of all, you've got talent to conceive.

GB: Yeah, I've got—I've got—I've got talent. . . . You're asking me questions. I'm able to answer them. That's talent. Uh, when I worked for Gracie—you know, you've got to time your jokes, you know.

LK: Hey, that's as much. A straight man needs timing.

GB: Yeah, yeah. Timing. Of course. So, I've got talent. But I haven't got that *kind* of talent. *Now* I've got talent—since Gracie retired. Gracie retired in '58, and I went into show business. *I* was retired when I worked with Gracie. I did nothing. And I went into show business. And now I'm an accepted commodity.

LK: In fact, you've gotten bigger as you've gotten older.

GB: That's right.

LK: In fact, you've *never* been bigger.

GB: That's right. I'm the— The best time of my career is right now.

LK: The biggest—right now. How do you explain that? What do you tell to Gracie?

GB: Well, I think, I think. Of course, working with Gracie didn't hurt. I lost— I wasn't allowed to—I—I had a lot of timing.

LK: But most people who see you now don't know Gracie. . . . I mean, most people alive may not remember your act, right?

GB: Well, because I tell the truth. I tell my age. I talk like a ninety-three-year-old man would talk. I don't get, you know, when I talk about sex, I have fun with it. I don't, you know, I don't— They know I can't *do* anything—which is not true. [*laughs*]

LK: [*laughs*] Do you go to . . .

GB: You see? When I lie, I tell you it's a lie.

LK: [*laughs*] Did you like Groucho?

GB: I liked Harpo.

LK: [*laughs*]

GB: I'll tell you why. Uh, Harpo—I liked Groucho. I didn't hate— I never *danced* with Groucho. But I liked Harpo and Susan—were wonderful. They adopted four kids. And I said to Harpo and Susan, "How many kids are you gonna adopt?" They said, "As many windows as we have in the house. So that when we leave, we want a kid waving to us from each window." You know, they were charming people. . . . Tell you a good Groucho story—a good Marx Brothers story. The Marx Brothers are playing a theater, and their father is in to see the show. And the fellow in back says, "Harpo Marx"—who's on the stage with the Marx Brothers— "he's deaf and dumb. He can't talk." The father turned around, and he says, "No, no, no. Harpo can talk. He talks." The guy turned around and says "Don't tell me Harpo talks. I know Harpo! He doesn't talk." His father says, "I know him better than you know him. He talks." The guy says, "I'll bet you $25 he doesn't talk." The father says, "If you lay me odds, I'll take the bet."

LK: [*laughs*]

[*Commercial break*]

LK: . . . We only have two minutes left. The *film* career of George Burns. *Oh, God*: one of the great movies ever made.

GB: Why shouldn't I play God? Anything I do at my age is a miracle.

LK: You were a great God—a great God.

GB: The first *God* movie was good. . . . That's because John Denver was good. It was good casting. If God came down and looked for a nice man, he'd have picked John Denver.

LK: But, George, don't downplay yourself. You were a good God.

GB: Yeah, well.

LK: How about *The Sunshine Boys*?

GB: Great.

LK: Did you like working with [Walter] Matthau?

GB: Oh. Great actor. And Dick Benjamin. And Herb Ross, the director. And Neil Simon, the writer.

LK: How did you like—how *do* you like acting?

GB: I love it.

LK: Because that's different, isn't it?

GB: That's the easy, uh, it's easy to do acting. You know, you sit down and you act. You don't have to stand up all the time.

LK: I don't follow you.

GB: Well, on the stage, you walk out there. You stand there. If you asked me to get up here and stand for an hour, I couldn't do it. But with an audience out there, they applaud, and the love comes over the footlights and gives you vitality, and you can stand.

LK: Right. But in acting you can sit. [*chuckles*]

GB: In acting, I can sit. And if I can sit and get paid, I'm in the right business.

LK: You have—wait a minute. You have summed up—

GB: How do you feel, sitting?

LK: Fine.

GB: Fine. There you are.

LK: [*laughs*] You have summed up a whole major art form by saying you can sit. . . . In other words, in *The Sunshine Boys*, when you walked into the room, you could sit down and talk to—

GB: I could sit down and talk. Sure.

LK: What a way to make a living!

GB: Of course! I won an Academy Award.

LK: [*laughs and extends his hand across the table to Burns*] What an honor.

GB: [*smiles broadly, takes King's handshake*] Thank you.

LK: George Burns, ladies and gentlemen.

GB: [*acknowledges the applause of the studio audience*] Thank you. Thank you.

LK: The book is *All My Best Friends*. It is published by Putnam. And, uh, we did tonight's show in New York. This book is destined to be a major bestseller. Most of his books were. The Gracie book, in fact, went through the roof. . . . One of the proudest things I am now proudest of is that George is out in the audience, live, watching us.

GB: No he isn't.

LK: I heard him.

GB: [*slaps King's hand*]

LK: Whoa! Good night, George Burns.

Ronald Reagan

January 11, 1990

Born above the general store in Tampico, Illinois, on February 6, 1911, Ronald Wilson Reagan became interested in acting while at Eureka College, worked as a radio sports announcer, then went to Hollywood as a Warner Bros. contract player.

Through the 1950s and the first years of the 1960s, Ronald Reagan was a committed liberal Democrat. In 1964, he abruptly turned to Republican conservatism and campaigned on behalf of Barry Goldwater with a speech that prompted Reagan's successful run for governor of California in 1966. In 1980, Reagan swamped incumbent Democrat Jimmy Carter, winning the first of two terms as president. Reagan introduced "supply-side economics"—or just plain "Reaganomics"—reviving (at least temporarily) a sluggish economy and earning him unprecedented popularity. The so-called Iran-Contra scandal threatened to wreck his second term, but he emerged relatively unscathed, leading detractors and admirers alike to call him the "Teflon president." Nothing bad seemed to stick.

"I don't want to hear anyone tell me what the political ramifications are of some decision that has to be made. We will discuss only: Is it good or bad for the people?"

LARRY KING: Our special guest for the full hour tonight is a gentleman very familiar to this city, the former president of the United States, and a man who had an effect on the decade second to none. . . . What do you miss the most? It's been almost a year. What do you miss?

RONALD REAGAN: Well, really, the people, the very fine people that you worked with and all of that.

LK: Don't miss the trappings? Don't miss the White House itself?

RR: No. If I had to pick places or anything like that, I have a great many happy memories of Camp David, where you lived in a normal-sized house and could go out the door and take a walk if you wanted to, or ride a horse.

LK: Those were disadvantages to the White House, then?

RR: Well, the thing is, there was a certain amount of bird-in-a-gilded cage atmosphere there. You could look out the windows at the people walking on Pennsylvania Avenue, and you knew that you couldn't go out and do that. You were kind of in there for security reasons, but—

LK: And are you the kind of person who wanted to go out?

RR: Oh, sure.

LK: Because Harry Truman liked going out. Those were different days.

RR: Oh, yes, yes. He used to walk consistently, I know. It was a different time, though. Incidentally, though, I have to wonder about as we start here, I've heard a great deal from Nancy about a little problem with a cold metal microphone that wound up being against her flesh.

LK: Her body, yes.

RR: Yes, she didn't have clothes like this on, so—

LK: She was at our studio in New York, and we put the microphone down. It went down her dress, and then hit all sorts of parts of her. Anyone in New York, they know your wife intimately. She was a real trouper.

You were telling me something interesting before we went on, I think the audience would really be interested in. We know that you're hard of hearing, but it's not due to the aging process. Tell that. This is really fascinating.

RR: Well, I began finding that, particularly with the one side, I was having a great deal of difficulty in hearing, and, finally, I went to the very distinguished Dr. House, and he did find that, yes, the hearing was very low there. And so he started asking me about things that might have happened, because it was something that had taken place in the nature of an injury. I didn't know how far back he wanted to go. Finally, when he said, as far back as I could remember, I remembered a movie that I made many years ago, and me and another actor were running from the bad guys, and went to get behind a tree and start shooting at them. And I'm afraid that my fellow actor didn't know much about guns, because as we turned around the tree, he was just behind me, he put that .38 right up on my shoulder and pulled the trigger. And you know, the concussion actually knocked me three or four feet to the side. And then Dr. House said, "Say no more. That's what did it." And it was a deterioration then of the nerves that took place over the years.

LK: Because you sure have handled the aging process well. Do you feel as good as you look? I mean, you look incredible.

RR: Well, thank you very much. I feel just fine.

LK: You don't—it seems that you are in—you know, everyone's envious. Like, the hair is real. It grows back, right? . . . They have surgery, and it grows back.

RR: I can't take credit for that. That has to be by the genes, because my father died with a very handsome head of hair, and my mother also. So I guess I just inherited that.

LK: You know, you're very good at describing things, and something has fascinated me and, I'm sure, the audience. What is it like to be shot? I mean, we all think about that. We've watched it in movies. You've played it in movies. You've been shot, and shot others. What's it like to be really, like, to be really shot?

RR: Well, I'll tell you what it was like. What it was like was, *I didn't know I was shot.* I heard a noise, and we came out of the hotel and headed for the limousine. The next thing I knew, one of the Secret Service agents behind me just seized me here, by the waist, and plunged me head-first into the limo. I landed on the seat, and the seat divider was down, and then he dived in on top of me, which is part of their procedure to make sure that I'm covered.

Well, as it turned out later, the shot that got me careened off the side of the limousine and hit me while I was diving into the car, and it hit me back here, under the arm, and then hit a rib, and that's what caused an extreme pain, and then it tumbled—it turned, instead of edge-wise—and went tumbling down to within an inch of my heart. But when I got in the car, I hadn't felt anything. And he landed on top of me, and then the pain, which now I know came from the bullet hitting that rib—that terrific pain—and I said, "Jerry, get off. I think you've broken a rib of mine." And he got off very quickly, and just then I coughed, and I had a handful of bright red, frothy blood. So I said, "I guess evidently the broken rib has pierced the lung." Well, he simply turned and said, "George Washington Hospital." And we were on our way.

But—and all the way I was—I used up my handkerchief, and then I used up his, but when I got to the emergency entrance, I got out of the car and walked in, and a nurse met me, and I told her I was having a little trouble breathing, and what I thought it was. And the next thing I knew—then when my knees began to turn to rubber, and I wound up on a gurney. And I was wearing a suit like this, for the first time I'd ever worn it—it was brand new—and they were taking scissors and cutting it off of me.

LK: And you were thinking, *What are they doing?* Did you ever think you might die?

RR: No, although I didn't just leave it to chance. I talked to my friend upstairs about that.

LK: But you never thought that this was the end? . . . Because some people in that situation, in a trauma situation, think it's over.

RR: No. I found out afterward that a lot of those people there at the hospital thought it could very likely be the end. They said that I was very near going into a state of shock, and I had also lost more than half the blood in my body. . . .

LK: Were you angry?

RR: Well, I didn't know for quite a while, until they began to tell me about the young man that had done this and what his problem was—that he was not exactly on a normal basis. And so, then, I added him to my prayers—prayers for myself that, well, if I wanted healing for myself, then maybe he should have some healing for himself.

LK: The Pope forgave the man who shot him. Did you forgive John Hinckley?

RR: Yes. I found out he wasn't, he wasn't thinking on all cylinders, yes. . . .

[Commercial break]

LK: You've had two careers. Not many people have had that, either. A full career in one profession, a full career in another. All the time you were in the White House, did you read *Variety?* Did you keep up with the goings on out here? Did you stay aware of the business?

RR: Well, I never had a chance at any of the trade papers. I was always interested in what was going on, because I started out as a radio sports announcer.

LK: So you had three careers. But you didn't stay in touch while president with the old career, the old—

RR: Well, as I say, I tried to keep interested, but I never had any access to the trade papers. But I tried to keep up with, you know, what was being made in Hollywood and so forth.

LK: Was there a good comparison between the two—politics and acting? Did you utilize one with the other? I mean, critics would say you did. Do you feel you did?

RR: Well, I'll have to tell you this one thing. I know that I took an awful lot of abuse when I was running, because people said, *What is anyone who had the nerve to be an actor and think they could be president of the United States?* I have to tell you there were a number of times when I thought, *Could you do that job if you* hadn't *been an actor?* . . . First of all, just like you have the reviewers that pan your pictures and so forth, and then the constant publicity seeking in that business; well, there's much of the same thing in the business of being president.

LK: There is a comparison. There's a comparison between the two cities, isn't there, Hollywood and Washington?

RR: And you're familiar with the public and the people and so forth. I think one of the things that probably was a help in the presidency was, you can't be an actor without liking people. They're your stock in trade. You are out to please them.

LK: Because if you don't please them, you don't make it.

RR: That's right. So the people are what you're thinking of in the presidency. I told every cabinet member and every staff member that I appointed, that I wanted to hear from them, without any shading, on all of the decisions that had to be made. I wanted their thinking on it. But the thing, I said— There is one thing I *don't* want. I *don't* want to hear anyone tell me what the political ramifications are of some decision that has to be made. We will discuss only: Is it good or bad for the people?

LK: Bill Casey, the late Bill Casey, told me once at a lunch, if Ronald Reagan has one fault, it's an inability to dress people down. He doesn't fire people well. He can't knock someone down well when they deserve it. Was he right?

RR: Well, I guess there was some right in that. Yes, it was difficult for me to fire someone, or to be mean to them in any way.

LK: You also don't bear grudges, do you? You seem not to have a meanness. . . . Well, let's take, like, Donald Regan. You don't seem to have animosity toward— Your wife has more.

RR: Well, that's on my behalf. She feels a little bit about the same way you are in asking these things and saying these things. But she sometimes thinks that someone's taken advantage of me, and that fires her up more than if they were taking advantage of her.

LK: But it doesn't fire you up?

RR: I've sometimes had the staff tell me they know I'm upset when I throw my glasses.

LK: You've thrown— I can't picture that.

RR: Well, yes, sitting at the desk, and throwing them across the desk, the reading glasses.

LK: The liking of Gorbachev. Was that a real sense of affection? Did you "*like* like" him?

RR: Yes. I'll have to tell you that, as you know, there were— He was the fourth. There were three leaders before him in the Soviet Union, and I didn't have much to do with them. They kept dying on me. But he was totally different than any Russian leader that I had met before, and I have to say I think that there was a kind of a—of a chemistry there, that set up. Now, on the other hand, I knew too much about communism to believe in words. I said that I would make my decision as to whether we're getting along on the basis of deeds. Every meeting that we ever had, I presented him with a handwritten—my handwriting—list of people that had been brought to my attention, who wanted to emigrate—and for reasons— to get out, and I would give it to him, and in every instance, very shortly, he—

LK: He came through. . . . Do you think he would have been a successful politician in this country? Was he just good at it?

RR: Yes, because I think—he is a likeable person. You find yourself liking him. But again, knowing the difference between our two systems, I had a—I'm not a linguist, but I learned one little Russian phrase, and I used it so often that he used to clap his hands over his ears. And that was "*doveryai no proveryai*," which means "trust but verify."

LK: Do you, with all the changes that have occurred in this decade, especially the last year, this incredible year—do you feel a personal sense of accomplishment?

RR: Well, I think that perhaps I had something to do with it, because I believe, number one, that in seeking peace with the Soviet Union it could only be done through strength, not just through words or pleading. And I also believed in the necessity of being frank about how I looked at them and their expansionism, and so forth, and the things that they were doing, and had done, here in our own country. And that's why I used some terms like the "evil empire" and things of that kind.

LK: Do you think that all paid off?

RR: I think it did, yes. Because in talking about peace and armament, I remember in our first meeting, I said to him that here was a very unique situation. Here probably were the only two men in the world that could start World War III, or maybe bring about peace, and I said that I knew we were going to talk about could we reduce arms and weapons, but I said I have to remember that we don't mistrust each other because we're armed. We're armed because we mistrust each other. So maybe we should see if we couldn't find out ways to reduce the causes of the mistrust between us. . . . Well, he accepted that, and I think—you see—there's one thing. He had a need for achieving something. He had discovered that he had inherited an economic basket case, and much of that was due to the military build-up. So, if he was going to fulfill the responsibilities of his new job, general secretary of the Soviet Union, he had to find an answer to that basket case, that terrible economic situation, where they couldn't provide enough food for their own people. . . .

[*Commercial break*]

LK: Mr. Gorbachev in Lithuania.

RR: Well, he's there, of course, because of the desire of those Baltic countries to have their nationalism reinstated, and I think that he has a great opportunity. The only reason that Stalin and the Soviet Union seized those Baltic states was to save them from Hitler, but now there's no Hitler. And it just seems to me he has a great opportunity to call the attention of the world to the fact of why they were taken over, and now there is no longer any need, and then restore to them their nationhood.

LK: You think he might do that?

RR: I don't know, but I think it'd be—I think it'd be smart if he did.

LK: If he asked your advice, that's what you'd tell him?

RR: Yes.

LK: The Noriega situation. Would you have done what President Bush did? Would you have gone in?

RR: I think, on the basis of all that I know about it and all of the facts—you know, I'm not privy to everything now that I'm not there— But, yes, I think that the facts as they were— We had tried everything we could domestically and without force before, and we weren't able to move him. And so I—yes, I think that this is the proper thing.

LK: Do you miss not being in the know?

RR: Well, no, because having been there, I know what the situation is, and I know how difficult it would be . . . for them to try and keep me apprised. Now, I must say that they do. I get reports from them, just as I sent reports to the pervious presidents. But for making a decision, no, I know how that comes up at such a time.

LK: So you don't personally miss it?

RR: No.

LK: How, in your opinion—you can be honest now, you don't need the job—how's Dan Quayle doing?

RR: I think Dan Quayle has been badly abused by much of the media. I think they've ignored looking at his record as a senator, and he has a fine record, and he was looked up to and respected by a great many people. And now this just trying to find every misuse of a word or something—I think he doesn't deserve that.

LK: Is that a tough job?

RR: Oh, sure. Yes, it has to be.

LK: Because all the power depends on what the president gives to him?

RR: Yes. And I think that a vice president has to be aware that there's a limit to what they can say or do, because of the presidency. But I have to tell you—and I think George is doing the same thing with him—when I became governor of California, I had a feeling that the lieutenant governor was a position that had been abused, that it was like letting someone sit on the sidelines in case they were needed in the game if something happened to the player. And so the same thing with the vice presidency. I thought that the vice president—it was a waste of talent, unless you used him like, say, the vice president of a corporation. So George was a part, a major part, of every thing we did.

LK: Ollie North said yesterday you are the man of the decade. Now, how do you react? I'm sure you heard that. How do you react?

RR: Well, now, I have to admit that gives you a warm feeling inside to hear someone say that, particularly someone who was around when it was going on.

LK: Do you—how do you feel about him?

RR: About Ollie North? . . . Well, I have difficulty in talking about this situation that he was directly involved in, because it is still before the law and all, and I could create some problems if I made statements here.

LK: Did you personally like him?

RR: Yes, and he had a great military record of courage and, certainly, of taking care of his men. . . .

[*Commercial break*]

LK: What we're going to do now is include some of your phone calls. This is, like, only in America. The former president of the United States, Ronald Reagan—your chance to talk to him. And, naturally, the first call is *not* from America. San José, Costa Rica, hello.

CALLER: [*San José, Costa Rica*] Yes. Hello, Larry, Mr. President. This is, indeed, an honor. In regard to your actions while president and regarding the Contra activities, do you think that it's possible that there will ever be a verifiable free election in Nicaragua? And, two, in regards to our activities in Panama, why do you think that the news media has not mentioned the large number of Cuban, Libyan, PLO, and other such groups that have had a strong military presence in Panama?

LK: All right. Let's handle the first one first. Think we'll ever see that in Nicaragua?

RR: Well, I think we can, but I think some things have to be done. Nicaragua, the revolution against the dictator, the revolutionaries, at one point in that, asked the—that dictator to step down in order to save lives and stop the killing. And he said, *Well, what are the revolutionary goals?* And—well, incidentally, I'm ahead of myself. He—they asked the Organization of American States to ask him to do that. And this question then came back, and the Organization of American States asked the revolutionary goals, and they were listed as being everything that we have: pluralistic society, freedom of the press, all of these things that go for democracy. And these were promised by the Sandinistas.

Now, the Sandinista organization has that name because of Sandino, a man, and it was a communist organization. When he stepped down—the dictator stepped down—and the revolution was over, they were the only really organized group in the revolution. They took over. They even exiled and got rid of some of the other leaders of the revolution, and they have not kept a single promise about this being a democracy.

LK: So you are not optimistic?

RR: Well, I'm optimistic in the belief that if the Organization of American States, if the—all the other Central American countries and ourselves—if we will ensure that it can be—there can be a team to watch this election, and not just leave it to the Sandinista government, because then—no, it's not—it's not going to happen. But if they are there, and can ask for it, I have confidence that the people of Nicaragua will vote for democracy.

LK: To Kalamazoo, Michigan. Hello.

CALLER: [*Kalamazoo, Michigan*] Hello, Mr. President. You're looking very good, sir. Do you think a black or a woman will ever be elected president? If so, will it be in your lifetime?

RR: Well, I don't know whether it'll be in my lifetime or not. I would hope so. But I think that both things can happen. You only have to look at the progress that has been made already, and one of the things that I could point out right now, that I think should—there should be more—in looking for presidential candidates, there should be more looking at governors. For a time in our history that's where you found the presidents, and I can tell you, having been a governor and having been a president, the only job in the United States that is similar to the presidency—and *very* similar—is the job of governor.

LK: Is this a statement for the new governor of Virginia?

RR: Well, what I'm saying is, we now have had some experience with black governors, with women governors, and we can match them with anyone else. And if we set out to look at the record of governors with their states, we could judge on the basis of what they've done for their state, what they could do for the nation. Because, as I say, I was surprised, as president, in the first forty-eight hours, I was surprised to realize how *un*-different this new job was than what I had done in California.

LK: I know he's not in your party, but are you a little encouraged by the election of a black governor in Virginia? Is this a good sign? I know I'm taking you away from partisanship here.

RR: Well, I would like to point out that race should no longer be the consideration. The consideration should be political philosophy. Now there I have to get into Democrat and Republican—I've been both in that regard. . . . And I have to ask, how many Democrats, if they really pin down the policies of their party, how many of them can still be supportive of them. I didn't really leave the party, I don't think. It left me.

LK: To Santa Rosa, California, with former president Ronald Reagan.

CALLER: [*Santa Rosa, California*] Hi, Larry King. Hi, President Reagan. . . . My daughter, when she was eighteen months old, and we were in a poster shop, she saw your face on a Van Heusen shirt commercial, a print ad, and she said, "Oh, there's President Reagan!" They didn't even recognize you. But she did. Anyway, my question is if you were interested in getting back into show business at all—commercials, or movies, or TV? And do you watch *Falcon Crest?*

RR: Fair question. Let me start with the other. I happen to believe that to return to show business—and I loved show business—but I happen to believe that returning to that now would seem as if I was trying to capitalize on the presidency. And besides, now that I'm out, I have some other things that I very seriously believe I should be doing, and I'm trying to do, and that is to get back on the mashed-potato circuit, the after-lunch and after-dinner speaking, and speak up to the people for some of the things that we didn't get done while I was there. . . . For example, this country needs a balanced budget amendment to the Constitution.

LK: Boy, you've been fighting for that for a long time.

RR: Yes, and it needs the line-item veto. Forty-three governors had it. I had it. Where you can pick out of a big hodge-podge bill certain things that are simply costly and are just pork and shouldn't be done and veto them, and then the legislature would have to override your veto to get them back. Well, I was one of the forty-three governors that had that when I was governor of California. I used the line-item veto 943 times—and was never overridden once. Now, for a president not to have that same authority—and I have to tell you that the Congress, over a great many years, has continued to nibble away at the authority of the president, until when I hear some of them accuse me of having the budget deficits, a president of the United States can't spend a dime. Only the Congress can spend money. So who's to blame for the deficit?

LK: Now, we're going to get Tip O'Neill mad again. Do you miss the Tipper? He misses you.

RR: Well, yes. I must say, Tip was one who kept the politics and the personality separate. In other words, as he once said to me—when I caught him saying something pretty rough about me—well, he said "That's politics, old fella." He said, "Old buddy, after six o'clock, we're friends." So every once in awhile, when I knew I had a meeting with him, I set my clock ahead to six o'clock.

LK: You want to answer the *Falcon Crest* question? . . .

RR: I don't know that I've had time to watch that so much. . . . No, other than the news and trying to follow the news, I can't say that—

LK: Do you watch films a lot?

RR: Sometimes I like to turn to that channel that puts on the old ones, just in case they might be putting on one of mine.

LK: Do you watch it? Do you watch yourself?

RR: Well, if I see the movie and think it'd be interesting. Because I'm surprised to learn how many movies I didn't see.

LK: Really?

RR: Yes, you'd think living in Hollywood, and then suddenly you see a movie and say, I remember that title and all, but I never saw that movie.

LK: I like the one you did with Nancy, the navy one. . . . That was a good film. . . . I liked that movie. See that a lot.

RR: Well, that was from a book written by Admiral [Chester] Nimitz, and it was about an operation that took place in World War II, in which a whole flotilla of our submarines went into the Sea of Japan, went to the bottom, and laid there until a signal to come up, and then they came out to virtually wipe out the Japanese merchant marine, which was getting the supplies for Japan from the mainland, from China. And it was a very successful operation.

LK: What was the title of that movie?

RR: Well, the title of the book was *Operation Hellcat*, but the studio decided to change the name to *Hellcats of the Navy*, and I thought they should have stuck with the first title.

[*Commercial break*]

LK: We just showed that clip of the Berlin Wall—"Mr. Gorbachev, tear down this wall." Now you can't tell me you figured that would happen?

RR: Well, I meant what I said when I said tear it down. It—you know, it was such a— how can you—how would we feel if you wanted to put a wall down the Mississippi River from Canada to the Gulf?

LK: Now, do you think they're going to unify that country?

RR: I don't know, but I do believe it's up to them, and I—I don't think there should be too much interference from the outside with them.

LK: Tarzana, California, for Ronald Reagan. Hello.

CALLER: [*Tarzana, California*] Hello, Mr. President. As a political science student, it is indeed an honor to talk to you. My question is: Do you believe that the campaign Bush conducted in 1988 involving Willie Horton and Boston Harbor—did you feel it was a little too negative, too personal, and how do you feel about negative ads in general?

RR: Well, I think that he was goaded into this, and I think it was a case of trying to remind the people that—Massachusetts, first of all, their own people were calling it "Taxachusetts," and many people were moving across the state line to live in another state because of their, their tax—

LK: You don't think it was at all dirty—

RR: Well, I think you have to realize what the other man is saying, including your response. It isn't just an open attack on someone who has not opened the subject himself. But I think, yes, to hold with a program in which a man is freed and then goes out and commits dastardly deeds, and against his fellow human beings—

LK: Is fair game?

RR: Yes. . . .

[*Commercial break*]

LK: We go to Oslo, Norway. Hello.

CALLER: [*Oslo, Norway*] I wonder very much about, has it ever, during your time of presidency, been a chance of nuclear war between Soviet Union and America?

RR: I don't think so. Because while I disagreed with the policy that was called the MAD policy—M-A-D [Mutually Assured Destruction]—it at least had seen both countries armed to the point that neither one wanted to take the risk of starting that war, because each of us knew how well armed we were. But I did feel that we could not keep on doing that, and that it was a foolish policy. And so when the opportunity came to get an intermediate range treaty on the weapons, the missiles that the Soviet Union had aimed at the cities of Europe . . . well, that led them to a meeting, and thank heaven, a meeting with Gorbachev, where I said the answer, then, is zero-zero. You get rid of yours, and we'll get rid of ours.

LK: But we were never close to conflict in your eight years?

RR: I don't think so, no. . . .

[*Commercial break*]

LK: We are running out of time. A couple of other things: AIDS, were we late on that?

RR: I don't think so—no, certainly, we were not unnecessarily so. It was a plain case of catching up with things, and I immediately appointed a commission to get into the whole problem of AIDS and come back with the recommendations of what we could and should be doing.

LK: Do you think Rock Hudson focused a lot of our attention on it?

RR: I think that brought a lot of attention to it.

LK: Did you know him well?

RR: Well, I knew him as we knew each other in Hollywood, as fellow actors and all, but not more than that.

LK: Are you hopeful about it?

RR: Well, yes, I think we have to be hopeful about it, or we'll find ourselves back in those days of the plagues that wiped out millions of people.

LK: Sandusky, Ohio, for Ronald Reagan. Hello.

CALLER: [*Sandusky, Ohio*] Hi. Real quick, Ronnie. I just want to tell you I love you, and I just want to know what your favorite actor or actress was that you worked with. And I wish you could run again for many more years.

LK: Not a bad call.

RR: Thank you for your call, and I appreciate it. And obviously, I have to tell you that my opportunity to act with an actress, Nancy Davis—

LK: Didn't turn out too bad.

RR: No, she was a nurse, and I was a naval officer, and so forth, and we went home together because we were married.

LK: What actor did you like working with most?

RR: Well, now, there were a lot of them. That's pretty hard.

LK: Was Flynn fun?

RR: Yes, although I can tell you an unusual thing about Errol. Errol, with all that figure and all that he had, and that ability in the action films and so forth, actually had an inferiority complex about his acting ability. . . . Yes, and so he was always kind of looking for a way to maybe get an advantage, which he thought he should have, because the other actor—for example, if you were playing as a costar, as I did with him in *Santa Fe Trail* and pictures of that kind—he never bothered about the people who could really steal scenes, the character actors, that didn't bother him. But it was another leading-man type—

LK: He'd move in on you?
RR: Yes, and he would try to want the camera a little favoring—
LK: Stay well.
RR: All right.
LK: Thank you.
RR: Well, thank you.

William Henry Cosby was born (July 12, 1937) and raised in Philadelphia. During his college days, a friend offered him five dollars a night to tend bar and tell jokes at the Cellar, a Philadelphia coffeehouse. In 1962, he toured clubs around the country, achieving enough success to make him a regular on Johnny Carson's The Tonight Show. *This led to* I Spy *(1965–68), with Cosby as the first African American actor to star in a weekly dramatic series. Next came* The Bill Cosby Show *(1969–73), a series of films, and then the hit sitcom called simply* The Cosby Show.

Cosby has received multiple Emmys and Grammy Awards (for eight comedy albums), and he is the author of The Wit and Wisdom of Fat Albert, Bill Cosby's Personal Guide to Power Tennis, Fatherhood, Love and Marriage, *and* Childhood. *The publication of* Childhood *occasioned this interview.*

"A guy asked me, he said, 'How much money do you want to make?' I said —and this was 1962— I said, 'Three hundred sixty dollars a week, $35,000 home, and two cars.'"

ANNOUNCER: Welcome to *Larry King Live* from New York. Tonight: America's favorite television father, Bill Cosby, looking at life after the Huxtable household. Now, here's Larry King.

LARRY KING: Good evening from—

BILL COSBY: Whose voice is that?

LK: Wait a second— It's an announcer. Good evening from New York—

BC: Whose voice is that? Somebody— Who is it?

LK: Tomorrow night—

BC: Good evening—

LK: Tomorrow night—

BC: Oh—Oh—

LK: Tomorrow night, Colonel Ollie North will be our special guest for the full hour. Now, this is a quinella: Bill Cosby tonight, Ollie North tomorrow, and then Thursday night, back in Washington with the commissioner of the Food and Drug Administration.

You know, for a kid who had to share a bed with his brother Russell in North Philadelphia [*King strokes Cosby's head*], Bill Cosby grew up to do pretty well. His NBC sitcom, *The Cosby Show*, ranks as one of television's most successful programs ever. He is now a one-man entertainment conglomerate. In his latest book, *Childhood*, memories of north Philadelphia come shining through, and it is bound to be a bestseller. . . . Thanks for joining us, Bill. Good to see you.

BC: Okay, that's enough of that.

LK: What is it? We're done now?

BC: Let's have fun. Enough of that.

LK: All right. *Childhood*. You did *Fatherhood*. You did *Time of*—

BC: *Time Flies*.

LK: *Time Flies*. And now—

BC: Which was about aging.

LK: And now you reversed it.

BC: And then I did *Love and Marriage*, which is about that, and now, as all people do when they get old, you revert.

LK: So what could be next? Birth?

BC: Almost: childhood.

LK: Yes, you are reversing back.

BC: Yes, reversing back, but we're gaining yardage! Going down the 75-yard line.

LK: Where did you grow up?

BC: North Philadelphia, with parents—obviously. I'm one of the few writers who will say, "My parents moved to—" Did you ever read these books, and they say, "I moved to Kansas at age four"? . . . You know, you see a picture of a little four-year-old with wagons and oxen and stuff, you know. "Where are you going?" "Well, going to Kansas. I'm going by myself. I left my parents." *I* stayed with the folks.

LK: [*laughs*] In other words, they moved; you stayed with them?

BC: I stayed with them. Larry, I *could* have left them. I could have left them. . . . Any kid has a right to leave. I've been a parent for twenty-six years, and I say the same thing my parents said: "You don't like it here? Get out." And you can go if you want to, but I stayed with them.

LK: Did they offer you the right to leave.

BC: Yes!

LK: Were you a good kid?

BC: Yes. It depends on what old person was watching me. See, I come from that time in the neighborhood when old people would watch out for your parents, so your mother or your father would come home and she'd say, you know, "Today you left the house, and I told you to stay here." "Well, how'd you know?" She'd say, "Well, a little bird told me." Well, it wasn't a little bird. It was some old person who had nothing better to do than spy on little children, and so, when mom came home, the old person told.

LK: Is this a collection of stories?

BC: Yes. Some of them are from the albums, the old albums that I did, but some of them are just new stories. For instance . . . there's a thing about Spanish Fly. Do you know anything about Spanish Fly?

LK: When we were kids we used to—

BC: There you go. There you go. That's all. I just wanted the recognition.

LK: Yes.

BC: Spanish Fly.

LK: We knew what it was.

BC: Spanish Fly was the thing that all boys from age eleven on up to death: we will *still* be searching for Spanish Fly.

LK: [*laughs*] That's right.

BC: And the old, the old story was, if you took a little drop— It was on the head of a—

LK: Pin.

BC: —pin! And you put it in a drink—

LK: That's right. Drop it in her Coca-Cola. It don't matter.

BC: It doesn't make any difference. And the girl would drink it, and—

LK: And she's yours.

BC: Hello, America! And there's a story in there about Spanish Fly. So I think that everybody, any guy picking it up, will just have a ball reading about that.

LK: Why is childhood difficult? I mean, you've studied this a long time. You've raised kids, you *were* a kid, you have good memory of childhood, you did a Fat Albert cartoon series dealing with childhood. . . .

BC: It's difficult because you're under a microscope. There's supposed to be a certain amount of freedom. People call it rebelling. "Rebelling" may be just an over-simplified term, coming from an over-simplified speaker, but I think the important thing is that children have to perform. They don't want to always do. They don't want to be graded. They don't want to be judged. So they're constantly trying to get off of that particular step and move on, and so the cry for freedom within themselves, and a lot of things happen with kids. And so it's kind of painful for them, but in the long run, as you and I both know, there comes a time in our life as we get older where we turn around, and we almost blame the parent for not having made us do what we said we didn't want to do.

LK: That's right.

BC: That old ad that used to sell on the back of the comic books—remember?—"I wish my parents had made me play the piano, or take the lessons . . ." You know, "I wish my parents had made me—"

LK: That's right. I say that a lot: "I wish my mother had made me do this."

BC: Yes. But, see, you were such a tough kid, Larry, you put her up against the wall, and you made a good case in point, and that was it, and so she said, "Okay, you don't have to."

LK: "I don't want to go to the dentist. Okay, here's why I don't want to go—" She didn't take me. . . . She should have taken me.

BC: Rot-mouth.

LK: Rot-mouth.

BC: She said, "You are going to get rot-mouth." You said, "Let me worry about it. . . ."

LK: That's right.

BC: And so with all of that—what the psychologists or behavioral scientists call rebellion—is a kid's crying to have that freedom to play, that freedom from having to perform.

LK: Your mother recently passed away, right?

BC: Yes, August seventh.

LK: I think we have a picture of Bill and his mom. . . . There it is. [*photograph of Bill Cosby, in mortarboard and gown, with his mother*]

BC: Now, this is—all right—when I graduated from the University of Massachusetts. I think this was one of my mother's happiest moments. She's only four-foot-eleven, so she's just about standing there. And, man, she came running down out of the stands and just went horizontally for about forty feet—"zzzzz-BOOM!"—and hit me, and that was— I just wanted everybody to take a peek at what my mother looked like at her happy, happy, happy moment.

LK: Bill Cosby is our guest. His new book is *Childhood*. There's lots to talk about. He's leaving, finally: *The Cosby Show* ends this season, and next season he brings back *You Bet Your Life*, the old Groucho Marx quiz show. . . .

[Commercial break]

LK: What an extraordinary career Bill Cosby has had. We forget what a great monologist he is. Arguably the best. Just standing on the stage, cold, with that cigar, making people laugh. . . .

BC: No more cigar on the stage.

LK: You don't use it? You smoke it, but you don't use it as a prop.

BC: Right.

LK: Because of people smoking?

BC: Well, people don't care for smoking any more.

LK: And Bill, of course, is the author of *Childhood*, a new book from Putnam, which is going to be a major bestseller. They all have been. And this is the last season of *The Cosby Show*, finally. . . . Three straight years you've been coming here saying, "This is it."

BC: No!

LK: Yes.

BC: Do you have tape of me saying that?

LK: I think so.

BC: I don't think so.

LK: You know what I'll never forget? Right before my heart surgery . . . you were the last guest, and you had that big panda dressed as a doctor and introduced him as my doctor. . . . I never forgot that.

BC: "Dr. Panda. . . ." But the main thing is, you cannot say you'll never forget.

LK: What do you mean?

BC: Because you *will* forget. Something will happen to you, and you will forget, and people should never say that. You should never say, "I'll never forget," because you will forget.

LK: What are you getting on this tirade for?

BC: Larry, I want you to tell the truth!

LK: In other words, people do forget?

BC: No, just you! You're the only one who's going to forget!

LK: *[laughs]* Okay. *The Cosby Show* is going off?

BC: It's going off, Larry.

LK: Why, Bill?

BC: Because I'm tired. I have nothing else to say on that show. I love it. Shut it down—please! . . .

LK: And then it's over.

BC: I don't go to work that morning.

LK: All right. Now, you don't *have* to work.

BC: Yes, I do.

LK: Why?

BC: Because I love it.

LK: Yes, but you don't have to economically, right?

BC: Yes, but what difference does that make? Did Exxon quit pumping?

LK: [*laughs*] No, I don't mean— No, no no—

BC: Huh? No, I'm talking about money.

LK: I know that. Money is why you work.

BC: No, I don't— No—

LK: You don't need the money.

BC: Yes, I do! Yes, I do!

LK: Bill.

BC: Larry.

LK: You're one of the wealthiest men in the history of show—

BC: One! There are more to catch. Got to catch more of these guys. Do you know that there's a man who's at $86 billion?

LK: All right, what are you going to do with that?

BC: What? With his money?

LK: Yeah.

BC: Ooooh! Well, if it's his money, I'll have big fun with it. . . . I may pay off a few rings that people haven't paid for.

LK: I'm leading up to a question.

BC: I'm sorry.

LK: You don't need the money—*need*-need the money—so why do other things? Why not watch the dancers, sip the wine?

BC: I don't drink—

LK: [*laughs*] Okay.

BC: —and I have bad knees. [*laughs*] No, the reason for it is because I'm in a business where you can really continue to perform until you can't get booked, and I enjoy what I'm doing. The thoughts are always turning, churning, and there are things that I want to say. At times there are certainly— I just finished playing Purdue University, Saturday night at a homecoming. It was a wonderful, wonderful time that I had for an hour and forty minutes non-stop—talking, people laughing, I was ad-libbing. I got into— I was ad-libbing so well, I was talking about a priest, and then I said something, and the audience went "Whoa!" and then I said, "Okay, wait a minute, I apologize." You know, I had gone off the deep end. [*laughs*] I was having so much fun, I forgot to edit myself, and I apologized. They said, "Okay," and then we went on, and we had a ball. I enjoy that. I really enjoy it. And Larry, if I wasn't working, I would still be out of that house about 150 days a year, because people would call, "Come and be the emcee at a benefit," "Come and perform at a benefit," "Come and do this at a benefit—" I would be doing benefits, so I might as well work and do the benefits as well.

LK: Do you ever pinch yourself over all you've attained? I mean, we read so much about that kind of wealth that is—I mean, as a kid in north Philly, this had to be beyond any dream you ever had.

BC: I have to tell you over and over and over. You don't pay attention to me.

LK: [*laughs*] I forget.

BC: My original—I told you, you see? My original goal— A guy asked me, he said, "How much money do you want to make?" I said—and this was 1962—I said, "Three hundred and sixty dollars a week, $35,000 home, and two cars." That was it. Larry, I passed that. I've passed it. It is working in this business that I love, entertaining people. There are people who don't want *The Cosby Show* to go off the air because they feel that it's very, very entertaining, and I think that if there was a ninth season, I'd still be able to generate ratings—up against Bart Simpson, which is one of the strongest draws we've had to go up against. And Bart has to go up against us as well. The strongest draw is we're still holding seventeenth place, sixteenth place. Once in a while something will happen—I don't know, a whole lot of people will turn the lights on—and we shoot up to twelfth place or something like that. So there's enough juice for us to stay in for a ninth year. . . . What I'm saying is, it isn't just the keeping score. I'm saying, I could still be in the ballgame if I wanted to.

LK: All right, I want to talk about *You Bet Your Life.* You talk about Bart like he's a real person.

BC: Oh, Bart is. It's just that they won't put him up for an Emmy. But I just want Bart to know that winning an Emmy, or even being nominated, is no big thing, Bart—please. Because if you look, Bart, at the way the people vote for whatever person's going to be in there, Bart, it's no big deal.

LK: [*laughs*] Don't take it personally.

BC: Absolutely. You may win one year, Bart, without even being nominated, the way they give those things away. . . .

[*Commercial break*]

LK: You're watching *Larry King Live.* Our guest for the full hour tonight is Bill Cosby. We'll be going to your calls in a little bit. *You Bet Your Life*—

BC: Yes.

LK: Why?

BC: Because it's a comedian's ultimate lemon meringue pie. Any stand-up comic will eventually—while working out a routine in front of an audience—will say to somebody: "Oh, where are you from? What do you do? Where do you go?" Well, with *You Bet Your Life*, they come right to you. Two people sit down. You already have a card on them. You talk, and you have a good time with them. And we're using real people. When I say "real people," I mean people who have never been on television before. . . .

LK: And you're doing it in Philadelphia? . . . What took you back there?

BC: That's my home town. I think that Philadelphia is a city that needs a good perker because it's, I mean, it's the cradle of independence. Independence Hall: we've got an awful lot of good historical things. We've got Pennsylvania, which is a beautiful place to ride through and see, and I just think that Philadelphia deserves to be brought back.

LK: So this is by design for the city, to bring it there?

BC: To bring it back to my home town, to give something . . .

LK: And I guess this is your own baby, your own business?

BC: You shouldn't really be thinking that much, because you have Oliver North tomorrow. This should have been a respite for you, but you're thinking too much.

LK: I treat every show individually. I'm not thinking about Oliver North—

BC: You're not?

LK: —I'm thinking about you.

BC: No, I'm not saying that. I'm saying that you are working too hard. You know, ease up! Because, you know, you have a little—on this side there's a hair or something that's hanging over—

LK: Over my ear? . . . Why did you have to point that out? Why do you humiliate me? Every time you come you humiliate me.

BC: I'm—I'm sorry. . . . I'm really sorry, see? You withdrew—

LK: That's right.

BC: —and you got sympathy—

LK: That's right.

BC: —from the viewing audience.

LK: You know what I'm doing here.

BC: Of course. I mean, I'm in the business myself—

LK: [*laughs*] I've heard.

BC: —*You Bet Your Life*. I've got six shows in the can.

LK: Are you supporting— Is Jesse Jackson going to run?

BC: I don't think so. I'm not— Camille and I are not going to put one penny into anybody's political coffers.

LK: Why? I thought you were going to be more active?

BC: No. Who told you that?

LK: Somebody told me that.

BC: No. I know "somebody" must have told you that, because I don't know "somebody. . . ." Mrs. Cosby and I are not putting any money out for any political people.

LK: I think I read somewhere you're going to be involved in Doug Wilder's campaign.

BC: You may have read that—

LK: So you're through with political donations and endorsements?

BC: From now till I see America become a place where people are working. And I don't want to sound political. And the other thing is, why does the media continue to write that [David] Duke is an ex-Klansman? If the guys a—

LK: Oh, you mean you're never an ex—

BC: But what's important about being an ex-Klansman? Why do they continue to write "ex-Klansman"?

LK: What should they say?

BC: Just say his name, Duke.

LK: Duke?

BC: Yes, and then put down what he believes in. . . . No, and then what does it look like? It looks like Bush, doesn't it?

LK: We'll be right back with Bill Cosby, who's left politics, as you can tell. . . .

[*Commercial break*]

LK: Our guest: Bill Cosby. His secret desire is to be Bernard Shaw. One day, we will let him be Bernard Shaw. . . . Oh, one other thought I wanted before we start taking calls. . . . Your overview of the [Clarence] Thomas [–Anita Hill] hearings, that whole— I don't think I've heard your—I *know* I haven't heard your thoughts.

BC: Well, first of all, I didn't, I really didn't watch it.

LK: You're the only one.

BC: Good. Then somebody is walking around, and I didn't miss anything. I took a look, and I saw a whole panel of white people looking down at two highly educated African Americans and asking them about their sexual awareness—

LK: [*laughs*] Putting it that way, it's funny.

BC: Yes, yes, and I said: and what was it about? About this fellow getting into the Supreme Court. Made no sense to me. Should have been done where you would take that kind of talk, or put it on Channel 36 here.

LK: You were embarrassed for the—

BC: No, I was embarrassed for the United States of America.

LK: Let's go to your calls for Bill Cosby. New York City, hello.

CALLER: [*New York, New York*] Good evening, Mr. Cosby, sir. I'll never forget how, when your wife was—

BC: It's not my baby!

CALLER: [*New York, New York (laughs)*] When your wife was pregnant with your first child, you told the world that it was going to be a boy, and you were wrong. And your second child—again. And you used to make very disparaging remarks and say things like, "Well, we think we'll keep her," and say something about her being like a German Shepherd or something. And I'm wondering now, as you look back, are you embarrassed by these kinds of sexist comments that you used to make?

BC: Yes, the answer is "yes and no," because I think now if you look at *The Cosby Show* for the eight years that it's been on the air, if you've paid attention to many of the messages that have gone out, I think I've more than come total full-circle. And you're absolutely correct. I realize where I was wrong.

LK: Milwaukee, for Bill Cosby. Hello.

CALLER: [*Milwaukee, Wisconsin*] Mr. Cosby, I was just wondering, where did you find Raven-Symoné, who plays Olivia? She's just a doll.

BC: Didn't have to find her. Her parents said that when she was, I think, two years old, she pointed to the set and said she wanted to be on my show, and her parents took her to the Hughes/Moss casting agency, and she auditioned, and we needed someone that age, and she got the job. She's just absolutely brilliant.

LK: Yes. You've got no problem working with a kid that young?

BC: She's a professional, and her parents have set it up that way—that she knows she works, the parents know she works, and that's the way it is.

LK: Winnipeg, Canada, with Bill Cosby. Hello.

CALLER: [*Winnipeg, Manitoba*] Larry, great show. Mr. Cosby, before my question, I'd just like to commend you for your comment on Duke before. I think it's— I wish more people would stand up and point out that President Bush is a racist, and I commend you for that.

LK: I'd rather have a question. Go ahead.

CALLER: [*Winnipeg, Manitoba*] Anyway, I'd just like to ask you a question about the Coca-Cola and the Pudding Pops. I'm trying to get my kids to eat healthy, and when they see you trying to sell them soda, they want to go out and get that soda. How do you feel about that?

BC: Turn it off, and tell them that Bill Cosby is not their father. No, I'm very, very serious. Turn it off. Tell them Bill Cosby is not their father and that he—you know— and that's enough, really. And I don't mind you doing that, if that's what you believe in.

LK: Interesting, what the public would object to. Have you heard this before?

BC: Sure.

LK: That . . . Jell-O and Coca-Cola are non-healthy products?

BC: Yes.

LK: What? Sugar content?

BC: Yes, but I've also read that now they're saying that children who don't eat sugar are the most hyper people in the classroom, you know what I mean?

LK: How long have you been with Jell-O?

BC: I don't know. Fourteen—twenty years?

LK: Charleroi, Pennsylvania, for Bill Cosby. Hello.

CALLER: [*Charleroi, Pennsylvania*] Bill? How old were you when you decided to get into entertainment, and how did you realize that you had the talent that you have?

BC: I think I was about twenty-six years old when I decided. I knew I had the talent when I was tending bar, because I was telling jokes to people, and they were laughing, and I didn't care how many people were in the room, and then I started to ad-lib.

LK: Where was your first professional engagement?

BC: In a bar in Philadelphia, at Broad and Spruce, called the Cellar Bar.

LK: You got paid?

BC: Five dollars—for the whole night—and tips under the ashtray.

LK: Did they laugh?

BC: Yes, the people laughed, and then they told me jokes.

LK: We'll be right back with Bill Cosby. . . . He'll be entertaining us when he's one hundred years old. Bill Cosby will be the next George Burns. I predict this. I've been wrong before. We'll be back after this.

BC: George what?

LK: Burns.

BC: Oh, I thought you said "Booth."

[*Commercial break*]

LK: Camp Hill, Pennsylvania—

CALLER: [*Camp Hill, Pennsylvania*] Hello. Good evening. A great answer to Winnipeg, Bill. That was great. I have two questions. In my opinion, being the funniest man in the business, the fact that you have comedy that does not use foul language makes it funny for all ages. Having said that, what is your opinion on why comedians, today's comedians, feel they have to use foul language? Is it because they can't be funny otherwise or not? My second question is, out of all the characters that you had in *Cosby*, in the cartoons, do you have one favorite?

BC: "Mushmouth." And now for the answer to the other one, everything has opened up—not only stand-up comedy. Movies have opened, I mean, you have actors who are saying four-letter words like never before. You have sexual shots that are like never before. So the censors have really opened up. And I don't think you have to worry about people who use what you call foul language—and I'm not putting you down for that—because, generally, they don't last that long.

Take a guy like Sinbad. He's a comedian. . . . And you will watch some of these newer comedians. They will watch him, and they will tail-in behind him. A lot of these newer comedians will now come up behind Sinbad and throw off the four-letter words.

LK: Have you ever been tempted to use it?

BC: Sure. Sure. And when I went out and did it, I just felt embarrassed that I had done it.

LK: Gleason used to think that in the main it was cheap laughs.

BC: Yes, we all would think that way. I know Red Skelton will tell you in a minute that he doesn't appreciate that. Milton Berle will also say that. But . . . you just can't get rid of the change. There's a way to use curse words with class and with intelligence. However, when an eight-letter word becomes the sole punchline, you have not written anything funny. You've made a funny moment, which is going to be worth only about six minutes on the stage for you.

LK: Calgary, Canada, with Bill Cosby. Hello.

CALLER: [*Calgary, Alberta*] Hi, Bill. As you know, you're really popular up here in Calgary, and I just wanted to ask you, does it still bother you when somebody asks you a question and you answer them truthfully, and they say to you, "You're kidding"? Does that still really bother you?

BC: [*laughs*] Sometimes, yes. No, but, you know, when people do that, they say, "You're kidding," and then you have to say, "No, I'm not kidding. . . ." And they say, "Well, really?" and you say, "Really." And then they keep going, you know.

LK: Have you ever wanted to do a serious piece: a drama?

BC: I did one, called *To All My Friends on Shore*, a wonderful movie with Gloria Foster.

LK: Never saw it.

BC: It was on television, but it was at the time, I think, Nixon was coming back—seriously—coming back from China.

LK: Or played the same night, you mean?

BC: Yes, and I think we went out somewhere. But it was about this father who was always working, working, working and never paid attention to his son. Then his son was diagnosed as having sickle cell anemia, and they thought—Gloria and I thought that the son was going to die, and then I began to pay more attention to the son.

LK: Houlton, Maine, with Bill Cosby. Hello.

CALLER: [*Houlton, Maine*] Hi, Larry, Bill. Thank you for the years of laughter, Bill. I wanted to ask you, out of all of the things that you have done—the brilliant comedy albums and the series and the films—what are you the most proud of?

BC: All of them, really. It's a matter of putting things together with a thought that you have and then beginning to execute the things. I enjoy performing on the stage. I enjoyed the television series because certain ideas came out, and I was able to play them, and then I saw that people laughed at them. The book I enjoy because that's taking some of the routines from the stage and then putting the written word in where, while I'm talking to people, it would lose the flow. So there's a difference in the written—

LK: So you like everything you do?

BC: Yes, I'm enjoying the business I'm in. . . .

[*Commercial break*]

LK: Back to the calls. Great Neck, Long Island, New York, hello.

CALLER: [*Great Neck, New York*] Hi. Mr. Cosby, I've been a fan for many years, and I've also been a fan of Groucho Marx. I wondered if maybe you were a fan too, in choosing *You Bet Your Life*?

BC: Yes. Let me give you a story. I don't know if Larry has the time. Mrs. Cosby and I entertained quite a few times a fellow by the name of Eubie Blake. As you know, Eubie lived till be was one hundred. And we were in California, and Eubie came to the house. My mother was there and some of the children and Eubie and a man by the name of Mr. Browning. Erin Fleming, who was looking after Groucho at the time—I called, and I invited Groucho, because I thought that these two great icons would sit, and we would have a ball. Well, Groucho was fragile, and [*speaks in frail voice*] when he talked, he was kind of like this just a little bit, but, you know still had that— That twinkle was still there, man, the life.

LK: Yes.

BC: So I sat him down. The two guys did not talk. They did not talk. They ate. And after dinner the ritual is that Eubie goes to the living room and plays the piano. His wife likes to see him do that, because that means he's practicing, and he would play for a half hour. My mother, Camille, the children would come in. Groucho comes in, he sits with Erin, and Eubie is playing all of this and doing the thing, and Eubie started to play "I'm Just Wild About Harry" [*hums tune*]. And he's playing it, and to my right I hear "Rooor-rooor-rooor—" and I said, "What in the world is that?" And I turn around, and there's this fragile Groucho pushing Erin out of the way and walking off-balance and singing. And Eubie looks up, and Eubie sees Groucho, and he starts to play slower, and Groucho, in the best way, began to sing "I'm Just Wild About Harry." And to see those two guys, who before could never have worked together on Broadway when they were coming up, to see those two working together, and Eubie was playing and Eubie saying, "Sing it! Sing it!" you know, and then Groucho starts with the foot and the leg across—

LK: He did the walk?

BC: —back, absolutely crossed—and he started to dance and Erin came up. She's about two feet away, man. She's ready to catch him. He never stumbled. He looked like he could fall, but I think that was one of the best moments this guy had before his death.

LK: Gleason said he's the only comic who lasted all those years and never asked for your sympathy.

BC: Absolutely. Absolutely.

LK: Never asked you to care for him, hug him, hold him.

BC: Absolutely. . . . You know why? [*laughs*] Because he had a cigar.

LK: He had a prop.

BC: No, he loved his cigars.

LK: And you didn't matter.

BC: Absolutely. . . . But he was wonderful, though. All you had to do was bring over two or three, you know, beautiful, young and that twinkle.

[*Commercial break*]

LK: Okay, listen, tomorrow night Colonel Oliver North will be our guest. This will be the first time—

BC: He should be a general by now, shouldn't he?

LK: [*laughs*] I don't think so. He's not in the Marine Corps.

BC: He's been around a long time—Huh?

LK: He's not in the Marine Corps any more.

BC: Where is he now?

LK: He's a civilian—

BC: In the Navy?

LK: No—

BC: Well, did he go to the Salvation Army?

LK: —anyway, think about and call in early with questions because this will be Colonel North's first time ever taking phone calls on a national hook-up. That's tomorrow night with Colonel Oliver North.

BC: He hasn't spoken to anyone since then?

LK: No, he's spoken to people, but not on the phone.

BC: Well, what did he—just go out from his bedroom?

LK: He hasn't done like, you know— No, no—

BC: He was always in a van whenever I saw him.

Oliver North

"I would have

died for

President

Reagan, but I

wasn't

prepared to

go to jail

for him."

Oliver Laurence North was born (October 7, 1943) and raised in upstate New York. An Annapolis graduate, he became a gung-ho marine, who received two Purple Hearts, the Bronze Star, and the Silver Star for heroism in Vietnam.

North was assigned to the National Security Council at the White House in 1981, where he specialized in counter-terrorism. North was seen as the architect of the "Iran Scam" arms-for-hostages scheme that nearly torpedoed President Reagan's second term.

North battled to exonerate himself from criminal charges and appeared on Larry King Live *to tell his story for the first time as he wrote it in* Under Fire: An American Story, *the autobiography he had secretly penned.*

Three years after this interview, North narrowly lost to Charles Robb in the race for Senator from Virginia.

LARRY KING: For nearly five years, Lieutenant Colonel Oliver North has held his peace and listened to what the rest of the nation thinks of him. For his central role in the Iran-Contra affair he has been dubbed a hero and a renegade. Some called him a loose cannon. North himself said nothing until now. The wraps have just come off—an autobiography written in secret, *Under Fire: An American Story*, just published—and finally, the man himself is talking. . . . How did you pick that title? Is that your title? That's a great title.

OLIVER NORTH: It is my title. It comes from a note I got from our president, Larry. The note goes—

LK: Current or previous?

ON: Our current president. The note goes like this. [*reads note*] "En route to Kennebunkport, 11/27/85. Dear Ollie, as I head off to Maine for Thanksgiving, I just want to wish you a happy one with the hope that you'll get some well-deserved rest. One of the many things I have to be thankful for is the way in which you have performed under fire in tough situations. Your dedication and tireless work with the hostage thing and with Central America really give me cause for great pride in you, and thanks. Get some turkey. George Bush."

LK: The president gave you the title.

ON: Indeed.

LK: I want to touch a lot of bases. You're all over the news, naturally, and your thoughts about President Reagan. We'll cover all that, but let's go back a little. Why did you choose a military career?

ON: Well, I had grown up in a family where my dad had—like a lot of folks in our generation, Larry—my mom and dad had been through the Depression, born at the back end of World War I, had been married just before World War II. My dad went off to World War II, and, of course, that was the great war that we won for democracy in the world.

LK: And you were a war baby?

ON: And was a war baby in 1943, born while my dad was overseas. And I guess the whole thing about growing up in that environment was one of being instilled to the idea and ideals of service and wanting to in some way give back a little bit of what we'd gotten.

LK: So you knew you wanted it as a career when you went to the Naval Academy?

ON: I got to the Naval Academy by being in the marine reserves, and I'd gone to college before that. I'd had a remarkable coach in high school—a fellow by the name of Russ Robertson—who'd been a World War II marine, terribly wounded, and yet made a remarkable recovery and was the high school athletic director and my coach. And I got to college, and the dean of men, Harold Raykoff, was the son of Russian Jewish immigrants and also a marine. And between those men and my dad's influence and the kind of upbringing I'd had, it became something I really wanted to do. I went to the marine reserves and from the reserves got the appointment to Annapolis.

LK: What do you think, if you hadn't chosen that, you'd have done?

ON: Well, I also wanted to look at the possibility of medical school. My dean, Harold Raykoff, encouraged me to look out and reach out and to use everything that education could possibly bring to you.

LK: Was the Marine Corps what you thought it would be? Was it all that you thought it would be?

ON: It was. I had the great blessing of serving with wonderful people. Before the show, you and I were talking about loyal people, and I had the great blessing of serving with wonderful people. One of the things that disturbs me so much is the way some of them have been portrayed. I can recall one of your guests who was on that's made some movies about that era and that war that I take strong issue with. He's also named Oliver.

LK: Oliver Stone.

ON: Yes.

LK: But he was there, too.

ON: True enough.

LK: You came back with two viewpoints.

ON: Yes, and both Olivers have a different perspective on that experience. Mine was that these young men that served with me were not the pot-headed marauders that they'd been made out to be, not just in his movies, but by much of what's been written—by other movies, like *Apocalypse Now* and the like.

LK: But you do understand why the other side felt the way it did about that war?

ON: I do, but I somehow missed all of that experience. The ones that I served with were remarkably brave, incredibly resourceful, and died for a cause that this nation basically abandoned.

LK: Now, you were a warrior. "Warriors don't like war" is what a general said to me once. But you also appeared—there are stories about you, and I hate to reflect just on that—to like secrecy. You liked what happened. The kinds of things you got into in the White House were the kinds of things you enjoyed. True or false?

ON: Well, I don't think that's an accurate perspective. I know that kind of thing has been said, but a marine is wont to serve in the capacity to which he's been assigned and, in this case, I was told by my superiors to work on some very, very sensitive projects. It wasn't any particular infatuation that I had with secrecy. The job required it, and I tried my best to carry it out.

LK: In other words, if they'd have assigned you another job, it would have been that job to do?

ON: Sure.

LK: All right. Bill Casey: worked with him. Did you like him?

ON: Great man.

LK: What was special about him?

ON: Oh, I think his vision is one of the things that I admired; his ability to reach out and grasp the essence of a problem, to come to a quick conclusion based on all the information he could gather in at once; his remarkable, insatiable appetite for books.

LK: His incredible New York accent. [*laughs*]

ON: Absolutely.

LK: Did you understand him all the time?

ON: Oh, yeah—as long as he didn't have his tie up and chewing on it or something.

LK: Do you believe that he spoke to Bob Woodward at the end—as an aside—that he gave him all those facts for that book? [*Veil: The Secret Wars of the CIA: 1981–1987* (1989)]

ON: I don't have any reason to disbelieve all of that. I really don't know, but there is no doubt that the Bill Casey I came to admire and came to know quite well was a man who had the best interests of this nation at heart and carried out a remarkably difficult rebuilding of the Central Intelligence Agency at a time when it was absolutely essential.

LK: How did you get into all of this, you and Iran-Contra? I mean, you couldn't have run this show, because you didn't have that high a position. How did you get in the swirl?

ON: I was basically picked by [Reagan aide] Bud McFarlane from the staff to start working in 1984 to help the Nicaraguan resistance at a point in time when the Congress had decided that no more tax money was going to be allocated for that purpose.

LK: Well, didn't you say, "If they're not allocating the money, how can we do this?"

ON: No, the law was very specific. It simply said that no money that they're going to make available in this particular act could be used for that purpose any more, but it didn't say "You can't do anything." And so what the administration did was—lawfully—go out and find other ways to support the resistance. And so the president and Bud went to the Saudis. Bill Casey had earlier arranged for the shipment of significant supplies of captured Palestinian weapons from Israel. Other steps were taken to get private contributions, like that of Joe Coors and other generous Americans who wanted to support the resistance.

LK: Was there ever a time when you said, "I think I'm doing something wrong here"?

ON: It didn't come in the course of doing what we were doing, Larry. I don't believe to this day that any of those steps that we took to provide support for the resistance were illegal. I know that there's others that have a very strong difference of opinion on that, and I respect it.

Where I feel like I did wrong—without putting the burden on anyone else—was when I went into the White House situation room on the sixth of August 1986 and sat there and looked them in the eye. I didn't tell them the truth. I told Congressman Hamilton that. I don't believe that it was illegal because that kind of informal exchange between a member of the executive branch and a member of Congress had never before been declared to be illegal, but I also—

LK: You weren't testifying?

ON: No sworn oaths. No testimony. Informal meeting in the sit. room, not up on the Hill—all of those things. But I know the difference between right and wrong. My mom and dad taught me that well before I ever thought of going to the White House, except as a school kid. I know that it wasn't right. In the end result, that's the kind of thing that I don't feel good about. . . .

[*Commercial break*]

LK: Our guest is Lieutenant Colonel Oliver North, United States Marine Corps, retired. His book, published by HarperCollins—one of the great secret stories in the history of publishing—*Under Fire*. How did no one know about this?

ON: Well, when we first signed the contract with Mr. [Rupert] Murdoch and the folks at HarperCollins, we agreed mutually that it would be a very confidential matter. I, on my side, wanted to be able to finish the book without all this attention and publicity. I'd gone through a good bit of that in the course of our ordeal since 1986. And second of all, Larry, I wanted to make sure that before it went to the publisher that it got a good careful security review. And so we did it that way.

LK: How did they pull it off, though? I mean, secretaries had to know. A lot of people had to know. This is a book.

ON: There's no doubt that there's a lot of good folks in the publishing business. HarperCollins keeps a better secret than the U.S. Congress.

LK: Were you surprised that it didn't leak?

ON: Not really. I think that they saw it to their benefit. Certainly, it was to mine. And it helped us get a better product out on the market.

LK: What was it like for someone obviously expressive—sense of humor, affable—Everybody here liked you, meeting you. You're cordial. You're wonderful to be around. You're a storyteller. You're kind of a raconteur. What was it like to be quiet all this time, I mean, to not come forward—hear people talk about you, and not want to get on? How could you not?

ON: A mutual friend of ours, Edward Bennett Williams, used to have to just about sit on me. Of course, he was the man that brought Brendan Sullivan into that great law firm. I can recall one time when there was a particularly outrageous article about something to the effect that anonymous sources close to the investigation had revealed that I'd purchased Fawn Hall's [North's secretary] sports car with Iran-Contra money. And I took this article and raced into Ed Williams, and I said, "I know you've got a policy of 'no comment,' but my wife will see this, my mother will see it, my children will see it," and old Ed Williams said, "Sit down, son." He said, "You're getting to be like a dog chasing fleas, and you're never going to get rid of the fleas until you take a flea bath, and, son, you're going to take a couple of them." He said, "What you have to understand is that the anonymous sources telling these stories, the reporters who are writing them, all believe it's true." I said, "Ed, you and I have known each other since 1981. How can that be?" He said, "Has nothing to do with your honesty and your integrity. They have to believe that you did it because they know that if they could have stolen a million dollars and had an affair with a beautiful secretary, *they'd* have done it. They have to believe you did it. You've got to stop reading this stuff. You've got to stop watching it on television."

LK: But how about emotionally? . . . I mean, your kind of makeup. The makeup of that guy that ran into Ed's office is the same kind of makeup that wants to go on, and so how did you handle that?

ON: I was blessed—unlike most others in this long ordeal, not just for us, but for the nation—I was blessed to have enormous physical resources. I was in very good shape, as a marine. I was blessed to have a very, very loyal and tough family, because we'd been through some tough times. I was blessed to have the prayers of literally thousands of people. And I was blessed, after the hearings, to be able to raise the kind of financial resources that were necessary. Those four things— those assets that I had, those resources—were something that gave me the—that, along with the discipline of twenty years as a marine—the ability to bite your tongue and clench your teeth and take it for as long as we did. . . .

[*Commercial break*]

LK: You said something with Charles Bierbauer this morning on CNN. I never heard anything said quite like this, and you ought to elaborate. You said, "I would have died for President Reagan, but I wasn't prepared to go to jail for him." One would think the former was worse than the latter.

ON: There's nothing that I think bothers me more than to have been described as a criminal. In all of what transpired, I never once thought that I was doing something criminal. I think anybody who's in the service to their country is prepared to do anything legal, to include the possible sacrifice of one's life. You try not to, of course. I certainly ducked every time somebody shot at me.

LK: But you aren't prepared to say you did something wrong—

ON: When I didn't do it.

LK: Okay. All right. He didn't pardon you, he didn't speak up for you, and yet you say you like him. Why would you like him, if loyalty is big to you?

ON: Because— Loyalty is important to me, and I can't tell you that I'm anything but disappointed, but I also look at it from the perspective, Larry, that the good Lord lent my best friend and me four lovely children that today have a better future because Ronald Wilson Reagan was president for eight years. We have a more peaceful and tranquil world. There are many people in this country and elsewhere that don't agree with Ronald Reagan and what he stood for, but it's impossible, I think, for a thinking person to accept that the world didn't change because of his tenure. And because of that, because of the opportunity for a more peaceful future and a more prosperous future, the spread of democracy— That foundation that we've seen grown in the last three years is really the result of his presidency.

LK: Now, you go around speaking out for candidates, don't you?

ON: I have.

LK: You support Republican conservative candidates.

ON: I've supported some; I have actually gone out and supported some Democrats—who were conservatives, I have to tell you.

LK: You were a fan of "Scoop" Jackson, Senator "Scoop" Jackson of Washington, the late "Scoop" Jackson.

ON: Absolutely.

LK: How do you feel about David Duke in Louisiana?

ON: I think it's an outrage, and I think what's happened—because I went down, and I campaigned very hard for one of the Republicans that ran against him early on. I'm very disappointed with what's happened down there. I think what you're seeing is not the political process that you and I believe in. There is no room in America for the politics of hatred in either party, whether you're a Republican or a Democrat. That's not what this nation is about. Most of us live right here in the middle. We may be a little to the left of center, a little to the right of center, but we're not way over here, and we're not way over there. And I'm very concerned that what we have happening down there does not represent the best of American politics.

LK: Do you think it means there's still a lot of racism in the country?

ON: There is a lot of racism in America, and there ought not to be. You know, one of the things that I have encouraged the Republican Party—that I have gone out and campaigned for and raised money for—is to reach out to Hispanic and black and Asian and other minorities in this country, because I happen to believe that the Republican Party is the party of opportunity. And you and I might disagree on that, but I think it's crazy to put a controversial person like me in a room full of blue-haired, very nice, generous old ladies to raise money, when the other party has people like Jesse Jackson out registering voters. I think we need to be out registering more voters.

LK: Why not run?

ON: Well, I've been asked to run. I don't think it would be responsible for me at a point in time when my family has been through an incredible ordeal, before we're back on our feet financially, with a company I've just started out there becoming successful. . . . We make ballistic-protective equipment. We're the life-saving company. We make a new generation of protective equipment.

LK: Now, when that gets rolling and everything's back—things get to normal, eventually they get to normal—might you run?

ON: My daddy used to say, "Son, never say 'never.'" That's probably good advice. I cannot envision today running for any particular office. I have gotten a great deal of satisfaction out of going out and encouraging good candidates and most of all, I hope, encouraging the American people to be involved in the process.

LK: Now, all charges were dismissed against you.

ON: Yes, they were.

LK: So you have your rank—

ON: I have my retired status—

LK: Did you lose your rank?

ON: I retired from the Marine Corps shortly after I was indicted. I did not feel that it was proper, as a serving officer, to have my attorneys—with good reason—handing out subpoenas all over the government of the United States, and so I very reluctantly retired, rather than be an active-duty officer with that process going on.

LK: Do you like what you see in Nicaragua today?

ON: I do. If there was ever a vindication in what we did, it was to bring about the democratic process that elected Violeta Chamorro, and I know that we had a role in that. . . .

LK: We're ready to go to your calls for Ollie North, and we start with Huntington Beach, California. Hello.

DAVID JACOBSEN: [*Huntington Beach, California*] Larry, I'd like to talk with Colonel North. . . . Ollie, this is Dave Jacobsen.

ON: David Jacobsen.

CALLER: [*Huntington Beach, California*] How are you, friend?

LK: Is this *the* David Jacobsen?

CALLER: [*Huntington Beach, California*] *The* Dave Jacobsen.

ON: David, how are you?

CALLER: [*Huntington Beach, California*] Just fine.

LK: Former hostage.

CALLER: [*Huntington Beach, California*] You know, I take a chance to call in tonight, because I don't think the public is really aware of the many good things that you have done. You know, when Colonel Qaddafi offered $10 million to murder [hostages] Terry Anderson and Tom Sutherland and Father Jenko and me, you heard about it, and you reacted promptly and urgently, and you saved our lives. And in addition to saving my life, you made a free man out of me and brought me home to my family, and I'll always love you for that.

And the other thing the public doesn't know, Ollie, is that you were the man— you were the force behind the capture and the conviction of the men who murdered poor Leon Klinghoffer on the [terrorist-held cruise ship] *Achille Lauro*. You made justice happen, and you're to be commended for that.

And I tell my friends that, you know, you're a classical marine. You see a problem, you analyze it, you identify the options, and you respond with a sense of urgency. You're a man of conviction, not of consensus. And no wonder the power brokers in D.C. are afraid of you. So I just want to wish you well. I think you've been a victim of a worse form of terrorism than I was. You were subject to legal terrorism, and I wish I could do something to give you freedom. And I've got a couple of questions for you.

ON: Fire away, friend. . . .

CALLER: [*Huntington Beach, California*] Why did you care so very much about the hostages? . . .

ON: Well, first of all, David, I very much appreciate your kind statement. Let me answer the first question, if I can get out without—

LK: That was really emotional, yes.

ON: It was very emotional. David Jacobsen is a man that I struggled mightily to get free.

LK: He asked a fair question. Why did you care so much about these people you didn't know?

ON: Well, I came to know them through their families, Larry. I had to meet with them, as did the president and Vice President Bush and Admiral Poindexter, and I guess the way I was raised was to cherish human life. I had, certainly, the experience of seeing what it meant to have others lose it. I had young marines die in my arms. To come to know those families, to see the anguish that was in their eyes when they would come to meet with us, whether it was Peggy Say, the sister of Terry

Anderson, who is still a hostage, or whether it was the sons of David Jacobsen who came to see us. It was very clear that we needed to do everything we possibly could to make them free, and my prayer is that those that are still held will soon be home with their families.

LK: Boy, that kind of call makes a lot of things worthwhile, no matter what anybody's feelings are. . . . Next caller for Ollie North is . . . Washington.

CALLER: [*Washington, D.C.*] Hi. How do you do, Mr. North? I have read how you feel about [Special Prosecutor Lawrence] Walsh for what he's done to your family and yourself, but I was wondering, how do you feel about Senator Inouye and Mr. Hamilton? Because, basically, because of their rush to put you on television and get themselves on television, you're a free man.

ON: Well, I can't say that Congressman Hamilton or Senator Inouye were doing anything other than what a lot of politicians do, and that's try to get as much face time as they possibly can. It was their quest to televise the hearings that created the circumstances in which a real travesty of justice was worked. Our system was never set up in such a way that we would compel a person to go and give testimony against themselves and then take and use that testimony to prosecute them in a court of law. It wasn't meant to do that.

LK: Can you quickly straighten out this Ross Perot thing? I know you mentioned that he called you, that he didn't want you to harm Ronald Reagan. Was that in essence what he asked you to say?

ON: Well—and I relate this in the book, and I'm sorry that Ross is so upset about it, but the fact is when Ross Perot came to see me and my attorneys— He's not just taking me on, he's taking on Brendan V. Sullivan, and if he wants to bite off a hunk of that potted plant, then I hope he has a mouthful. But when he came to see us, he didn't say, "Talk about the truth." What he said was, "I don't think it looks good for a marine to be taking the Fifth. That's a fact. And I think you ought to go out there and exonerate the president."

LK: His statement today was, "I strongly urge Lieutenant Colonel North to step forward and tell the whole truth. The action I took would have, in all probability, been detrimental to the president. I have no idea why Lieutenant Colonel North makes up this false story that appears in his book."

ON: I can only say that both my counsel, Brendan V. Sullivan, and I stand by the words in the book.

LK: And still stand by them?

ON: Amen.

LK: To Boston, for Ollie North. Hello.

CALLER: [*Boston, Massachusetts*] Hi, Larry. My question for Mr. North. He just spoke of cherishing human life, and yet his activities in support of death squads in Central America have resulted in thousands of innocent civilians being killed, and I wonder how he reconciles those two facts.

ON: Well, let me just clarify my activities on death squads. I spent a good bit of my time dealing with the process of getting rid of the death squads in El Salvador. That's something that never came out during the hearings, and it didn't get the kind of attention that some of the other things I did were given.

LK: You worked against that element?

ON: We went a number of times—both I and others on the staff of the NSC and in the State Department and our military and our CIA—working very hard to bring about a real democracy in El Salvador. And I relate one of the events in the book where then-Vice President Bush went into a room full of armed men with a transitional president—President Magana—sat down with people who were truly opposed to our telling them this, and said, "Look, you've got to do away with the death squads. You've got to stop this business. You've got to bring to justice the murderers of the nuns and the American labor leaders, and get these people to justice." And the facts are that the democratic process that began after that, that resulted in a real election—86 percent of the people going to the polls, walking through enemy fire to get there—began as a consequence of that emphasis to do away with the death squads. . . .

[*Commercial break*]

LK: Our guest is Ollie North. Back to your calls. Houston, Texas. Hello.

CALLER: [*Houston, Texas*] Hello. Colonel North, I just wanted to say, before I ask you a question, I was with SEAL teams a few years back, so I imagine we've seen a few of the same exotic places around the world. *Semper fi*, sir. Job well done.

ON: *Semper fi*. Thank you.

CALLER: [*Houston, Texas*] My question is, do you still have any contacts with any of the intelligence communities, either here in America or abroad, that are keeping you abreast of people like Abu Nidal or anybody else whose toes you may have stepped on that may want to come look for you?

ON: Well, I do get regular reports from the Federal Bureau of Investigation to look out for various people. In 1987 our government—the same one that was prosecuting me for taking a security fence—provided thirty-five federal agents to protect my family and me, and that continued until the Congress decided to cut off the funding for it. We have got several notices since then of things that we need to do, and, since the federal government withdrew the protection against the terrorists for my family, what has happened is that the American people, with their generosity, through our defense fund, have provided for that security.

LK: Your threats still come?

ON: We still get them, Larry. The thing about Abu Nidal—who operates probably the most vicious terrorist organization in the world—is it's not the kind of threat that goes away. He has taken anywhere from seven to ten years to track down the people that he's targeted, and it's not something you take lightly. . . .

LK: To San Jose, California, with Ollie North. Hello.

CALLER: [*San Jose, California*] Hi, Larry. Hi, Mr. North. I just wanted to state, you know, I supported Ronald Reagan, and I supported you, but I do believe Reagan did know what was going on, and I think that you were kind of the fall guy in it. Don't you think that you're doing a disservice to the presidency and to the Marine Corps to now come out and state to the contrary and make him look bad?

ON: Well, I don't— I hope this is not something that's coming as a shock to you or to anyone else, because what I have said in the book is exactly what I've said in the hearings in 1987: that I believed then that President Reagan knew and approved of what I had done; otherwise, I wouldn't have done it. And all I've said now is that I've seen increasing evidence that confirms that even more in my mind.

LK: How do you regard McFarlane?

ON: Oh, I think Bud is a sad, tragic case. I don't know why Bud suddenly and precipitously resigned in 1985, what it is that prompted him to do some of the things that he's done. I had enormous regard for Bud McFarlane. He was a man that I respected, a man that I had traveled not just to Iran with but to Central America with him. And I quite clearly believe that the things that he had me do had the president's endorsement.

LK: Do you think he may have some problems beyond which we may understand?

ON: Well, I— Obviously, the world knows of his attempted suicide, and obviously we need to, I think, be understanding of that kind of a problem.

LK: How depressed did you get, at its worst?

ON: This ordeal was not as depressing as some might have wanted it to be, I guess, Larry.

LK: This was not the saddest time of your life?

ON: Oh, no. The saddest time in my life was when I had marines die in combat. I don't think anybody who's ever really been to a war ever wants to go to another one because of that. But it was not a picnic, but I truly did have enormous spiritual support in this. I try to lay that out for people in the book. I went through a very, very tough time, but I never once doubted the outcome. I don't truly understand why it is that a lot of these things happen, but I truly knew all the way through that it was going to be positive. . . .

[*Commercial break*]

LK: Are you optimistic naturally?

ON: Oh, I think so.

LK: Is that from faith?

ON: Yes. I don't think the good Lord put us here to simply complain. I think He gave us the chance—each one of us in our own way—to affect the future in a positive direction.

LK: Do you miss the marines?

ON: I don't miss the Marine Corps as a thing. I miss being with marines. I miss being with people who get up every morning intent on going in the same direction, accomplishing a certain set of objectives. I do miss that.

LK: I know you're taught to love your enemies. Do you?

ON: Well, I'll tell you, I'm probably a little more forgiving of some of my adversaries than, perhaps, my attorneys might be. Brendan and his team are as tough as anybody I've ever met, and they're just absolute straight arrows. Someone sent them a little bunch of buttons here the other day that said "Lawyer From Hell." In fact, Brendan and his whole team went after this with the absolute faith that they were right, that what was happening to me was wrong, and fought it all the way to the end.

LK: Do you dislike Mr. Walsh, or do you think he was doing his job? Like a marine, let's say.

ON: Well, I have some very strong feelings about Mr. Walsh and the vigilantes he's brought into town. These are volunteers. These aren't like U.S. attorneys out here in New York chasing down drug criminals. These are people who saw a highly visible, politically charged case, came in to make a name for themselves and get their name in the paper, their face in the news, and go back out into private practice, having profited from it. That's what they're doing. and this whole thing has gone on far too long for the good of the nation and, certainly for the good of the people who—

LK: In other words, they were parasitic, you think? They're just jumping on for their own benefit?

ON: I think that that's what's happened in a lot of cases, yes. . . .

[*Commercial break*]

LK: By the way, you met with the president a lot. He never mentioned what was going on directly to you?

ON: In what way?

LK: You know, "What's going on with Iran-Contra? What is happening?"

ON: Oh, we gave him lots of briefings on what's happening. Iran and Contra were two separate things, and I was involved in both.

LK: So you know he knows?

ON: Oh, yes.

LK: This is not just through thinking he knows?

ON: No. No.

LK: You know he knows. . . .

Fort Myers, Florida, hello.

CALLER: [*Fort Myers, Florida*] Hi, Colonel North. How are you doing? From what your family's been through and what you've been through, you're obviously a man of tremendous substance and inspiration to a lot of us Americans. I have one question for you. The panels that sit in judgment—like this Senate judiciary panel that sat in judgment of [Supreme Court nominee] Judge [Clarence] Thomas— what are your emotions? What are your feelings about that? Do you think that that's the way to handle such conditions?

ON: Well, let me just tell you this. I had great empathy for what Judge Thomas went through. That whole process, I think, is an example of what's happened with— for lack of a better word—an imperial Congress, and I think the end result of that is going to be a lot more of what we've already seen happen in Oklahoma, in Colorado, and California, where the voters have decided, "We're going to limit the terms of our legislators." In Colorado, it already applies to the—

LK: Do you favor that?

ON: I do. I wouldn't have before. As a conservative that doesn't believe in dickering with the Constitution, I would have initially said "no," but I think it's gotten to the point now where we're in a skewed imbalance.

LK: We're almost out of time, Ollie. Do you like the limelight?

ON: No, I cherish my privacy, Larry. I am grateful beyond words to express it for the support and prayers of the American people that helped us in ways that are hard to describe, and if this is a chance to say thank you, if this book is a testament to that, then I welcome it. But I also cherish the time that I have with my best friend and our children.

LK: And the wife is the best friend?

ON: She sure is.

LK: Thanks, Ollie.

ON: Thank you, Larry.

Richard Nixon

The thirty-seventh president of the United States was born in a modest house in Yorba Linda, California, on January 9, 1913. Richard Milhous Nixon practiced law in Whittier, California; served in the U.S. Navy during World War II; then was elected to Congress in 1946. He gained prominence as a relentless Cold Warrior, and in 1950 was elected to the Senate. Two years later, he was the Republican nominee for vice-president, brilliantly dodging a campaign slush-fund scandal with his televised "Checkers" speech.

Nixon lost his 1960 presidential bid to John F. Kennedy, and two years later, failed to become governor of California. He triumphed in the 1968 presidential race against George McGovern and was highly successful in beginning to thaw the Cold War. Nixon's second term was smothered by the agonizing Watergate scandal, and on August 9, 1974, he became the first president of the United States to resign office. He devoted himself to writing books and was widely regarded as an elder statesman. King interviewed him immediately after the fall of Russian leader Mikhail Gorbachev.

Nixon succumbed to a stroke on April 22, 1994.

"I don't live

in the past."

LARRY KING: For forty-five years, the resilient Richard Nixon has been with us: candidate, president, notorious figure, and elder statesman. Think what you will of his career, his expertise on both foreign policy and stateside politics remains widely respected. The man who opened China and won the first tentative period of détente with the much-feared Soviet Union is still talking about how the United States ought to conduct itself. His new book: *Seize the Moment: America's Challenge in a One-Superpower World*. It's a great pleasure to welcome a return visit to *Larry King Live* for President Nixon. . . . Yes, and happy birthday. Tomorrow, Richard Nixon is seventy-nine years young.

RICHARD NIXON: [*laughs*] Don't remind me.

LK: Do you celebrate them when you get over seventy?

RN: Not if I can avoid it. [*laughs*]

LK: [*laughs*] Let's deal right away with the things at hand and the occurrences in Japan with Mr. Bush. He apparently is okay. It is intestinal flu. You know of these things. He collapsed at a dinner. First, what's the first thing a vice president thinks of when this happens? Because it happened to you with Eisenhower.

RN: It actually happened to me three times. President Eisenhower, as you know, had a heart attack in 1955. He had a stroke, and he had ileitis—an operation that was very serious, in which he had to go under an anesthetic. And for a vice president, you don't think about, "Well, gee, I'm going to be president pretty soon or I may be, and what am I going to do?" But you really think about, "We just hope that the president gets well." You're concerned about it. That's the way I felt, at least.

LK: You don't give any thought that it could be you?

RN: Not at that point. Later on, you can be sure that as the media descends on you and as the political people descend on you, in fact, you can be sure at that time— The *moment* President Eisenhower had a heart attack, I heard from people that I had never heard from before, and once he got well I didn't hear from them again. That's the way it goes.

No, honestly, you *do* think of the fact that you might have the responsibility, but when you have a close relationship with the president you primarily think, "Well, I just hope that they're doing everything they can to get him well and that he will survive." And in this case we can be very thankful that the latest reports, as I understand, from Tokyo are that President Bush is doing very well. If you have later information—I guess CNN always is up to date on these things.

LK: But this is a difficult day for Dan Quayle.

RN: Yes, it is. It's a difficult day for him and, naturally, the spotlight will be on him again, as it has been for some time. I know that the conventional wisdom is, "My, if something happens to George Bush the country is going to be in a terrible condition." But let's look at Dan Quayle for just a moment. He has been through a lot, and when a man is tested— You don't know what he's made of until he really goes through fire. Dan Quayle has been through fire. He has handled himself with poise, with dignity, and with intelligence, and I think, under the circumstances, therefore, that the concern about whether Quayle would be a good president is not nearly as much as it would have been early on when, as you know, he got very, very bad publicity—almost as bad as I got on occasion.

LK: Is President Bush, in your opinion, pushing himself too much?

RN: If I were making up his schedule, I would lighten it up, but he's a man that likes to be on the move. He's an outdoor man, you know. He plays tennis, he plays golf, he drives that motorboat around—the cigarette—and, of course, he does a lot of running and other things. I, personally, feel that he could cut back on some of the appearances that are made simply for PR purposes. I think people would be more comfortable if he were seen doing what he has to do and which only he can do: handling the domestic affairs and the foreign affairs, the foreign issues, which are the president's responsibility.

LK: But the PR aspect is part of that job.

RN: Yes.

LK: Some people are saying this trip is PR.

RN: Yes, and I realize that some are knocking the trip because they feel that it's too commercial. I think his recent speech, though, or his statements that he made when he was in Tokyo put it in a better perspective. We shouldn't be going to Japan asking them to help us out. Let's understand one thing. There was a very unfortunate statement—which the president didn't make, but somebody in his cabinet did—to the effect that the recession may have been caused, to an extent, by the Japanese. That's nonsense. There would have been a recession whether there were Japanese quotas or tariffs or not. That's a very different problem. Now the Japanese need to be brought up short on some of their restrictions, but we have some problems, too, in that respect. But let's not assume that the Japanese are responsible for our problems. We've got to look to ourselves and *then* look to them.

LK: Taking [Lee] Iacocca and the head of General Motors and the head of Ford: your thoughts on that?

RN: I think the reason was that, when we look at the trade deficit which, as you know, is about $60 billion to $65 billion, that three-fourths of that deficit is in automobiles and automobile parts. There then comes a reason to try to get the Japanese to make some sort of arrangement, where we could sell more to them and maybe cut back on what they sell to us. I don't like that idea myself. I'm a free trader, and I think that, as far as our automobile companies are concerned, that they make very good cars. I think they have to do a better job of selling them. And I think the Japanese, of course, have got to make their market more available than it currently is, but the problems of the automobile industry are not due just to the Japanese. They're due to the industry itself.

LK: What does this illness do to the trip?

RN: I think, actually, it's going to help the president because it's— I found, for example, during President Eisenhower's illnesses that the country—who liked him already, as they like George Bush—they liked him even more. They liked him even more, because a great wave of sympathy came out. And also it brought home another point. I've known a number of presidents, and I've studied about a lot of them. There hasn't been a president in my lifetime who has worked harder at the job and who has had a more intense schedule than George Bush. Every time you turn on the tube you see him doing something, and this is apart from the tennis and all these other things. That's simply for the purpose of keeping him well. *He* thinks that.

LK: How do you react to this concept of late that he has no philosophy? You know him very well. You appointed him to some key posts.

RN: I would never have appointed him to key posts unless I felt that he did have a philosophy. People say, "Well, George Bush is not a conservative." Well, he may not be a conservative according to, maybe, Pat Buchanan, but on the other hand, there's no question about his conservative credentials, coming as he does from a Texas district which is conservative. He is what I would call a responsible conservative, and in the field of foreign policy, Larry, there's no question—as he demonstrated so eloquently by his actions during the Persian Gulf War—he's a strong leader. He believes in freedom, he believes in democracy, and he believes in doing what is necessary to deter and punish aggression. So that tells me he's a man of principle.

LK: And you have said also—was it true?—that you thought [Mario] Cuomo would have been his toughest opponent.

RN: Yes. I still think that. I have not talked to the governor. We correspond now and then. He wrote me a very nice letter about my book. I must tell you, it's about this— When I wrote him a little note on it, I said, "To Governor Cuomo, one of the rare politicians who reads books." He said, "Well, I don't read them all, but I'll read yours." And the greatest compliment you can pay an author—you know, as an author—is that he reads the book. But apart from that, Governor Cuomo, of all the Democrats, is the only current heavyweight—and he *is* a heavyweight, without question.

LK: Might he still be the nominee?

RN: Possible, but remote. Possible, because there is a chance still that there could be a deadlock at the convention due to the fact, as you know, under the new rules, the votes in the primary states are apportioned. In other words, when you win California, you don't win all the electoral votes.

LK: That's right, yes.

RN: Now, that means that, when you got to the convention, it might be that no one has a majority. I don't think that's likely. I think what's going to happen is that Governor Clinton will be nominated, without question. He will be a formidable candidate. He will be built up by the media. The media will give him what I call "media steroids," and they can take a middleweight—which he is today—and make him a heavyweight overnight the day that he's nominated. I think he will be a formidable candidate, but I think that President Bush will beat him. But it *will* be a much closer election—due to the recession, primarily—than was the last one. . . .

[*Commercial break*]

LK: I know *Seize the Moment* talks about this moment [in history]. Did you at all foresee this moment?

RN: No, I did not. I have a comment in my book, which you will find particularly interesting, when I said that in the debate that I had with Khrushchev in 1959—the so-called "kitchen debate"—he said to me, jabbing his finger into my chest, "Your grandchildren will live under communism," and I responded, "Your grandchildren will live in freedom." At that time, I was sure he was wrong but, I must admit, I wasn't sure *I* was right. And now these last three years, particularly the developments in 1991, have proved I was right because his grandchildren do live in freedom. I am pretty good at predicting elections and fairly good at predicting foreign policy. I would not have predicted it would have happened. Eventually, it would have happened, but that it would happen this soon and—very important—that it happened peacefully. People forget, this revolution occurred peacefully.

LK: And the obvious question is, "Why now? Why peacefully? Why so quickly?"

RN: It happened now due to the fact that the communist system had been totally discredited. And whatever you want to say about Gorbachev, you've got to give him credit that back in 1985, when he came into power, that he realized that the system wasn't working. But his purpose at that time was to save communism. His purpose was to keep the empire together, but he thought he had to revitalize the Russian people to do it, so he opened up the system politically. He allowed freedom of press, freedom of speech, and the rest. By opening it up politically, the Russian people—the Soviet peoples—were able to see the failures of the system and, when they saw the failures of the system, rather than making it survive—which was his purpose—it made it fall. I would say, too, that what made it happen this fast was the fact that the system finally simply failed because, whereas Gorbachev did provide for political reforms, his economic reforms did not go far enough, and, as a result, the system hadn't worked. Russia was an economic basket case.

LK: How much of a part did communications play—television, seeing freedom?

RN: An enormous part. Let me put it in terms of China. When I was in China in 1972, when we left we decided to leave back— The networks worked with us, and we left back in China the television communication system, the satellite system, and so forth. You know, that was like leaving a Trojan horse behind because, as a result of that, China saw the world—the Chinese people—and the world saw the Chinese people. Tiananmen Square, for example, was in living color on television. If it hadn't been in living color, there wouldn't have been the reaction against it.

Now, looking at the Soviet Union, at the present time, when you find television from Western Europe, from the United States, and so forth, being shown in the Soviet Union, it has an enormous effect on the people. As long as the Soviet Union was a closed society, it would survive; but when it opened up, when the people were able to see—to compare their lot with the situation in other countries that were not communist, they turned against it. What happened here in this revolution, it was not a revolution necessarily for democracy. It wasn't a revolution for freedom. It was a revolution against communism, because it failed. Now we've got to make freedom succeed.

LK: Is it going to succeed? Because in China it's not, is it?

RN: Well, first, as far as the Soviet Union is concerned, it is a close call, but it is the best bet that we have because Yeltsin has a very good group of people around him. He has done what Gorbachev would not do. He has adopted free-market policies, and he is going to try to unleash the creative abilities of the Russian people.

I would say that, as far as China is concerned, though, don't write that off, because what has happened today, over 50 percent of the Chinese GNP is from private enterprise. And you cannot have private—or what I would call "private freedom"—or free markets, without having eventually political freedom. Freedom is indivisible. -

LK: But why did they do what they did in Tiananmen Square?

RN: It was a terrible mistake. It was a mistake by frightened old men who felt that, unless they punished these people who were demonstrating peacefully for freedom and against, basically, communism, that their jobs would be imperiled. We have to continue to condemn that mistake, but we must not, on the other hand, close off our communication with them. We must continue to open up because you want to remember, if we hadn't opened up to China in 1972, there would have been no Tiananmen Square.

LK: Yes. Gorbachev's future: You know, a lot of people said, "When Richard Nixon waved good-bye in 1973, what future was there?" And here we are, nineteen years later—dignified elder statesman, writing successful books, appearing on national television, and being sought out by world leaders. What happens to Gorbachev— a *young* man?

RN: Gorbachev is only sixty years old. I must say, a few years ago I thought that was very old. But he's a very vigorous sixty. I know, from having seen him back in March. I think the way I'd look at it, to paraphrase MacArthur—and I heard that famous speech that he made when he addressed the joint session after being relieved of his command in Korea—but to paraphrase MacArthur, old politicians sometimes die, but they seldom fade away. Gorbachev is not going to fade away.

LK: We'll hear from him?

RN: But he cannot come back in the Soviet Union. He cannot come back in Russia. Unless—unless he repudiates communism, which he will not do. He is a true-believing communist.

LK: So where will we hear from him?

RN: I think we will hear from him on the world stage. He may be a critic of the policies in Russia and in the balance of the Soviet Union, but I wouldn't write him off in another role. But he must not— We must not expect that if Yeltsin fails, the Russian people are going to turn to him. They will not turn to him, because he failed. . . .

[*Commercial break*]

LK: Ben Bradlee, the former editor of the *Washington Post*, said one of the tough problems when you're the only voice in town—and for a while the *Post* was; now we have, of course, the *Washington Times*—it's harder. It's easier, when there's competition, to produce a great daily newspaper, because when there's no competition, there's no competition. We're the only superpower. Is that harder for us now?

RN: The responsibility is greater. It is greater because before, when we had the rivalry of the Soviet Union, it meant that we could mobilize the West against what they were doing, and people could get charged up to do what we needed to do to keep ourselves strong economically, politically and, of course, militarily. Now, with the enemy gone, in effect—although we cannot assume that five centuries of Russian expansionism is forever gone simply because we've had for one year, or almost a year, a democratic government in power—but with that danger gone, it is much more difficult to mobilize the people of this country in support of an effective foreign policy. But we need an effective foreign policy now because we are the only superpower, because there are other dangers in the world. Let's look at the world. Since the end of World War II, there have been one hundred forty wars, and in those wars, eight million more people were killed than were killed in World War I. Now that's going to continue. Nuclear weapons are being—

LK: Wars are going to continue?

RN: That's right. The wars are going to continue in the future. Iran-Iraq, the Iraqi war that we've been through just recently: all over the world today there are places that can explode. The Mideast is explosive.

LK: Yugoslavia.

RN: Yugoslavia we know is a problem. The possibility of the Koreas: it's still there, despite this temporary truce they have. And then, of course, there's the possibility of war between India and Pakistan. Who knows where it will happen?

LK: What do we do, then? How do we seize that moment?

RN: Well, we have to seize the moment by providing the leadership for the whole world, and not just the free world. And one way to seize that moment is to develop a good relationship with the new republics of the former Soviet Union. Yeltsin must not fail because, if he fails, it means not just that the communists will come back, but an authoritarian old guard will come back.

LK: So we must help?

RN: We must help, without question.

LK: Financially?

RN: We must help financially, but, Larry, this time, as compared with after World War II—and I was there—John F. Kennedy and I—we voted together for the

Greek-Turkish aid program in the 80th Congress, and that was the beginning of containing communism. But then we were the only player. All of our allies were devastated by the war, and the Germans and the Japanese were our defeated enemies, and they were devastated, and we had to put out the money. We've put out $400 billion over the past forty years in foreign aid. Now it's a different game. Those that we helped—the Japanese and the Germans—are the next two strongest economies in the free world. The rest of Europe—Japan and the rest —must assume the primary burden for providing the transitional funds, the humanitarian aid that Russia and the Soviet Union needs at this time. The U.S. cannot do it alone. We should simply provide, however, the leadership.

LK: Are we going to sell that well to the American public?

RN: It will be difficult, but it can be done. And I think here is perhaps the best advantage that President Bush will have over his opponent.

LK: Mr. Clinton.

RN: Yes. His opponent is an able man and has some good credentials domestically, but in the field of foreign policy, while he did support the Persian Gulf War—which most of, I think, his competitors did not—in foreign policy he isn't in Bush's league. . . .

[*Commercial break*]

LK: Our guest: former President Richard Nixon, who, I think, has forecast that Pat Buchanan, his old friend, compatriot, may get 40 percent of the vote in New Hampshire. That would be like a win, wouldn't it?

RN: Well, it proved to be somewhat of a win when Eugene McCarthy got that back in 1968. Of course, he didn't get the nomination. And, on the other hand, I would say that in the case of Pat Buchanan, while it would appear like a win, it isn't going to be one, because nobody is going to beat George Bush for this nomination. He's a cinch.

LK: Does Pat Buchanan have a case?

RN: Pat Buchanan: we have to look at it from his standpoint. You know him.

LK: Very well.

RN: Very well, and Pat—I know him perhaps even better. He is a true-believing conservative, and he doesn't believe that this administration is conservative enough on some issues. Whether you believe that—agree with that or not, he has a right to do everything he can to get the administration to move toward his point of view. He thinks this is the best way to be heard and, of course, he is being heard now, and he'll be heard at the convention if he makes a good showing—as he will—in New Hampshire. . . .

LK: How do you react to the anti-semitism charges?

RN: I think that it's really a very bad rap. I know him in a way that many others don't, and he's talked to me in confidence. I've talked to him in great confidence, as well. He knows how I feel. Pat is not anti-semitic. He is not, frankly, anti-anybody. He's very heavily pro-American. Getting back to the anti-semitic thing, I remember very well that in the 1973 Yom Kippur war, he was totally pro-Israel— all the way—in part because the Soviets were, of course, supporting the—at least behind the scenes, they were supporting the nations, the Egyptians and the others, that had started the war. I think that with the Soviet equation out of it, Pat now looks at the Israeli-American relationship solely in terms of what is best for the United States. He—incorrectly, in my opinion—but he sincerely believes that it is not in the interest of the United States to tie its policy as closely as we do to Israel.

LK: But he is not anti-semitic?

RN: But anti-semitic—in terms of being anti-semitic to an individual who happens to be Jewish—that is an absolutely false charge, and it shouldn't muddy the water.

LK: Concerning that area of the world, the Middle East, how do you look at that in the '90s?

RN: I would say the Middle East in the '90s will be the area of the greatest opportunity for progress toward peace and the greatest opportunity for disaster. It is the prime candidate for nuclear war, because the Israelis have nuclear weapons. I'm not going to tell you how I know, but I know that. And others—

LK: As a former president—I'm going to take your word.

RN: Others in the area are going to get them—there's no question about it—by hook or crook. That is why it is vitally important that Israel make its deal now, rather than waiting until later, when its potential adversaries will have the power to threaten its existence. This is an optimum time for Israel to make a deal, because look at what has happened: Iraq is out of the game; Egypt is out of the game; Jordan is out of the game—all of the ones that have attacked them previously. The Syrians don't have any money, and the Saudis now are not supplying them as they had previously. But most important . . . we have to have in mind that the Soviet Union, rather than supporting all of those that are attacking Israel, as they have in every other Arab-Israeli conflict, they're now supporting the peace process. So now is the time to make the deal.

LK: So this is Israel's time to seize the moment?

RN: It is.

LK: All right, will Shamir do it?

RN: No. I say no. That's too categoric. I do not know him. Because we've got to remember that Begin was also a hardliner, but he did it. Shamir may be the one that can do it. Just as they said Nixon was the only one that could go to China, maybe he's the only one that can make the deal, but he's got to get off of this high horse to the effect that there can be no concessions on the occupied territories. He's got to get off of this view that they've got to build all these settlements in it. That will not fly. It will not work, and it isn't right.

LK: Back to the isolationism aspect of Pat Buchanan: You're opposed to that, although the Republicans and conservatives of your past—the 1940 Republicans—were isolationist to the core. Why is it a mistake now? Why is Pat wrong?

RN: Well, he is wrong because we live in one world today. Wendell Wilkie, as you may know— You can remember this far back.

LK: I was a child, but he wrote a book called—

RN: He wrote a book called *One World*, after he had traveled around. It wasn't true then, but now, today, because of communications, because of trade and so forth, there *is* one world. The United States today— We cannot have peace in a world of wars, and there are forty of them going on right today. We can't have a healthy American economy in a sick world economy. If the world economy gets sick, we're going to get sick, too. And, frankly, we can't have freedom survive here if it is lost in too many other areas of the world.

I'm very pro-American. If I thought it was in the best interest of the United States to be isolationist and say, "As far as the Japanese are concerned, cut off all our alliance with them, don't do anything to help the Russians out of their problems, and forget the Europeans, because they're going to be looking after themselves—" it would be a terrible mistake. The United States is the one superpower in the world, the one that can provide the leadership which will make Europe, the Soviet Union—the former Soviet Union—Japan— We can all work together in building peace, freedom, and prosperity in the next century and, also, we can help that very poor southern hemisphere. . . .

[*Commercial break*]

LK: Our guest: the former president of the United States, Richard Nixon. I want to touch other bases. Senator Kennedy said yesterday—drastic cuts in the military budget and a lot of emphasis now—almost a kind of war in the domestic area— on the plight in America. Buy any of that?

RN: Not the drastic. Cuts, yes, but not drastic cuts. That would be very detrimental to the United States. We're moving into uncharted waters. We don't know what's going to happen in Russia after just one year, for example—or less than a year— of a democratic government there. We don't know what's going to happen in other parts of the world. We've got to retain a significant military capability. Let me say, also, that we *can* make cuts, however, in Europe. We have approximately 300,000 [troops] there now. That'll be down to 200,000. That can be cut back to 50,000, because the Warsaw Pact has disintegrated. We can make those cuts. I think we should cut our strategic nuclear weapons—the big ones, you know— because the Soviet Union no longer exists as an enemy of the United States. We could cut that not by 50 percent, as I indicate in my book, but by 75 percent. We do not need to have that capability which existed only for the purpose of deterring the Soviet Union. . . .

LK: Would you take that and get to national health insurance in America?

RN: Let me tell you the way I would see this sorting out. These cuts will not provide a huge peace dividend immediately, because it takes time to make the transition, as you know. On the other hand, over a period of time, it will be significant. I imagine that we're talking about $50 billion. Fifty billion dollars should be applied to health, particularly. It should be provided, also, for tax relief—some tax relief for the middle class. The capital gains tax should go in, because that's going to provide jobs, which we very much need. There are domestic issues—domestic areas where it can be used. But we have to realize it isn't going to be a huge grab-bag. What is really needed more is a change of behavior in many of these areas, rather than a lot more money.

LK: Behavior?

RN: Behavior, behavior. Well, let's take, for example, the situation on health care. Many people are not aware of this, but we have the best health care in the world today. Where do people go when they want an operation, as you had, for the heart or something like that? Do you go to a place that has compulsory health insurance, state health? No, you come to the United States. We've got the best health care in the world. We spend more money per capita on health care than any other country in the world. The question is, how do we properly spend it? Because there are thirty-eight million that aren't even covered by it.

LK: Our delivery system is poor.

RN: That's right, the delivery system. For example, health-care consumers have got to have more of an obligation to see that they get their money's worth. Also, you've got to have competition between health-care providers and health-care insurers, which you don't have today. I would say, in other words, it is not just a question of we need more money for a system that is not already producing. The same is true of education. We spend more per capita for education than any other country in the world, and yet 25 percent of our young people don't even graduate from high school.

LK: Do you see the recession ending soon?

RN: The recession, according to the experts, will end in the spring or summer. Now, most people don't have much confidence in that because that's what— They didn't, because the same experts—

LK: They've been wrong.

RN: —at the first of last year, they hit it wrong. My view is—for whatever it's worth— that we are at the low point today. The recession is primarily one of confidence. Let's look at it for just a moment. It is the smallest recession that we have had since the end of World War II, and yet it is the longest, and in terms of consumer confidence, it is the worst—and that is what matters politically. If people are not confident about their future, then you're in recession, no matter what those economists tell you.

LK: That's right. Perception is reality.

RN: So that's why it's very important that the president, as he is planning to do, comes before the Congress and comes up with a program on the tax front and other areas, which will give people hope.

LK: This is a very important State of the Union address, then.

RN: A very important one. And, incidentally, you want to remember, every time you tend to write off George Bush he makes the big play. Remember before the convention? Many people were saying that Dukakis was going to lead—he was leading in the polls by—

LK: Nineteen points.

RN: —nineteen points. And George Bush made a brilliant speech—the best speech, I think, that he has made. Then he had this time when he was going, beginning to go down somewhat in the polls. Remember, it was a very tough time when they had the budget deal and he went down below 50 percent. And then he provided that splendid leadership there in the Persian Gulf War—over the objections of most of the establishment, most of the media, and most of the Congress, and some in his own administration. As a strong leader, he came through.

George Bush makes the big plays. He's now down. He's at 47 percent approval, but let me tell you, historically, I was at 49 percent at this time before the '72 elections and won with 61 percent. He's going to come back. He's not going to win with 61 percent, but his State of the Union will be a very effective speech, because George Bush—incidentally, like Dan Quayle (they're different in many ways)—he's an intense competitor.

LK: You predict that Clinton will be the nominee?

RN: Yes.

LK: Who will be his vice presidential nominee?

RN: The vice presidential nominee will be the one who runs second, I believe, in the primaries and comes to the convention with that kind of a showing. Now, who that is likely to be, I wouldn't know at this point. I doubt if it's going to be Jerry Brown. I would doubt, for example, if it's going to be Tsongas. I would doubt if it's going to be Governor Wilder. But let me say, in saying that, I doubt if maybe this is going to help him—

LK: You're down to Harkin and Kerrey.

RN: Harkin is a very tough campaigner. There's a possibility. And, of course, the other one is Kerrey who, with his war record—

LK: Vietnam veteran on the ticket.

RN: That's right, and that would be formidable. But I'll tell you, they don't vote for vice presidents. They vote for president. And incidentally, as far as Quayle is concerned, Quayle this time will be an asset on the ticket because he is the one that can reassure the conservatives. Those that think that George Bush has become a flaming liberal, Dan Quayle will be out there preaching the old-time religion. . . .

[*Commercial break*]

LK: Vietnam. Should we recognize Vietnam? Have we come to this now?

RN: No, I would not recognize Vietnam. Vietnam has not complied with the peace treaty of 1973. It still is engaged in aggressive actions in Laos, for example, imperialism or colonialism—call it what you want—and it has adopted economic policies that make it one of the five poorest nations in the world, and has been particularly repressive to those who fought beside us from South Vietnam. Until they change their policies, we should not recognize them, because it is in no interest of ours to do so.

LK: Are there POWs there?

RN: That's another area which gives us reason not to recognize them. I don't know whether there are or not, but it has been obscene, the way that they have just dribbled out information to these poor families who simply want to know what happened. They've got to know a lot more than they've done, and they're trying to dribble it out and get brownie points for it. They should get none, whatever.

LK: On November 22, 1963, you flew out of Dallas. You were attending a convention of PepsiCola.

RN: That morning.

LK: Your law firm represented PepsiCola.

RN: That's right.

LK: Do we know that whole story?

RN: I am not one of those who saw the motion picture [*JFK*], but its credibility was questioned in my mind when I read an op-ed piece by the director, Oliver Stone, in which he made the statement that President Johnson in 1965 sent the first combat troops to Vietnam. Well, now, that wasn't true. President Kennedy sent the first combat troops—1,600 of them—to Vietnam when he was president—which I think, incidentally, was the right thing to do and supported at the time—and there were 400 casualties while he was president. So I would say that anyone who was that off-base historically is not, perhaps, the best expert as to whether there was a conspiracy or not.

LK: That aside, did you believe the Warren Commission?

RN: I did not study it carefully, and I have never questioned it before, and I don't question it now. A lot is being written— But the reason that I don't is that nothing's going to happen as a result. If I thought it would be useful to try to dig into it, I would do so.

LK: Are you surprised that 75 percent of the American public don't accept it?

RN: Not at all surprised, because people think usually that there's a conspiracy about most everything. In fact, there's a conspiracy about the Lincoln assassination still, you know—the stories are out. But in this case, I know the people don't believe that, but I don't see a useful purpose in getting into that, and I don't think it's, frankly, useful for the Kennedy family to constantly raise that up again, so I'm not going to get into it.

LK: And do you agree with keeping the files closed, then, for another, I guess, twenty-three years?

RN: Keeping the files closed is another matter. I see no reason to keep the files closed, unless there's a national security problem involved, and I can't see any national security problem involved because, for example, if the Cubans were involved or some other foreign power, that has all changed. I think at the present time there would be no reason to keep the files closed.

LK: Are we going to do better with Cuba?

RN: Only when Castro leaves. Castro should be cut off totally, and that's one of the things we've got to negotiate with Yeltsin right away. They've begun to cut him off, but he must not be subsidized in any way. And let him sink or swim, which is the very thing which, as you know—coming, as you do, from Florida a few years ago—is what hundreds, thousands of Cubans have had to do as they tried to leave the place.

LK: Do you think Yeltsin will be receptive to that?

RN: I do. One of the advantages of Yeltsin is that he wants to cut off all foreign aid to all of these losers in the world. He wants to cut it off to Cuba. He wants to cut it off to Korea—North Korea. He wants to cut it off to Afghanistan. And we should get him to do that—lock him in on that right away—because we should-n't help the Soviet Union unless it helps itself— We shouldn't help Russia, I should say, unless it helps itself. And that's why we should lock in the arms control right now. Cut the arms now before some new person comes in who might be aggressive. . . .

[*Commercial break*]

LK: Are we going to learn anything from the KGB files?

RN: Oh, yes. I think we could learn a great deal, unless the KGB—and I guess this happened—has probably destroyed a lot of them already.

LK: Super Bowl: okay, are Washington and Buffalo going to win Sunday?

RN: I would predict that both would win, although Detroit will give Washington a good game due to the strength of their offensive line. But Washington's too good all-around not to make it to the Super Bowl.

LK: And who wins the Super Bowl?

RN: I would give it to Washington by about a point . . . but I would say don't bet the ranch on it. Don't even bet the outhouse on it. I would say it's even.

LK: Pete Rose: Hall of Fame?

RN: I think he should be put in. I think he has paid the price and, like Ty Cobb—who also had some problems like this, Larry, as you know from your history—Ty Cobb is in the Hall of Fame. Pete Rose should be in the Hall of Fame.

LK: Mr. President, finally, is it hard to come back to this city? Is it hard to drive by the Watergate?

RN: Well, I've never been in the Watergate, so it's not hard for me— [*laughs*]

LK: Never been in? Never been in the restaurant?

RN: No, no, no. Other people were in there, though, unfortunately, and so—

LK: [*laughs*] But is it hard for you?

RN: No. I don't live in the past. As a matter of fact, one of the problems older people have is when you get together with them, they always want to reminisce about the past. I don't do that. I like to think about the future. . . .

Robert McNamara

Robert Strange McNamara was secretary of defense under John F. Kennedy. In this interview, King relives with McNamara the chilling hours thirty years earlier in 1962, when the United States and the USSR very nearly went to war over Soviet missiles in Cuba. McNamara reveals just how close the world was to thermonuclear armageddon.

"There was a 100 percent chance of nuclear war in the event we attacked, and we came very close to that."

LARRY KING: Good evening from Washington. The post-Cold War thaw is uncovering information that'll make you shudder. In a conference earlier this month with Cuban and Soviet officials, Americans learned just how close the world was to nuclear holocaust thirty years ago. During the tense days of the Cuban missile crisis in 1962, the Soviets had nuclear warheads in Cuba, and the CIA didn't know it. Even more chilling, Soviet field commanders in Cuba had authorization from Moscow to fire if provoked—a move that would have led to an all-out nuclear counterattack from the United States. So says our guest, Robert McNamara, who was President Kennedy's secretary of defense at the time of the crisis and was at that conference in Havana. Were you shocked?

ROBERT MCNAMARA: I was totally shocked, and you're absolutely correct in your appraisal of the danger. It was much greater than we thought.

LK: Why?

RM: Because you're correct, the CIA—and I give them great credit; they knew an awful lot about what was going on, but— And, by the way, they discovered the missiles in Cuba before Khrushchev was ready to disclose them, so the CIA performed well. But they stated they believed there were no nuclear warheads there. We were told in Cuba last week by the Soviet general, who was sent by the defense minister to Cuba with instructions to the commanders as to how to handle them, there were thirty-six nuclear warheads for strategic missiles that were capable of destroying the U.S. East Coast. But the really frightening and chilling fact was the one you alluded to. There were nine *tactical* nuclear warheads there. We had absolutely no knowledge of that. And the most important point is the one you mentioned. The local field commanders had authority to use those against a U.S. attack without further consultation with Moscow. There was a 100 percent chance of nuclear war in the event we attacked, and we came very close to that.

LK: We were embargoing, right? We were circling—

RM: We had a quarantine.

LK: Quarantine. We were searching ships.

RM: Exactly. And we had stated publicly we were determined to prevent further importation in Cuba of Soviet weapons of any kind, and that's what the quarantine was designed to prevent.

LK: Except they were there.

RM: The warheads were there—exactly. We didn't know it.

LK: As you look back, that was—what—twelve days, right? It took twelve days, that crisis?

RM: Exactly.

LK: From get-go to stop?

RM: That's right. It lasted, essentially, from the time we got the U-2 photographs, which were taken on a Sunday— We were informed of them on Monday, and the president went on the air the following Monday. And on the Sunday after that, which was exactly fourteen days after the U-2 took the photographs, Khrushchev announced publicly— And, by the way, he held open the radio transmitter in Moscow to announce it publicly over the transmitter. He was so concerned that we were about to invade, he didn't wish to take the time to encode, decode, transmit, and so on through diplomatic channels. He held the radio transmitter open and announced it over the radio, fourteen days after we'd had the U-2 photographs.

LK: He knew he had warheads there, and he knew he had commanders who could use them—

RM: You're damn right. And more than that, he knew that we had an invasion force poised to invade. The first days' aircraft sorties were scheduled for ten 190 sorties. Now, to tell you the truth, had Khrushchev not announced on Sunday the 28th he was withdrawing the missiles, I believe President Kennedy would have found a means of deferring the invasion for a time, because neither he nor I wished to accept the risk of invasion, and yet we didn't know *how* great the risk was.

LK: In retrospect now, after you've heard this, you must have given thought. You were there every second of this.

RM: I lived in the Pentagon for twelve days.

LK: How close were we to taking an overt action that would have had that reaction? How close?

RM: We were that close [*holds thumb and index finger, nearly touching*]. We were that close. The majority of President Kennedy's advisers were recommending that if Khrushchev did not remove the missiles or announce he had removed them on that Sunday, the 28th, we should authorize an invasion on Monday or Tuesday. We were that close.

LK: And had we invaded, of course, he'd have—

RM: He would have fired his nine tactical nuclear warheads. Our force, by the way, was not authorized to be equipped with nuclear warheads, so we would have sent a force in without nuclear warheads confronting his force with them. Now, what would we have done? We would immediately have put tactical aircraft in the air equipped with nuclear warheads to respond. We would have had to. And where would that have ended? Who knows?

LK: We may not have been here.

RM: We may not have been here. You're absolutely right.

LK: That means they had to move warheads off that island.

RM: They did.

LK: Thinking about it, that's a little scary.

RM: Well, it's not as scary as having them there without our knowledge. That's what's frightening. And most of all, what was frightening was the authority in the field commanders to use those tactical warheads without authorization from Moscow.

LK: Supposing you knew that?

RM: That's a good question. That's a good question. I've thought some about it. I don't want to speculate. I don't think it would have deterred us. I think we would have perhaps moved in some other way. We surely would have equipped our force with tactical nuclear warheads, which we had not. But I think the conclusion is— What we should concentrate on today is not what we would have done then had we known it. What we should concentrate on today is how to avoid this. And the lesson, I think, is *human beings are fallible*. We all make mistakes. I make mistakes in my everyday life. I've spent ten years of my life in association with the military, and I can tell you in conventional wars—World War II, North Korea, Vietnam, whatever—we make mistakes. The mistakes cost lives—thousands of lives—but they don't destroy nations. You make a mistake with respect to nuclear weapons, and your nation is at risk. That was the risk.

LK: Given today's society—CNN, cameras, worldwide microphones, satellites, communications—and the same set of circumstances, would the result have been different?

RM: I don't think so. I think it depends on the president. It is said that today a president couldn't hold in confidence for six days the knowledge we had that the missiles were there while his advisers examined all the alternatives. We held that in confidence for six days. It's said that couldn't be done today. I don't agree with that. I think it can be done, and I want to tell you, I think it *should* be done. Had we acted on the first day, the majority of the advisers would have said, "Attack immediately." By the end of the sixth day, the majority recommended the quarantine.

LK: We're going to take a break and go to your phone calls. I must ask you this: . . . Have you seen the movie *JFK*?

RM: I haven't. I haven't.

LK: Okay. Any desire to?

RM: No, because I don't believe at all what I understand to be the underlying premise: that there was a conspiracy involving senior leaders.

LK: One of the key principles you would know, though, is the movie contends that Jack Kennedy unequivocally was going to pull out of Vietnam.

RM: I can't speculate on what—

LK: Did he ever say that to you?

RM: No, he did not. But I want to tell you this, that in October of 1963—roughly four to six weeks before he was killed—he did authorize and publicly announce he was beginning to withdraw our advisers. We had about 16,000 advisers—trainers—training the South Vietnamese to defend themselves. He authorized and directed 1,000 be brought out as the first step toward removing them before the end of the year.

LK: So there would have been—

RM: I don't want to speculate what he would have done after that. Very quickly the situation changed. [President Ngo Dinh] Diem was killed, for example. There were all kinds of changes. I don't know how he would have reacted. . . .

[Commercial break]

LK: Indeed, another thing we learned, Bob McNamara, was that the Soviets had 42,000 troops in Cuba, not 10,000.

RM: The CIA had reported 10,000. We were told in Moscow, and it was repeated again in Havana last week, they had 42,000.

LK: You defended the CIA.

RM: Well, I did.

LK: Didn't they do some bad work here?

RM: They did very good work.

LK: *Good* work?

RM: This was a closed society. Both the Soviet Union and Cuba were closed societies, and the CIA penetrated it. They did very good work. We didn't know everything.

LK: Before we get some calls, your thoughts on the new Russia, the new confederation.

RM: They're in the deepest of trouble, the deepest of trouble.

LK: Do you like this air lift idea?

RM: I do, I do. I think we should provide humanitarian relief. We should provide additional—"we," the West—should provide additional financial assistance if—if—there's a political structure, an economic structure that assures us the financial assistance can be well used. We're not certain of that yet, but we are absolutely certain they will need, and we should provide, humanitarian relief. . . .

LK: Castro had full knowledge of this—warheads?

RM: Partial knowledge. . . . He didn't, in my opinion, know that the Soviets had nine tactical warheads there and that their field commanders had authority to use them.

LK: That might have frightened him a little.

RM: I think it would have. It *should* have.

LK: All right, we go now to Pensacola, Florida, with Robert McNamara. Hello.

CALLER: [*Pensacola, Florida*] Secretary McNamara, looking back at some of the errors the CIA made in that intelligence, how should we feel about the intelligence today concerning Iraq and nuclear weapons?

RM: Well, I think it's apparent that none of us—CIA or anybody else—knows everything about nuclear weapons in Iraq. And the lesson is not that the CIA is imperfect—my impression is they have done an outstanding job—but our information is always incomplete. And the point I want to make is incomplete information relating to nuclear warheads that can destroy nations is a recipe for disaster, and the conclusion is not that we should get rid of the CIA and replace them all. The conclusion is we should restructure the globe's nuclear forces and rid the globe, as best we can, of this terrible danger.

LK: Columbus, Ohio, with Robert McNamara. Hello.

CALLER: [*Columbus, Ohio*] I was just wondering. You had said that all Kennedy's advisers were telling him to attack. I wonder what your advice was?

RM: Well, I don't think I said all Kennedy's advisers were telling him to attack. I said the majority of them believed he should attack on Monday, if Khrushchev didn't take them out on Sunday.

LK: What was your opinion?

RM: Well, I—

LK: It's fair to ask. Come on, Bob.

RM: Well, to be frank with you, I did recommend, and would have continued to recommend, we defer attack. There were other things we could have done had Khrushchev not moved on Sunday. For example, we could have what I called "tightened the screws" on the blockade. At that point we were blockading the importation of weapons into Cuba. We could have blockaded the importation of petroleum and put increasing pressure on Cuba. Wouldn't that have been a wiser course than attacking? Even if they hadn't had nuclear weapons, if we had attacked and killed 42,000 Russians and 200,000 Cubans, what would the soviets have done elsewhere in the world—against Berlin, against our Jupiter missiles in Turkey? It was a very risky situation.

LK: You did not go home during those twelve days?

RM: I spent twelve nights and twelve days in the Pentagon.

LK: Rochester, New York. Hello.

CALLER: [*Rochester, New York*] Good evening, Mr. King and Mr. McNamara. We were wondering whether or not you agree with entering and opening up the new assassination files on the JFK assassination?

RM: Well, I'm not an expert on the cost of that in terms of exposing confidential sources, but, excluding that, I would definitely favor it.

LK: That day, November 22nd, 1963—

RM: Yes.

LK: —were you flying to Japan?

RM: No. No, no, no, I was not.

LK: You weren't? There were a lot of the cabinet that was on that flight.

RM: You're absolutely right. Dean Rusk, for example, was in the air, along with most of the other—

LK: Pierre Salinger.

RM: Exactly—most of the other cabinet officers.

LK: Where were you?

RM: I was not, because Japan didn't have a defense minister, so I was in the Pentagon meeting with McGeorge Bundy, the chief of the Bureau of the Budget, and the chairman of the joint chiefs. We were getting ready to take the following year's budget to President Kennedy at the Cape the following weekend.

LK: How did you hear about it?

RM: Bobby Kennedy called me out of my meeting. The meeting was in my office. He called me, and the first call stated, "The president has been shot." It was believed he had not been seriously injured. The second call from Bobby said he'd been killed.

LK: What did you do?

RM: He asked me to go out with him to Andrews [Air Force Base], which I subsequently did. We met the plane bringing the body back from Texas.

LK: That must have been incredible, for him to have to—

RM: It was terrible. It was just awful. And then, of course, he went with the body out to the naval hospital in Bethesda, and he called me and asked if I'd come out there. I went out there. I spent the night with the family, and we took the body to the White House about five in the morning.

LK: When did President Johnson ask you to stay on?

RM: [*laughs*] The first day. His office was then in the Executive Office Building, and he retained that office for a day or two after President Kennedy's death, and in our first meeting, which was the morning after the president was killed, he asked me to stay on.

LK: Cambridge, Massachusetts, with Robert McNamara. Hello.

CALLER: [*Cambridge, Massachusetts*] Hello. Mr. McNamara, the CIA had the covert plan for Operation Mongoose out of New Orleans in 1963. Apparently, [Lee Harvey] Oswald was hanging around some members down there—David Ferry and Guy Bannister, two members of Operation Mongoose. This was the covert plan to retake Cuba. Can you shed any light on that?

RM: Yes, well, you're right— You're *half*-right. There was a covert plan named Mongoose. It wasn't operating out of New Orleans. It was operating more out of Miami. I don't believe—to be absolutely frank with you—I don't believe there was any connection between Mongoose and Oswald.

LK: Topanga, California, hello.

CALLER: [*Topanga, California*] My question is, why are the Soviets still building weapons, according to Secretary of Defense [Richard] Cheney? And they just tested two of the ICBMs. One went 4,000 miles. Why are they still doing this, and we're still giving them—want to give money to them?

RM: Day before yesterday, the general in charge of the Defense Intelligence Agency and Mr. Gates, the director of CIA, reported publicly that the Soviets had cut their weapons procurement in the first quarter of this year 80 percent.

LK: Eighty percent?

RM: Eighty percent.

LK: Madison, Wisconsin, for Bob McNamara. Hello.

CALLER: [*Madison, Wisconsin*] Does Secretary McNamara think that his recommendations to President Kennedy at that time played a critical role in the course the President took? And what does it feel like to play a pivotal point in all of human history? And I think we have maybe a debt of gratitude to Secretary McNamara that we are still here today, for his steady, clear counsel back in—nearly thirty years ago now.

LK: Yes, how do you feel?

RM: Well, you're very kind to credit me with that. Quite frankly, I think President Kennedy was determined to avoid war if he possibly could. It happened that I was advising him to do what I think he would have done anyhow. So I can't take the credit you give me, but I appreciate your thought.

LK: How about the second part of the question—to be a part of history?

RM: Well, the implication of the question is that these responsibilities weigh heavily on you, and he's absolutely right in that.

Judith Exner

Judith Campbell Exner, born in 1930, was the daughter of an architect and grew up in the glitter of Hollywood. In 1960, she went to Las Vegas with friends Jeannie Martin and Tina Cahn—the wives of Dean Martin and composer Sammy Cahn—to attend one of Sinatra's shows. Also attending was Jack Kennedy, the Democratic nominee for president. A romance quickly developed between Exner and Kennedy, which lasted well into his presidency. Later, Exner became friendly with Chicago Mafia boss Sam Giancana and, subsequently, became Giancana's contact with Kennedy, passing messages and money between the two during 1960 and 1961. Exner claimed to have arranged ten face-to-face meetings between Kennedy and the crime kingpin. This revelation contradicted statements she made to Congress in 1975.

At the time of this interview, Exner was ill of cancer and was anxious to set the record straight. The interview took place in a secret Los Angeles location.

"[Giancana] would call Jack a spoiled brat, and he would say, 'Your boyfriend wouldn't be in the White House if it wasn't for me.'"

LARRY KING: She is older now, out here in southern California. She's fighting cancer. Camelot feels like another lifetime. Washington was glamorous, the president was young and dashing, and the air was rich with hope. Judith Exner would add intrigue, plotting, and fear. The younger Judith Exner knew John F. Kennedy well, and she knew of connections between Kennedy and the Mob. She was a go-between. She had the trust of the world's most powerful man and some of its most feared criminals. Now, when Exner has talked before she says the story has never come out right, so a few days ago, here in a private place near Los Angeles, I sat down with her, and Judith Exner talked for the record.

With Judith Exner. Why are you here?

JUDITH EXNER: The main reason is, I think, to separate the fact from fiction.

LK: Any reason you chose *Larry King Live*, this show?

JE: I think that you are very fair with people, and I think that you're very credible. And it's good. That's of utmost importance to me.

LK: Give me life for Judith Exner today. First, how are you?

JE: Well, I consider myself well, because I'm still standing, and I'm still on my feet. I've had two cancer surgeries, and I've lived a year and a half beyond what they said the time that I was supposed to have had.

LK: And what do they say now?

JE: I'm taking a drug called Taxol, which is an anti-estrogen drug that is specifically for breast cancer after you've gone through chemotherapy and had a recurrence. And they are just watching, you know. It's gone to my spine, but it's moving slowly, and that's due to the drug Taxol.

LK: You have cancer of the spine?

JE: Yes. It's metastatic breast cancer. I've had a mastectomy and a lung removal, and now it's gone to the spine.

LK: Are you tired of seeing your name all the time in the press?

JE: Yes, I am.

LK: Tough to live with?

JE: Very hard to live with. I am as close to a recluse as you can get.

LK: If you had to do all this all over again—and we'll touch a lot of bases—what did you do wrong?

JE: I'm sure I've done a great many things wrong, but had I told the whole story when I was subpoenaed to appear before the Intelligence Committee, the Church committee, in '75, and—

LK: You didn't tell them the whole story?

JE: No, I didn't.

LK: Why?

JE: Sam Giancana had been— He was killed a week or two before he was to appear before the committee. I knew what the committee was investigating, and I was afraid. I was terribly afraid, and I was in a position where no one really seemed to know, although the Church committee did— They felt I was the go-between, that I was the link—

LK: Between Kennedy and Giancana?

JE: —between Jack and Sam. But they couldn't prove it, and when I went back there— My husband and I had long discussions about it, and I felt that I just couldn't safely tell the whole story. But it's also partly protecting Jack.

LK: In retrospect, you should have?

JE: Yes.

LK: Because it all comes out anyway, right?

JE: I think there are two sides to that. I don't think anyone was ready to hear it then, and my waiting as long as I have to really reveal the whole story is simply because I have access now to documents that were not available then. I didn't even have my own FBI files then. I didn't know they existed.

LK: That can back up, then, what you've asserted, as well?

JE: Yes.

LK: All right, let's start from the beginning. You grew up here in southern California, right? And knew a lot of famous people, didn't you?

JE: I was brought up within the entertainment industry—

LK: Your father was—what—real estate?

JE: An architect.

LK: Architect. You knew Frank Sinatra early on?

JE: Yes, because I married early, and I married an actor, and, of course, you know, in those days, in the '50s, my husband was under contract to studios, and you are required to attend the premieres and the parties and do the *Photoplay* layouts and all of this.

LK: What is Frank's part of this story—just the introduction of you to Kennedy?

JE: I went out with Frank for a short period of time and—very short period of time—and we just then became friends.

LK: And this was after you were divorced?

JE: Oh, yes. Yes, long after.

LK: And he introduced you to Kennedy, and what were the circumstances? How did you meet John Kennedy?

JE: I went to Las Vegas with some friends of mine to see a show that Frank was doing at the time. He was shooting a picture called *Oceans 11*, and it was really an incredible show. Everyone that was in the picture was on stage at night: Peter Lawford and Dean Martin, Sammy Davis Jr., and Joey Bishop, and Frank. And it was an incredible show. So I had gone up with friends of mine a couple of times, and on this one weekend I went up on the plane with—not at anyone's request, which has been written. I went up with some friends of mine, and also Jeannie Martin was on the plane—

LK: Dean's wife.

JE: Sammy Cahn's wife, yes.

LK: Tina Cahn?

JE: No, his previous wife.

LK: And this was what year?

JE: 1960.

LK: Jack was elected or running?

JE: He was running, but it was February, and it was the very beginning. . . .

LK: And he was there?

JE: Yes. I was at Frank's table, and there were— In the lounge there was a big group. And, as it's been suggested, this was all set up from the beginning. He was introduced to many people at the same table, and then Frank went to get ready for his show, and some of us went into the Garden Room for dinner—about six or seven of us. And Jack was there, and Teddy and Sammy's wife at that time—Sammy Cahn's wife.

LK: Did you like him right away?

JE: Yes.

LK: Did he like you?

JE: Yes.

LK: Was that obvious?

JE: Slowly. We saw the show later, and then I went over to one of the casinos with Teddy. It was just, you know, when you're with—and some other friends.

LK: You were how old at this time—twenty-five?

JE: I'm fifty-eight now, so in 1960—[*laughs*]

LK: You were a young lady.

JE: Yes, yes.

LK: When did a spark— How did it start that you would see John Kennedy? Did you see him, by the way, romantically, before he was elected?

JE: Oh, yes. Yes.

LK: So, while he was running you were seeing him?

JE: Yes. He asked me to go to lunch the next day, and he told me what time to meet him out on the patio, outside the Sands. And he was having a press conference at the time, and he called over to me, "Judy, I'll be right with you," and everyone turned around, and I sat down and waited a few moments, and there were a number of people there at his press conference.

LK: No one reported it?

JE: And no one reported it.

LK: And you knew he was married?

JE: I had a hard time in figuring out when I figured that out, but it was within the first month, because we were talking on the phone almost every day, and he wanted me to meet him in different places that he was campaigning in. And finally, in March, I was going to New York, and I told him that I was going to New York, and he said, well, we would meet there. . . .

[*Commercial break*]

LK: Did you, Judith Exner, think twice about starting a physical relationship with not just a United States senator running for president but with a married man?

JE: Yes, I had—I had great pangs of guilt. I'm from a very strict Irish-Catholic family, and my heart really did rule my head, and it's—

LK: You fell in love with him?

JE: Yes, I did. And the next time we met was in March of '60.

LK: And that's where it began?

JE: Yes.

LK: In New York?

JE: Yes.

LK: Would you call it ardent? I mean, were you intense romantic lovers—calling each other, as happens between people having this kind of relationship when one is married? Were there secret calls and meetings at ten in the morning and four in the morning, and, "I can't be here, I'll meet you there," and that?

JE: Well, it was very intense, and you have to remember that in 1960 he was campaigning so there was— Somehow, he always found time to call me and our meetings were really not as frequent as once he was in the White House but—

LK: More frequent *after* he was in the White House?

JE: Yes, but we saw each other, really, a great deal. That shows really—

LK: Where were you the night he was elected?

JE: I think I was at my mother's home, because I sent a telegram to Evelyn.

LK: Lincoln?

JE: Yes.

LK: His secretary—who knew you well, right?

JE: Yes, very well.

LK: How often after elected did he call you?

JE: Oh, the same—really, the same amount of time.

LK: I mean, did he call that night? Next day?

JE: No, no, it was probably a couple of days before I got to—

LK: Did you ever discuss seriously his ending his marriage?

JE: Only twice did he discuss with me his wife at all, and it was before he was nominated. He said that they were going to— If he wasn't nominated, the marriage would end. But it didn't have anything to do with the fact that I was seeing him. It didn't mean that he was leaving his wife for me. That was something they had already decided and he had more or less the same conversation with me before the election.

LK: And after elected, did he ever say, "I'm going to—"

JE: No, we didn't— It never came up. He knew that I wouldn't discuss his wife, and that wasn't Jack's nature. He wouldn't sit and discuss his wife.

LK: It's one thing to be in love with someone, Judith, who's married. It's another thing to be in love with someone who's married and president. I mean, he's on television. *She's* on television. You see them—the first lady. They walk; they're happy; they're smiling. You're in love with this man. What was that like?

JE: Agony. Agony. I think that any woman that finds herself in the position of falling in love with a man that's married goes through tremendous pain. And this is not excusing the behavior, but you do go through tremendous pain. Your holidays are not with the person you care for.

LK: But he's also president.

JE: You see, that never— As far as that was concerned, I was never politically oriented, and that was something that, for me, was in the way of our being together.

LK: It was a hindrance?

JE: Yes, a tremendous hindrance.

LK: Did you date other men?

JE: Just friends.

LK: Was he jealous?

JE: Oh, very.

LK: Possessive?

JE: Very possessive. That's why the amount of phone calls, and he would want to know what I was doing twenty-four hours a day. In fact, he would call my mother if he couldn't locate me. He had a telephone relationship with my mother. He completely won my mother over.

LK: Did you ever say to him, "I can't take this any more," as happens with people in this situation? "I want you to leave your wife," or, "Make me a promise— something?"

JE: No. . . .

LK: That changed things a lot?

JE: It changed things a lot, and it—

LK: Did it change your feelings?

JE: It made the situation more impossible for me to go on with. I couldn't handle it any more. And he wanted me to move to Washington, and we started bickering on the phone, and he said, "Well, if you would just move to Washington, it would be easier for you." And he said, "I could keep closer watch over you." And I wouldn't.

LK: Did Robert know about this? And Ted? And close people around him?

JE: Robert—yes.

LK: Did people in the White House know about it?

JE: Dave Powers—

LK: Evelyn Lincoln?

JE: —and Evelyn Lincoln were the main links for me.

LK: He [JFK] had Addison's disease. Did he have much back pain, by the way? Because he never talked about it publicly.

JE: Some, but he didn't discuss it.

LK: Didn't complain?

JE: No.

LK: Didn't say his back was hurting a lot?

JE: No.

LK: Because some said his back hurt every day.

JE: No, he didn't discuss that. You have to remember that when you're— This is not a relationship where people are spending as much time together as they want to spend together. And your discussions are very limited.

LK: Well, it's a lot sexual, isn't it? I mean, you're having an affair. You're seeing someone on Tuesday, you're not going to see him till a week from Thursday, and you've got two hours. A lot of that is going to be consumed with things other than talking.

JE: Yes, some of it.

LK: Would you say you were, Judith, madly in love with him?

JE: I was very much in love with him.

LK: Since having learned that there may have been others, does that pain you more?

JE: If I had known at the time, I would not have seen him. It was hard enough for me to deal with the fact that he was married, but if I had known that he was seeing anyone else or there were other women in his life, I would have stopped seeing him, no matter what.

LK: Do you think a lot less of him now?

JE: I don't think— It's not— No. I don't think less of him. I think that Jack was very reckless. He took tremendous chances in many areas, not just with me. But I think that that's the way he was brought up. I think that Jack emulated his father a great deal and in a great many ways, and it hasn't lessened my feelings or my opinion of him. . . .

[Commercial break]

LK: Before we talk about Giancana and things in that regard, now when you see things like one dalliance—[*snaps fingers*]—a career is ruined. Gary Hart says, "Follow me," and—bam—it's over. How do you look at that as compared to what was going on then?

JE: Well, I think that things have become very distorted. In the '60s everyone was turning a blind eye, and now I think they have— They're overreacting. Somehow, we have to find some middle ground, where we accept our leaders, or anyone else. We stop putting them on these pedestals and realize that they're just human beings. Yes, I think that there is— Any of our leaders do have a responsibility in how they conduct themselves.

LK: Should they be above reproach with regard to sex?

JE: As much as possible, yes, I think as much as possible. I think they're setting examples, and I think that it goes more or less with the territory. If you are going to be making our laws and setting examples, I think you have to—you have to be—

LK: So Jack had— President Kennedy had a character flaw?

JE: Yes.

LK: And it was with regard to women.

JE: Yes.

LK: Yes. So you're saying that kind of flaw should be known by the public, and we should judge it accordingly when voting for people—whether it's Senator Hart or whomever.

JE: To a certain extent. . . . I certainly don't believe all of the stories but, as well as I knew him, his reckless behavior I believe was a detriment to the office that he held.

LK: And now the public lives—the private lives of public people are everybody's business, aren't they?

JE: They really are.

LK: You think the pendulum has gone too far—where we know everything?

JE: Yes, I think it has gone too far. . . . It's tabloid news now. It's not weighed, the good against the bad.

LK: Did you have an opinion, by the way, on the William Kennedy Smith trial? Was that funny for you? "Funny" is the wrong word, maybe. Was it difficult for you to—

JE: It was difficult in that I think that any woman that becomes involved in any kind of scandal when it comes to the Kennedys, she'll live with it. I feel for her. I don't know what is true and what isn't, but I think there is an arrogance and—

LK: To the Kennedys?

JE: —about—that the Kennedys have.

LK: They do? Jack had it, too?

JE: Yes, and—

LK: A kind of—what—"It's coming to me"?

JE: It's a kind of being above the law, above—

LK: Oh, in other words, you can—

JE: "I can get away with this."

LK: "We're the Kennedys. We can do anything."

JE: Uh-huh.

LK: And that was prevalent in others you knew? Did you ever talk to him at all about Marilyn Monroe?

JE: Never.

LK: Did you ever suspect anything with Marilyn Monroe?

JE: No, and I still don't believe that that was a great involvement.

LK: All right, Kennedy–Giancana. How did you get to know Sam Giancana?

JE: That same show that Frank was—

LK: In Vegas?

JE: In Vegas, appearing in Vegas. When he went to Florida, to the Fontainebleu, the whole group went down for some of the shows.

LK: And saw them there.

JE: And so I went down. I was in New York, and I went down with some friends of mine, again.

LK: To see the show. Did you stay at the Fontainebleu?

JE: Yes, I did. And the night after the last show, Frank gave a tremendous party for— There could have been two hundred, five hundred people there. And just before going into the—I think it was called the Versailles Room . . .

LK: And who introduced you to Sam?

JE: Frank called me over to him. I came in with my escort, and Frank called me over to him just— He introduced me to Sam.

LK: An innocent introduction?

JE: Very innocent.

[*Commercial break*]

LK: You took a liking to Giancana right away?

JE: Well, I really— The only reason I remembered him was he made some comment. I had, I remember, a pale blue *peau de soie* dress on, and I had had some jewelry made to go with the dress, and he said to me, "A woman like you should be wearing real jewels," and I— He thought he was giving me a compliment, and I was rather offended by it—[*laughs*]—because I loved the piece that I had on. And I ended up the next night having dinner with him and a woman by the name of Betty Winnipis. And that was accidental that that happened.

LK: So nothing was set up here by Sinatra or Kennedy or anyone?

JE: No.

LK: Did you date both? Did you date Giancana when you were seeing Kennedy?

JE: No.

LK: Did you talk to him at all?

JE: Oh, yes. I had a lot of contact—

LK: And what was the purpose of that?

JE: Well, when I— As I said, with Jack, he wanted to know what I was doing every day, and so Sam's name— I was introduced to Sam as "Sam Flood," but I have to say that if I had been introduced to him as "Sam Giancana," it wouldn't have made any difference. I wouldn't have known the name.

LK: So you told Jack about Sam?

JE: I told Jack about Sam and—

LK: Who would call you as a friend?

JE: Yes, and he— His name— Sam's name came up when I went to dinner at Jack's home—

LK: As president?

JE: No, this is before—in fact, before he was nominated.

LK: His home where?

JE: In Georgetown, and I was so uneasy. This was the first time I had been to his home, and I was so uncomfortable. This is another woman's home, and I'm going to have dinner with—

LK: It wasn't the first time you were together, though, physically?

JE: No.

LK: That was in New York?

JE: Yes. But I arrived at his home, and there was another man there having dinner with us—that was going to have dinner with us. All I could remember for years was that his name was Bill, and he was a railroad lobbyist. Well, he since has been identified as Bill Thompson, but I was so nervous about the evening and being in his home. I didn't want to be there. I wanted to be with him, but I didn't want to be there.

LK: And how did Sam come into that?

JE: Well, they were talking about the campaign, of course, and towards the end of the dinner Jack asked me could I set up a meeting with Sam for him, and I said, "Well, yes, if you want me to, but why? Or should I ask why?" And he said, "I think he can help me with the campaign." So I—

LK: Was that financially?

JE: Well, I didn't know that first it was money until later on in the conversation, and he asked me would I take this satchel to Sam, and he said—

LK: From Jack to Sam?

JE: From Jack to Sam, and Bill Thompson was there the whole time.

LK: What would Jack be sending Sam?

JE: Well, he told me that it was money, and he said, "It's a great deal of money."

LK: That Jack was sending to Sam?

JE: Yes.

LK: To do what with?

JE: That he— It was for the campaign. Now, through wiretaps and things that are available now, we know that it went to West Virginia—

LK: For the campaign?

JE: For the campaign, but all that I knew—and I usually only like to address what I really knew—

LK: The West Virginia campaign was where Kennedy was a big underdog, spent a lot of money, and beat Hubert Humphrey—

JE: Yes.

LK: —and Humphrey was a big favorite, but Kennedy was giving Giancana the money? . . . You knew there was money in the satchel?

JE: Yes, and the reason Jack told me there was money is he said that if I— He wanted me to have the opportunity to not do it, if I was uncomfortable. And what I was concerned with was the safety factor. Would I be safe? Would the money be safe? And Jack said someone would be with me at all times. When I asked him who, he said, "You're better off not knowing." He said, "This way—"

LK: You mean, they'd be there, but you wouldn't know—

JE: Yes. He said, "You won't be looking over your shoulder."

LK: Now, over the three-year period—'60 to '63—was there a constant going-on between— Tell your story. What *didn't* you tell the Church committee? What can you tell us, between you, Giancana, Kennedy?

JE: Well, the most important aspect of it is that Jack *did* know about the assassination plots against Castro, because I carried the intelligence material between Jack and Sam, and I have to state that this was always at Jack's request.

LK: Sam was going to take care of— The Mafia, in a sense, was going to take care of killing Castro, with Kennedy's approval?

JE: Well, they had already been hired by the CIA in 1960.

LK: You *knew* that?

JE: I didn't know that in early '60—

LK: You subsequently knew it?

JE: —but I know now that they were hired during the Eisenhower administration.

LK: And that Kennedy knew of this?

JE: Yes.

LK: And Kennedy would give what information—

JE: Once he was briefed, once he was—

LK: What would Kennedy give you to give to Sam?

JE: He told me that it was intelligence material. He never used the word "assassination." He used the word "elimination." And again, the reason that he told me was that I would have the opportunity to say "No, I'm not comfortable with this."

LK: But you were okay?

JE: Yes, and for the reason being—and the same is with setting up the meetings and carrying the money for him, because that happened on two occasions—is that he was, in my eyes, he was making me more a part of his life. I was doing something that I felt was very important to him, and I was very proud that he asked me to do it. I didn't think that—

LK: You felt more like you were getting closer to a man who you were in love with, who was married, more than you were doing something for your country? You weren't particularly political at all.

JE: No, I wasn't.

LK: You weren't thinking about what it— Did you ever look at the material?

JE: No.

LK: Did not?

JE: No.

LK: Never tempted to?

JE: No. No. It wouldn't— That part of it would be my—part of my upbringing. It just would not— It wouldn't enter my mind—not for fear of getting caught doing it. It wouldn't enter my mind to— That trust that he had in me to do this for him, and then to betray it by examining whatever it is that he has given me would have been unthinkable for me. . . .

[*Commercial break*]

LK: By the way, we'll be showing some logs, White House logs, that back up phone conversations and visits and the like that have come into your possession, that you didn't have before. Do you feel righted now?

JE: Well, I feel that at least when I— I guess vindicated a little.

LK: All right, I want to get this right. Robert Blakey, who was former counsel to the House Subcommittee on Assassinations, says—he said this to our staff—that "you were clearly a mistress to both men at the same time, but neither man would have confided in you because you wouldn't be credible." The Mafia may have had a reason to want JFK killed. He buys that concept.

JE: I think that that is just— That idea was planted in people's minds from the Church committee, because when they promised me that they wouldn't use my name, they said in their report that a very close friend of the president's was also a very close friend of Sam Giancana's. So the end result of that was that the press linked me with both of them at the same time.

LK: Has Mr. Blakey ever talked to you?

JE: We had a terrible time with Mr. Blakey, and he got even with me, in a sense. I was to be subpoenaed to appear before the committee. I said I would gladly appear before the committee, but it had to be in Washington in an open forum. I was scared to death that the same thing was going to happen to me that happened to me with the Church committee—that selected material would be leaked. And we had this ongoing— He had this ongoing—

LK: What did he have against your testifying publicly? What would Blakey have against your—

JE: I don't know. He said, "I will not give her the publicity." I mean, we have the letters and everything to this effect. He said, "I will not give her the publicity," and my attorney said, "That's not what she wants. She wants the truth to come out."

LK: So, unequivocally, you're saying you were not sleeping with both men, or having a relationship with both men at the same time?

JE: Absolutely not, and there isn't— I have documents that the FBI— They were watching me twenty-four hours a day, and there isn't a document that exists that says that I had a relationship with Sam Giancana.

LK: Never, even after Kennedy's death?

JE: After Kennedy's death, yes.

LK: You did?

JE: And in '62 for a short period of time—for about a month—and the reason that it happened, I know now—in fact, I realized then—was that I had become very close to Sam when I couldn't—when Jack was away, and I was doing so much of this going back and forth for Jack; that Sam became a friend, and I could call and talk to Sam.

LK: And then, eventually, a lover?

JE: Eventually, a lover, and I turned to him. He was more or less— It was like an emotional security blanket.

LK: Were you in love with him?

JE: No, and when— He asked me to marry him, and it was at the end of '62, and I said no, and that's when I realized that this wasn't right—you know, that I was unhappy, and this was someone that I just felt close to. But I think that Sam always knew that I would say no when he asked me to marry him, because I believe the true love of Sam's life was Phyllis Maguire.

LK: Yes? And Jack yours.

JE: Yes.

LK: Where were you when Jack died?

JE: I know that shouldn't be hard now, but it still is. I was in Beverly Hills, and my mother called me.

LK: It was the morning, then?

JE: Uh-huh.

LK: And told you?

JE: And told me that Jack— She said, "Turn your television on."

LK: Had you spoken to him before that? Any recent time before?

JE: Not for—

LK: Or had it ended then?

JE: Yes, it had ended. But, we're looking through the logs, and there are some calls—

LK: In '63?

JE: —into '63, uh-huh.

LK: You felt, of course, the loss of a great love.

JE: It was devastating to me.

LK: What did you feel for Jackie?

JE: The pain that she was going through, and I feel that today for her. I'm so sorry that my name became public knowledge, that my relationship with him—

LK: You're sorry that she knows? . . .

JE: Yes. I don't want— You know, I don't want to cause that heartache for someone. I don't want to cause the pain for her that I'm going through.

LK: Do you buy any of the stories about [Jimmy] Hoffa being involved in the death of John Kennedy?

JE: I believe in a conspiracy theory.

LK: Hoffa? Mafia?

JE: I believe in the government and the Mafia.

LK: Government and the Mafia?

JE: Yes.

LK: That's almost the Oliver Stone theory.

JE: Not quite. I think that he's really done a great service to our country. I don't agree with that particular theory, but I do believe there was a conspiracy and I do—

LK: And the Mafia was involved?

JE: I think so, but, you know, a lot of this is because of the knowledge that I have—personal knowledge that I have.

LK: Did Sam Giancana ever say to you that he or friends of his like Trafficanti and others were angered at John Kennedy because of what Kennedy was doing to the Teamsters?

JE: Well, Jack and Sam really didn't like each other. I mean, this was business, and Sam very often used to— In fact, he would do it just to tease me or to irritate me or to get me riled. He would say— He would call Jack a spoiled brat, and he would say, "Your boyfriend wouldn't be in the White House if it wasn't for me." And they hated Bobby. They— This was— There was no love lost between these people, but it was business.

LK: Did Sam say anything to you after Kennedy was killed?

JE: No.

LK: Nothing? Do you have any information, or is it just a feeling?

JE: It's just a feeling because, as I look back now, I realize just a couple of days after, Johnny Roselli said, "You need to get away."

LK: After the Kennedy—

JE: After Kennedy was killed.

LK: "You need to get—" "You," Judith?

JE: Yes, and he said— I went down to Palm Springs with Johnny and his girlfriend and another couple, and I was by myself, and people are always trying to say that Johnny also was an intimate friend of mine. Johnny was just a friend and, again, it was the end result of the transfer of documents.

LK: So him telling you, "You need to get away," you think now—

JE: I question that now, yes.

LK: We'll be right back with Judith Exner. Don't go away.

[*Commercial break*]

LK: You mentioned the FBI following you around a lot. Did they question you when Marilyn Monroe died?

JE: No, not at all, but in my files that we—that have been released to me, they watched— They had an apartment that they took across from me, across the street from me, and watched my place twenty-four hours a day. And they watched a break-in into my apartment by two men, and they—in the report they say, "It doesn't seem that they've taken anything," and they got the license plate number. And later on there's another report that they've identified this—one of the men as being the son of an ex-FBI agent, and that was two days after Marilyn was killed. And it's only recently that I've realized that the only phone bills that I *don't* have were for that period of time.

LK: So what do you gather from that?

JE: Someone ordered a break-in into my apartment, and the FBI were already—

LK: You didn't connect it with Marilyn Monroe, though?

JE: No.

LK: You do now?

JE: I think it's possible.

LK: Looking for what?

JE: Well, my phone—my telephone information was gone, my telephone bills that would have shown my calls.

LK: What kind of relationship did you have with Bobby?

JE: None.

LK: Never spoke to him?

JE: I noticed in my testimony, which I've only just received—I was supposed to get two weeks after I appeared before the Church committee. Sixteen years later they finally released my testimony to me. It was at the top-secret level. And I notice, with my trying to cover everything up, they do ask me about Bobby and, luckily, this is testimony that wasn't sworn to. And I said yes, I had met him. And I think that probably I met Bobby at a couple of parties. I know there was a fundraiser out here at Barry Sullivan's house, and I think, probably, that's what was in my mind, but I didn't know him well.

LK: We'll be right back with Judith Exner after this.

[*Commercial break*]

LK: The movie [*JFK*] you haven't seen, although you praise Stone's having made it?

JE: Yes, I praise his courage for it.

LK: You haven't seen it because of personal feelings?

JE: Yes.

LK: It would be too tough for you to see it?

JE: It would be very hard for me to see it.

LK: How do you feel now, Judith?

JE: That is— Is that physically how do I feel?

LK: No, no, no, emotionally. Do you feel better now, telling more of this now?

JE: Oh, yes. I, of course, have mixed emotions. I'm a reluctant—you might say, a reluctant witness to what went on in history, but I think that it's very important that— So many cover-ups have existed within our government that I really think that it's important. For historians to evaluate Jack, to evaluate his presidency properly, the truth has to be out there, and then let them study it. But without the truth, without our people knowing the truth about any given presidency, we're bound to just stumble and fall and make the same mistakes again.

LK: I wish you good health, Judith.

Barbra Streisand

Barbra Streisand was born Barbara Joan Streisand in Brooklyn on April 24, 1942. Supporting herself as a telephone operator and theater usher, she developed a nightclub act built around the song styles of vaudeville comedienne Fanny Brice. The act caught on and landed her Broadway roles in I Can Get It for You Wholesale, *and then, as Fanny Brice, in* Funny Girl. *Barbara dropped an "a" in her name and became, simply, Barbra.*

She went on to a fabulously successful film, recording, and concert career, then directed herself in Yentl, *which garnered mixed reviews. In 1991 she directed and starred in* The Prince of Tides, *which drew seven Oscar nominations.*

"You have to understand this, and maybe it's hard to. I never listen to music."

LARRY KING: Good evening from Los Angeles. We have a whole room full of guests tonight. First, one of Hollywood's leading directors, currently acclaimed for her hit project, *The Prince of Tides*, and nominated for a Directors Guild of America award. We're also honored to welcome a legendary singer, who, as an ingenue, electrified Broadway in *I Can Get It for You Wholesale*, and then came west to take this town by storm. We have a comedienne who won laughs and hearts in *Funny Girl* and *Owl and the Pussycat* and *What's Up, Doc?* Also with us, an acknowledged Hollywood power broker—probably the industry's most influential woman—who produced *Yentl, A Star Is Born*, and *Nuts*. We're also pleased to welcome an Oscar winner, a multiple-Grammy winner, an Emmy winner, a Tony winner, and a multiple-Golden Globe recipient. Ladies and gentlemen, that's a lot of people. They are all here as one—Barbra Streisand.

Two Jewish people from Brooklyn, sitting here, worldwide, Barbra. Don't be nervous.

BARBRA STREISAND: [*laughs*] You just scared me with that intro. I've got a lot to live up to now, right?

LK: All right, let's start with that. Are you an actor who directs and sings? Are you a singer who directs and acts? Are you a director who acts? What are you, first?

BS: Do I have to label myself?

LK: How do you think of yourself?

BS: I just don't think that way, you know. I don't think in terms of words—one word to describe me or two words or three words. I mean, I know you have to. I guess the world has to—to just categorize you.

LK: You don't categorize you?

BS: I can't.

LK: All right, when you started back in Brooklyn, that little girl wanted to be a—

BS: An actress.

LK: Not a singer?

BS: No. I liked singing. I mean, my identity was the kid on the block who had a good voice, so that was my identity at the time but, no, I always wanted to be an actress.

LK: When did you know you were good? In other words, was there a time—? Was it in high school? Was it back at Erasmus Hall in Brooklyn that you said—

BS: Well, one time my mother got mad at me. I did something bad, probably. I said something bad, whatever—and she kind of hit me a little bit. So I pretended I was deaf, and it got her. And I did it for hours and hours, you know? And I did it well, and I thought, *Hey, I can act!* [*laughs*]

LK: You scared her?

BS: I scared her, uh-huh.

LK: You knew you could act, but when did you— There was a time when you knew—right?—"This is going to be my life. . . ." Was that early?

BS: Yes. I mean, I remember going to two acting classes at the same time. I didn't think one was enough, right? So I changed— I had a pseudonym in one class. My name was "Angelina Scarangella," and I had two different teachers, you know, and I went to two different classes with two different names. And very early on I think I knew I wanted to act. I loved Shakespeare and Chekhov—things that I discovered very late in life. I mean, I was about, well, it was late in life when I discovered these wonderful things.

LK: Can you remember why you liked being other people, why you wanted to be the girl, the sister, the mother, the brother the lover, the aunt? . . .

BS: It's funny. You know, I have said before that I wanted to be Scarlett O'Hara, not Vivien Leigh. In other words, I did— I must have wanted to escape my life in some way, because if I did see something in the movies, I thought, *This is wonderful. Like, you know, people love each other, and they get married, and isn't that nice to be in that world?* It wasn't so much even acting as it was to sort of be in that world—be those people. It was a little odd, a little strange [*laughs*]. . . .

LK: Was there a lot of knocking on doors early? I mean, were you the kind of kid that we saw in New York—

BS: No, no, never. I only made rounds—you know, as an actress, where you knock on people's doors—I only did that for two days, and I remember feeling very humiliated and very degraded by a sense of a power play that I felt was operating with people, and I couldn't go through it. I could not knock on people's doors and say, "Do you have anything for me today?"

LK: So, then, how do you get into—

BS: So I gave it up. That's why I sang. That's why I became a singer. . . . Yes. I said, "You know, this is too humiliating, to ask for a job." I remember going and asking— There was a part of a beatnik, and I used to walk around with black stockings and a trenchcoat. I looked like a beatnik. I guess I was a beatnik. And I remember going up for a part—wasn't even a speaking part. It was a walk-on. And the woman said to me, "We have to see your work," so I said, "Well, why? I mean, first of all, I'll never get work if people like you keep saying you have to see my work. When do you get that first shot? And second of all, I could be a lousy actress or I could be Eleanora Duse. It doesn't matter. In other words, do I look right for the part?" The principle got me. I couldn't understand it. Why did they have to see my work, you know, for a walk-on? And I thought, *This is too degrading.* I couldn't do it. That's why, you know, when I see things like—about chutzpah, I mean, I guess I had chutzpah in other areas, because I had something I felt I needed to express, you know? But I would never ask anybody for a job— except one time I did. . . . And that was because after I sort of made a hit at the Bonsoir— I was eighteen years old and I—

LK: I remember that.

BS: —a kind of a hit, right? And they kept extending my engagement, till finally they had another female singer booked in so they had to let me go, and I didn't get work for months and months and months. In other words, nobody hired me. I thought, "Well, what was that all about?" So my agent at the time, Joe— Who's the famous agent?

LK: Glazer.

BS: Joe Glazer, right, Joe Glazer. I never used to go up to anybody's office, but this one day he told me that Enrico Beneducci from San Francisco, who had the Hungry Eye, was going to be up in his office, and I wanted to meet him—and I thought, *I'm going to put on an act*, because I could never ask someone for a job in real life—you know, say, "Would you hire me?"

LK: That's amazing.

BS: I couldn't. But I remember putting on this—you know, playing the part of a person who would ask for this job, and I did this whole number on him, and he hired me. And that's how I got the Hungry Eye job.

LK: Did you know that your voice was different? Sinatra told us that he didn't think he was very— He didn't know what he did that was so different. Did you know your voice was unique?

BS: No. . . . I mean, I thought it was nice. It sort of sounded nice. I remember singing in the hallways of my Brooklyn apartment, you know, with the brass rail, and there was a great echo sound in this hallway, and I thought, *Oh, that doesn't—you know—it doesn't sound bad.* And we all used to sing with the *Hit Parade*—all the kids at the time—but I didn't know how special my voice was. . . .

[Commercial break]

LK: The rap on you—

BS: The rap on me—

LK: The anger that you seem to have at—for example, *60 Minutes* and Mike Wallace and those kind of things that you feel offended you—what happened there? What went wrong?

BS: *[laughs]* Well, I'm very naive, I suppose, you know, because— In other words, I like Mike. I like him. I feel him. I feel his own pain, even, you know? He's a complex human being. And I was just very naive in terms of thinking, *Well, you know, he's part of my life, my history. We started together thirty years ago, and when I was nineteen I was on his show.* And I thought, *God, isn't this wonderful?* So I was kind of shocked to be attacked, you know, but—

LK: And hurt?

BS: I was hurt, yes. I was hurt. But that's my naiveté, I guess. You know, in other words, he's looking after getting a terrific show, I suppose, and—or I don't know exactly what in me touches off that anger in him. I don't know what issues he has unresolved with his own mother or, you know, being with a powerful Jewish woman or . . .

LK: So you think he brings his own problems to it?

BS: I do. I think every interviewer brings themselves to the person they're interviewing, and preconceived notions and so forth. . . .

LK: Do you think people want to know the bad side of Barbra Streisand, do you think? Or you don't think they want to know that? And do you think that the media wants to give—

BS: I don't think it's either/or. I think there is an "and" here. In other words, maybe people want to hear certain negative things about people like me—me and people like me—in order to feel better about themselves. And there's the other thing. I think they want to hear the truth, and they want to hear positive things, and they want to be inspired, and they want to feel good. So I guess both—

LK: But now we have an age of tabloidism. . . . Like, look at the Governor Clinton concept. . . . How do you feel when you see something like that or when you— How have you felt when you've read about yourself?

BS: I have felt outraged in the past. I really— I'm getting to a deeper level in myself, I hope, which is to be a little bit more immune to this stuff. In other words, as I read somewhere, nothing real can be threatened, and nothing unreal exists, which means that— The truth is, I have been around a long time. I've been very fortunate to have wonderful fans, who've supported my work. And with all the b.s. that floats around and the made-up stories and all that stuff, somehow some truth in what I do permeates to these people.

LK: Now, when you read about pain of others, when you read about a Clinton or any figure, do you tend to sympathize with them, having been the victim of it yourself?

BS: Yes. . . .

LK: Do you feel sorry for Clinton?

BS: Do I feel sorry for Clinton? Well, he's not my first choice as a candidate, so—

LK: Who is?

BS: I'd like Cuomo, to tell you the truth. I like Harkin, too. I like his voting record. But that's beside the point. I mean, there is an issue here that's about the right to privacy. I mean, would Roosevelt have been elected if they knew about his mistress? What about President Kennedy? . . .

LK: Why don't you sing more? Why aren't you out in concert?

BS: I'm thinking about doing—

LK: Why don't you give us your gift?

BS: I'm thinking about doing it, but it is very scary. You know how we were talking before about some people— The surgeon who operates would be afraid to be on this show with you. . . . It's the same thing. In other words, I have this—

LK: You're afraid?

BS: Yes.

LK: Of what?

BS: I mean, this scares me—being on this show with you.

LK: You're not afraid to go on stage and sing?

BS: Oh, yes.

LK: Of what?

BS: I don't know—that I'll be less good than the people expect; that I'll forget my words; that I'll— You know, this happened to me. I was singing in front of 135,000 people, and I got a death threat from the PLO because it was during the Arab-Israeli war, and I was making the movie with Omar Sharif, whose films were banned in Egypt—

LK: Who loves you, by the way.

BS: That's very nice.

LK: He said on this show you're the best person he ever worked with.

BS: That's very nice. He was wonderful to work with, too.

LK: So that fright—

BS: I forgot my words, in front of 135,000 people. I went blank. It was like—because I figured I'd better keep moving around, in case there were snipers out there. It did scare me, I must say.

LK: Someone said, though, if you did a concert tour right now you would be, probably, the highest-paid and the biggest-drawing person who could go on concert because we haven't— When was the last time you did a tour?

BS: I never did a tour, but when I was—

LK: When was the last time you worked Vegas, or in public?

BS: The last time I charged for singing was at least twenty years ago, oh, more than twenty years ago. . . . Twenty-five years ago was the last time I charged.

LK: Twenty-five years. You've got this great album out—

BS: I only perform for charity.

LK: —this great album, which is a package set—maybe the best package set ever done. Why don't you want to stand on a stage and—

BS: Well, I *may* want to. I'm saying it's a challenge. You know, we all have to grow. I am a work-in-progress here, you know? I mean, I—

LK: You may come back soon? . . .

BS: I'm thinking of it. I'm thinking this might be very exciting if I could. And a growth process for me, to see if I could stand up in front of people. Look, the truth is I love directing movies, so that— You know, it's taken me three years on this movie. It's taken me five years on *Yentl*. In other words, I don't have much time in between to make the records and to also do tours.

LK: And you like directing better than standing on a stage singing?

BS: God, yes. It's in private. I like recording, too. Remember that. It's in private. . . .

[*Commercial break*]

LK: Our guest is Barbra Streisand—who didn't finish her thought on the Clinton thing involving privacy and sexuality, right?

BS: Well, yes, I just think that what goes on in a person's sex life is a very private issue, and are we going to deny ourselves some great politicians because of their sex lives? I don't know about that. In other words, what I'm saying is, we might not have had some great presidents.

LK: When they say it goes with the business, do you think— Buddy Rich once said— I think Sinatra, too—"All I owe the public is my best performance. That's all I owe the public. I don't owe them anything more than that. I don't owe them a smile backstage. I don't owe them anything but my best—"

BS: Well, that's just—but that's just human kindness. . . . I think you owe people human kindness.

LK: Do you think you also owe us—"us"—your private life?

BS: Yes.

LK: You do?

BS: I do, but I also know that, being a public person, you give that up. That is the price of fame. It's hard to live with, but that's the truth. That's the way it is.

LK: In other words, you've got to pay that price. If you go into the business—

BS: That's the way it is. . . .

LK: So when you walk down the street, if they hawk you or paparazzi take pictures, you—

BS: I don't— No, I don't like that. That scares me—you know, on a dark night and bulbs go off. Or I understand them wanting the picture, and I'll say, "Listen, please, let me pose for you. Take your picture, then will you please leave me alone to walk down this street?" And if they're nice, they will honor that. If they're not, they follow you anyway. It's like you don't exist.

LK: If your image is power and you're known as strong and you like to direct—directing means "You go there. You go here. Camera goes here"—what would you be frightened of?

BS: You know, life is full of paradoxes. I mean, it's not that simple. "A" doesn't just add up to "B." I mean, one and one is three sometimes. In other words, it's not that simple. How do I describe that to you? What does that mean? It's like I can direct a movie, but I have no sense of direction. In other words, if I'm in a car, I don't know where I am.

LK: [*laughs*] But you can say, "Put the camera there."

BS: I can say, "That's how the movie goes, and that's the vision I have, and that's the dream I have, and this is the way things should be," but I can't—I am totally unmechanical.

LK: How much a part of success in your head is financial? When you hear things like, "Here's what Madonna's making, here's what Michael Jackson is making," and you know what you could make. I mean, tomorrow you could decide on income beyond belief.

BS: Uh-huh. If I were just interested in money I would, obviously, tour. That's where you make a lot of money. That's how people make a lot of money.

LK: So that's not your driving force?

BS: No. not at all.

LK: Is it because you have enough?

BS: I have enough to live with and give enough away. I like to give money away.

LK: Don't you need applause?

BS: No. I don't need it on a large scale. I mean, I like it because people are going to see *Prince of Tides*. I mean, people are going to see the movie that I love—

LK: That's a reward—

BS: —that I made. People write me letters about how the movie touched them, how it made them feel. That's the reward for me.

LK: And that's more of a reward than 40,000 people going "Bravo" at the end of a magnificent singing—

BS: Yes. I mean, to get nominated for the Directors Guild of America is a great honor. I am very thrilled about that.

LK: Only the third woman, ever. . . . Do you think you'll be nominated for an Academy Award?

BS: I have no idea.

LK: Do you expect it?

BS: I don't expect anything like that. I don't know. . . . I have no idea. I don't know what's in people's minds, in their hearts.

LK: Our guest is Barbra Streisand. As promised, you'll get the chance to talk with her. Here's what Pat Conroy says about her: [*reads*] "To Barbra Streisand—" He inscribed this in the *Prince of Tides* book. [*reads*] "You're many things, but you're also a great teacher—one of the greatest to come into my life. I honor great teachers. You've made me a better writer. You rescued my sweet book. You've honored me by taking it all with such seriousness and love." Pat Conroy, the author of *Prince of Tide*s. . . .

[Commercial break]

LK: Sometimes people get an interesting rap or image in the business. We're going to go to your calls in a moment, but this is a letter from the entire crew, by the way—you can see that clearly—of *Yentl*. They all worked on *Yentl*, and it says, [*reads*] "The undersigned are currently working on *Yentl*, directed by and starring Barbra Streisand. Because she's subjected to so much adverse press, we thought it might interest you to know that during the last three months of rehearsal and filming she has completely captivated us all. Though undoubtedly a perfectionist in her dealings with everyone—producers, camera, sound, electrical crews, props, wardrobe, makeup, et cetera—she has shared jokes, chats, and pleasantries each and every day. She appears to have no temperament. Her voice is scarcely heard on the set. Her smile is seen constantly. We have all worked with directors and stars who were the complete antithesis of Barbra Streisand, but whose antics don't reach the newspaper. This letter is entirely unsolicited and is the result of our collective affection." No one printed that, right? [*Streisand laughs*] Why do you have this image of the opposite of—the antithesis of this, do you think?

BS: I never understood it. Really, when I was doing *Yentl*—again, I was very naive, you know. But I guess it's because, you see, as a singer, when I was singing, I never experienced any chauvinism. I don't mean just males, but anything about being a woman, you know. What was so odd about being a woman? I didn't get it.

LK: Until you directed?

BS: Until I directed.

LK: Because?

BS: Well, actually—

LK: You were in a man's business?

BS: —it probably started when I started to act, too, you know.

LK: You were entering a man's domain?

BS: Because I had opinions, and I think people weren't used to women with opinions in the early—in the '60s, when I made *Funny Girl* in 1967, because I adored Willie Wilder, I adored Harry Stradling, my cameraman. And I was shocked by what I read in the paper—you know, that I was telling Harry how to light. Well, Harry was a genius. Harry lit my first four pictures and, you know, he had done *Camille* or something. He was—

LK: So are you saying you're not bossy, you're not difficult, you're not temperamental?

BS: You know, I'm not temperamental, no. But it depends what you call "difficult." If that means striving for excellence, if that means doing it till it's right, then you can call me difficult. In other words, I don't want to call anybody a liar, because it depends how you define these words, you know? . . .

LK: Toronto, as we go to calls for Barbra Streisand. Hello.

CALLER: [*Toronto, Ontario*] Hi, Barbra. Hi, Larry. Barbra, if you perform live again, do you think you'll consider a performance in Toronto?

BS: Well, of course! Absolutely. I would love to go to Toronto.

LK: On a scale of ten, what are the chances that you will perform live again?

BS: Fifty-fifty. . . .

LK: Houston, for Barbra Streisand. Hello.

CALLER: [*Houston, Texas*] Hello! How are you, Barbra? I'm wondering what the status is on the reunion with Robert Redford for the *Way We Were* sequel?

BS: I would love to work with him again. I'd love to work with Sidney Pollack again. I don't know. We have to, like, have meetings again and talk about it, because it's hard to do sequels, you know, when the first film was so successful, but I do think there is a sequel there.

LK: What's special about Redford?

BS: Always interesting, always fascinating—good guy, good guy.

LK: How good an actor?

BS: Wonderful actor. I think he's a wonderful actor.

LK: Staten Island, New York, for Barbra Streisand. Hello.

CALLER: [*Staten Island, New York*] Hello. Hi, Barbra. I just wanted to say I've been a faithful fan for twenty-eight years.

BS: Twenty-eight years, huh?

CALLER: [*Staten Island, New York*] Yes. [*laughs*] But my question is, do you have any plans on working with your son Jason again? . . .

BS: Ah! Wasn't he good in my movie? I'm so proud of him. Yes, I want him to work near me, by me, for the rest of my life.

LK: Did you want him to be an actor?

BS: Not particularly, but I—

LK: Were you surprised when he wanted to?

BS: A little bit, because—he made a brilliant film. He directed his own film—wrote it, directed it, edited it—and he's absolutely amazing. But I want to support him in anything he wants to do, so if he loves acting— You know, I don't think it's his passion in life but—

LK: No?

BS: He likes to explore all different kinds of things. He's building a house now—

LK: Was he easy to direct? . . .

BS: Yes. You know, when you do something with love, it's easy.

LK: Los Angeles, hello.

CALLER: [*Los Angeles, California*] Hi, Barbra. I wanted to say you were a really important and dignified role model for me as I was growing up. . . . And I was wondering who your inspirational role models were and are. And also, how do you feel about the opportunities available for women today in Hollywood?

BS: Role models.

LK: Did you have any?

BS: God, I don't know.

LK: No? Do you have any heroines or someone you emulated that you wanted to be? No? Did you want to be Barbara Stanwyck? Did you want to be Joan Crawford?

BS: No. [*laughs*]

LK: No?

BS: With wire hangers?

LK: [*laughs*] You wanted to be you?

BS: Yes.

LK: So you didn't have that? Role model in the family?

BS: I don't remember that, no.

LK: Interesting.

BS: Sorry. What was the second part of your question again? . . .

LK: Hollywood and women in Hollywood now—getting in—easier?

BS: Oh, I think it's easier now, yes. When I did *Yentl* it was like, you know, "*What?* An actress wanting to direct?"

LK: Yet, interesting, they will criticize you for, let's say, doing close-ups of yourself in a movie, and they won't criticize, say, Kevin Costner for doing close-ups of himself in a movie, right? There still is a double standard.

BS: There is a hidden agenda behind statements like that, because that's just nonsense. I mean, it's like, you know you would— I would shoot me the way I would shoot any actress playing the role—the way I would shoot Blythe Danner, the way I would shoot Kate Nelligan. . . . And you want to make everything look as beautiful as it can be in a movie. You're not going to try to make it look bad. So I don't understand criticism like that. It's very personal—trivial commentary.

LK: Did you see in Nick Nolte a great actor?

BS: Oh, yes.

LK: When you cast him in *Prince of Tides*?

BS: Yes, I think he's a wonderful actor. Yes, absolutely.

LK: Was he easy to work with?

BS: What do you mean by "easy"?

LK: Was he a perfectionist?

BS: He wants the best out of himself, yes.

LK: Was he difficult?

BS: I don't— See, I can't describe it as difficult. It's like somebody saying, "Well, you don't want to work with Marlon Brando—" who happens to be the greatest actor who ever lived, in my opinion. I would work with him in a second. I don't care what the rumors or the stories are.

LK: Well, let's put it this way. Was it fun each day to go to the set and say, "I'm working with Nick again today"?

BS: You know, some days were fun and some days were less than fun, but it was always interesting, always fascinating. . . . Never dull, because it was alive and, you know, he has his issues with women, and that was interesting. I like parallel issues that go along with the film and reality. I was his therapist in the movie—playing his therapist—and, in a sense, he had to come to trust me as a woman.

LK: As well, yes.

BS: That was interesting.

LK: Toronto, hello.

CALLER: [*Toronto, Ontario*] Hello. First, I'd like to wish you success with an Oscar nomination. . . . Win for best director for *Prince of Tides*. . . . Personally, I think you were robbed for *Yentl*.

BS: Oh, that's very sweet.

CALLER: [*Toronto, Ontario*] However, my question focuses on your music. Which album were you most satisfied with and which album were you least satisfied with?

LK: Is there an album you were least satisfied with?

BS: Couple. . . .

LK: What didn't you like?

BS: Can I say the one I liked first? . . .

LK: Sure.

BS: [*laughs*] I loved doing the Broadway album—really loved that. These were songs that I just loved and that had stories attached to them, you know—really intelligent lyrics, gorgeous melodies. And it was really fun to have an artistic success when I didn't plan on it at all. It was just—it was a total labor of love, and then when it was a commercial hit, that was like icing on the cake. That was fabulous.

LK: And what, if you could remove from the shelves, would you?

BS: I think my album called *Butterfly*. I thought that was pretty lousy.

LK: Why?

BS: I don't know. I just had no— *Butterfly* and— I think that's the only one, actually, that I didn't love. I just don't remember the songs. I can't remember what was on it. I don't remember doing it.

LK: Do you like to hear your recordings?

BS: No. God, no.

LK: Are you very critical?

BS: Ten years later I put it on. If I happen to hear it in a store or something, it doesn't bother me, but if I hear it too soon, then I just hear the imperfections. . . .

[*Commercial break*]

LK: Our guest—Barbra Streisand. The caller is from Atlanta. Hello.

CALLER: [*Atlanta, Georgia*] Hi, Barbra. Congratulations on a great movie. . . . I was really impressed with the performances that you pulled from everyone—Jason, Kate, Blythe Danner, Nick Nolte, and yourself. But my question is, how did you go about getting such effective performances from the children that were in the movie? Did you approach them differently than the adults?

BS: Well, first of all, you have to love them, you know? I mean, people thrive on being loved, especially children, and so everyone that was picked, were kids also that I saw how they interacted with Nick—I did a lot of improvisations with them and Nick—who naturally responded to one another. In other words, there might have been one kid I wanted, but she didn't take to Nick. I couldn't hire her if she was to play his daughter. . . . So it was fun to find these children, and I really go by their own lives, so they don't have to act, and then try to create an atmosphere where there's fun. Like Nick was really off-camera talking to these girls on a phone when they're supposed to be on a phone, and they were carrying on, and we created an atmosphere. . . . Yes. He was really hiding behind a couch, you know, because I wanted it to be very real. Children are so gorgeous, so beautiful—

LK: And honest.

BS: And honest. Just to capture them, you know—they're just fabulous.

LK: How about directing yourself?

BS: I don't pay attention to myself much. I mean, I do my scenes. Like, my office scenes are all done at the end of shooting. I was the cover set, which means if it rains outside we go in and do my scenes. I just don't— I *know* her. I lived with this character for three years. When I read the book, I said, "Oh, my God, except for the hair color, this is me." I mean, it could be me—down to the jewelry I wore, down to the way I feel about life.

LK: Did you want to do that movie when you read the book?

BS: Uh-huh.

LK: Yes? Washington, D.C., hello.

CALLER: [*Washington, D.C.*] Hello. Barbra, I've got to tell you, this is one of the high points of my life. I am your number-one fan. I have two questions for you. First of all, you looked fabulous in *Prince of Tides*. . . . I mean, there were some scenes where you were wearing some pretty tight-fitting clothes. And I was wondering—

BS: I was watching my diet.

CALLER: [*Washington, D.C.*] —what have you been doing lately to keep yourself in such great shape?

BS: Well, when I was making that movie, I didn't eat dinner. I ate a nice lunch and a nice breakfast, but I just didn't eat dinner. I had so much work to do to prepare for the next day's shooting anyway—but that's the only way I could stay thin.

CALLER: [*Washington, D.C.*] The second question is, I've always wondered, who do you enjoy listening to, musically, in your spare time? Who do you enjoy?

BS: You have to understand this, and maybe it's hard to. I never listen to music.

LK: *What?*

BS: I listen to the news. I mean, I watch the news—

LK: You're a CNN freak, right?

BS: Yes, I'm a CNN and C-SPAN freak. [*laughs*] I just got the C-SPAN newsletter now that tells me what's on. But, because I spend so much of my time making albums, I just can't stand to listen to music, except maybe classical music now and then or sometimes film scores. I love beautiful film scores. . . .

LK: You don't listen to music?

BS: No. I don't. I can't. I can't.

LK: This is very strange, Barbra.

BS: It is?

LK: Music is not your favorite thing. If you'd started as an actress, you might never have been a singer. You used singing as—

BS: [*laughs*] If they would have hired me, right?

LK: And you don't listen to music.

BS: [*laughs*] Isn't that terrible?

LK: Do you watch movies?

BS: Oh, yes, I watch movies. I love movies.

LK: Was this a good year for movies?

BS: Yes. Oh, yes.

LK: Did you agree with the attention paid *Bugsy* and—

BS: Oh, yes. I mean, there were a lot of other movies that were not recognized, too, but they're wonderful films. I mean, look, you have to understand this, too. I don't like to be put in contests with my colleagues.

LK: Yes, there's something wrong— George C. Scott said there's something wrong with that.

BS: In other words, you know, when I was nominated for the Academy Award for best acting, there were five fabulous performances. I couldn't tell you mine was the best. I mean, Katherine Hepburn was great—which we tied, you know, at the time. And Joanne Woodward was great. Vanessa Redgrave was— There were five great performances.

LK: You all played different parts.

BS: I felt embarrassed by being in this contest. I wish they would just give us plaques—say, "These are the best performances of the year." The Directors Guild gives you plaques. This is great.

[*Commercial break*]

LK: Our guest is Barbra Streisand. Before we take the next call, you're not—I gather, since you said you would perform for the Democrats—you're not a great fan of President Bush's?

BS: I think he lives in denial, you know—denying certain things—and you can't fix things unless you acknowledge them. But I've heard that he comes from abused—he had an abused childhood. Like Reagan, I heard, had an alcoholic father. . . . I don't know if these things are true. . . .

LK: It wouldn't surprise you, though?

BS: It wouldn't surprise me.

LK: Orlando, Florida, for Barbra Streisand. Hello.

CALLER: [*Orlando, Florida*] Hi, Barbra. I just want you to know that I love you, and all my family members love you. . . . I wanted to know if you had a special place in your heart for Daisy Gambel, the role that you played in *On a Clear Day You Can See Forever*?

BS: Yes. Yes, I do. I do.

CALLER: [*Orlando, Florida*] Really?

BS: I really do, yes. It was a really interesting piece about reincarnation and this kind of Jewish Brooklyn girl who, in another life, was an English woman. Yes, I loved doing that movie. I loved Vincente Minnelli. . . .

LK: Do you believe in reincarnation?

BS: I believe we'd better make the most of today. . . .

LK: You're going to London for *Prince of Tides*, right? It hasn't opened there yet?

BS: Uh-huh, yes, with Princess Di. The opening's with Princess Di.

LK: You're going with her to the opening?

BS: Well, I'm not going in her *car*, but, I mean, I'm going to meet Princess Di.

LK: By the way, how many times have you seen this movie?

BS: A lot.

LK: A lot? Don't get tired of seeing it again?

BS: [*laughs*] Of course I get tired of it.

LK: [*laughs*] But you've got to go with the Princess, right? Barbra—with the Princess. From Brooklyn, hey!
      Los Angeles, hello.

CALLER: [*Los Angeles, California*] Yes, I just had a question for Barbra about how she manages to choose the work that she's going to direct. Do you read a lot of novels? Did you read *Prince of Tides* and decide that this is a movie that had to be made? Do you read movie scripts, or how do you go about that?

BS: I don't like reading movie scripts, by the way. It's really hard to read movie scripts—for me, anyway. No, I was just—I was reading that novel, and friends had recommended it to me, and then I just thought: *Wow, this is such a powerful book about childhood and the consequences.*

LK: So it struck you. Did you ever turn down anything you regret?

BS: Well, I turned down a lot of roles that I would have liked to play. But Jane Fonda thanks me.

LK: What did you turn down?

BS: Like *They Shoot Horses*, her role in that; *Klute*, you know, but she was wonderful—

LK: You turned down *Klute*?

BS: Yes.

LK: You turned down *They Shoot Horses*—?

BS: *Cabaret.*

LK: *Cabaret* you turned down?

BS: But before Bob Fosse was attached to it—only after I saw the play. But had I known Bob Fosse was attached to it—

LK: You would have done it?

BS: Yes.

LK: Back with our remaining moments with the great Barbra—I think we can safely say that. "Great" gets— Do you want to say something?

BS: I was going to say that, you know, in my thirty-year career of being a movie star I've only been asked by six directors to be in their movies—four of which were foreign. See: paradoxes. You know what I mean? You'd never believe this, right? You'd think I have all these offers from directors. No. From producers and writers, but not directors. [*laughs*]

[*Commercial break*]

LK: We're running real close on time. Quickly—Los Angeles, hello.

CALLER: [*Los Angeles, California*] Hello. I wanted to tell her my name really is Susan Lowenstein, first of all—

BS: Wow! Really?

CALLER: [*Los Angeles, California*] —so, thanks. So I loved the movie. . . . And would you ever run for political office? . . .

BS: No. . . . I'm too afraid of crowds. [*laughs*]

LK: [*laughs*] That's right, you don't want to appear in public.

BS: I like the babies, though. [*laughs*]

LK: How about the battle against AIDS? You're very involved in that, right?

BS: Yes.

LK: Think we're going to lick it?

BS: God, I hope so. We have to. We have to. We have to. Everybody has to give their support. Again, President Bush was a little remiss with that one, you know. That's a project I may do, *The Normal Heart*, because it's a story about—

LK: It was a great play. . . .

LK: Barbra, thank you for a wonderful hour. You were very difficult, very hard to put up with, you were just—

BS: Oh, I'm so sorry.

LK: We love you, Barbra—

BS: Can I beat you up more? [*laughs*]

LK: What? We love you.

BS: Thank you.

LK: Will you come back?

BS: Yes. You were very nice. Thank you.

LK: Thank you. Barbra Streisand.

H. Ross Perot

H. Ross Perot was born on June 27, 1930, in Texarkana, Texas, and grew up learning about finance and trading by listening to his horse-trader father. After four years in the navy, he went to work for IBM, then founded his own firm, Electronic Data Systems, in 1962 with $1,000. Six years later, he floated a stock offering that netted him over a billion, and in 1984 he sold it to General Motors for $2 billion.

This interview, in which Perot announced his third-party candidacy, marked the beginning of Larry King Live *as a major political platform for presidential candidates.*

"If you want to register me in fifty states, number one, I'll promise you this: between now and the convention we'll get both parties' heads straight."

LARRY KING: About a third of the voters in New Hampshire's primary said that they wished somebody else were running, and some undoubtedly have this guy in mind. The idea of pulling the lever for H. Ross Perot seems to get peoples juices flowing. A Tennessee businessman is trying to talk him into it—even sent Perot rules for getting on the ballot in all fifty states. A retired PR man in Florida wants to draft him because, in his words, "Perot's the only guy in the country who owes no favors to anybody." The pragmatic Texan keeps his distance, but keeps talking to his fans and would-be organizers, so the White House talk keeps coming. And we certainly welcome him to *Larry King Live.* . . . Are you going to run?

H. ROSS PEROT: No.

LK: Flat "No"?

RP: But we've got an hour tonight to talk about the real problems that face this nation, and you, in effect, have sort of an electronic town hall, so I think we can serve the country by really getting down in the trenches, talking about what we have to do, and then doing it.

LK: Why not serve the country by running for its top office?

RP: I feel very strongly that my contribution, if any, in this country is to create taxpayers, and I know we need more taxpayers. I would do anything I could to help this country because it's been so good to me. If I could come up here for nothing and spend the rest of my life and contribute in a very tangible way, I'd do that in a minute. I owe this country that.

LK: But?

RP: Getting all caught up in a political process that doesn't work—and we'll be talking about that—I don't think would be— I wouldn't be temperamentally fit for it.

LK: I know John J. Hooker, a former gubernatorial candidate, Senate candidate, in Tennessee, is strongly urging you to do it. Have you told him the same thing: you don't want to?

RP: Well, people call me, and I get a tremendous number of calls and letters, and these are very, very kind. There's no nicer compliment people could pay, but it's important in this old world to play to your strengths.

LK: Your strength would not be as president?

RP: My strength is creating jobs and fixing things.

LK: Well, isn't that what a president could do?

RP: Well, I'm not sure in our present system.

LK: All right, what about this system would keep someone like Perot away from wanting to lead it?

RP: It's a system that doesn't work. For example, right now we have fundamental economic problems. We owe $4 trillion that we admit to. We *really* owe more than that. We are going to run up a huge budget deficit this year "jump-starting the economy." Now, let's just talk about jump-starting. I'm stalled on the side of the highway. You come by, and you say, "Ross, what's the problem?" I say, "My battery's dead." You jump-start me. With luck, I'll get to the filling station, right? . . . What I really need is a fundamental fix for the problem. See, whoever called it "jump-starting" did the country a favor, if we think about it. Now, these guys must really think we're stupid. For example, in effect, they're coming to us and saying, "We'd like to buy your vote with your money this year." See? Well, that's when I say, "No, no." They don't *think*. Then the guy says, "Well, I'd like to really buy your vote with *your* money this year. Plus, I'd like for you to borrow a lot of extra money this year so I can give you more this year, so that you'll be sure to vote for me this year." Now that's the system we have right now. That's a bad joke, Larry.

LK: But wouldn't a good president—presidents have changed systems and concepts. Roosevelt came in, changed a lot of things. Lincoln changed things. Couldn't a good, forceful, effective leadership president change things?

RP: Oh, I'm certain if you had the right person in the White House and if, on day one, everybody agreed they're going to stop acting like little boys in the schoolyard— fight all day—and if everybody would read the Constitution— And this will come as a heck of a shock to the White House, but Congress does not work for the president. [*laughs*] Do you follow me? You cannot order Congress to pass a law by a certain date. For example, if you and I are equals, we'd better link arms and work together, because you can't order me around. I can't order you around. Why are we having this mud wrestling operation?

LK: So like giving Congress a deadline is—

RP: No. Mud wrestling won't work. We've got proof of that. Right now, you go over to those tax hearings, and it's just sad. We've got *work* to do. We've got *business* to take care of. . . . If you're bleeding arterially, first thing to do is stop the bleeding.

LK: Give me something Ross Perot would do if he were king.

RP: No, if I could have one wish for this country— May I say it that way?

LK: All right, an edict.

RP: No, no—

LK: If you could issue one edict—

RP: I'm going to have one wish.

LK: Okay.

RP: If I could just wish for one great thing for this country, it would be to have a strong family unit in every home. It's the most efficient unit of government the world will ever know.

LK: The family unit, okay. Well, you can't do that.

RP: We will wipe out most of our problems right there. But now, I would say this. Let's go down to grassroots America—

LK: That sounds like Mario Cuomo. . . . He talks about the family unit as the basis of America.

RP: Anybody that thinks it through understands. You can't replace that unit. It's fundamental. Now, let's go down to grassroots America, where the people are hurting, and everybody's saying, "Why are we in this mess?" The first thing I'd like for you to do—all of you—is look in the mirror. We're the owners of this country. We don't act like the owners. We act like white rabbits that get programmed by messages coming out of Washington. We *own* this place. The guys in Washington work for *us*. They are our servants. It's interesting—

LK: They are civil servants.

RP: Yes. They're *our* servants. . . . Now, they act like they're our kings and emperors, and so on and so forth. And since they're picking our pockets five months a year—five months a year the average guy works just to pay his taxes—and since they vote themselves all kinds of special privileges and perks—et cetera, et cetera, et cetera, et cetera—you start saying, "Wait a minute. Who is working for whom?"

LK: No, but give me some—

RP: So you get down to brass tacks here. Step one: The second wish is that everybody in this country would start acting like an owner. Now, I've got a great mom and dad in every home or great parents in every home. Everybody rises up and says, "We run this place, you guys. Listen to us."

The third thing I'd ask for is the electronic town hall. We're very close to it. This program here is a forerunner of it. We saw another piece of it right after the State of the Union—the CBS call-in. With interactive television every other week, say, we could take one major issue, go to the American people, cover it in great detail, have them respond, and show by congressional district what the people want. Now don't you think that would kind of clear Congress's heads about whether or not to listen to folks back home or listen to their foreign lobbyists on an issue? Sure, it would.

LK: What went wrong? What went wrong? You saw this recession early. Others did. You said it. You saw it long before the president, long before a lot of politicians. What went wrong in the '80s?

RP: We spent a whole lot more than we took in and—

LK: But we've always done that, haven't we?

RP: Yes, but now stay here. We started out as a huge land mass as a country: a tiny little population, loaded with minerals, natural resources, timber, oil and gas, so on and so forth. We'd go through one area in the country in a very creative way and then shout, "Go west, young man. Go west." Now we have populated our country from shore to shore. We now, at this point in time, are a mature country. When you're a small growing company, you can bury your mistakes. When you're a small but rapidly growing country, you can bury your mistakes. Once you mature, you've got to be a little more sure-footed. That's where we are. We have gone through all the easy ways to make money in this country. It's brains-and-wits time now—our biggest challenge in this country. So, now, if I could have another wish, it would be that we had a growing positive tax base, rather than a shrinking tax base.

LK: Meaning?

RP: Meaning that our companies are thriving, our companies are making the best. Now, can we do this? Absolutely. Why aren't we doing this? We don't have it as a goal. Do you hear anybody in this country saying— The people who create jobs in this country are the coaches in business. Their mission in life is to make sure their team wins. Their team can only win if their team has the best products. There is no excuse for every company in this country not to make the best products.

LK: Well, but some say if we lower their taxes—like capital gains—and give that guy the chance or that lady the chance to pump it back in, you'll get better products.

RP: Well, it's not that simple. I wish it were. Step one, when they were rich, why were they making fifth-rate products? Do you follow me? When they had plenty of money, they were making fifth— One company I can think of spent $90 billion and never got in the game. Well, you can't spend that much money intelligently and not get in the game.

[*Commercial break*]

LK: Okay, you owned one percent of General Motors, right? You merged EDS into General Motors?

RP: Yes, and it's complicated.

LK: Okay, but eventually they bought you out for $700 million for one percent?

RP: Well, most of what they paid me— They paid me when we did the merger, and they bought 80 percent of my stock. The last 20 percent was converted to series E, which had the General Motors votes, which gave me roughly one percent of the General Motors vote.

LK: What went wrong at that company—the company that, as they go, so goes America? . . . Because they're a good way to structure this, right? We could look at them and look at this.

RP: General Motors. When you've got companies of the quality of General Motors and IBM downsizing, that means they're saying, "We're no longer in the game at the size we were. We're going to reduce the size of the company," and thousands and thousands of people get laid off. See, that's a really strong signal that we have a problem, right?

LK: But what caused that?

RP: That always is caused by leadership at the top. If we were— See, we understand sports in this country; don't understand business. If we have a losing football team, we know what to do. Get a new coach, get a new quarterback, start with basics, clean it up. That's what we have to do in business. Now, the sad thing—you can't really blame the fellows in Washington. Most of them don't understand business. If you ask me to do brain surgery this afternoon, I can't do it. Our primary problem in this country now is to create taxpayers. You create taxpayers by building strong, growing companies. That should be the highest priority.

LK: Are you saying GM should not have downsized, should not have—

RP: See, back in the mid-'80s, when I was there, when we were still rich, when we had time, we should have optimized our position. We should have moved heaven and earth to improve the quality of the product. We should have been first and best. We were spending almost $4 billion a year on research and development, and our first car came in at seventeenth place. So we didn't even have as a goal to be first and best. So you need to get your product up there while you're still strong.

Now there's a great parallel here. Our country is still relatively strong. If the owners of this country—the American people—will say, "Wait a minute. We're going to fix this thing while the watch is still ticking, and we're not going to be programmed by white rabbits, by a government that comes *at* us instead of government that comes *from* us, the way it's supposed to," then we can fix it, because we still have the resiliency to fix it. But look, the clock is running against us.

LK: All right, give me some fix-it ideas.

RP: Okay, fine. All these guys—

LK: Some concrete fix-it ideas.

RP: Let's just clean up the system first.

LK: All right.

RP: All right, first thing you've got to do in business is get rid of all this crazy stuff we do on international trade. The way you get rid of that is to get rid of all these ex-government officials that cash in and become lobbyists for 300,000 bucks a year. We pass a simple law. We, the owners of this country, tell the guys—pass a law that if you were elected or appointed or worked in Washington, you cannot be a lobbyist for a foreign government, foreign individual, for ten years. You go to Washington to serve, not to get rich. If you want to get rich, don't go to Washington. . . . Do you follow me? Now you've just shut—

LK: What do you do about Japan and the trade imbalance?

RP: Well, I just cured a lot of it right there. Do you follow me? The second thing we do is get people who know how to negotiate. We cry for trade negotiators. When our international competitors compete with us—or negotiate with us—they stake out an extreme position. They expect us to stake out an extreme position. They expect us—the two of us—to negotiate a position that works. In many cases, we buy their extreme position and that creates stress. Well, one thing, as a negotiator you'd say this in a minute. In a case like that, if it's that one-sided, say, "Okay, you set the rules, but let's do it for both sides." Now, if it's an unfair deal, the other side sure doesn't want you to have half of it, right?

LK: Agreed, but if we're strong, why do that? Why capitulate?

RP: All right, they know how to negotiate, and we don't. When they do a negotiation for an industry, the most experienced people in their industry put together the plan. We've got a bunch of young people that blew up balloons in the election, I guess. I don't know who puts together the plan, but the result is chaos.

Now, my favorite story is when they brought trucks into the United States and got them declared cars and cut the import tariffs from 25 percent to $2\frac{1}{2}$ percent. That's like getting an elephant declared a horse at the dock. Then, when they got to the lot they got them redeclared trucks so they wouldn't have to pay a penalty.

LK: And you don't knock Japan for this? You're not a Japan basher?

RP: No. Japan is our rival, not our enemy. Japan is a competitor. The saddest thing that can happen to our country as we lose our competitive position is to start hating our competitors. That leads to great stress and leads to very unproductive thinking. Bashing a Toyota won't make a better car—just bluntly put—with a sledgehammer. You know what I'm talking about.

[*Commercial break*]

LK: A couple of other things I wanted to get to. Japanese real estate investment in the United States—way down from last year. . . . Like 61 percent. Surprise you?

RP: Not really. They've got a downturn in their economy. Land values are dropping. Stock prices are dropping. They're bringing their money home. Now, I hope everybody will listen to this part. Between the Japanese and the Arabs, they've been buying a lot of our debt. The last thing we want them to do is take the money home, with the debt we have: $4 trillion.

LK: You don't want them to pull out?

RP: Well, not buying our government debt. See, we've got $4 trillion in debt. I wish we didn't have the debt, but we have the debt. Somebody's got to buy those T-bills, right? In business, the first rule of finance is: Never finance long-term projects with short-term money.

   Now, to Larry King's audience, listen to this: sixty-eight percent of our $4 trillion debt is due and payable in the next five years. Now if I haven't gotten your motor going till now, surely at this moment you understand. We can't waste a year on stupid jump-starts, Novocain-in-the-knee shots, that sort of thing. We'd better get to fundamentals, because within five years that debt rolls over, and if these guys go home with their money, we're in deep trouble.

LK: Do any of the current political figures impress you? The incumbent and the challengers?

RP: I'd say I certainly respect them for running, and I would appeal— There's some wonderful people in this country who ought to be running who are not. I wish they would run. They could make a tremendous contribution now.

LK: Going to name any?

RP: I don't think it's appropriate for me to name any. But certainly, people who are willing to climb into the ring and get cut to pieces and slug it out—you have to respect that.

LK: Yes. You were a critic of the Gulf War. . . . Any regrets over that?

RP: No. My only regret—

LK: Would you criticize it again?

RP: Well, let's net it out. Our objectives were to get Saddam Hussein—his nuclear, chemical, bacteriological capability. It's all still intact.

LK: And get him out of Kuwait, which we did.

RP: Well, but wait a minute, Larry. If we didn't want him in Kuwait, we shouldn't have told him on July the 25th, when Ambassador Glaspie met with him, that he could take the top part of the country. You know the meeting. And if anybody listening to this questions that, go through Nexus or Lexus and pull every *New York Times* article from July 25th forward, through her testimony at the Senate Intelligence Committee, or the Senate Foreign Relations Committee—

whichever it was—at the end of the war. There's a total disconnect between what she was saying on the record back in July, August, and what-have-you, and what the other key people in the State Department were saying, and what they said under oath to that committee. Now this is *my* country. It's *your* country. It's *our* country. And this is aimed straight at the White House and the State Department. Why don't you just release those written instructions you gave her? Because a lot of fine young men and women lost their lives over there, got cut to pieces. Just lay the instructions signed by the secretary of state and the president of the United States to Ambassador Glaspie for the July 25th meeting on the table. They won't do it.

LK: We know they're there?

RP: They know they're there—

LK: I mean, these written instructions—

RP: —we know they're there. They admit they're there, but they say, "We don't release that." Well, I can understand politically why they wouldn't want to, but when you tell a guy like Saddam Hussein, who you spent ten years making what he is—ten years— We spent billions of dollars creating this bad guy, then we decided we didn't like him after he took all of Kuwait. If he'd just taken a little up there by the border, apparently we were going to finesse it. When he took the whole thing, then we got nervous.

LK: Oakton, Virginia. We'll start including phone calls for H. Ross Perot. Hello.

CALLER: [*Oakton, Virginia*] Hi, Mr. Perot. . . . Mr. Perot, since it's corporate America that's been dumping thousands of people on the unemployment line, and it's Democratic-controlled Congress and Senate, do you think George Bush is taking an unfair blame for the poor economy?

RP: I would put the guts of the blame for the economy in terms of the people who run the companies. Just go back to your athletic team. If you've got a losing team, you start with the coach, right? People at the top determine the strategy, the tactics, what products to make, how the money gets spent. The silliest thing in the world is to blame the working American. That's kind of like blaming the water boy, but we do that. Now then—

LK: But we are told that private industry is what built America. Keep government out; government doesn't work; private industry works. You're saying private industry failed.

RP: I'm saying now we have another problem. I'm coming to step— Most of these problems have several layers. Let's look at our international competitors that are successful. They have an intelligent supportive relationship between government and business. So if I could put my wish list, I'd say let's cut out the adversarial relationship between government and business and have an intelligent supportive relationship. I don't mean subsidize business. I don't mean burp them and diaper them. But I mean, let's stop breaking their legs first thing every morning.

LK: Do you think President Bush sees this problem?

RP: In all candor, I don't think he understands it. He's interested in international affairs. Doesn't understand business. Doesn't like to work on domestic issues. I think he realizes now he's got to get into it. My unsolicited advice—and I hope it doesn't offend him—is to get a bunch of people around him that understand this and go to work on it night and day.

LK: Would you volunteer?

RP: Only if they're serious. And I will not be used as a Hollywood prop, and, believe me, the guys in the key places know exactly what I'm saying there. . . .

LK: Holland, Michigan, hello.

CALLER: [*Holland, Michigan*] I'd like to, first of all, say that I really back a lot of the things you're saying. When you sit down and you look at them logically, they do make a lot of sense. My question was, though, I was going to ask who out of the country you would propose to run a plan like you're talking about; but a better question is what should the American people be looking for in a candidate?

LK: Okay, if you won't tell us *who*, what *qualities* would you look for?

RP: I would look, personally, for a person who is dedicated to seeing that our children live in an even better country than we have, that we leave a better country to our children.

LK: They all say that.

RP: That's top. That's one of our problems. If a guy says it, you know, then we turn—

LK: Okay, so what would you look for?

RP: But step one, that he is— Now, he's thinking long-term—

LK: Or "she."

RP: Or *she* is thinking long-term. Secondly, that this person has got to understand how you get the economy under control, how you stop this profuse deficit spending that we have that's not producing utopia. When you're $4 trillion down, we ought to have a perfect country here, and we don't. Drive through any big city. Drive through this town. You can see there's work to be done.

LK: How do you recognize that? Does Paul Tsongas's program impress you—his eighty-two-page program?

RP: If you read his book, he is thinking. It is orderly. It is logical. It involves pain. It involves sacrifice. That's another thing—not to aim it at any one candidate—look for a candidate that has the guts to look you in the eye and tell you, "This won't be pretty." You know, going to the dentist to get your teeth fixed has a little pain attached to it, but it has a long-term benefit. We cannot go from where we are to where we need to be on a pain-free trip. This needs to be carefully thought out, logical. It needs to be presented— I'd look for a candidate that talks to you as adults; that talks to you as thinking, reasoning people and doesn't assume that he can buy your vote with your money.

LK: Plano, Texas, hello.

RP: Getting right back to home. How are you?

CALLER: [*Plano, Texas*] I'm fine. Hey, I used to work for Perot Systems.

RP: Right.

CALLER: [*Plano, Texas*] I was laid off.

RP: What were you laid off for?

CALLER: [*Plano, Texas*] Because your company merged with another company that merged with another company.

RP: Well, I—

CALLER: [*Plano, Texas*] That's what's the problem in America.

RP: Our company is—

LK: Mergers: What about mergers?

RP: We didn't merge with our company. We take over accounts. Now the thing I can't do here on television without knowing your name and having access to your file— Our company is growing rapidly.

LK: You're hiring people?

RP: Oh, absolutely, all the time. I'm not familiar with your particular case, and I'm sorry.

LK: We go to Plattsburg, New York, with H. Ross Perot. Hello.

CALLER: [*Plattsburg, New York*] I heard Mr. Perot earlier say something about that we are the owners of this country, and that the civil servants work for us. . . . Okay, what I wanted to know was, how exactly would us, as the owners of this country, tell the people in Washington and all the other bureaucrats, I guess, to do what we want them to do without just putting them in office? What exactly would your suggestion be?

RP: Well, it's this simple. You know, I go back to when people are always asking me to run, and I explain to them that one of the reasons I don't want to run is I don't think any one person can do this job. For example, whoever you decide to back, you're going to have to stay in the ring after election day. You will not be able to go home. Just that one person—I don't care how gifted he is and how able he or she might be or what-have-you—he has got to have your organized visible support to make this system work. Otherwise, the special interests or the PAC money moves in after election day, you go back to work, and the rest is history. You're going to have to be buried at the local, state, and national level. You'll never get your schools cleaned up unless you're willing to put your shoulder to the wheel, know who's on the school board, attend PTA meetings, et cetera, et cetera, et cetera.

We can have a revolution in this country. I urge you to pick a leader that you're willing to climb in the ring with, stay with, stay the course. Then that leader, with the Congress that allows us to work together as a team, as a nation, and go from where we are to where we want to be— But you're going to have to be very, very active at grassroots level, and not just be some sort of puppet that dances to Washington's string. And I'm saying that to upset everybody that's listening. I hope I am.

LK: Would you help the Russians? Would you spend money overseas? Would you be as involved as we are in the Middle East?

RP: I would love to have a country that could always reach out and help other countries. It is a whole lot cheaper to help Russia right now than it is to have a new cold war pop up in eighteen months because we didn't.

LK: You can't turn away from the world.

RP: We cannot turn away from the world. It costs so little to help Russia go from where she is over to a free economy and a stand-alone country, and it costs so much to have her regress, because her people are hungry. Now if I were in United Europe, I would really be nervous because, you know, if Russia gets hungry, guess where the nearest food is?

LK: We go to Potomac, Maryland, hello.

CALLER: [*Potomac, Maryland*] Yes, hi, Mr. Perot. . . . I'm a fellow businessman. The only difference between us is I'm about one-millionth the size of you. I'm a small businessman here in Maryland, and a lot of my peers are getting squeezed by the credit problems and the problems with lending to small businesses, and I wanted you to comment on that. I think there's a lot of— The banks are just not lending to the small businesses across the country, and it's hurting a lot of people. And the small businesses are the people that employ a lot of the people in this country.

RP: You employed over 125 percent of the growth in the workforce in the last ten years—businesses with twenty-five employees or less. And you're right, you can't get money. You can't get capital. You can't get loans. You can't get anything you need. We've got Congress up here working on all kind of tax fixes to give the average guy three-hundred bucks, which won't mean a thing.

Here's what we could do to really make this economy work long-term. We ought to— Now, see, everybody gets turned off by the term "capital gains." A lot of folks don't even know what it means. I'm not going to call it "capital gains." I'm going to call it putting risky money into your little business. If that money goes into the treasury of your company and is used to build your company and create jobs, that's high-risk money. It's like wildcatting. I can explain that to anybody in America, that it makes sense for that money—which is high-risk money, which is going to stay there for a long period of time—to be taxed on a favorable basis.

LK: But it's got to be invested that way, or you don't get that?

RP: Absolutely. Now then, let's go to— If we had any sort of intelligent relationship between government and business, we would take the industries that are in trouble. We would develop ten-year plans like the Japanese do, to get them out of trouble and get them back king of the hill again. And in those companies that needed a capital infusion, money going directly into the treasury of the corporation—now you've got to make sure, in order to get this kind of tax benefit, you've got to have a killer plan that'll get you there and stay the course. You've got to know how much money you need, the money going in there—fine. Now, where the average guy gets upset—and he *should* get upset—is folks shooting dice on Wall Street. They say, "If you're going to give those folks a big break, why don't you give the fellow that wins at Atlantic City a big break?" You see what I mean? . . . Wall Street has a useful purpose. That's the scoreboard of how well the company is doing. You can have a step-down capital gains tax in that case for long-term holders.

LK: But you want people who want government out of business, who want government out of their hair? You're saying invite government in.

RP: No, no, I'm saying—government *is* in.

LK: I mean, there are a lot of people who want government out.

RP: We're dealing with a point in time. We're dealing at a point when our fighter is on the ropes, see? And we're trying to get him up on his feet so he can finish the fight and win, so we've got some work to do. At this point intelligent tax policy could really help. Now, as far as patching our existing tax laws, that's the biggest joke in Washington. If you have a minute, go down there and watch these guys with their alligator shoes and their briefcases running up and down the halls getting their special deal cut. My advice—very simple—to Congress: throw your old tax law out. It's like an old inner tube—full of patches. Let's replace it with a complete new set of tax laws. Number one, it's got to raise revenues. Number one-A, it's got to be fair. And there's nothing fair about the present tax laws, and that's what upsets the average guy.

LK: Don't you think the ultra-rich get a big break?

RP: Yes.

LK: Yes, you do?

RP: No, no, I was against the bubble. Now, if anybody can give me one reason why I should pay a lower percentage of taxes on just regular income than a guy making less than me, I want to meet him. . . . Keep in mind, I started out in life— Until I was thirty-eight, the only money I ever made was through sweat. Now I'm in the interesting position—I still make money through sweat, but I also can make money with money. Given a choice, ten guys out of ten would rather make money with money than money with sweat.

LK: And the government, therefore, is helping your welfare by letting you do that.

RP: No, I would say this. The government is getting more than its fair share of taxes out of me. If you look at the taxes I've paid in my life, I don't think I have to tip my hat to anybody. But I am really frustrated about how they were spent, Larry. [*laughs*] I bought a front-row ticket to utopia—

LK: [*laughs*] But the show ain't on.

RP: —and the show didn't hit the road. Right.

LK: What were your taxes last year?

RP: Oh, millions. I'd have to go get it. But in terms— I looked one time. I've paid close to a billion personally, and my companies have paid—

LK: What was the largest check you ever signed?

RP: Oh, well, let's see. Oh, I've signed individual tax checks—$30 million, $40 million, $50 million. . . . No, but I mean, the point is—I felt good about that, see? I felt really good that I could do that, but then I would really like to see every penny of it spent for people who need it. I'd like to see every penny of it spent intelligently. I'm tired of seeing $180 billion a year wasted, and the president's own staff has made that statement. We waste $180 billion a year—fraud and mismanagement. That's inexcusable.

LK: The hotel the president lives in in Houston—his legal residence—filed bankruptcy today. Comment? The Houstonian Hotel.

RP: Well, that's sad. Just another indication. Keep in mind: go to Rome, go to Paris, go to London. Those cities are centuries old. They're thriving. They're clean. They work. Our oldest cities are brand new compared to them, and yet our cities— Go to New York, drive through downtown Washington, go to Detroit, go to Philadelphia. What's wrong with us? Why is it that the Italians and the French and the Germans and the English— And let's go to Hong Kong and Singapore, and we're looking—wow! We're looking at tomorrow. Our challenge— This country should be tomorrow. And it's inexcusable if we're not, because we can be.

[*Commercial break*]

LK: Brooksville, Florida, for H. Ross Perot on *Larry King Live*. Hello.

CALLER: [*Brooksville, Florida*] Yes, I'd like to say that I agree with Mr. Perot 100 percent about our relationship with Japan. Japan's not our enemy. They're our competitors. . . . I was wondering if he agreed that our problem is in the bureaucracy of the way products are moved through the retailing methods, or if we'd need to change to an alternative, more efficient method of moving products, such as networking?

RP: Yes, all of these things should be— See, the market, I think, will handle the distribution. Our core problem— See, we're selling Chinese shirts made by prison labor, and China has a most-favored-nation status. Now let's assume you're Einstein running the greatest textile plant in the world in South Carolina, and you're getting slave-labor shirts dumped on you. You cannot compete. . . . And then, when the guys blow the whistle, and everybody says, "Ooops," we let China send them through Korea and, for a few pennies per shirt, put on a "Made in

Korea" label, and the rest is history. And all those folks making shirts in this country are out of work. Now, I cannot live with that any longer. I don't care whose favorite nation China might be. I think we ought to cut—

LK: [*laughs*] They're not yours.

RP: No, I like the Chinese. I'm not against—but we're back to trade. I say, "Okay, China. You want to dump? We're going to dump two ways, baby." Now, we're not going to take— Now just bear with me here. Study the Mexican trade agreement. Philosophically, I'm for free trade, but down in Mexico they pay workers one dollar an hour.

LK: And how do you compete with that?

RP: You can't compete with it. I have called a Who's Who in this country and said, "If this agreement goes in place, when will you build your next factory here?" They're going to build it in Mexico. When will the Japanese build their next factory here? They're going to build it in Mexico.

LK: Would you build yours in Mexico?

RP: No. Absolutely not—

LK: Because you're a patriot—

RP: —but the point is just hard, pragmatic, you know, next quarter's bottom line. They're going to head for Mexico. Now here's the thing, Larry. This is going to implode the tax base when we need the money. Do you follow me?

LK: Yes.

RP: You can't do that. Now just bear with me just a minute here. I've talked to a Who's Who of people who are for it and they explain, "Oh, there will be disruptions." That's pretty vacant. In other words, if I go home tonight, lose my job, lose my house, kids can't go to school—don't call me a disruption. Jesus, that's a catastrophe for me! Now then, they say, "But over a period of years, that one-dollar-an-hour wage from Mexico will come up to seven dollars an hour, and our workers will get used to working for seven dollars an hour, and then we can go back in the manufacturing business." Now watch my lips on this one [*King laughs*]: We owe four trillion bucks. We just cut ability to pay taxes in half after a ten- to fifteen-year delay while nobody has a job. Is anybody going to cut the debt to two trillion bucks? No. This is a recipe for disaster, and please, please, please— all of you guys in the federal government—if you can explain that to me, call collect. Thank you.

[*Commercial break*]

LK: By the way, is there any scenario in which you would run for president? Can you give me a scenario in which you'd say, "Okay, I'm in"?

RP: Number one, I don't want to.

LK: I know, but is there a scenario—?

RP: Number two, you know, nobody's been luckier than I have. And number three, I've got all these everyday folks that make the world go round writing me in longhand—

LK: Is there a scenario?

RP: Now that touches me. But I don't want to fail them. That would be the only thing that would interest me, and so I would simply say to them and to all these folks who are constantly calling and writing, if you feel so strongly about this, number one, I will not run as either a Democrat or a Republican, because I will not sell out to anybody but to the American people—and I will sell out to them.

LK: So you'd run as an independent?

RP: Number two, if you're that serious—you, the people, are that serious—you register me in fifty states, and if you're not willing to organize and do that—

LK: Wait a minute. Are you saying—? Wait a minute.

RP: —then this is all just talk.

LK: Hold it, hold it, hold it, hold it, hold it—

RP: Now stay with me, Larry—

LK: Wait, wait, wait. Are you saying—?

RP: I'm saying to the ordinary folks—now, I don't want any machine—

LK: This is a "Draft Ross Perot on an independent—"

RP: No, no, no, no. I'm not asking to be drafted.

LK: Okay.

RP: I'm saying to all these nice people that have written me—and the letters, you know, fill cases—if you're dead-serious—

LK: Start committees—

RP: —then I want to see some sweat—

LK: —in Florida, Georgia—

RP: —I want to see some sweat. Why do I want to see some sweat? I said it earlier. I want you in the ring. Why do I want you in the ring? Because I can't do the job, and nobody can do the job, unless you will go in the ring—

LK: Well, wait a minute. Are you saying groups all across America—all across America—can now, in New York, Illinois, California, start forming independent groups to get you on the ballot as an independent, and you would then— If this occurred in fifty states, with enough people, you'd throw the hat?

RP: I am not encouraging people to do this—

LK: If they did—

RP: —but the push has come from them. So, as Lech Walesa said, "Words are plentiful, but deeds are precious." And this is my way of saying, "Will you get in the ring? Will you put the gloves on? And do you care enough about this country to stay the course?"

Now recognize, you're listening to a guy that doesn't want to do this, but if you, the people, will on your own— Now, I don't want some apparatus built. I don't want two or three guys with big money around trying to do it. If you want to register me in fifty states, number one, I'll promise you this: between now and the convention we'll get both parties' heads straight. Number two, I think I can promise you're going to see a world-class candidate on each side. And number three, by the convention you might say, "Cripes, you know, it's all taken care of."

But on the other hand, we're set, and if you're not happy with what you see, and you want me to do it, then I don't want any money from anybody but you, and I don't want anything but five bucks from you, because I can certainly pay for my own campaign—no ifs, ands, and buts—but I want you to have skin in the game. I want you to be in the ring.

Now then, God bless you all who have written me and called me. The shoe is on the other foot.

LK: Other foot.

RP: The shoe is on the other foot.

LK: Okay, now we have to know something!

RP: I expect everybody to go very silent at this point, Larry.

LK: No, no, we have to know—

RP: That puts it to bed.

LK: We have to know something very important.

RP: That puts it to bed.

LK: Now that you're a potential—

RP: Yes.

LK: —what does "H" stand for?

RP: Henry!

LK: We'll be right back with—HENRY! [*Perot laughs*] right after this.

[*Commercial break*]

LK: We're running quickly out of time. Okay, let's say you're in. You're elected, independent, president of the United States. First thing you do? First thing you do?

RP: I would create an electronic town hall where, say, every week or so we would take a single major issue to the people. We would explain it in great detail and then we would get a response from the owners of the country—the people—that could be analyzed by congressional district so that the Congress—no ifs, ands, and buts—would know what the people want. Then these boys running around with briefcases representing special interests would be de-horned—to use a Texas term.

LK: You trust the people, in other words?

RP: Well, the people—

LK: I'm out of time—

RP: But here's the key—

LK: Will you come back, Ross?

RP: You bet. You mean trust the people over elected officials?

LK: Yes.

RP: Absolutely. That's the foundation of our country.

LK: Will you come back, Ross? Maybe like once a month we ought to have you here.

RP: I'll come back. Some time I'd like to come back and talk about how you make a business work, because we need taxpayers out there. It would be fun to get all the entrepreneurs on one night.

LK: We're out of time. Thank you, Ross—Ross Perot. I won't say "Henry."

RP: Great.

LK: His name is "Ross"—Ross Perot.

Terry Anderson

Terry Anderson became famous in a way nobody wants to be: as the U.S. hostage held longest by Islamic terrorists. The AP journalist was kidnapped on March 16, 1985, in Beirut. He would remain captive for 2,454 days. During this period, Anderson's sister, Peggy Say, worked tirelessly to keep the plight of her brother and other hostages before the American people.

At the time of his abduction, Anderson was in the process of divorcing his wife, having fallen in love with a young woman who was pregnant with his child. During his captivity, Anderson's father and brother died, and his daughter, Sulome, was born. This interview took place four months after his release.

"There were times when I wished I could die. There were times when I thought I wouldn't last. But I never gave up."

LARRY KING: After nearly seven years in captivity in Beirut, former hostage Terry Anderson is home, released last December—walked straight into a hero's welcome. And now, after four months of rest with his family, Terry is able to recount the details of his imprisonment. And we welcome to *Larry King Live*—a program that didn't exist when Terry was—[*laughs*] This program is six and a half years old—well, we're going to be seven years old June first—and you were taken what date?

TERRY ANDERSON: March 16, 1985.

LK: We started June 1, 1985. You just missed us, Terry. You could have been here for the— Those are the breaks of the game.

TA: What can I say? Yes. . . .

LK: What was the—for want of a better term—weirdest or most difficult thing about freedom after imprisonment?

TA: Well, weirdest—I mean, you can imagine what it's like to try—to all of a sudden be put back in charge of your life. I mean, I had virtually no decisions to make for a very long time, and all of a sudden I've got a million decisions to make—some of them minor, some of them important. I think the most difficulty I had at the beginning was with the minor decisions.

LK: Like?

TA: I was very disorganized. You know, an ordinary person has a lot of skills that he's developed over the years in just kind of managing his day—when to get up, shaving, where he put his tie, where his wallet is, what he's got to do next, keeping appointments, that kind of thing. I just couldn't keep anything organized. I was late. I think in Wiesbaden we were there—what? Five, six days? I was late for every single appointment I had [*laughs*]. I couldn't get myself organized worth a darn. Now, I write everything down. I'm getting better at it.

LK: Waking up the first morning of freedom: Is there a disbelief about it when you're held that long?

TA: Well, I don't know. I wouldn't call it a disbelief.

LK: I mean, it's got to be—

TA: It's incredible. I mean, the emotional high was just—was just enormous. I spent those first few days just kind of bathing in love, I guess you could say. I had my lady and my daughter, and my family around me. And it wasn't incredible; I was just enjoying it. I was just having a great time.

LK: Have psychologists talked to you?

TA: Yes.

LK: And have they discussed with you what might be the most difficult aspect of all of this?

TA: Well, we had two psychiatrists—Royal Air Force men, actually, strangely enough— that the AP borrowed from Britain. They treated the British hostages. They were also specialists in hostage/POW decompression things—very, very wonderful men. In fact, one of them happened to be in the States last night. We spent some time with him, just chatting. And excellent people. They knew what they were about and, because they were so nice and so easy to talk to, they did an awful lot for us. Mainly, what they talked about—what they urged on us—was priorities.

LK: Meaning?

TA: Meaning, when you get out from a thing like that, the world is pretty confusing, and it goes pretty fast. And there are a lot of people tugging at you and a lot of things you want to do, let alone the things people want you to do. And they said— the first thing they said was, "Get away. Get away. Go off by yourself. You know what's important." I know what's important—my family. That's number one, far ahead of anything else. So we went away for three months and spent that time being together, getting to know each other again, working out things.

There were other problems. There are readjustments to be made by everybody. I mean, Madeleine, my fiancée, was—unhappily—independent for seven years, leading her own life, making her own decisions. She had to. And now, all of a sudden, I'm back, and we've got to make decisions together again.

LK: Yes.

TA: And we've got to consider each other.

LK: And you were separated from a wife, right?

TA: Yes, I was undergoing a divorce at the time.

LK: Yes, so Peggy, your sister, had that tough time almost carrying the mantle for you. We never heard from your wife. That was probably difficult for her, too.

TA: Well, it was very difficult for her. She's Japanese, and it's a different culture, and we were undergoing a divorce. I have a sixteen-year-old daughter now, who's a beautiful girl—a wonderful lady.

LK: You missed seven years of her, though, right?

TA: Missed seven years of her life. We are back again. I've spent some time with her. I'm going to spend some more time with her, and that's working out very well.

LK: Were you aware of all Peggy was doing? Peggy Say became the best-known hostage relative in the history of this country.

TA: Yes. I heard from time to time on the radio. I mean, I wasn't aware completely. I didn't have all the details, but I heard from time to time on the radio of Peg's efforts and the efforts of everybody else. All my colleagues were fantastic. The other members of my family also worked hard. Peg—being the most outspoken, the most well-spoken, and very forceful—was always on your show and on the other shows.

LK: Yes.

TA: But my other family members also were working. My little brother and sister—the twins—my older brother, who died, and my father, who also died.

LK: And I guess, knowing Peg, everything she did didn't surprise you—or did it?

TA: Well, in a way it did. I mean, I never quite expected that—to see her kind of striding the world stage like that. I mean, Peg—there's no doubt about it, Peg is a capable woman and an intelligent woman, but to see her with presidents and prime ministers and things like that was a little—was a little strange.

LK: And often critical of them. Did that surprise you?

TA: Often kicking them in the shins.

LK: Yes.

TA: No, no. I mean that—our family is not known for being gentle and kind when we disagree with somebody. We tend to be a little aggressive. [*laughs*]

LK: Terry, are you—to you—a hero?

TA: No, absolutely not.

LK: What are you, to you: a victim?

TA: No, I don't—I wouldn't use that word. I don't think so. I mean, strictly speaking, I'm a kidnapee, I guess. I'm a former hostage now, although I hope I won't be that for a very long time.

LK: You'll be it for the rest of your life. It's going to be in the first paragraph of your obituary—hopefully, when you're 126—but it'll be there.

TA: Well, let's hope I do some things that make that a—you know—second or third or fourth paragraph. I don't know. We'll see. But I'm not a hero. Okay? I didn't do anything that any of the other hostages didn't do. There were a lot of us, and they got through, too. They got through with dignity and with courage and came out. The men I knew in there, there were nine of the— How many hostages were there? A great many—that I was kept with, all helped me, as I helped them. So what's with me?

LK: You were in the press, and you were the longest. . . . That's a fact. What part did you play—as you look at this—in your own capture? In other words, why did you stay there?

TA: What part did I play in getting myself kidnapped? [*laughs*]

LK: Yes.

TA: A major part. I mean, I made a major mistake in judgment. Look, I relied on my own judgment as well as close people's judgment, for a long time. Two and a half years I was in Lebanon, and it was always dangerous. I'd been in dangerous situations before. I made a mistake. My judgment went bad. I should have been more careful, especially after they tried to kidnap me once and missed. I don't know. What can I say? Arrogance—I mean, you know—

LK: You're the kind of journalist who liked the— You know, are you like Peter Arnett? You want to be where trouble is?

TA: Don't all journalists?

LK: No! Some of them are chicken!

TA: Oh, now, come on! That doesn't have anything to do with it. Look, yes—

LK: All journalists want to be where trouble—

TA: Not all, but most of them—the good ones, anyway; at least the ones I know. When there's a hot story going, I can tell you, AP foreign desk phone is ringing off the hook with people wanting to go.

LK: By the way, is that still in you?

TA: What?

LK: Do you want to cover a story now?

TA: Yes. Yes. I'm still a journalist. I still think it's the most marvelous job going. I've always loved it, and I still do. There are things that I used to do that I probably won't do again. I'm forty-four. Running up and down the street, watching people get killed—I think I've had enough of that. And it's not just because I got kidnapped, and I wouldn't—you know, I'm a little more aware of the danger. When you get hit, you're a little more careful. It's also because that's a job where—although we get cynical and we don't talk about it—all that pain and all that violence you see affects you. It piles up inside. And you can only do that for so many years.

LK: You can't stay jaded, in other words.

TA: Yes, if you're jaded—if you don't feel anymore—then you're a lousy journalist, as well as a pretty poor person. . . .

[*Commercial break*]

LK: I read somewhere that the thing that kept you going was your faith.

TA: That was the primary thing, yes.

LK: Why, though, didn't you say, "If there is a God, why did He let me get caught?" In other words, how do you use that faith when you're in a situation in which you could blame the faith?

TA: Well, when I was first kidnapped and when conditions were bad and I was very depressed and very low, as you can well imagine—still in shock an awful lot—I went through all the things that you would expect in prayer. You know, "Why me? Why me? What are you doing to me, God? Why did you let this happen? These are evil men. I'm not an evil man. Why is this happening?" And then, when you have time to think about all the things you've done and all the things you've said, you come to the conclusion, "Okay. Okay, I deserve it—you know, maybe. I've done some bad things, and you're punishing me. Okay."

LK: Guilty.

TA: "I'm sorry. Now, can I go home?" [*laughs*] "I'll never do it again"—and the promises, and the bargains, and all that. But you get through that eventually.

LK: Then what?

TA: Then—I don't know how to describe that. I don't know how to say that. Then you just pray.

LK: To?

TA: You just feel. You just accept, mostly. "Okay, that's what I am. That can't be changed. The things I've done can't be changed. I'm sorry, and that's not going to make any difference to anybody. I'm going to try and do better, but I don't know if I will because, you know, we won't know until that comes around. But that's just what I am, God, and you're supposed to accept me for that. I mean, that's what it's about." And it works, I guess. It helped.

LK: And then did you actually feel watched over? I mean, did you feel a kind of force caring for you?

TA: I felt—yes, I felt at times—very brief times, and not very often—that when I prayed and when I was in the proper frame of mind, God was listening, and God was touching me.

LK: Little things in life that are life—favorite foods—you didn't have that.

TA: [*laughs*] Although we sent them out for ice cream once.

LK: And they got it?

TA: And they went and got it. [*laughs*]

LK: [*laughs*] Accommodations, sexual desire— What do you do with normal things that people have?

TA: Oh, Lord! Most of it you just put away. There isn't much you can do. If you don't have things, you do without. You do what you have to. You're chained to a wall. You can't run down to the store and get the things you want. You can't go have a drink. You'd be surprised what you can do without when you have to.

LK: Why, Terry, were they oftentimes cruel to you, do you think? I mean, they had you. That was the purpose. Why go beyond that?

TA: There were different kinds of guards. Some of them were cruel and vicious. Some of them were kind, within their limits. Most of them were just doing a job, taking orders—same as any other group.

LK: Good and bad in everything?

TA: Good and bad—I wouldn't say, you know, "good." A man who chains you to the wall, no matter how kind he is, is not good. But he may not be vicious. He may do what he can for you. I don't think the chiefs ever meant to do us great bodily harm.

LK: You used the word "abuse," though.

TA: Yes, certainly, there was abuse. . . .

LK: How bad?

TA: Sometimes very bad.

LK: Physical?

TA: Both physical and psychological. Some of the guards were what I would call—within my limits of what I know of psychiatry—psychotic. They were crazy. Some of them were just mean or stupid. Some of them, as I say, were reasonable human beings. Even a couple of them, if you met them elsewhere, you would think you would like them—if it's fair to like somebody who does that to you.

There was unnecessary beating going on. Many of these people were—not many—some of them were very paranoid. They would take for an offense something that was not meant as an offense, or was imagined, and the result would be a beating. Sometimes the treatment was sheer laziness. I mean, can you imagine what it's like to be locked in a small cell with gastroenteritis, and the guard goes away for eight hours? I mean, that's not much fun.

LK: Were there times you gave up?

TA: Never gave up. There were times when I thought I might. There were times when I wished I could die. There were times when I thought I wouldn't last. I always knew I'd be free. I never thought the day wouldn't come. But I thought sometimes that the day would be too far away for me to reach. But I never gave up, no. . . .

LK: Are you bitter towards your captors?

TA: No.

LK: Why not?

TA: Well, for a couple of reasons. I think people have heard me say this before. I don't have time for it in my life. I don't have space for it. My life is very good. I am very happy. I've got a lot to be grateful for right now. And being bitter or angry is wasting my time, is wasting my life, is hurting me. It's not hurting them. They're in Lebanon.

LK: Did you ever know why you were held?

TA: Yes. At least the particular group, or sub-group, or faction—or whatever it was that was holding me—specifically wanted the seventeen prisoners in Kuwait who were taken after the attack on the U. S. Embassy and other facilities. They wanted them released. They wanted them swapped.

LK: And did you want that to happen? Did you say every day, "Please, swap"?

TA: At the beginning, yes. At the beginning, I wished the U. S. government would give anything to get me out. I just wanted to go home, and I didn't care who was right or wrong. After a while, when you have time to think and you have time to settle down and be rational again—no, it's not the right thing to do. It's not. You're going to release people who are going to kill again? Funny.

LK: So you can safely say that, even while held, you would say to a president, "Don't make deals for me"?

TA: Yes. I think I believed that for a long time. We talked about this a lot and, you know, you have to fight between the two ideas: You want to go home. It's miserable, it's a lousy place to be. It's horrible, and if somebody can get you out, more power to them. And the idea that, you know, you don't make deals with kidnappers. You don't pay them, because they'll do it again.

LK: So Iran-Contra was wrong?

TA: Iran-Contra was wrong, and I am very happy that Father Martin Jenko—whom I love dearly—was released, and David Jacobsen was released. I'm sure that was a good thing. But the Iran-Contra thing was wrong.

LK: Did you know anything about it? Did you know about Ollie North or any of those things?

TA: Yes, we heard about it. We heard about it when it broke, through a guard who translated the Arabic radio—and who got in trouble for that, by the way, because we weren't supposed to have any news. And later, when we had access to radio and magazines, of course, we read everything about it.

LK: And what did you think of it, as you read it?

TA: As I said, I think it was a mistake. I think it was a mistake in conception, and I think it was a mistake in execution, and I think, certainly, the confusion between the hostage deal and what was happening in Nicaragua was a real bad mistake.

LK: Yes, but when they say, "We were caring about you. We were trying to get you out—"

TA: Of course, they were caring about me, and that's great. An awful lot of people cared about me, and I'm very grateful for that, and it makes me feel very good. But that doesn't make it any more right. . . .

LK: Did you know before you were getting out? How much time before you knew you got out did you get out?

TA: Well, we thought we were getting out from about three weeks after I was kidnapped. We were told regularly by our guards: [*speaks with accent*] "Everything is good, and very good. The negotiate is good. Don't worry. You are going home." And there were several times through that seven years when I was given clothes and shoes and actually expected to go, but it didn't happen. Something always went wrong.

LK: When you were the only one left—

TA: For the last year, we knew that things were actually moving toward an end. The situation in the Middle East had changed. Our captors were accepting that they weren't going to get anything more out of this and, therefore, they had to draw it to an end and were telling us, "We want to end it, if we can just work out the details." When John McCarthy went home, we were certain it was getting very close. When Tom and Terry Waite went home, they told me exactly, "You're going home in five days." It turned out to be like eleven days, or something like that. Well, they don't exactly keep to schedules very well.

LK: Did they say good-bye to you?

TA: Indeed, they did. . . . They also said they were sorry. They gave me a new watch to replace the one I lost.

LK: Are you wearing it?

TA: No. [*laughs*] No. And six carnations to give to my fiancée, and said they were sorry.

LK: What did you say?

TA: "I'm sorry, too."

LK: What surprised you the most, coming back, about the seven years away?

TA: Oh, how good it is—how good everything is. And everything is very, very good. . . .

[*Commercial break*]

LK: The impact of television: you weren't aware of what was going on, were you?

TA: No, not really.

LK: You didn't see television?

TA: I mean, all these things—CNN and worldwide television are new to me, until right toward the end when we had a television. And even the local Arabic stations were using CNN clips. [*laughs*]

LK: Let's go to calls for Terry Anderson. By the way, we mentioned him. He's going to be here Tuesday. What do you think of Ollie North? Fellow Marine.

TA: I think Mr. North was a fine Marine and, from what I understand, an excellent combat leader. He earned some medals—and *really* earned them. I mean, you want to talk about heroes, those are the guys that are heroes. I don't know too much about the rest of it. My impression is he got into political waters that were too deep for a Marine.

LK: Shreveport. Hello.

CALLER: [*Shreveport, Louisiana*] Hi. Good evening, Terry, and welcome home. I was curious if you ever had the opportunity to escape that Terry Waite had during his capture?

TA: Well, there were opportunities, but the problem was, of course, weighing the chances against the probable outcome. Security was very heavy, and I never saw an opportunity or a chance to escape that I thought was worth it. And at the very least, I knew that I would have to probably kill a guard in order to get out, and I didn't think I could do that.

LK: Didn't think you could?

TA: No, I didn't. See, you have to remember, though, that nobody told us we were going to be there for seven years. We all always thought we were going to be there a few months. . . . It was going to be six months. And, I mean, is it worth killing somebody for that? . . .

LK: Were you moved around a lot?

TA: A lot. A lot.

LK: Yes? Did you ever get deeply into the Stockholm syndrome, of totally supporting their cause?

TA: I never got anywhere near the Stockholm syndrome. I don't agree with these people at all. I don't even like them very much.

LK: So it never happened to you? Because we keep hearing that the captor becomes—

TA: No. No. I don't know where that came from. I was asked that very early, and I've been asked it several times. Some of these guys were not terribly bad guys, except for what they were doing. They didn't seem bad. That was one of the confusing things. You know, when you talk to someone who's doing what you know to be an evil thing and he doesn't seem to be an evil man, it gets very confusing.

LK: Like Hitler petted his dog. . . . I'm sure there are people who had evenings with Mussolini and said he was a terrific guy.

TA: Yes. But I don't sympathize with these people. I don't agree with them. I think what they did was terribly wrong. And I didn't like most of them.

LK: Indianapolis, for Terry Anderson. Hello.

CALLER: [*Indianapolis, Indiana*] Terry, I just want to tell you what a powerful influence for good you have been in my life. I was diagnosed as being in the last stages of exhaustion just before you were released from captivity. Listening to your story helped me stay on track. When I would ask God for a quick recovery, I'd remember, "Terry had seven years. I've only had three." Last Tuesday, my doctor told me he was proud of me. I'd made it back without medications and in great time. I feel I owe it all to you and the example of your courage and belief. I thank you more than words can say.

LK: Whew!

TA: Well, God bless you, ma'am. I'm very happy to hear that you're getting better. I'm very pleased. I feel very proud if I've helped you in any way, but you don't find that kind of strength from me. You find it from yourself and from God.

LK: Northfield, Vermont, with Terry Anderson. Hello.

CALLER: [*Northfield, Vermont*] Hi, Terry. Welcome home. Those of us in the beautiful green mountain state of Vermont are very proud of you. Terry, during your captivity, were you ever in touch with, or did you know anything about, any of the non-American hostages, like Terry Waite or any of them? Had you communicated with any of them at all?

TA: Yes. I spent a year in very close contact with Terry Waite—in the same room, chained to the same wall—also, with John McCarthy. And I spent some months with Brian Keenan, the Irish captive. All fine men, by the way.

LK: You would sit chained—one arm chained to a wall?

TA: One arm or one leg, yes.

LK: Okay, and you'd sit? And he'd be chained to a wall over there?

TA: Right, there were four of us in the room at that time.

LK: And they just chained you? And they'd come in, give you food—

TA: Uh-huh.

LK: Exercise?

TA: We were supposed to get exercise, but we rarely got it.

LK: You just sat there and talked all day?

TA: Talked; we played cards or chess. I taught John McCarthy—well, I taught several people how to play chess. John turned out to be very good at it, you know. In about two months—he'd never played before—he was matching me pawn-for-pawn and giving me a hell of a game, and I was quite enjoying it.

LK: When they were all gone—how many days were you there before you got out—the last one left?

TA: Was it eleven or fourteen? Something like that.

LK: Loneliness—big thing, loneliness.

TA: Well, I'll tell you. I knew I was getting out. And after that long being in those close quarters with men—even though I may have liked them—it was a bit of a relief to be by myself. [*laughs*]

LK: [*laughs*] We'll be back with Terry Anderson. By the way, he is writing a book. It'll be out in 1993. Crown will be the publisher. There are film offers. You recently— is it true?—got $245,000—$100 for each day held.

TA: From the Freedom Forum, yes.

LK: From the Freedom Forum. You were named a Columbia University fellow at the media studies center, effective June fifteenth. Are you going to teach?

TA: No, I'm not going to teach. I'm going to write and do some seminars. They're nice people. They're giving me a fellowship and not making me do anything for it. [*laughs*]

LK: We'll be right back with Terry Anderson. That's the journalist's ultimate wish. [*laughs*] Don't go away.

[*Commercial break*]

LK: New York City, with Terry Anderson. Hello.

CALLER: [*New York, New York*] Hello, Mr. Anderson. We want to say that we were all very happy when you returned. I wanted to ask you whether you think it's at all possible that, during your long imprisonment, the Lebanese government, such as it was, or the Syrian government, or the PLO, did not know where you were.

TA: Difficult question. I don't know what other people knew. We were prisoners. Okay? Our guards did not discuss these kinds of things with us, and the situation in Lebanon changed over the years. I don't think it's a good idea for me to try to say who was responsible or who knew where we were and who didn't.

LK: Did you think about rescue attempts?

TA: Sure. Sure. There were times when we fantasized. We dreamed of Delta Force coming through the wall, guns blazing. In actuality—and I think we all agreed— it would have been a bad idea.

LK: Why?

TA: Well, first, because they were more or less ready most of the time. There were drills, and there were alarms when they thought they heard something, when the door would be flung open, and there'd be a guard with a grenade in his hand or a machine gun ready. They had orders to kill us if anybody came in. In fact, at one point they told us the building was wired with explosives—which it may well have been. I don't know. There was also the problem that there were a lot of hostages there, and we weren't all in the same place. If there are a dozen hostages and you rescue six, what happens to the other six? Are you going to run four different raids at the same time and hope all of them will be a success? It was a very difficult idea, and I think the administration waited and abandoned it.

LK: Do you ever get used to it?

TA: Used to what—being a hostage?

LK: Yes.

TA: Yes, you do in a way. . . . You learn how to do time—one minute, one hour at a time—and you don't think about the painful things, and you don't think too much about getting out, and you don't think too much about—oh, about the really emotional things, if you can. You try to just float through the days. That's hard, and it doesn't last very long. You do chunks of it. And if you can do it for a week, you're happy. And then you fall off the tightrope, and it gets very painful again.

LK: Do you lose all concept of days, months? Do you lose that, or do you always know pretty much?

TA: We always knew what time it was. Tom Sutherland, of course, was a fanatic about it. [*laughs*] He had to know what the date was, and he always kept reminding me, you know, "It's been 1,200-and-umpty days." And I'd say, "Tom, don't tell me. I don't want to know. . . ."

LK: Were there ever laughs in captivity?

TA: Absolutely. We laughed a lot. And that may sound strange, but we did. John, as I say, is funny. He does imitations of the guards that used to freak us out and send us rolling in stitches. Tom Sutherland does—used to do long scatological songs—[*laughs*]—and great, better, reams of Robert Burns. Tom is from Scotland originally, and he still can do a fantastic Scottish accent. Brian Keenan—the Irishman—was into shaggy-dog stories. He could go for an hour and a half and never get to the point, you know? You'd want to strangle him before you laughed. [*laughs*]

LK: [*laughs*] I guess, even though you're in captivity, you still want the story to end, yes? And Terry Waite, of course—he was—what?—6' 7", right?

TA: Six feet, seven inches, and I guess he was about 280, or something like that, when he came in—although he got skinny. He was very ill for several months after he joined us.

LK: He was CIA-involved, wasn't he—Waite?

TA: Why do you say that?

LK: That's the stories we hear. Did he ever talk—

TA: I don't—Larry, I don't think that's accurate, and I don't think it's fair.

LK: Okay. It's just stories we hear. I'm just telling you that was the— We had assumed here— There were stories here that he was involved.

TA: As I understand it, he met with Ollie North. Ollie North was a designated American representative to deal with hostage problems. To accuse Terry Waite of being involved with the CIA—

LK: I'm not accusing him. It may not be an accusation. They're an American organization.

TA: Well, no, we didn't talk about it much. He talked about a few of the things he did. I think Terry Waite's an honorable man. He's a churchman, and I don't—

LK: And a brave man.

TA: And a very, very brave man—much braver than I am. I don't think I would have done the things he did. And you know, after we managed to get him moved in with us— He was in solitary for three and a half years. They kept him in solitary confinement with no radio, no news—nothing. And then we finally persuaded—

We knew he was next door to us. We finally persuaded them to put him in with us, and he was with us for a year, and I never heard him express a word of regret or bitterness about having taken those chances and having been kidnapped.

LK: Because he came to try to get you out.

TA: And he came to try to get us out. He's a very, very brave man.

LK: We'll be back with more of Terry Anderson on *Larry King Live*. Don't go away.

[Commercial break]

LK: I said to Terry, he's been away—fax machines. Suddenly, everybody's got a fax machine.

TA: Everybody's got a fax machine. Everybody's got an answering machine—which really bugs me, because I call somebody, and they're not there. You've got to talk to the machine. You pay for the call anyway, you know. And the telephones themselves are too complicated for me.

LK: Have you operated a fax machine?

TA: No, never in my life.

LK: Neither have I, and I've been *here*. *[Anderson laughs]* Alexandria, Virginia. Hello.

CALLER: *[Alexandria, Virginia]* Hi. My question to Terry is, while you were in captivity, were you actually personally ever taped head-to-toe and transported from place to place in wheel wells of trucks or other vehicles?

TA: Yes, a number of times. I was moved about twenty times, and the majority of them were done in just exactly that manner. . . .

LK: Whew! Houston, Texas, hello.

CALLER: *[Houston, Texas]* Terry, from one Terry to another, welcome back. My questions is, last year we had the war against Iraq, and I know you were in captivity last year, but now that you're back, what's your opinion of that entire affair?

TA: Oh, boy. Well, I followed it on the radio and what little television we had then. We did have a radio all the time. I think I agree with most Americans. It was a necessary war. I don't know enough about it to say whether it was prosecuted properly or not. We seemed to win it fairly handily, and it's a little disconcerting to see Mr. Hussein still in charge—Saddam Hussein still in charge there. But I'm afraid I'm not an expert on that particular area. That's a little way away from me.

LK: Kingston, New York. Hello.

CALLER: *[Kingston, New York]* Terry, when you were first released, you said that your faith required you to forgive your captors, and I admired you for that. It seems it's been so easy for you to forgive when so many people would be angry. How have you been able to heal so easily?

TA: I wouldn't say it's been easy, ma'am. Forgiving is not something you do and then walk away and say, "I've done it." It is a process that you have to go through every day, every time you think about it, and every time you pray. I'll probably be doing it for the rest of my life. If there has been any easy healing—and I must say, you know, the recovery has been a lot faster than I thought it would, and coping with the problems has been easier than it might have been—it's because of the support I've had; because of the AP, my colleagues, my family, and certainly, my lady, and just the love and care that's surrounded me.

LK: Are you surprised that we still have major racial problems?

TA: When you ask it that way, I have to say no. I mean, racial problems in the United States have been something that have been around for a long time, and probably will. I was surprised at the Los Angeles riots and—

LK: The verdict?

TA: Well, like most of us, I didn't pay enough attention to realize that the same kind of problems that were there in the 1960s remain, and nobody's done anything about them. And that's a shame. We should be ashamed of that. . . .

[*Commercial break*]

LK: We're practically out of time. Are you optimistic or pessimistic about peace in that area?

TA: I'm optimistic and cautious. I mean, two things: Lebanon—they seem to have grown tired of fighting each other, and seem to be at least moving toward something that might be a real country. In the Middle East, at least they're talking with each other. I mean, that's new.

LK: We're about out of time. Is there anything you'd like to say?

TA: Thanks to everybody. There are an awful lot of people out there who cared about me and the other hostages, who did an awful lot, who prayed for us, mostly—I mean, how can God ignore all those prayers? And I just have to say, thank you very much.

Arthur Ashe

Arthur Robert Ashe grew up where he was born on July 10, 1943, in Richmond, Virginia, next door to the Brookfield Park public tennis courts. He began practicing when he was seven and later attended UCLA on a tennis scholarship. At the age of twenty-five, he became the first African American to win a major tournament: the 1968 U.S. National Amateur singles. The next year, Ashe won the U.S. Open and became a member of the U.S. Davis Cup team—another first for an African American. In 1969 he turned professional, only to have his tennis career ended in July 1979 by a heart attack. In 1988, he discovered that he had contracted AIDS from tainted blood used in the 1979 triple by-pass surgery. Within days of publicly announcing his medical condition, Ashe appeared on Larry King Live *in this landmark interview. He died on February 5, 1993.*

"I know that my odds of, say, being here in five years are not very good. That's just a fact of life. Those are just the numbers."

LARRY KING: Whether he wanted the job or not, Arthur Ashe has always been a role model. In the '60s and '70s, he electrified the tennis world by winning the U.S. Open, then Wimbledon—the first black to do so. He shattered the color barrier and opened doors for new generations of black athletes. Throughout his tennis career and long after, he has spoken out for political causes, racial justice—from his own efforts in the sports world, to attacking apartheid in South Africa. But in April, he unwillingly announced to the world that he had AIDS, contracted from a blood transfusion during heart surgery in 1983. He has spoken against the media for invading his privacy and forcing him to go public, but he's rising to this as he did with all earlier challenges, fighting his own illness and helping to educate others. And, once again, Arthur Ashe is a role model. Arthur Ashe just got in from Albany. I thank you very much. What was going on in Albany?

ARTHUR ASHE: Well, we're up there asking the mayor to help us with a public park sports program, tennis program, and we think we'll do very well this summer. It's our third summer coming up.

LK: Your activism has not ceased?

AA: No. These are some things that I've been involved with for a long time. This is a continuation of a project I've been involved with, and our lead project in this vein is in Newark, New Jersey.

LK: We all wonder, Arthur. We've talked about this when there was heart surgery and the time—

AA: Right. Sure.

LK: I remember you making a speech.

AA: Yes.

LK: Because we both had bypass surgery.

AA: Yes.

LK: So we know what it's like to think this. What is it like—we can only imagine, and you've had it—to be told something so earth-shaking?

AA: My wife and I were talking about that moment back in September of '88. My neurologist at New York Hospital suspected, after looking at scans, brain scans, that it might be toxoplasmosis, which at the time was developing a reputation as a marker for AIDS. So they thought I might have AIDS even before the brain surgery.

LK: So you had brain surgery for a tumor?

AA: Well, there was this abnormality on the CAT scan. It looked, even to me as a layman, real serious. [*laughs*]

LK: And they told you you might have AIDS?

AA: Yes. The neurosurgeon said, "Look, I mean, we've got two choices. One is, we can wait to see what happens next—" and my hand had gone dead "—or we can go in there now and see what's there and biopsy a piece of whatever it is and then go from there." And I elected to be a bit more active about it, so we had the surgery. And then it was toxoplasmosis, so that sort of confirmed the AIDS diagnosis.

LK: All right, can you remember what your thoughts were? You're facing brain surgery, which is, in and of itself, no walk around the block. And then, you're also thinking about what you might hear when you wake up, if you wake up.

AA: That's true. I thought I would wake up. It wasn't so much that that I was concerned about. Heart surgery, I think, would be a bit more daunting than brain surgery. And brain surgery doesn't hurt. You know, you hurt the inside of your brain, you don't really feel it unless it's pressing against the cranium, or whatever. But anyway, back to your question—

LK: You wake up.

AA: You wake up, and there was a time when Thera, my wife— Doctors were confirming what we had suspected.

LK: How did they say this? Were you in your hospital bed?

AA: Yes. Yes. "It's confirmed. You have AIDS." But later on, they thought it may not have really sunk in with me, because I had just, obviously, come out of brain surgery. I think it was a day later. And, as if to have no doubt at all about it, about a month ago, my wife and a friend came by just to make sure that I knew, because they thought maybe I thought I was HIV-positive or had ARC—not quite full-blown AIDS. But toxoplasmosis is a marker for AIDS.

LK: Did you know what they had said?

AA: Yes.

LK: Were they wrong? Did you know all along?

AA: No. No. No. I really didn't think that I had full-blown AIDS. I certainly wasn't sick. Didn't feel sick.

LK: Didn't feel sick. What about anger, Arthur? In other words, it's one thing to— The only comparison we could make is someone telling someone who has never smoked a cigarette—

AA: That you have lung cancer?

LK: "You have lung cancer."

AA: [*laughs*] Yes.

LK: Now, you have never had a homosexual act and never taken intravenous drugs. You had a transfusion in '83 before they started testing. So this is a total freak accident. What do you do with the anger?

AA: I really wasn't angry. It sounds crazy, but I really wasn't. And I think that even my wife would tell anyone honestly that I wasn't angry.

LK: What were you?

AA: I was disappointed. I was frustrated. But I think I, a long time ago, learned—probably too well—to control anger. You learn in some ways, growing up in Virginia as a black person, that you have to control your anger or else you will, you know, find yourself in dire circumstances if you don't, in the 1950s. Later on, as a tennis player I was literally taught early on by my tennis coach to, "Control your anger on the court. It would be in your interest—" *my* interest "—to do." And so I guess I developed an ability to adjust to tricky situations rather quickly. And I thought, "Well, so I'm in this situation." I didn't want to view it as a tragedy. Crisis, yes; tragedy, no.

LK: Meaning, then, that, if it's crisis and not tragedy, then you have hope?

AA: There's always hope. Yes, there's always hope.

LK: Based on?

AA: Based on just my personal experience with heart disease. I had a heart attack in '79. I had two heart bypass surgeries. But the advancements and the improvements in the treatment of heart disease, just since 1979, have been astounding. And it always amazes me that the national death rate from heart disease has only come down about a half a percentage point with all those improvements. But still, as far as I'm concerned, there have been a lot of improvements.

LK: So you're in crisis, and there could be an improvement in AIDS or a cure.

AA: Yes. Yes, there even have been some improvements since I found out I had AIDS in the fall of '88. They've come up with some medicines that are just as good, they say, as AZT—not nearly as toxic. Certainly, in the area of research they are able to eliminate some avenues of possible breakthroughs, based on past experience. Certainly, a lot of AIDS activists, especially in the gay community and especially here in New York and in San Francisco, have made it possible to speed up the FDA approval of some drugs. I'm not sure whether that's correct or not, because I would like to know that, if there is some prescription drug out there which is supposed to do what it says it's going to do, that it has been proven in clinical trials to do what it says it's going to do.

LK: You don't want to be a guinea pig?

AA: You don't want to be a guinea pig unless you don't have any other choice, yes.

LK: Are you taking a lot of medication?

AA: I take a lot of medication for my AIDS condition and for my heart disease. I take a *lot* of medication—and then you add both those sets of medicines to vitamins that I take.

LK: And none of these are counter-indicatory?

AA: I don't think so; at least, no one has told me, no.

LK: Concerning anger, I remember our first time we were together was 1968 in Miami, at Channel Four. You were in your lieutenant's uniform. You played for and represented the United States Army. It was "Lieutenant Ashe," and I remember then you said that if an opponent was crazy and wanted to win and banged on the— Give him the match.

AA: That's right.

LK: "If you want to win that much, forget it, Charlie."

AA: Yes.

LK: So you have always kept this kind of cool attitude. Has it now become part of you, or is it an attitude?

AA: No, it is part of me. And sometimes I think it's healthy, and sometimes I think it's not. I don't know to what extent my ability to adjust or to control the anger may have contributed or not to my heart condition. Most people say that—

LK: You mean holding it in?

AA: Oh, sure. If you internalize anger to a great extent, I think there are a lot of studies to show that, you know, you're leaving yourself open for all sorts of maladies.

LK: How old are you now, Arthur?

AA: How old am I? Almost forty-nine. [*laughs*]

[*Commercial break*]

LK: I mentioned earlier that Arthur, when he first learned of this, had not had a homosexual relationship, had not taken intravenous drugs, and had also not had unprotected heterosexual relationships outside of marriage, right? So you knew it was the transfusion?

AA: Yes.

LK: Because you can get it heterosexually, as well.

AA: Yes. We're almost convinced that it was just after my 1983 bypass surgery.

LK: And you never thought anything then, that something could go wrong?

AA: No, not immediately. But we did start to see some things right after that about tainted blood transfusions. But you didn't think too much of it. Of course, then, I think in the spring of '85 was when all blood donated was tested for HIV.

LK: All right, so you've known you've had this four years?

AA: Almost four years.

LK: Are you a little surprised you feel good?

AA: Yes, I am, because, as I've recounted earlier, I remember reading the October '88 issue of *Scientific American*. The entire issue was devoted to AIDS or what medical science knew about AIDS at the time. And there are a couple of things that hit me. One—very quickly—the chances were about nine out of ten that three years after diagnosis you wouldn't be here. And secondly, there was a sentence in one of the articles that said, "Almost invariably, once you are infected with the HIV virus, it will lead to death." And that was—obviously, you sit up and take notice when you read that.

LK: And you feel how?

AA: Now?

LK: Right now.

AA: I had a rough night last night, but—

LK: And "a rough night" is what?

AA: Diarrhea, basically. I may have to get up two or three times.

LK: Have you had pain?

AA: No, no, no, never had any pain.

LK: Do you get tired easy?

AA: Yes, but, you know, up till now it's never lasted very long. But for most people with AIDS, there's no question that diarrhea and a malady called thrush—which is basically a yeast infection in the mouth and maybe some other bodily openings—may be a problem. But you can control those things.

LK: Knowing you, Arthur, you've learned about everything. Have you done this?

AA: Oh, yes. Oh, yes.

LK: Have you gone to see AIDS patients?

AA: I have had some come up to me. I had one come up to me on the street the other day and just— He was freaking out, he told me. His wife has AIDS, his son has AIDS, and his mother didn't want to have anything to do with it—his *mother*. This is a young man, a Hispanic gentleman, on the Upper West Side of New York.

LK: Do you notice any people not—like, afraid to touch?

AA: No.

LK: Has that happened to you yet?

AA: No. No. That was one of the things that I was genuinely worried about, and I have found out that, thank goodness, at least from my standpoint, that has not happened. In fact, I would say it's the other way around. Today in Albany, I mean, the kids couldn't have been nicer. They came up and they wanted autographs, and they were touching me. One lady wanted to kiss me. It was— That makes you feel pretty good.

LK: How's your wife handling all this?

AA: My wife is—is terrific. Yes, I mean, I just literally could not have gone through this without her. I mean, just— I couldn't have done it.

LK: Does your daughter comprehend it?

AA: She knows daddy has AIDS. She doesn't know too much more about it. And, thank goodness in a way, she's at an age where she's always under adult supervision, and so I don't worry about anybody coming in saying things that, really, she shouldn't be hearing at this age. . . .

[*Commercial break*]

LK: Okay, almost four years. How did we not know about this? How did this— Because you told friends.

AA: Yes, I told a small coterie of friends and family. Some of them were journalists. I just—I guess I had this human nature problem of trying to lay off some of this burden on some people that I figured could help me carry it.

LK: And nobody leaked it?

AA: Nobody leaked it.

LK: Did you ever run into anyone who said to you, "There are rumors about you, Arthur"?

AA: Oh, I heard that a lot, yes. I heard that a lot, and I always chuckled. I had people, friends from various parts of the country—California, New York, Florida, Cincinnati—say, "You know, the people have strong rumors that you've got AIDS." I'd say, "That's interesting," and I let it go at that.

LK: When the call came from *USA Today*, then, you were not shocked?

AA: Well, I actually made the call.

LK: Oh, you had heard they had—

AA: Yes, well, I was talking— My good friend Doug Smith, whom I've known since high school—we're both from Virginia—is a tennis writer for *USA Today*, and he came up a few days after they got the tip to talk to me about this. And I could tell halfway into his explanation he, himself, was very physically distressed. I mean, he was extremely uncomfortable. And I could just tell after a while that, you know, he had been sort of holding this in for a couple of days. But anyway, I asked if I could talk to his boss. And so I made the call to his boss, and then we jockeyed back and forth over the phone.

LK: Now, did they give you a day?

AA: No, no.

LK: They ran it the next day?

AA: No, they did not run it. I thought they were going to do so. Gene Polichinski—

LK: Sports editor.

AA: —right—told me on the phone that they had a policy of not going with anything like this that was under the category of rumors unless they could get a positive confirmation from a credible source. And I was neutral at best. I was, basically, trying to tread water.

LK: Yes. But you knew it was going to break?

AA: Yes. That is really what I meant when I said I felt forced to go public with it, because the rumors now are just so strong that it's just a matter of time before some publication puts it out there. And again, my wife and I had three plans that we thought might eventuate in a situation like this. The best situation for us—plan A—was to make the announcement when we wanted to make it. Secondly, was to be able to make it as we did in this case, even if we were forced to make it. We are doing it unilaterally. Thirdly, is to read it in the paper and have to react to it. We did not want that alternative, obviously.

LK: If you were the editor of a paper, is this a story?

AA: Oh, it's a story, but I wouldn't print it. It's certainly a story, but you—

LK: Explain that. That's like a contradiction. It's a story, but you—

AA: No, no, no, there are lots of stories out there—

LK: But they're none of our business?

AA: Right. Yes.

LK: In other words, it's a story. Sure, it's a story—

AA: Oh, no question—

LK: Once it's out, it's a story.

AA: No question, it's a story. No question. I agree.

LK: But it's not our business.

AA: It's not your business. In fact, as I have also said before, if part of their rationale for saying, "This is newsworthy, and you're a public figure, and you might even enhance the public's understanding of AIDS"—that would only happen, even in this situation, if I cooperated. Gene Polichinski may have said, "Well, we're going to run it anyway." I said, "All right, maybe they run it." I'm not now picking on him. "Maybe they'll run it." Now, I can then just clam up. And you can even call my doctor at New York Hospital, and if I tell my doctor, "I don't want you to release any information," professionally, he's got to keep his mouth shut. So only if I cooperate and come forth and do what I'm doing now would the public be more enlightened.

LK: So you decided to do that?

AA: Yes. We were going to do it anyway. But, obviously, I just strenuously objected to being forced to do it just to satisfy the public's need for titillation.

LK: Do you think you can help?

AA: Oh, yes. There's no question I can help. And I knew that all along, yes.

LK: By awareness? Talking? Will you be talking—

AA: Certainly, yes. The public was certainly waiting—and I'm not saying with baited breath or on edge—but the public was certainly waiting for the first heterosexual HIV-positive individual to come forth, without that person being on his or her death bed. Magic Johnson did that.

LK: Right.

AA: Yes. November of last year. Here's a heterosexual. Forget how he got it now. He's heterosexual, so he's like the "rest of us"—supposedly.

LK: Now, when he came forth, did you say, "Now maybe I will?"

AA: No. No.

LK: What did you think when he did?

AA: Well, first of all, he was also forced to come forth with this.

LK: He had an insurance exam.

AA: Yes, and a Magic Johnson can't now be in a position of having to resign from the L.A. Lakers and not explain it. So he did it.

LK: But did you think, "Well, now he's done it, maybe I will?"

AA: No, I was— No. We still—when I say "we," I mean my wife and I—still were going to decide with our doctors when we thought the best time to do that was. But certainly, my wife and I looked very, very closely at his press announcement out in Los Angeles—very closely.

LK: You were watching differently than the rest of us.

[*Commercial break*]

LK: One other thing. You mentioned, and I think you mentioned earlier here, being black was more difficult than having AIDS.

AA: I meant being black and having to maneuver through society as a black person. I don't mean actually being black. I mean—

LK: Being black in society?

AA: Yes, yes, in our society. It's very draining. It's very energy-sapping. It's enervating.

LK: When you saw Los Angeles, when you see the anger—

AA: You know, L.A. was—with some of the friends that I've been talking to— entirely predictable. I knew some people—like Dr. Maulona Karenga predicted it would happen, and that's exactly what happened. You know, the people have become so disaffected, so unconnected, feeling so alienated from the rest of society. In fact, Dr. Karenga tried to correct the semantic description of what happened. He said it wasn't a riot; it was a revolt. And the two are quite different.

LK: And they were doing what Arthur Ashe all his life has not done.

AA: What's that?

LK: Expressing anger.

AA: Oh, yes, yes. But also, in this country, a lot of special-interest groups now believe that the only way, really, to get any action out of federal, state, or local government is to be as loud and as boisterous as possible. No justice, no peace.

LK: Let's go to calls for Arthur Ashe. Wichita, Kansas, hello.

CALLER: [*Wichita, Kansas*] Thank you for what you're doing. Mr. Ashe, what can a person such as myself do to protect myself from a situation that's happened such as yours?

AA: Well, abstinence is certainly the first line of defense. I don't think anybody would argue with that. And if you're HIV-positive, well, certainly, you have got to protect yourself and your sexual partners, no matter what. If you are not HIV-positive, and you're worried about it, I would seriously advise you to be tested, because finding out you are HIV-positive is not the end of the world, even if you are.

LK: Port Washington, New York, for Arthur Ashe. Hello.

CALLER: [*Port Washington, New York*] Hi, Mr. Ashe. I'm twenty-two years old, I'm gay, and I'm HIV-positive. And I have a couple of questions. I have one really good question for you, actually. The question is: Do you feel like a victim, being that you got it from a blood transfusion, rather than having contracted it as a sexually transmitted disease? I mean, society would view you more as a victim; whereas they would view me more as, like, "criminal" for having gotten this through an illicit sexual act.

LK: "You brought it on yourself," they would say.

AA: Yes, right.

LK: Arthur, is there any difference between you and him?

AA: Yes, there's no question that there is. I started reading about the "good" ways and the "bad" ways of contracting the HIV virus. A "good" way was the way that Ryan White got it—a hemophiliac—or myself. A "bad" way, obviously, was if you're an IV-drug user, you're a homosexual, or even as Magic Johnson said he was: It was promiscuity that did it. But to answer your question, yes, I do feel like a victim. But, as you were asking me earlier about being black and living in America, what I don't want to do is to wallow in my victimization. I don't want to use that as a crutch for inactivity. Yes, I'm a victim, but I'm going to move on, and I'm not going to dwell on it.

LK: New York City for Arthur Ashe. Hello.

CALLER: [*New York, New York*] Hi, Larry. Hi, Arthur. Arthur, I'm an admirer of yours. I've had the good fortune of seeing you play a number of times. There's a new study out that says adults are not reaching teenagers, and I deal with teenagers all the time, and they don't really want to listen. How is it possible to reach them? What can we do to save their lives?

AA: Certainly, I think—with a daughter, I think about these things myself now. We need to find more creative ways of connecting and communicating, parents and children. In the minority community, I know rap groups are very, very influential. They are now, as I have seen it, next to parents in influence over children. Disc jockeys are very influential. Athletes—especially—if you're someone like Magic Johnson—are very influential. So if we can get the people that youngsters will really listen to, get them involved, in a very organized way and not just in any one particular avenue or route, with explaining situations like this, I think we can do quite a bit.

And there's also the moral qualms of doing some things. I mean, just this morning in the metropolitan section of *The New York Times*, I was reading that Washington was at odds with Mayor Dinkins in New York and Mayor Kelly in Washington over distributing needles. And I'm thinking, "Hey, wait a minute, now. Do you want to make the problem bigger? If you don't distribute—" Just practically speaking, that makes sense, although I understand the moral qualms about it. But if it is part—in answering this lady's question—of an overall program of trying to wean drug addicts off drugs or trying to get American young-sters to more fully understand sex education and all that's involved with it, well, then, a condom or a needle may not be so bad. It won't be taken in isolation.

LK: When a disease, Arthur, has this kind of image, what is it like? Because you know when you walk into a room—you used to walk into a room and people would look up, "Arthur Ashe, tennis champion." Now, they look up, and you know what they think.

AA: I have mentioned before Susan Sontag's book *Illness as Metaphor*, and she followed up a few years ago with *AIDS as Metaphor*. And cancer and tuberculosis she talked about—that had this sort of stigma. But, obviously, leprosy was certainly one.

LK: People didn't say "cancer" at one time.

AA: That's exactly right. They just wouldn't want to say it. And tuberculosis was even given another name, "consumption."

LK: Yes, that's right. But how does it feel when you go into a room?

AA: Practically speaking, people stare a bit more, as they did up at Albany today. But that's—

LK: Or at airports or—

AA: Yes. Oh, yes, there are a lot more staring. But it's sympathetic staring, and I under-stand it, even though I'm not looking for sympathy or empathy. I want people to learn and to be comprehending and to understand. But, certainly, there is a differ-ent look now, and I appreciate the concern they show. I really do. And thank you.

[*Commercial break*]

LK: The next caller is from Stockholm, Sweden. Hello.

CALLER: [*Stockholm, Sweden*] Yes, good evening, Mr. Ashe. Mr. Ashe, my question is not concerning your great calamity, but it's another—concerning something else. Why don't we have—almost no top black athlete in tennis these days—I mean, excepting Yannick Noah. I know there is racism in tennis because I myself write about tennis. But can you please explain to us, why don't we have any top athletes in tennis these days that are blacks?

AA: Interesting question. I'm asked that quite often. As African Americans, we have done best in those sports that are stressed in the public school systems, because they are free—the big-four team sports: football, basketball, baseball, track. And you throw in boxing, you've got the big five for African Americans in sports. Relatively speaking, it costs a great deal of money to become a Jennifer Cappriati or a John McEnroe. I doubt if Michael Jordan's mother spent more than a thou-sand dollars, total, in getting Michael to the player he is. Shoes—and that's it. So it didn't cost much at all. But then again, the sport of tennis, like a few others, is not exactly very hospitable towards some minorities in some places. I'll give you an example. It's the example I give most of the time. We have a hell of a time try-ing to place black teaching professionals in private clubs—very difficult.

LK: Because the private club doesn't want a black around all day?

AA: Well, you get that opinion. And they've got credentials to hang all over the wall. Yet, when you do walk in a lot of private clubs, you see a lot of foreigners who have never taken a USPTA course, have never taken a USPTR course, never gotten a degree in tennis management from a university, but they have a foreign accent and—

LK: You had the break, as I remember it, of a doctor—a doctor in Richmond who liked you, right?

AA: In Lynchburg, Virginia.

LK: Who financed you, right?

AA: Yes. Yes. I spent eight summers with him.

LK: He got you into clubs? He got you playing?

AA: Yes. He sort of took care of everything.

LK: Or you would have not been able to do it?

AA: Oh, no, I would not have been. No, my father was a policeman.

LK: Now, one would think, if tennis were made wholly on a wide circle available in public schools and everywhere, there would be a lot of blacks competing and doing very well.

AA: I was always amazed because, if you look at the group of individuals who supply the great athletes for the popular team sports that we have—in particular, football, basketball, to a lesser extent, baseball and track and field—you're looking at an incredible—

LK: Out of whack with their percentage of the population.

AA: Out of whack, highly motivated, very athletic. My question was always: If you're tennis, why don't you go after them?

LK: It's crazy not to—

AA: It's crazy not to go after them.

LK: Windsor, Connecticut, hello.

CALLER: [*Windsor, Connecticut*] Hello, Arthur. I just wanted to know, being on the board of directors of Aetna Life Insurance Company, how did they, as an insurance company, react? And will you stay on the board?

AA: Yes, I will stay on the board. I've been on the board now for ten years. Several Aetna senior officers knew about my AIDS condition. The former champion— [*laughs*] champion—former *chairman* Jim Lynne, who has now just retired—he knew. The present chairman, Ron Compton, knew, and some other executives there knew. I also was very aware, because I was on the board at the time, when Aetna stopped writing individual health insurance policies for any individual because the risks— Actuaries just told us, "Hey, this is crazy." So now, we only write health policies under group plans.

LK: And if a person has AIDS, they're covered?

AA: Oh, yes. If you're part of a group . . .

LK: You take—what—AZT?

AA: I take AZT, and I take Daraprim Lucovar, and there are brain-seizure medications and some other things.

LK: Heart, brain, AIDS—and you look great. Explain this.

AA: [*laughs*] I take care of myself.

LK: Vitamins?

AA: Vitamins.

LK: That's the answer?

AA: Yes. Yes.

LK: Do you take a lot?

AA: I do take a lot of vitamins, and when you asked me the question about balance and contraindications of crossing groups of medicines, that's a very important consideration. But you must also keep in mind that I was in a sport that was an individual sport that called for a lot of personal self-initiative, a lot of self-discipline, a lot of having to depend upon myself, and so I was able to translate that to dealing with my heart problem. And then, when this came along, for me to develop or to summon the personal self-discipline to do what the doctor says and to go even a little further is much easier for me, because I've been doing it all my life, first as an athlete and then as a heart patient. . . .

LK: Do you take multiples?

AA: I take very specific vitamins now. Interesting, you know a *Time* magazine cover story a few months ago on vitamins— Of course, a lot of people who were vitamin apologists and adherents before are saying, "Hey, it's about time," but there is no question that the evidence now shows that even megadoses of some vitamins may be very good for you—in particular, obviously, vitamin C. . . .

[Commercial break]

LK: I was asking Arthur during the break if there were doctors who were AIDS specialists, and he said, "Yes, doctors who treat nothing but AIDS victims." In fact, his wife's best friend is a female doctor who treats nothing but women with AIDS. But also, there's the reverse side, and you said what about your dentist?

AA: My dentist lost some patients.

LK: Because they knew you were his patient?

AA: They found out later that I was one of his patients, yes. . . .

LK: New York City, hello.

CALLER: [*New York, New York*] Yes, which player was the most satisfying to win off of? And which player did you dislike playing the most, and why?

AA: [*laughs*] Well, I wasn't crazy about playing Rod Laver.

LK: Because he was so good?

AA: I lost to him eighteen times in a row before I finally beat him.

LK: Was he the best you ever played?

AA: Yes. I think he was the best a lot of people ever played. Yes, he was—

LK: He may be the best-best.

AA: Yes. Yes, you wouldn't get too many arguments there. He was right up there.

LK: Columbus, Ohio, hello.

CALLER: [*Columbus, Ohio*] Good evening. Mr. Ashe, I just, first of all, want to say I think you're a fabulous person. I watched your speech at the National Press Club, you know, the other day, and was very impressed, and being that you're one of the more articulate, intelligent people I've ever seen in my life, I think you've got an excellent chance of at least getting a major message across. And I was curious to ask you, what kind of results are you looking for and have you tangibly received from that speech?

AA: I did get a lot of reaction from the speech at the National Press Club and the question-and-answer session afterwards. I am now, in answer to your question about how I can be effective, I've been talking to and have sort of assembled my own think tank of people that I call on: I mentioned my wife's best friend, who's a doctor here at Bellevue, treats nothing but female, and mostly indigent, HIV patients; Dr. Irwin Chin, who is head of UCLA's AIDS Institute; my own doctor here at New York Hospital, Dr. Henry Murray; even Dr. Tony Fauci down at NIH, and Dr. Bill Roper, head of CDC, and some others, who are in clinical trials involved in this. They have all said, if I need to call them and ask them something if I'm coming on a show like this, to get the right information out, please do so. And that really is a big plus for me, to be able to call on them.

LK: There's no other way to ask this, Arthur. Do you think about dying?

AA: I think about dying a lot, yes. I think about it, yes. But I—

LK: And is it frightening?

AA: No, it's not frightening. No.

LK: What is it?

AA: Realistically, I have to face the fact that that is a possibility, and a strong possibility. But, no, I don't think I'm afraid of dying. And you can also get ready for it. . . . I am one who likes to mix hope and optimism with a good dose of reality. I mean, I'm left-brained, so to speak—[*laughs*]—logic. But I know that my odds of, say, being here in five years are not very good. That's just a fact of life. Those are just the numbers. They don't look very good. Yet I think that there may be breakthroughs that will allow me to live longer than I think or, as you were saying earlier, better while I am here.

LK: But do you look at the sky, and is it bluer now? Do flowers smell better?

AA: Yes. One thing I did notice, which I reported in a couple of interviews, was that I felt, for me, uncommonly more creative in the time I found out that I was HIV-positive or had AIDS.

LK: Uncommonly more? You mean like painting or—

AA: No. I like to write, and just making connections with things that maybe previously had been not connected. I have just felt incredibly prolific and creative.

LK: Are you spiritual, Arthur?

AA: Oh, very much so. Very much so.

LK: Do you think you're going to another place?

AA: Yes. Yes. I think, yes. I am— Growing up black in the South, I spent— The church was a very heavy influence on me. No question about it, yes. . . .

[*Commercial break*]

LK: We only have thirty seconds. Anything you'd like to say?

AA: No, other than I think education is the key to understanding and containing the spread of this disease. And I think America is in the forefront of finding a cure and treatment, because the rest of the world—especially in Africa and some other places—certainly doesn't have the resources to do so. So we are the leader in this fight.

LK: Is it going to get worse before it gets better?

AA: From what I read, yes. Yes. They're expecting ten million-plus HIV-positive individuals by the year 2000.

LK: Thanks, Arthur.

AA: Thank you, Larry. Good luck.

LK: Arthur Ashe—what a man.

H. Norman Schwarzkopf was born on August 22, 1934, and graduated from West Point in 1956. He did two tours of duty in Vietnam, earning the Silver Star, a Distinguished Flying Cross, a Purple Heart, and a Bronze Star.

Schwarzkopf was deputy commander of the Grenada invasion (1983) and was made commander in chief of Operations Desert Shield and Desert Storm, the campaign to drive invading Iraqi troops from Kuwait. He retired shortly after the completion of Desert Storm, spurning a flood of commercial offers to devote himself to writing an autobiography, It Doesn't Take a Hero, *the publication of which occasioned this interview.*

"Yes, I hate war. Absolutely, I hate war."

LARRY KING: Tonight, the story of a lifelong soldier, who spent most of his career in the kinds of low-profile jobs that guarantee a man's anonymity. Real soldiers don't mind that—and anyway, as this one happily admits, he is no politician. Then came an assignment to run the United States Central Command and, on August 1, 1990, when Saddam Hussein rolled south into Kuwait, General Norman Schwarzkopf was anonymous no more. . . . And now he gives us a peek inside the command tent, in his account of the Gulf War and his extraordinary life leading up to it. The book is called *It Doesn't Take a Hero.* . . . Did you like writing a book? Did you like all this?

H. NORMAN SCHWARZKOPF: Writing a book is hard work. You know that. But I've got to tell you what: I have a tremendous—I always had a great respect for authors. I've got an enormous amount—greater respect for authors, particularly prolific authors who write these thick books and turn them out one after another after another, because it takes a tremendous amount of self-discipline. I never understood that until I got involved myself.

LK: Was that the most difficult part?

NS: Doing it—making yourself do it every day. Because, you know, there were days when Peter and I—Peter Petre, my cowriter, and I—we would go on three weeks straight, you know, seven days a week, from 8:00 in the morning till 6:00 at night, and then preparing the night before, before you'd start all over again. And there were some mornings when you got up and you just said, you know, "The last thing in the world I want to do today is deal with that book again!"

LK: General, you're used to being in the need-to-know business, and, certainly, we at CNN know that from briefings—"need-to-know." Was it hard to let it out? You're not used to giving out personal things.

NS: Yes. Well, I've got to tell you that that's hard. This is hard. Going on the road and volunteering to promote something that you've done is absolutely the opposite of what the normal tendency is, and that's to work and not worry about promoting or anything like that. So, it was tough.

LK: Was it hard to write about early life?

NS: Yes. Yes, there were some tough decisions that we had to make—that I had to make, as far as what I would include and whether or not I would include— You know, my mother's alcoholism was a very good example, which is something that my sisters and I have dealt with. We have reconciled over it, but it wasn't easy. I mean, it was something that there were really three different opinions between my two sisters and myself as to how that should be handled.

LK: And we know so much more about it today, don't we?

NS: Yes, well, that's why I— You know, in my day and age, when I was a young boy— eight years old, nine years old—it was something you didn't talk about. I mean, my God, you did not tell anyone that you had an alcoholic parent. You just lived with it. And I think the problem in our household was compounded by the fact that it was going on at a time when my dad wasn't there, you know. He was gone for four solid years. So the only parent you had, you know—

LK: And your father was a radio regular—one of the great radio shows of all time— in fact, it was the number-one radio show for a while—*Gangbusters*. . . . [*imitates sound of machine gun*] "The sirens of prison!" And your father interviewed the gangbuster of the week, right?

NS: That's it. That's exactly right. And he was the man that would say, "Now, Sheriff Smith, what happened on the night of so-on-and-so-forth?" And then the sheriff would start to narrate his story, and they would kind of fade into the dramatization.

LK: What made you choose a military life?

NS: You know, my dad graduated from West Point, 1917, April 1917; went to World War I; loved the Army, and always gave all the credit for everything he ever did in his life to West Point. I've got to tell you, the day I was born my father said, "That boy's going to West Point," and that's the only thing I ever heard my entire young life. I think a couple of times, I probably entertained the thought of maybe being a fireman or something like that, but that thought didn't last long. [*laughs*]

LK: Was the Point equal to its credentials?

NS: Absolutely, in every way. . . . It's a great school. It's a great school academically, but, more importantly, it's a great school in teaching you character, the funda- mentals of character, giving you focus for your life. The motto of West Point was "Duty, Honor, Country." Years later, I went to one of these touchie-feelie organizational-effectiveness courses and, after three weeks in the course, we were all supposed to write down our new motto for life. And I sat down and said, "What's my motto?" And I wrote down, "Duty, Honor, Country"—the same motto that I'd been taught years and years before at West Point.

LK: You were also a strong social liberal, right? . . . And still are, I guess, in the area of integration, civil rights.

NS: Absolutely.

LK: You were big on that. You were a JFK fan.

NS: Yes.

LK: Was that true of a lot of your compatriots at the Point?

NS: Some. I wouldn't say a lot. You know, we ran the spectrum there, just like you do any place else. But free thinking is not something that is prohibited in the military. You know, we have a lot of people that think freely and speak their own minds about issues, and care very much about social issues.

LK: Now, where along the line did you decide the type of career in the Army you wanted?

NS: Well, I think that probably happened about my third year at West Point, when I was— You know, I could have gone in the Air Force. I stood high enough in my class that I could have gone into any branch of service that I wanted to, but I decided I wanted to be an infantryman and—

LK: Why?

NS: I don't know. I think maybe it was sort of, "Well, if you're going to be an Army officer, you've got to be a complete Army officer, a total Army officer." But the challenge of leadership was there, and I got a taste of it, and I kind of liked it, and so I decided to go in the infantry.

LK: But that's the grunts, right?

NS: That's it. That's it.

LK: I mean, that's dirt and—

NS: That's the dog-faced soldier, you know. [*laughs*] We had a very famous instructor at West Point who was a tanker and held infantry in great disdain. And he used to say, "Infantry: you walk and think at 2½ miles an hour," is what he said.

LK: Ulysses S. Grant was your hero?

NS: Yes, he was one of them. My dad was my first hero—really was. My dad was my first hero. But Grant was a hero. Sherman was a hero. Certainly, Lee was a man to be admired. But I kind of liked Grant and Sherman because they were sort of muddy-boot soldiers themselves, who had a tough job to do and just went ahead and did the job the best they could.

LK: General Chappie James—the late General Chappie James—the first black four-star general, told me in an interview once that nobody hates war more than warriors. . . . Because they've been there.

NS: Right.

LK: But then there's the thinking of many that generals like it, because peacetime is anathema to what they do.

NS: That's crazy, though.

LK: You hate war?

NS: Yes, I hate war. Absolutely, I hate war. And you know, I am very proud to say that we probably faced down the Warsaw Pact with NATO without ever firing a shot. I mean, you could have a military force, and a military force can accomplish great things without ever having to go to war.

LK: So, you can win without shooting.

NS: Sure, and that's the whole philosophy of a deterrent force. Hey, those of us that have been to war hate it. Those of us that have been to war know that you might have to go to war, but I've got to tell you what: good generalship is a realization that you've got to try and figure out how to accomplish your mission, but you've got to try and figure out how to accomplish your mission with a minimum loss of human life. That's what being a good general is all about.

LK: They used to say that Eisenhower's first concern all the time was, "How many did we lose in this operation? . . ." And it was painful to him to hear any numbers. . . . Was it to you?

NS: Terribly. Terribly, you know. It scared you to death. You don't want to lose any lives. You recognized that life is going to be lost. But I've got to tell you what: most of the generals I know today—one single human life lost is one too many to them. I mean, they care that much. . . .

[*Commercial break*]

LK: Those who say that war was a piece of cake—?

NS: They don't know what the hell they're talking about.

LK: Why not?

NS: [*laughs*] Well, you know, they say it was a piece of cake because of the outcome. First of all, one of the interesting things is the same people that are saying that war was a piece of cake were the ones that, in November, prior to the war starting, were counseling that we shouldn't go in because we were going to take so many casualties and we were going to suffer so much. So it's a question of perspective.

The thing that people forget is that we waged a thirty-eight day air campaign that was specifically designed to break the will of the Iraqi military to fight and to reduce them down to a size where they could be handled readily through a ground offensive. Anybody who knows anything about correlation of forces knows that the attacker is supposed to have about a three-to-one or five-to-one advantage over a defender. You've got to remember, the Iraqis had 635,000 people in the desert, okay, at the beginning of that war, and we had a total of 800,000. That doesn't give you a three-to-one ratio or a five-to-one ratio. So we designed an air campaign to break their will to fight, to cause them to desert, to give them problems psychologically and reduce their strength.

LK: You never wanted a land war, then?

NS: Well, we were hoping— We never wanted a war, period, okay? We never wanted a war. Once the war started, we were hoping that, you know, in the first, initial phases of the air war they'd recognize—they'd come to their senses and stop right then. We continued to pursue peace, continued to ask them to withdraw. After thirty-eight days, we got to a point where we could launch the ground war, and, by that time, they hadn't withdrawn.

LK: The day it started, can you tell me the moments leading up to it starting, who you were talking to? Were you talking to President Bush? Were you talking to Colin Powell? How does it work?

NS: No. The moments right before—about twenty-four hours before it started, we weren't talking to anybody because by that time— I described it one time as like standing at a crap table, and you throw the dice in the air. Once the dice are in the air, they're going to land, and then it's only a question of how they land.

LK: But that would be twenty-four hours to land?

NS: Sure. You see, we had to start planes flying from very, very distant locations, heading out there long, long before H-Hour. So we had to have a decision forty-eight hours in advance in order for us to get the wheels rolling. So forty-eight hours prior to the launching of the war—the start of the war—was when we had the decision: "Okay, it's a go." And that became D-Day. We knew what H-Hour was. H-Hour was going to be, you know, 3:00 A.M. over Baghdad—twenty minutes to 3:00 in the morning, local time, back there. So, once we had the go-ahead, of course, we continued to communicate—Colin Powell, predominantly, with me. We continued to communicate, and we stayed in touch, and we always had the capability— See, we kept the capability to call it off right down to the very last minute. You know, "Okay, we're on a countdown to war, but—"

LK: It was a fail-safe?

NS: Sure. You want to make sure you can stop.

LK: How autonomous were you? How does it work—you, and the head of the Joint Chiefs, and the president—when you're running a war?

NS: Well, the way it worked was the way it *should* work, okay? And that is: I had my mission. I formulated the plan. I, of course, briefed everybody in great detail on the plan. They approved the plan. Then, they left the execution of the plan to me and my subordinate commanders.

LK: And then, do you talk only to Powell?

NS: I talked to Powell 99 and 44/100ths percent of the time. He is the person that is the interface between the military and the civilian world in Washington.

LK: How good an officer is he?

NS: On a scale of one to ten?

LK: Yes.

NS: I've said it before: ten.

LK: He's a ten. Kelly said the same thing. Why?

NS: Well, Colin Powell is the most effective general officer we've had in Washington, D.C., since George Marshall. You remember, George Marshall was someone that President Roosevelt depended upon completely for his military advice and judgment.

LK: And made Eisenhower the commander over thirty-nine people.

NS: Yes. But it was because Marshall had the confidence of the civilian leadership that he was able to get things done. Colin was the same way. Having been National Security Adviser in the White House before, he was part of the inner decision-making circle in the White House and, therefore, he could get answers for me in a matter of hours that would have taken anybody else days to do.

LK: The argument now is that we should have stayed longer: we came home two days too soon—wrong?

NS: I don't believe that. First of all, that thing got completely blown out of proportion. The question was whether we stopped at 9:00 in the morning, as we eventually did, or stopped at midnight that evening. We're literally talking about a half a day's difference.

LK: We were never going to go into Baghdad?

NS: Never. People ought to go back and look at the battle maps. We never went into a single city—by design. Because once you get into a city, you can't sort out the civilians from the military, the good guys from the bad guys. We didn't want to kill a lot of civilians. We deliberately avoided it. So we didn't go in any cities. . . .

[*Commercial break*]

LK: All right, now, you're not wearing the bars tonight, and you don't have to talk under any kind of cloak of protecting any army official. The war is over. What was wrong with the media? What got you mad?

NS: Nothing was wrong with the media. As a matter of fact, I take a lot of pride in the fact that— You've got to remember, before the war was started, there were zero foreign correspondents in Riyadh. We put together the first press pool. The first press pool went over there. They'd been over there about thirty days, and the Saudis said, "Thank you very much. Send them all back home again." And I was one of the guys that argued that, "Hey, you can't do that. You're not going to walk that cat back," you know. And I protected the media's right to be there, because I very much believe in the American public's right to know, and I believe in the First Amendment and the media doing what they want to do.

LK: How controlled were we? . . . In other words, the media.

NS: See, to my mind, they were not controlled. The word "control" bothers me. Statistics. Okay? The problem is a management problem. At the height of the Tet offensive in Vietnam, we had a total of eighty reporters in Vietnam. In the Gulf War, we had 2,060, I think is the latest, you know. So, you had a huge number of people over there. In Vietnam, when somebody reported what they saw on a bat-tlefield, they generally made it on the television screens or out in the papers thirty-six to forty-eight hours later. In the Gulf War, it was instantaneously broad-cast around the whole world and right into the enemy headquarters.

LK: Right here, from this network.

NS: Sure. And so, what I am saying is we have to figure out how you handle that sit-uation, because people— You know, it's nothing against the media, but they don't know many times when they're giving information that would be very helpful to the enemy.

LK: So, then, you have to control facets, is what you're saying?

NS: I think you have to.

LK: Especially when it's being seen everywhere. . . . All right, so Vietnam was a more openly covered war, wasn't it? I mean, those people who covered—

NS: I don't know. I don't know whether it was or not, because we had pools out there [during the Gulf War] in the field, and the pools were roughly—you know, added up to about two hundred people. The problem was, you had two hundred happy people who were out in the field, and you had 1,800 unhappy people that were kept back in the rear. There were rules that were applied to the pools, and there were public affairs people who accompanied the pools to try and get them to adhere to the rules. Those rules were the ones that had been agreed upon after the Grenada war, because of all the flack about the press not being able to cover during Grenada.

LK: Yes. Was Peter Arnett a hindrance to you?

NS: Yes and no. Okay? I've got to tell you, there were times when—you know, there were times when I saw the Iraqis leading Peter around. And by the way, I know Peter, and I consider him a good friend from the Vietnam days. But there were times when I saw the Iraqis leading Peter around, saying, "The Americans say they're trying not to damage civilian places. That's a lie. The Americans are dam-aging civilian places. And look-it here, here's all this bombing that took place, and this civilian place was destroyed. Therefore, obviously, Americans are lying." And that's, you know, coming right out over CNN, while we're trying to knock our-selves out to continue—and risking our pilots' lives—to avoid civilian damage. When you're looking at a building, you don't know whether it's an American bomb that destroyed that building or all this stuff that they're shooting up in the air at you that turns around and comes back down when it doesn't hit anything, and lands on their own places. When they were suppressing the Shi'ites, they fired at random into civilian areas and destroyed all sorts of stuff and then later tried to blame it on us.

LK: All right, that's the "Yes," where he was bad. What's the "No," where he was good?

NS: Well, you know, what he was doing was he was keeping the American public informed, and that's something that needs to be done. It's important in molding public opinion.

LK: All right. So, if you were running CNN, you'd have had Peter Arnett in Baghdad reporting, wouldn't you?

NS: No, I don't think I would have. I think I would have had—what I probably would have done was Peter Arnett would have been in Baghdad during the initial phase, just as he was when all the reporters were kicked out. And then, the Iraqis came back in and said, "Okay, we will only let you in if you abide by our rules." I would have told them to go suck an egg, because I don't know of anybody else that the media says, "Okay, we're going to abide by your rules and only broadcast what you allow us to broadcast."

LK: But isn't it better to be there than not there—as opposed to no picture.

NS: I don't know, okay? I come from it from a man who spent thirty-five years in the military, okay? And I've got to tell you what: it sticks in my craw when I see an American broadcasting what is obviously blatant Iraqi propaganda. It's the enemy propaganda, and that's what's being broadcast.

LK: But we kept saying that, that it was—

NS: Yes, but wait a minute. You know what you also did? [*laughs*] Every time a broadcast came out of my headquarters, the same disclaimer was down at the bottom. Okay? "We are broadcasting what we are being told by general," just as if it was the same stuff as the Iraqis were putting out.

LK: But Israel also controlled its transmissions, didn't it? So you had to say it with Israel.

NS: I don't know. I don't know.

LK: Well, I guess, to be fair, we just said it with everyone: "Make up your own mind. . . ."

NS: Yes, but, you know, you asked me if it bothered me. Yes, it bothered me. Sure, it did.

LK: Generally, did the media cover this war fairly?

NS: I think so. You know, if you go back and read a lot of the stuff that was written right after the war, there were many people in the press themselves that said it was covered better than the Vietnam War.

LK: What's television done to war?

NS: Television has brought war into the living room. That's a fact.

LK: Meaning? Does it affect how you fight it?

NS: I don't think it—no, it doesn't affect how you fight it at all—not in the least. But I think it's going to be a tremendous molder of public opinion, and public opinion is one of those things that it's absolutely necessary to have. You've got to have favorable public opinion to fight a war. If you don't have it, you have a Vietnam on your hands, and that's the worst of all possible situations, where you're over there fighting a war that the American people don't support.

LK: The pluses, though, are that it's hard to have concentration camps with satellites.

NS: Yes, but there's still a lot of them out there. I mean, you don't always get into the concentration camp. You know, the enemy doesn't always take you and show you what he doesn't want you to see.

LK: Do you miss the service?

NS: I miss the troops. That's what I miss. I don't miss the pomp. I certainly don't miss the bureaucracy. I don't miss the politics of it. I miss the troops.

LK: When someone died, did you write a letter home?

NS: In this war?

LK: Uh-huh.

NS: No. No, that—

LK: You have in the past, though?

NS: Oh, yes, but that's a job that is reserved, normally, for the commander, the immediate commander, someone very close to the organization. Frankly, one of the things that happened in Vietnam that I hated was there was one outfit I was in that, when I was the guy that should have been writing letters home, that privilege was taken away from me. It was written by somebody back in the rear and, you know, they sent the letter out and said, "Sign it."

LK: . . . How do you feel about enemy casualties?

NS: Hey, a human life is a human life—just that simple. And that's one of the reasons why you don't want to have war, because—you know—a person gets killed, a person gets killed. But in the final analysis, once the war starts, I mean, if it's something that's thrust upon you, then what you're worried about is the lives of your troops first and foremost.

LK: All right, and you do keep score, and you want it to end.

NS: You don't keep score.

LK: Well, I mean, you're happy when they have a lot of casualties, and you don't have any.

NS: Right. I mean, if that's what's going to get the war over very quickly, that's what you're happy with. Remember, the United States of America had a thing called atomic weapons. I mean, if we really were that cold and calculating that human life didn't count, we could have blown Baghdad off the face of the earth and killed millions of people and not had one casualty.

LK: Did you ever give a thought to that?

NS: No. . . .

[Commercial break]

LK: We're back with General Schwarzkopf and your calls. Bristol, Tennessee, hello.

CALLER: *[Bristol, Tennessee]* Hello. My question is for the General. During a speech before the American Legion, Bill Clinton said, although he didn't relish sending men into battle, neither would he shrink from his responsibility as commander in chief to send them into battle. Two questions: In your opinion, General, did he not shrink from his responsibility to serve his country? And do you think he should have been willing to serve in the military if he wants now to be commander in chief?

NS: Well, you know, that's a tough question, and that's one that's widely debated. But, first of all, he didn't shrink from his responsibility, because he used the law, and he used legal deferments. Now, there's a lot of questions about how that came about, and I don't think—in my mind and a lot of other people's minds—all those questions have been answered. But I think it's unfair to just state blatantly that the man deliberately shrank from serving his country.

The answer to the second question is very straightforward. You know, we've had a lot of presidents that have never served in the military, and they've been good presidents. So you can't say a president has to serve in the military before he can be a good commander in chief. On the other hand, you know, I've said all along that Clinton did say that he supported draft resistance, and he, in essence, was supporting people breaking the law. And the question that I have in my mind is, what happens if he's the commander in chief, he has to have a war, he has to institute another draft, and there are people out there who resist? Is he going to, in fact, enforce that law or does he agree with draft resistance?

LK: New York City, for General Schwarzkopf. Hello.

CALLER: [*New York, New York*] Hi. I was there yesterday at the book store in New York for three hours, and my question is, did the protesters there bother you as much as they did me? And also, how does it feel to be loved by not only your troops, but also as many civilians as you certainly are?

NS: Well, you just answered the question, okay? First of all, the protesters didn't bother me. One of the great things about this country is that we do allow protesters, and I remember shortly after I got home from the war, I saw a whole bunch of protesters out on the street, and I said to my wife, "Isn't that great! Gee, I'm back in America. It's wonderful!"

LK: That's what you fought for, right?

NS: Yes. But on the other hand, I have had so much love and affection poured out to me by the great American people all over this country that, you know, it's not going to bother me that a few people say something like that. And I really do appreciate that love that I've had from the American people. But you've got to remember, I'm loved by the American people not because of what I am. I'm loved because of what 541,000 fantastic young men and women did under my command. I just happen to have been lucky enough to be their commander.

LK: Did you have requests to serve politically? Did people try to urge you to run for office?

NS: Right. Sure. . . . Yes, I mean, you know, I got off the airplane, and they came after me to, you know, run for senator in Florida, and I told them no. And I've said openly that all three of the organizations came to me for various support.

LK: That's Perot, Bush, Clinton?

NS: Yes. But I'm not a politician. I'd make a lousy politician.

LK: So, you're not endorsing anyone?

NS: No, I—[*laughs*]—I told somebody the other day I have voted—I participated in the American political process for thirty-six years without having to endorse somebody. Why do I have to endorse somebody right now?

LK: [*laughs*] Because you're a public figure. Norm, you're famous.

NS: Yes, but I think that the important thing is that the American people pick for themselves. And, you know, we had a law in the military against me going down leaning on my troops to vote for somebody. That's a pretty good law.

LK: Las Vegas, Nevada, hello.

CALLER: [*Las Vegas, Nevada*] Hello. Good evening, General. I want to thank you for the brilliant leadership. And vis-à-vis the media, if anything, you were too liberal with them. [*Schwarzkopf laughs*] Getting to the tank situation, would it, in your opinion, have significantly weakened Saddam had you been given a day, say, to surround the remaining Republican Guards in the south, let the soldiers abandon them and scramble north, avoiding any further killing but depriving them of tanks and field guns? And a quick second one: were you ever attempting to go for the Republican Guard units in the north? Thank you.

NS: Okay, let me answer the first one. That's exactly, in essence, what was happening at the end of the war. You know, we had surrounded most of the Republican Guard units, and they were abandoning their equipment and running away. Oh, by the way, when you surround somebody and then you say, "Okay, abandon your equipment," the alternative is you've got to shoot at them. So, it doesn't necessarily follow that if all you're doing is surrounding them you're not going to end up having to fight them. The important thing is that this myth about the vast majority of the Republican Guard escaping is just plain and simply not true. By count, by statistics, 90 percent of all artillery that was in Kuwait was destroyed, 85 percent of all the tanks were destroyed. That's exactly what was happening. They were bailing out, running across. And I would say a large number of troops in the Republican Guard did escape, but most of their equipment did not escape. Fifty percent of all their armored vehicles were destroyed. So, I don't know how that myth has grown up.

LK: Does it annoy you that Saddam is still alive? He's still in power.

NS: Ahhh— You know, Saddam's irrelevant. As a matter of fact, it's probably the best thing in the world that Saddam is still in power in Iraq, because Iraq has no voice whatsoever in Arab politics, and that's one of the reasons why we're closer to peace than we've ever been in the Middle East.

LK: In other words, keep him there a while?

NS: Yes. I can give you some very good strategic arguments why. Leave Saddam right there, because if you replace him with somebody else, then that fellow, in the name of Arab brotherhood, is going to have to, you know, pay attention— The Arabs will have to pay attention to him.

LK: Bedford, Pennsylvania, hello.

CALLER: [*Bedford, Pennsylvania*] From beautiful, historic Bedford, two questions for the General: did you have any independent knowledge of the Iraqi nuclear capacity? And number two, did you have authority, independent of the president, to use nuclear weapons?

NS: No. Let me answer the second one right off the bat: absolutely not.

LK: Nor would you want it.

NS: Nor would I want it; nor do you ever want to give that authority to any military man. That's an authority you want to hold strictly within the hands of the president of the United States.

With regard to the first one, yes. We were pretty sure—as a matter of fact, we were positive—that he did not have a nuclear capability. For a while, we were getting reports that he might have been able to put together some kind of a rough device, and every time we looked out to the west there and wondered why he hadn't defended it, we got worried that maybe he had put some kind of rudimentary nuclear device out there. But we were quite sure he did not have a nuclear capability, per se, in the form of a bomb or a missile. . . .

[*Commercial break*]

LK: Livingston, Montana, hello.

CALLER: [*Livingston, Montana*] Yes, I have a question for Norm. You were talking about the media. Did the media help you when you were trying to fool Saddam about your amphibious attacks?

LK: Yes, didn't they help?

NS: Yes—

LK: Didn't you use them?

NS: No. No. That's a very important difference. The media focused on the deployment of the marines out of the United States of America when they first went over—as a matter of fact, gave figures that were much larger than they were—and definitely caused Saddam to think that we were going to come straight in over the shore. I was delighted with that, because I kept seeing him put more and more force along the shore. Obviously, I wasn't going to stand up and say, "Hey, we're not going to conduct an amphibious assault, so therefore, Saddam, move your forces anyplace else." But let me tell you something. One of the other misperceptions to come out of this is that the military used the media, and that's absolutely incorrect. As a matter of fact, very, very early on, in the very first days, the subject came up about deception planning. And one of the techniques that can be used in deception planning is to plant false stories in the press. Decisions were made at the highest level of the United States government that that's not the way we do business in this country, and we never, ever, to my knowledge, planted a false story with the press to use the press in deception operations. It just didn't happen.

LK: Were the feelings generally unanimous among the heads here and your people there? I mean, you had squabbles, obviously. And you have to have differences. You're human.

NS: Oh, yes, absolutely. I say in the preface of the book quite clearly, on every issue we were unanimous—unanimous in the ultimate course of action we took. And that's amazing. I mean, that's amazing, because we had input from everybody, but nobody was, you know, wanting to fall on their sword.

LK: How did you hold that coalition together?

NS: I think the coalition held itself together. Saddam kept doing a bunch of really stupid things that helped us keep the coalition together. I mean, I tried to get in that fellow's head for a very, very long time. After the war, in hindsight, I recognized the way to do it. All I had to do was think of the dumbest possible thing he could do. And he continued to do that, and that helped hold the coalition together. But the other thing was, we all had one common goal, one common goal: kick the Iraqis out of Kuwait. And that tended to focus us.

LK: When you say "dumb," do you really mean *dumb*-dumb?

NS: Hey, now, listen to this. Now listen, Saddam Hussein—if he had invaded ten kilometers into Kuwait, taken the Rumallah oil fields and stopped right there, I am convinced that the world would have accepted that. He would control all that oil; he would be intimidating every other Gulf country because he had invaded an Arab and gotten away with it; he'd be controlling the price of oil all over—which is exactly what he wanted to do. But instead of stopping ten kilometers in, he went all the way, and he blew it.

LK: Silver Spring, Maryland, hello.

CALLER: [*Silver Spring, Maryland*] Yes, I'd like to jump into a current event and ask the General what he thinks of the Navy Tailhook scandal, and what, if any, parallel does that incident have in the Army?

NS: I want to tell you, first of all, that sexual harassment is not new to the army, but it's something that we addressed many, many years ago when we heavily integrated the army. Back in 1976 to '78, when I was at Fort Lewis, Washington, as a colonel, we were bringing many, many females into the army. And at that time, we ran into this for the first time, and it surprised us very much. But it's something that we've been dealing with for a very, very long time and are very active in. I'm not saying that sexual harassment does not happen in the army at all, but I am saying that in the army—which is all I can really speak for—we've been very much aware of it, and we have had a strong program.

  The bottom line is simply this, you know. I didn't tolerate it as a commander—not at all. And you know, we integrated the army a long, long time ago racially. And I'll tell you what: anybody in the army who would say somebody can't do their job because they're black would get their head cut off in an instant. And I used to say to a lot of officers at that time, I said, "Listen, you know damn well that your career would be over if you said somebody couldn't do something because they're black. Why the hell do you think you can say that somebody can't do something because they're female?" And so, we've been on top of the problem for quite some time.

LK: How about women in combat?

NS: I am a supporter of women in the military, big-time. They are wonderful. They do great work. They are a combat multiplier. The problem is the defense of the nation. You know, we've always had times when two principles of the Constitution come into clash. Here's the way it goes: Ranger battalions—you know, the guys out there that fight in the trenches with bayonets and this sort of thing—if 50 percent of all your ranger battalions were female, and they were going up against a similar type unit that was 100-percent male, it would not be in the best interests of the defense of this country. But on the other hand, I'm one of the guys that—you know, unlike many of my contemporaries, I support women in the cockpit . . . because how can you say that it's all right for a woman to fly a medivac helicopter right into enemy fire, but it's not all right for her to fly an attack helicopter or a jet fighter? I don't understand that. The problem is, you've got to do what's best for the defense of the country first.

LK: How about gays in the service?

NS: Same thing. I support the government's position on that. The courts have supported it for years and years. It has nothing to do with sexual preference. It has nothing to do with discriminating against someone because they're gay. Once again, we learned a long time ago that when gays openly are in small organizations it tends to polarize that organization completely. Yet we know that when you go into battle, the most important thing that holds you is the cohesion in the unit—fighting for the buddy on your left or right. So polarization in units is not in the best interests of the unit. Now, I'm sure we've got a lot of gays in the military—not hundred of thousands, as people have said, but I'm sure there are—

LK: But you must have had some in the five hundred and—

NS: —and they've done a fine job. So it's not an issue of, "Gays can't do a good job in the military." It's this polarization effect that will cause you to lose cohesion and, therefore, lose fighting ability.

[*Commercial break*]

LK: Reston, Virginia, hello.

CALLER: [*Reston, Virginia*] Hello. General Schwarzkopf, I am the mother of a First Division Marine. He spent seven months there on the front line with First Tanks and First Tow. I think I probably speak for most of the mothers of marines and all the servicemen: Thank you from the bottom of my heart for bringing him home.

NS: I want to tell you that nothing I ever hear means more to me than when I hear that. But I want to thank you for *him* bringing *me* home, too.

LK: Ma'am, are you still there? [*silence*] I thank you. That was very touching. What does it feel like? What's it feel like to hear something like that?

NS: Well, you know, it—[*touches chest*]—it gets you right here, because that's what it's all about. You know, I hear that from three sources: mothers, who thank me for bringing their sons home; I hear it from spouses, who thank me for bringing their spouse home; and I hear it from kids, who thank me for bringing their father or their mother home. I tell you what, boy: it gets me every time.

LK: Is the hardest the relative of someone who didn't come home?

NS: Yes, and it's particularly hard in this war, because the casualties were so few. . . . And that makes it ten times harder for them to accept the fact that their loved one got killed.

LK: What's the worst part of a lifetime in the military?

NS: Hmmm—nothing.

LK: You liked everything?

NS: I didn't like it all, but it's— Life in the military is a series of emotional peaks and valleys, and if you're lucky, you get more peaks than valleys.

LK: What's it like having more money than you ever dreamed you'd have?

NS: It's like not having it at all, because it's all paper. You know, it's funny. It's funny. We've got a great lottery in Florida, and my family and I used to sit around—

LK: Did you buy tickets?

NS: We always— We *still* do. We used to buy tickets, you know, but we'd always talk about what we'd do if we had the money.

LK: Now you have the money.

NS: And our lifestyle hasn't changed one iota. . . .

[*Commercial break*]

LK: We're about out of time. What are you going to do now? Are you going to continue speaking? Are you going to go into private— You're in private life. What are you going to do?

NS: I don't know. I really don't. MacArthur said, "Old soldiers never die; they just fade away." I don't want to fade away just yet.

LK: You're not going to fade away. . . . How about the media?

NS: I want to make a contribution. I really do. I want to—

LK: I mean, would you go to work for a media outlet?

NS: Well, you know, some might say I'm already working for one media outfit— [*laughs*]—you know, in specials, limited specials. So, yes, I mean, that's—

LK: But I mean, a full-time— Would you like *The Norman Schwarzkopf Show*?

NS: Who'd want to listen?

LK: Come on, Norman! You know better.

NS: No, who'd want to listen?

LK: The sound of it— I saw the way you looked right then. As soon as I said it, *The Norman Schwarzkopf Show*, a little jump went through you.

NS: Yes, a little jump—it may have been a recoil, Larry. [*laughs*] Did you ever think about that?

LK: Do you want to host this show when I vacation? Do you like to interview people?

NS: Yes, well, that might be fun.

LK: *Norman Schwarzkopf Live*—Thank God. [*Schwarzkopf laughs*] Thanks, General. . . .

"That's what

this election

is going

to be about.

Who do you

trust to lead

this country?"

It has been observed that George Herbert Walker Bush had the perfect resume for the job of president. He was born into a wealthy Protestant family on June 12, 1924, in Milton, Massachusetts. His father was a banker and U.S. Senator. Bush graduated from Yale in 1948 after serving as the youngest dive-bomber pilot in the Navy during World War II. Following graduation, he worked in the Texas oilfields, then formed his own drilling company. He lost his 1964 bid for the U.S. Senate, but was elected two years later as the first Republican Congressman ever to represent Houston. He tried for the Senate again in 1970, and lost, but was appointed ambassador to the U.N. (1971–72), then ambassador to China. President Ford named him to head the CIA.

Bush served next as Ronald Reagan's two-term vice president, then defeated Michael Dukakis in the 1988 presidential race. He failed to win a second term, and Bill Clinton stepped into the Oval Office in 1993. This interview took place one month before that fateful election.

LARRY KING: We are broadcasting from the heart of historical San Antonio, Texas. The President was here today for that trade agreement—a historic day— an agreement, by the way, which your opponent, Mr. Perot, disagrees with. But Mr. Clinton the other night said he agrees with it, except he wants to clear up the part about the environment and jobs. Your comment?

GEORGE BUSH: My comment is that it's a most historic agreement. And you could hear President Salinas say that today, this marvelous neighbor of ours, the president of Mexico. You could hear our neighbor to the north, Brian Mulroney, say it. And all three of us felt that this was something that will be remembered in history, the initializing of this agreement. In terms of saying the environmental part hasn't been worked out, it's been endorsed by the largest environmental group in the United States. And for the jobs part being worked out, we have a $10 billion job-retraining program. So, I think that Governor Clinton ought to make up his mind and come down on one side or the other. But the fact is, he said he's for it, and I think that part is positive.

Labor unions don't like it. They think it'll export jobs, and I am absolutely convinced it will create good American jobs in the export business.

LK: A good agreement benefits everybody. It benefits all three equally?

GB: Oh, I'm convinced of it, and, of course, *they* are. We have a free-trade agreement with Canada itself. And since that agreement, exports to Canada have soared— meaning new jobs. So I don't see how they can take the argument that it's going to hurt. I'm convinced it will help. Now, if you're a protectionist, and you want to shrink markets, then you oppose it. But we're not. I am for free and fair trade. . . .

LK: Are you geared for the debate?

GB: Yes, I'm getting ready, Larry.

LK: Are you doing training?

GB: No, not yet. [*laughs*]

LK: Ho do you do that? What happens?

GB: We haven't done it yet. The way we used to do it was we had—when I was debating against Geraldine Ferraro—which has got to have been another historic first [*laughs*]—why, Lynn Martin played her, and she would ask— You know, I'd answer a question, and then she'd jump in and challenge me. It turned out, in terms of history, that Lynn was much tougher than Geraldine, you know. [*laughter*] So, you can over-train for these things. But it helps to get some questions—

LK: Can you over-think it, too?

GB: Well, you can get your mind cluttered up with facts—factoids—and I don't want to do that. I want to stay on the main principles of why our agenda for American renewal is the best to move this country forward.

LK: Governor Clinton said the other night that you're a terrific debater—[*Bush laughs*]—that you're looking to downplay it because you know you'll do well. You're a Yale graduate; he's a Yale graduate. Mr. Perot, he hasn't debated in a long time, but he debated at Annapolis. It should be interesting.

GB: Well, it should be interesting, I'll say that. I've never considered myself a star debater. I think I'm good on principle, and I think I'm good on making tough decisions, and I hope that comes through. But we'll see. . . .

LK: How much do you think, Mr. President, is dependent on these debates?

GB: I don't know. I think some, but not all. I don't know that a debate has ever decided anything. They always cite the Kennedy-Nixon debates, where people listening to it on the radio thought Nixon won, and people watching it thought Kennedy won. But I don't know. We don't think that it's, you know be-all-end-all . . . but it does give you a chance to stand up there and say, "Here's what I'm for." No filters. People don't need a Monday-morning quarterback: "You have just heard this or that. . . ."

LK: So, you're not nervous about it?

GB: No, I'm not nervous. I'm not particularly excited about it. [*laughs*]

LK: [*laughs*] In this city a couple of weeks ago, Leslie Stahl of CBS made a speech and said that there's a Bush blacklist, that there are people you won't talk to— Dan Rather, Peter Jennings—

GB: I've talked to Dan Rather. Don't you remember? [*laughs*]

LK: [*laughs*] I remember. She says *now*, though. Is there anyone you won't talk to? Is there any—

GB: No, but there's some programs it's not worth going on. I like to go where you get a fair shake. I like to go where you get the answers out there. And I think some are objective and some are pejorative, the way they ask questions. So you can be a little bit selective, but there's no blacklist. . . .

LK: But there are some programs that you wouldn't—

GB: Hey, listen, I'm human. I've got a list of people I respect in your business, and I've got a list that I keep inside of me for whom I've lost respect. But isn't that human? Isn't that the way nature should be? You don't love everybody, but you don't go around complaining about it or talking about them.

LK: The last four weeks: Are we going to take the high road here? The low road? How do you view this campaign? . . .

GB: I think you do two things. You make clear what you're for. You talk about your own agenda for America's renewal: "Here's what I'm for;" secondly, "Here's what I've done." That has been obscured by the Democratic primaries hammering me on the economy. So, you talk about what you've accomplished: world peace; getting interest rates down; inflation down; doing a lot of things for this country; child care—all of this. And then, reluctantly but nevertheless forcefully, you factually state the other person's record and why what he is proposing—or they are proposing—would not be good for America. So it's going to be a combination. And I have listened for about eleven months to the Democratic debate, and I stayed out of that—maybe too late—till the convention, after our convention, hearing them hammer me every single day. And I said, "Look, let them talk about my record, and I'm going to start talking about this man's record in Arkansas, because it's only fair. If he wants to be president, what has he done? He's misrepresenting what I've done. What has *he* done? . . ." His record is a sorry record. . . .

LK: What is it like to see yourself ripped up every night, though—I mean, emotionally? . . . Do you watch it?

GB: No, not so much any more.

LK: Barbara doesn't watch at all?

GB: Well, she doesn't watch much any more, because it's been an unpleasant year. They had a show in Houston that Ted Koppel put on and—much to Koppel's surprise—he said, "Do you think the press has been fair to George Bush?" The place went berserk—I mean on and on and on. And this came as a great shock to some. It didn't come as a shock to me, but I expect Ross Perot would feel the same way, or Governor Clinton. So, what I do is I—you know, I check the news early in the morning—

LK: But when you watch— Like, you were in Wyoming when the Democrats convened, right?

GB: Yes, I didn't watch that. You see, ringing in my ears was the voice of Ann Richards, the governor of Texas, and that was from four years before that: [*imitates Governor Ann Richards*] "Where's George?" you know. I thought, "I don't need that. . . ." I said, "I don't need that kind of stuff," and Barbara didn't. . . .

[*Commercial break*]

LK: We're back on the river front in San Antonio, on this historic occasion in this incredible year. We're ready to go to your phone calls for President Bush. We start with Arlington, Virginia. Hello.

CALLER: [*Arlington, Virginia*] Mr. President, this is such an honor to be able to speak to you. I've been an admirer of yours for years. A question for you: Do you believe that people in America have lost respect for the office of the presidency? You seem to be treated really poorly by the press and by some people at your events. And I was brought up to believe that you treated the president with an enormous amount of respect and looked up to that person as a role model. And it seems to me that people are losing that. . . .

GB: I'll tell you why I don't think that there's lack of respect. I can go—maybe not in a campaign time—but in areas where I knew I wouldn't get any votes and hadn't gotten votes in the 1988 election, and people come out to see their president, whether for you or not. And I think there is a proper respect for the presidency, and I sometimes see a lot of people out there, and I've never gotten to take it so personally that I think they all, you know, love me. But in a campaign, it's different. There's a certain ugliness. And I have told Larry, I believe that this year is the ugliest I've seen in all the time I've been in politics. But you just hang in there. You do what you think is right. But I think the fundamental respect for the presidency is still there, and it's a good thing, democrat or republican.

LK: So when you make an appearance, and if there's an anti-Bush sign, you don't regard that as degrading the presidency? It's part of a campaign?

GB: No, I think it just goes with the territory. I do think it's a little offensive, on either side, if a person isn't allowed to speak. It happens to be common these days that people try to drown out the speaker. And you try to think of a comeback, but you don't get angry about it. You just say, "Hey, wait a minute. Give me a chance."

LK: The next call for President Bush is from Tokyo, Japan. Hello.

CALLER: [*Tokyo, Japan*] Yes, Mr. President, as a Republican and an American businessman in Japan over here, trying hard to sell our American services in this, what I feel, for all intents and purposes, is a closed market, I'm extremely concerned about the continued reports of American trade negotiators who retire and then lobby for Japanese business and governmental interests for huge sums of cash over there in Washington. I understand there are a number of these—I like to call them "economic turncoats"—some of whom are in your own administration. Now, I am a troubled Republican, but I would like to know, sir, if you do have a second term, would this policy exist?

GB: Well, I don't think it's government policy. It's the policy of an individual. We have cut way down in our administration on this revolving-door thing. We put in the strongest possible rules, in terms of revolving door—working for the government and then lobbying the people that you just left. But, look, I'm as offended as you are by that, if people go out there and take their expertise and use it against American interests, if that's what your question is. On the other hand, I think people are free to lobby or do what they want. I don't think we want to have a totalitarian system, where you tell somebody, "You can't go out and lobby for whatever your interest is." That's the American way. So, what we're trying to do is to open markets, and frankly, we've made some— I hope you would concede, if you're a businessman over there, there have been some strides. We haven't gone far enough, but we've made some dramatic strides in opening foreign markets.

LK: In the worldwide picture, does Japan have an edge on us? . . . Do they have the better of the deal?

GB: We've got an imbalance with Japan, but it's going down under our administration. We're doing better, and we're going to keep on doing better. We're going to keep on fighting to access their markets. Cattlemen in Texas couldn't sell their cattle over there. Now you can get in there with cattle, or citrus, or whatever it is—glass, and computers, parts of the computer industry. So we're doing better, but we've got to keep on knocking down barriers, but not go back to some kind of restriction on who can talk to whom.

LK: With President Bush. El Paso, Texas, on *Larry King Live*. Hello.

CALLER: [*El Paso, Texas*] President Bush, with all due respect, four years ago you called supporters of Governor Dukakis radical liberals, out of the mainstream of American values. How can you convince me to vote for you, when you have been divisive towards these Americans?

GB: Help me with what you mean, "been divisive toward the Americans"?

CALLER: [*El Paso, Texas*] Well, you have called us radical liberals, and you have told us we're not in the mainstream of American values . . . and I feel—I haven't felt like an American.

GB: If you're a radical liberal, I disagree with you. I don't say you're not an American. I hope I've never said that. But I have a very different philosophy. See, I want to put less power in the hands of government and a lot more in the hands of the people, and that's why we want to hold the line on taxes and spending. And therein, I have a very different approach from Governor Clinton and, to some degree, with Ross Perot, who wants to raise taxes.

LK: But you're not saying that liberals are less patriotic?

GB: No, no, no. I didn't think that's what [the caller] meant, but—

LK: No, she felt like, if she's out of the mainstream, is she out of the stream entirely?

GB: No, no, absolutely not. I hope I've never said anything to convey that, and I don't think she could cite anything I have.

LK: Concerning labels like that, when President Ford was on this program at the Houston convention, he said he knows you a long time, he campaigned for you in Congress years and years and years ago—

GB: 1966 in Texas.

LK: He said, "George Bush is a moderate Republican. That is his greatness. He hears, he sees all sides, and takes in all areas, and he is a moderate." Do you agree with that?

GB: Well, I try to be reasonable to people. Like her question—I don't think I have ever tried to paint somebody as out of the mainstream; or never, as you asked about Leslie Stahl, had a blacklist. I have strong principles, in that when you're president you can't waffle. You've got to make decisions, and I've done that. But I appreciate what Jerry Ford says. Of course, labels are so confusing. I happen to think I'm conservative, but if he uses "moderate" in a pleasant way, meaning you're not unpleasant to people that you disagree with, I plead guilty.

LK: But an ultra-conservative might— When Pat Buchanan ran against you, he ran against you as if you weren't a conservative.

GB: Well, he ran against me on what he believed was principle, but all those wounds have been healed, just like the wounds in the Democratic— You ought to go back and look at all the things those Democrats said about Bill Clinton. [*laughs*] I mean, it is something. [*laughter*]

LK: [*laughs*] Why, they always heal, don't they? The day of the—

GB: Yes, it's amazing.

LK: Everything's forgotten.

GB: It's amazing. Well, in a sense, that's a good thing about our country. It's a good thing about it. . . .

[*Commercial break*]

LK: With President George Bush. Temple, Georgia, hello.

CALLER: [*Temple, Georgia*] President Bush, I'm forty-nine years old. I voted Democrat until twelve years ago. I've voted Republican since then. Neither party's done the job. Tell me and the USA why we shouldn't vote an independent party? I like his program.

LK: You like Ross Perot's program? Why should she not vote for him?

GB: Well, I'd like you to vote for me. [*laughter*] I think world peace is important. Maybe you're a mother and, if you are, your kids go to bed at night today with a lot less fear of nuclear war. I think that's a major accomplishment. If you're of Polish heritage, why, your home base is free. If you're a senior citizen here— maybe your mother or dad saved all their lives. Their interest rates are— Inflation is way down. Their inflation is so far down that their savings aren't being eroded. If you're a small businessperson, your interest rates are way down. And so, it depends what the category is. But the reason I'd like you to vote for me is I believe that this agenda for America's renewal offers the answer to how we can compete, how we can strengthen the American family, how we can save and invest, and how we can do some of what I did today—increase our exports. And it's a program: The answers, I think, are good and sound, and I'd sure like you to take a real hard look at it.

LK: Mr. President, a lot of newspapers are praising the Perot program while not endorsing him. What's wrong with the Perot concept that we all have to sacrifice—an austerity program, down the line, top to bottom?

GB: Nothing is wrong with that, except all I heard the program did—I didn't see it— was to say what's wrong, spell out the problems. And if that's the case, I can do that for you. And I think I could do it without tearing down this country and acting like we're a second-class power. What we need are the answers for the future, and I think he's onto something, in terms of getting spending down. But I think I'm the only one, Larry, that's proposing controlling the growth of the mandatory programs. Two-thirds of the budget does not come to me at all. Only one-third does. And so, I've said, set social security aside. Don't listen to these false ads by Clinton and Gore, who say what Democrats say every four years: "They're going to fool with social security." I'm the guy that stood up in the State of the Union and told the Congress, "Don't mess with social security," and they haven't. But what we have to do is control the growth of the mandatory programs. And that's not without pain, but that is the way you get the deficit down, not by going out, as Governor Clinton has said—raise taxes and raise spending.

LK: But there will— You're saying we will have to have some pain?

GB: Well, if you control the growth of the mandatory spending programs, obviously, you're not going to have that largess that we've had over the last few years, since the programs were invented. But we've got to constrain that growth. And that's the way to take the burden of the deficit off the backs of the young people.

LK: So, when Mr. Perot says, "Politicians are afraid to say you have to sacrifice," you don't agree with him?

GB: Well, I say you do have to sacrifice, but I'd like to hear some answers. He wants to—at least, he did at one point—tax social security, or go after social security. I don't want to do that, and I'm not going to do it.

[*Commercial break*]

LK: We go right back to the calls. Halmstad, Sweden, hello.

CALLER: [*Halmstad, Sweden*] Hello. This is Rolf Kampter. I was wondering, Mr. President, if you're think of reducing military costs, are you then thinking of pulling back people from abroad—military people—or would you still keep U.S. troops in Europe?

GB: Rolf, the U.S. troops have helped guarantee the peace in Europe for forty-five years. You look back to Europe's history, as I'm sure you do, and you see a history troubled before that with a lot of wars. And the United States troop presence there has helped guarantee the peace. NATO is the single most important peacekeeping organization in the world. And I am going to keep American troops there. Some are saying, well, the way we're going to spend for our domestic spending programs is to cut the muscle out of our defense and make too big a cut in our troop levels. And I'm not going to do that as president. And I think it's a good insurance policy for other countries, but I must consider the national security of the United States. And I am absolutely convinced it is in our security interests. And we saw what we were able to do with those NATO bases when we had to go to war to stand up against aggression. Some were waffling, some were talking about sanctions. You know, many people in your country, until it happened, were saying, "What's going to happen? How are we going to handle this?" NATO logistics played a very important part in that. And so, NATO has kept the peace, it will continue to keep the peace, and the United States will continue to be a key part of NATO.

LK: Even though there doesn't appear to be any apparent danger in Europe at all?

GB: Well, there's no danger in Europe, except if you look in Yugoslavia, you see consternation. I have vowed not to put one single American soldier into Yugoslavia until I know what the mission is, know how the mission ends successfully, and how they come out. There will be no more Vietnams, as long as I'm president. [*applause*] And that's one reason that the Desert Storm was successful.

LK: By the way, there's a story today. I'm interested in your comment. It was revealed that Ross Perot told a Senate panel that you called him in 1986—you were vice president—asking him to pay somebody $4.2 million for a videotape allegedly showing live POWs. And Perot said that an aide of yours later withdrew the promise to reimburse him. Do you know about that? . . .

GB: No, I remember having a talk with Ross Perot, which is all a matter of record, where he said he was going to go to Vietnam and bring back live prisoners. Look, Ross has done a good job, trying to go the extra mile. But I think our administration has had a very good record in trying to expose the phonies that are running around out there getting the hopes of survivor families up, only to have them dashed. And we're doing much better in getting the Vietnamese to account for the remains. I rode down with John McCain today—one of the prisoners that suffered in there—and he has a very clear picture, and he says, "You've got a lot to be proud of," and I think we do.

LK: Cleveland, Ohio, for President Bush. Hello.

CALLER: [*Cleveland, Ohio*] Hello, Mr. Bush. I have an article in front of me from *The New York Times*, which says that in 1981 you sold your house in Texas, told the IRS that you lived in Maine, to avoid paying capital gains taxes on that sale. However, since then, you have been claiming that you legal residence is in Texas. You've been claiming that to the state of Maine. And it says that you've avoided over

$200,000 in Maine state income taxes over the past decade. Now, isn't that tax evasion?

GB: Nice question. [*laughter*] The answer is this: I have voted in every election in Texas since 1948. I am the only Texan that is certified to be a voting Texan—you don't have to have that—because when the challenge was raised, the secretary of state certified that I am a resident of Texas. What you're talking about is, I was denied the normal capital gains rollover that you get, regardless of your legal residence, if you sell a house. You're supposed to get a rollover on the capital gains if you invest in another one. We sold our house in Houston—still own real property in Houston, still vote in Houston, still have a Texas driver's license. But in terms of that part of the tax law, I was denied what every other tax payer gets. And do you know why? Because they said— The IRS did this to me—they said, "Your residence is the vice president's house." That's what they said. So it has nothing to do with avoiding taxes. There's a nutty left-wing group up in Maine called the Clamshell Alliance— What that has to do with taxes, I don't know, but you see them carrying banners around, and then it's been picked up by a couple of wackos out there. But I am certified as a resident of Texas and have been.

LK: By the way, when was the last— [*applause*] That's interesting, because it's kind of an interesting life. When was the last time you drove? [*laughter*]

GB: I drive when I'm— I have my own truck, for example, in Maine. . . . I've got a car in Washington, but I don't drive it very much. I'll drive around the circle in the Oval Office—the oval in front of the White House. But I can drive when I go hunting, something like that. I go hunting every year here in Texas, and I drive a truck.

LK: And still a Texas driver's license?

GB: Still. You want to see it?

LK: Yes. [*applause*]

GB: Let me see. I've got to be sure I give him the right—

LK: Make sure it isn't expired.

GB: No, no, it's not expired. [*hands driver's license to King*]

LK: Hey, and I like that smile! [*applause*]

GB: [*laughs*] Does it say "President"?

LK: Wait a minute— Yep. [*reads*] "President George W. Bush, The White House, 1600 Pennsylvania Avenue, Department of Public Safety, Texas." It's a Class C driver's license—

GB: Hey, wait a minute!

LK: —Six feet, one inch tall; sex is male— [*laughter*] Eyes are brown; birthdate, 6/12/24. And this expires 6/12/93.

GB: I'm legal, see? Where's your car? Let's go for a drive. [*laughter*]

[*Commercial break*]

LK: As we continue to humanize the presidency, just for a moment, here's that famous American Express card, which President Bush showed that kid in school to prove that he was a member [*holds up American Express credit card*]. It does say, "George Bush, President of the United States," and it expires in 1994. The signature is on the back—and it's not a gold card. [*laughter*]

GB: [*laughs*] Modest credit.

LK: [*laughs*] Back to the calls for President Bush. Baltimore, Maryland, hello.

CALLER: [*Baltimore, Maryland*] I'm a gay army captain who is still in the U.S. Army reserves. Today, a navy seaman on the *U.S.S. Constellation* was given an other-than-honorable discharge for being gay, despite the fact that he had an exemplary service record and no evidence of misconduct. Now, this type of discharge is going to follow him for the rest of his life. And my question is in two parts: Can you explain how he and I adversely affect the morale of the military that you're in charge of? And, number two, how do you feel about this type of punitive discharge, as commander in chief?

GB: Well, I'm not sure I know the case, but I do know that I support the military's problems on gays in the military. And if the military comes to me with a changed recommendation, I'll consider it, but I back the military commanders, and I back those who have lived with this problem, struggled with this problem. . . . If you'd give me your name and serial number, here, maybe we can look into the case, but I—

LK: Well, we're going to put you on hold, and we'll get that to the president. But the second part of his question was: Do you think someone should be dishonorably discharged if the only fact is that they are gay?

GB: I think it ought to be looked at on a case-by-case basis, Larry, and I support the military. I make no bones about it. [*applause*] And I have a very different view than some have on service of gays in the military. And I support what our military has recommended to me, and I will stay with it. That does not make me discriminating. It makes me backing what we need for military discipline and military order.

LK: How about gays in government? Do you have any qualms about—

GB: No. . . . I'm sure we have some. My answer to that is: How would I know? We have no litmus test, none at all.

LK: Lisburn, Northern Ireland, for President Bush. Hello.

CALLER: [*Lisburn, Northern Ireland*] Hello, Mr. President. I am pleased to be speaking with you. I'd just like to ask, in your State of the Union address, you said that it was America that won the Cold War, and I was basically thinking that, surely, was it not Mikhail Gorbachev bringing down communism and the Berlin Wall that basically ended it all, and not, basically, anyone winning it?

GB: I'd give Gorbachev great credit—great credit. And I give President Yeltsin great credit for moving down democracy's path. I think most would agree because there were two superpowers, and the United States was one of them, and we didn't listen to the freeze people that were yelling ten, twenty years ago that the only way you're going to get peace in the world is to have a freeze of nuclear weapons, where we would lock in inferiority in some cases. We stayed firm, and we led, and the result is imperial communism, outreach communism, is dead, and former enemies are our friends. So I think we deserve great credit. But let me put it this way. Others deserve credit, too. Others deserve it. When I say, "We won the Cold War," we *did* win the Cold War—we, and our allies—and we stood firm, and we didn't go with the people that were running around this country, and maybe Ireland, saying, "Freeze it, lock it in," because we stood firm, and the whole thing crumbled. And it's been a wonderfully historic period. And the historians are going to look back and say, "Thank God, the United states under Reagan and Bush said 'Strength—Peace through strength, not through freezing and locking in inferiority.'" I'm very proud of what our country did and proud of what our allies did in supporting it. [*applause*]

[*Commercial break*]

LK: By the way, Bill Clinton the other night and Al Gore said that, even if elected, after elected they will continue to take bus trips around the country. They think it's good to get in touch. Do you have a comment on that?

GB: I think there's other ways to stay in touch instead of climbing on a bus. I don't think they're going to have the problem, but— [*laughter*] But, you know, everybody to his own desire. I remember Jimmy Carter was going to go out and do town meetings, and it, for some reason, didn't work out too well. But that's fine— take bus trips to stay in touch. I mean—

LK: You wouldn't do it?

GB: No, I'm not going to do that. I'm president, and I don't think you need to take a bus tour to stay in touch. I think you can stay in touch by—a lot of ways. [*applause*]

LK: How about the fact that some people are saying we see a lot of Clinton and Gore together, but we don't see Bush and Quayle together. Any reason?

GB: Well, I think we've got a pretty darn good system working. I am very proud of our vice president, and frankly, I think he'll do very well in the debate. [*applause*] You know, I read this thing that Gore is going to bury him. Let's wait and see. Let's just wait and see on that one.

LK: Back to the calls for President Bush. Tampa, Florida, hello. . . .

CALLER: [*Tampa, Florida*] I am not happy with you. For two years, you did not recognize that people were hurting out here and we were in a recession. I feel like you have not come clean on Iran-Contra. And I'm tired of your party and you preaching to us about family values.

LK: All right, don't make a speech. Do you have a question?

GB: I'll put you down as "doubtful," fellow. [*laughter*]

CALLER: [*Tampa, Florida*] Yes. How can we trust you?

LK: Okay, let's respond to those three quickly. Iran-Contra—fair issue?

GB: Fair enough. I've answered every question. If Bill Clinton would do on the draft what I've done on Iran-Contra, we'd have the facts out there. [*applause*] That Iran-Contra has been looked at to the tune of $40 million of investigation. I've testified to the commissions and everybody else, and leveled with the American people. Now I see a lot of distorted campaign rhetoric, like this, and I'm sorry, I don't— If this guy had a specific question instead of a speech—

LK: Yes, his question is trust.

GB: Well, trust: that's what this election is going to be about. Who do you trust to lead this country? I served this country, and I served it in uniform, and I believe I've earned the trust in that capacity from the American people. I have made tough decisions. I have not waffled, been on one side or the other—on the war, or on right-to-work laws, or spotted owls, or NAFTA agreements. Every position these guys take, they're on one side—"Oh, by the way, I see the point over here." You can't do that when you're president. So I think I have earned the trust of the American— This guy, I mean, you know, he's part of the campaign apparatus or something like that. [*laughs*]

LK: What do you make of the Clinton Moscow trip thing? Do you think that's a—

GB: Moscow?

LK: He says it was just a student trip.

GB: Larry, I don't want to tell you what I really think, because I don't have the facts. I don't have the facts. But to go to Moscow one year after Russia crushed Czechoslovakia, not remember who you saw, I really think the answer is: level with the American people. I've made a mistake. I've said, "I made mistakes." But don't try to— You can remember who you saw in the airport in Oslo, but you can't remember who you saw in Moscow—?

LK: So, in other words, you're saying—

GB: I'm just saying: level with the American people—

LK: —say you're sorry you went—?

GB: —on the draft, on whether he went to Moscow, how many demonstrations he led against his own country from a foreign soil. Level, tell us the truth, and let the voters then decide who to trust or not. [*applause*]

LK: How about the missing pages in the State Department records? He implied the other night that that may have been Republican hanky-panky. He didn't even know there were State Department papers.

GB: Well, I'm sure there are passport files. But why in the world would anybody want to tamper with his files, you know, to support the man? I mean, I don't understand that. What would exonerate him—put it that way—in the files?

LK: Do you really have deep-down suspicions about the Moscow thing? I mean, just gut suspicion?

GB: I'm just concerned about it. No, I don't have it as a federal case. I'm just concerned about it, because it's a pattern here.

LK: Judgment-wise?

GB: Yes. I'll tell you what concerns me, and I really feel viscerally about this: demonstrating against your own country in a foreign land. I have demonstrators in front of the White House every single day. If you go up there right now, there are probably some sitting out here. . . . In the war, when I was trying to mobilize world opinion and United States opinion, we had a lot of people marching and demonstrating in front of the White House—ministers and guys that opposed the war. And I understand that. But I cannot, for the life of me, understand mobilizing demonstrations and demonstrating against your own country, no matter how strongly you feel, when you're in a foreign land. I just don't believe it. I don't think you should do that. [*applause*] That's what gets me. Moscow—I don't know what he did in Moscow.

LK: Well, what you're saying is: do it at home, okay; over there, no?

GB: Maybe I'm old-fashioned, Larry, but to go to a foreign country and demonstrate against your own country when your sons and daughters are dying halfway around the world? I'm sorry, I—I just don't like it. I think it is wrong. I think it is wrong to do that. . . .

LK: Orlando, Florida, for President Bush. Hello.

CALLER: [*Orlando, Florida*] Hello . . . Mr. Bush, thousands of Bosnians have died. You can save it—again, holocaust—only through military intervention. Please act, and act now. So far, there has been a lot of talk and no action.

GB: May I tell you my position on that? . . . The United States probably at this very minute—maybe a few hours from now—will be landing relief planes in there. We've done that. I am proud that we've done that. It is an extraordinarily difficult situation, in terms of military. And I learned something from our lesson in

Vietnam. And no matter how much the anguish, you cannot go into a military situation unless you're sure what the mission is, and how you're going to win, and how you're going to back your soldiers to the fullest and then get out. And that is my theory, and that is my trust to every parent who has a son or a daughter in the American military.

Now there are forces in the U.N. over there that are trying to protect the peace. They are sniped at. They are there for a humanitarian role. They are sniped at from the mountains. These feuds have been going on for a long, long time. And one of the prices that the world is paying for the fact that we have won the Cold War and that the Soviet Union is now dismantled and that our former enemies are friends, is there are these areas where you have ethnically based violence. And, yes, it is terrible what's happening, but when you suggest that we send troops over there, I would say I can't do that until I am absolutely sure, on the recommendation of Colin Powell and [Richard] Cheney—who certainly have won the confidence of the world in military—that the military mission is sensible, not just put them in there. We could do that easily. But I want to know that we're going to put them in and win and do what the mission is. And see, I can't tell you, sir, that we can do that right now. And yet we agonize over the humanitarian side, and we're doing our part, as the United States always does, to help in that regard. . . . One other quick thing. Are you enjoying this—this campaign? Or is this the kind of year you're not enjoying it?

GB: I'm not enjoying it very much, but I feel so strongly about what remains to be done to help the American people, to help the families in this country. We've done such remarkable things, in terms of world peace, reducing the threat of nuclear war, that I just want to finish the job, in terms of this economy and hope for families. And we've got good answers to give. . . .

Mark David Chapman

December 17, 1992

Mark David Chapman was born on May 10, 1955, in Fort Worth, Texas, and moved to Georgia, where he grew up. As a teenager, he was swept up in the psychedelic-drug scene and at sixteen briefly embraced religion as a Born Again Christian. In the 1970s, Chapman went to Hawaii on vacation and remained there, marrying travel agent Gloria H. Abe in 1979. He got a job as a security guard and began to brood about John Lennon, who (he felt) had betrayed the ideals expressed in his songs. Chapman quit his job, purchased a .38 caliber Charter Arms handgun, flew to New York, and on December 9, 1980, shot John Lennon to death. He pled guilty to second degree murder and was sentenced to twenty years to life. This remarkable interview followed the publication of Chapman's book, Let Me Take You Down.

"John came out, and he looked at me, . . . and he walked past me. I took five steps toward the street, turned, withdrew my Charter Arms .38, and fired five shots into his back."

LARRY KING: Twelve years ago, shots rang out in front of the Dakota in New York City. The victim was an icon for a generation. The gunman was Mark David Chapman. As fans continue to mourn the loss of former Beatle John Lennon, many continue to wonder about the man who killed him—someone who was also a Beatles fan, someone who requested Lennon's autograph on the very night he pulled the trigger. After more than a decade in prison, the assassin says he's rid of the demons that drove him to kill and ready to tell his story. Chapman sat for hours of interviews with the author of a new book, *Let Me Take You Down*, which chronicles his life and his crime. Mark David Chapman joins us from Attica Correctional Facility on this, the twelfth anniversary of John Lennon's death.

Mark, why now? Why tell the story now?

MARK DAVID CHAPMAN: Well, Larry, I'm well now. I've had a number of years of wellness. I feel good. There's always been things inside of me that I wanted to get out, to tell people why I did what I did. . . .

LK: All right, your sentence was what? Twenty years to life?

MDC: Twenty years to life.

LK: You have served how long now, Mark?

MDC: Twelve years to the day—to this day.

LK: Okay, you're eligible at twenty years for parole?

MDC: I'm eligible for parole in eight years.

LK: Do you have expectations about that? You're how old now?

MDC: Thirty-seven.

LK: Okay, how do you deal with—twenty years to life, so you know you're going to be there till you're forty-five.

MDC: Right.

LK: All right. How do you deal with that period of time? You know definitely you're going to be there another eight years. In time frame, how do you deal with that?

MDC: As a lifer—which is what we call ourselves across the country, people that are in prison for murder or worse and who are doing life—we'll try to take it a day at a time, and that's what I do. I've learned to do that. You naturally learn to do that through the years. If you don't, you're in trouble. You have to do it a day at a time.

LK: You don't set a goal? You don't say, "Boy, eight years from tomorrow, I'm going to walk out of here and do this?"

MDC: No. I don't think about the [parole] board. I don't think about eight years from now. That's not any prerogative right now.

LK: Well, when you live daily, then, do you set daily goals? Do you say, like, "Today, I am going to finish this book, write this thing?"

MDC: Yes. I write now. I write Christian short stories. One of them is in the back of Jack [Jones's] book. It's called "The Prisoner's Letter." That took me three years. I've just started a new one. I don't know when that's going to be through, but that's a goal right now, is finish this next story.

LK: Are you saying, Mark, that the young man who shot John Lennon was not you? What are you saying?

MDC: It was me, Larry, and I accept full responsibility for what I did. I've seen places where I'm blaming the devil, and I hope that isn't kept going after this interview. I'm not blaming the devil. I'm blaming myself. But in the major sense, it wasn't me, because I'm better now. I'm normal, I'm functioning, I have a lovely wife, and we have a great marriage—as much as, you know, can be had from here, from Attica. But I'm not the same person in the major sense, because back then I was lost, and I didn't know who I was. But now I do.

LK: All right, so it *was* you, but the personality of you is different now?

MDC: Well, I didn't have a personality then, and I do now. I have a life.

LK: All right, who was Mark David Chapman?

MDC: On December 8, 1980, Mark David Chapman was a very confused person. He was literally living inside of a paperback novel: J. D. Salinger's *The Catcher in the Rye*. He was vacillating between suicide; between catching the first taxi home back to Hawaii; between killing, as you said, an icon.

LK: By the way, would you have killed someone else, do you think? Would Mark David have done that if it weren't Lennon?

MDC: The Secret Service asked me that. "If Lennon would have, unfortunately, died a few days prior—say, in an automobile accident—would you have stalked someone else?" I can't answer that question. I don't know. I was so bonded with John Lennon at that point. What I told them is I probably would be crushed, and at that point I don't know what I would have done.

LK: Therefore, you have to have daily regrets.

MDC: I have regrets. I'm sorry for what I did. I realize now that I really ended a man's life. Then he was an album cover to me. He didn't exist, even when I met him earlier that day, when he signed the album for me—which he did very graciously. And he was not a phony, by the way. He was very patient, and he was very cordial, and he asked me if there was anything else. So if that didn't register— And I had also met his son that day. If that didn't register, that he was a human being, then I wasn't perceiving him as such. I just saw him as a two-dimensional celebrity with no real feelings.

LK: Okay. Why did Mark David Chapman want to shoot the album cover?

MDC: Mark David Chapman at that point was a walking shell who didn't ever learn how to let out his feelings of anger, of rage, of disappointment. Mark David Chapman was a failure in his own mind. He wanted to become somebody important, Larry. He didn't know how to handle being a nobody. He tried to be a somebody through his years, but he progressively got worse—and I believe I was schizophrenic at the time. No one can tell me I wasn't, although I was responsible. Mark David Chapman struck out at something he perceived to be phony, something he was angry at, to become something he wasn't: to become somebody.

LK: Mark, will you relive for us those terrible moments for you, for the world, for a lot of people around and in circles close to John Lennon? What happened that night?

MDC: Well, if you want to pick it up from the night. I was standing there with a gun in my pocket—

LK: Knew you were going to shoot him?

MDC: Absolutely. Tried not to—praying not to—but knowing down deep it was probably going to come to that.

LK: Did you know it would be that night? Did you know you would see him again?

MDC: Yes, I knew that morning. Oddly, when I left the hotel I had some type of premonition that this was the last time I was going to leave my hotel room. I hadn't seen him up to that point. That's what makes it interesting. I wasn't even sure he was in the building. And then I left the hotel room, bought a copy of *The Catcher in the Rye*, signed "To Holden Caulfield, from Holden Caulfield," and wrote underneath that, "This is my statement," underlining the word "this," the emphasis on the word "this." I had planned not to say anything after the shooting. Walked briskly up Central Park West to 72nd Street and began milling around there with the fans that were there, Jude and Jerry, and later, a photographer that came there.

LK: Okay, and then John came out that day, right?

MDC: He came out. I was leaning against the gargoyle-studded railing and was looking down. I was reading *The Catcher in the Rye*, and I believe he got into a taxi and disappeared. And then, later that day, I had gone to lunch with, I believe, Jude. We came back—

LK: With who?

MDC: With Jude. She was a fan there that was there at the building, and we struck up a conversation about Hawaii, about John Lennon. She had been there a number of times. And at one point during the day she had left, and John came back out. I don't remember him going back in from the taxi, but he was obviously back in the building. He was doing an RKO Radio special. And he came out of the building, and the photographer that I mentioned earlier, Paul Gorish—he kind of pushed me forward and said, "Here's your chance. You know, you've been waiting all day, you've come from Hawaii to have him sign your album. Go!—Go!" And I was very nervous. And I was right in front of John Lennon there, instantly. And I had a black Bic pen, and I said, "John, would you sign my album?" and he said, "Sure." Yoko went and got into the car. And he pushed the button on the pen and started to get it to write—it was a little hard to write at first—and then he wrote his name, "John Lennon," and then underneath that, "1980." And he looked at me, as I mentioned earlier. He said, "Is that all? Do you want anything else?" And I felt, then and now, that he knew something subconsciously, that he was looking into the eyes of the person that was going to kill him.

LK: Why do you think that?

MDC: Well, his wife was in the car, the door was open, and he's a busy man. He's going to go to a radio—or to his record studio. And he's talking to a nobody, just signed an album for a nobody, and he's asking me is that all I want. I mean, he's given me the autograph, I don't have a camera on me. What could I give him?

LK: I would admit that is a strange thing to say. All right, so he leaves, right?

MDC: Yes, he leaves in the car.

LK: Now, what do you do the rest of the day?

MDC: I stand around like an idiot, waiting for him to come back.

LK: And what time did he come back?

MDC: He came back about ten to eleven at night.

LK: Had you eaten dinner?

MDC: No. I had not.

LK: For fear you might have missed him?

MDC: Probably.

LK: Knew you were going to shoot him?

MDC: Yes.

LK: How did that happen? What happened?

MDC: Well, the photographer left. In all fairness, I have to say I tried to get him to stay—

LK: Because—?

MDC: There were those that felt I wanted him to shoot pictures of the shooting, which is not true.

LK: Why, then, did you want him to stay?

MDC: I wanted him to stay because I wanted out of there. There was a part, a great part of me, that didn't want to be there. I asked Jude, the fan, before she left, for a date that night. She said no. If she'd have said yes, I would have been on the date with her.

LK: But you might have killed him the next day.

MDC: Oh, yes. I would have probably come back.

LK: Okay. All right, the circumstances of the killing—what happened?

MDC: I was sitting at the inside of the arch of the Dakota building, and it was dark, it was windy. José, the doorman, was out along the sidewalk. And here's another odd thing that happened. I was at an angle where I could see Central Park West and 72nd, and I see this limousine pull up and, as you know, there's probably hundreds of limousines that turn up Central Park West in the evening, but I knew that was his. And I said, "This is it," and I stood up. The limousine pulled up, the door opened, the rear left door opened. Yoko got out. John was far behind—say, twenty feet—when he got out. I nodded to Yoko when she walked by me.

LK: Did she nod back?

MDC: No, she didn't. And I don't mean to be so clinical about this, but I've told it a number of times. I hope you understand. John came out, and he looked at me, and I think he recognized [me]: "Here's the fellow that I signed the album for earlier," and he walked past me. I took five steps toward the street, turned, withdrew my Charter Arms .38, and fired five shots into his back.

LK: All in his back?

MDC: All in his back.

LK: Never saw it coming?

MDC: He never saw anything coming, Larry. It was a very quick— It was a rough thing.

LK: Had you shot that weapon before?

MDC: That weapon? No. I didn't even know if the bullets were going to work. And when they worked, I remember thinking, "They're working. They're working." I was worried that the plane—in the baggage compartment, the humidity had ruined them. And I remember thinking, "They're working."

LK: What did Yoko do?

MDC: She naturally—and I can't blame her—she dashed around the stair area. I don't know if it's still there at the Dakota today. But she just, you know, ran for cover, which is what anyone would do. John, according to what I've been told, stumbled up the stairs. And then I saw her come back around and then go up to the stairs, and then she cradled his body.

LK: Did she scream?

MDC: I don't think she screamed, but a few minutes after that there was just a blood-curdling scream from someone, and it put the hair on the back of my neck straight up.

LK: Were you relieved?

MDC: No. What happened was, I was in a— What happened before the shooting, before I pulled the trigger, and after, were two different scenes in my mind. Before, everything was, like, dead calm, and I was ready for this to happen. I even heard a voice—my own—inside of me say, "Do it, do it, do it," you know, "Here we go." And then afterwards, it was like the film strip broke. I fell in upon myself. I, like, went into a state of shock. I stood there with the gun hanging limply down on my right side. And José the doorman came over, and he's crying, and he's grabbing my arm, and he's shaking my arm, and he shook the gun right out of my hand—which is a very brave thing to do to an armed person—and he kicked the gun across the pavement and had somebody take it away. And I was just—I was stunned. I didn't know what to do. I took *The Catcher in the Rye* out of my pocket, I paced, I tried to read it. I just couldn't wait, Larry, till those police got there. I was just devastated.

[*Commercial break*]

LK: J. D. Salinger, who has not been heard from in years—he's reclusive—wrote *The Catcher in the Rye*, a book read by millions, admired by millions. I wonder what he must be thinking as he is—if he is—watching this? Mark, why are you blaming a book?

MDC: I'm not blaming a book. I blame myself for crawling inside of the book, and I certainly want to say that J. D. Salinger and *The Catcher in the Rye* didn't cause me to kill John Lennon. In fact, I wrote to J. D. Salinger—I got his box number from someone—and I apologized to him for this. I feel badly about that. It's my fault. I crawled in, found my pseudo-self within these pages, and played out the whole thing.

LK: But Holden wasn't violent.

MDC: Holden wasn't violent, but he had a violent thought of shooting someone, of emptying a revolver into this fellow's stomach, someone that had done him wrong. But you're right, he was a basically very sensitive person, and he probably would not have killed anybody, as I did. But that's fiction, and reality was standing in front of the Dakota.

LK: What, Mark, got you better? What cured what you believe was schizophrenia?

MDC: Well, not medication and not doctors, but the Lord. I've walked in the power of the Lord now for a number of years.

LK: How did that happen?

MDC: Well, I became a Christian when I was sixteen, Larry, and that lasted about a year, of genuine walking with Him. Through my life, off and on, I have struggled with different things, as we all do, and at those times I would turn to the Lord. The night of the death of John Lennon, I was far from Him. I wasn't listening to Him. I wasn't reading the Bible any more. Today, I'm different. I read the Bible, I pray, and I walk with Him. He forgives me. He doesn't condone what I did, and that's a very important thing. He didn't like what I did twelve years ago. He didn't like all the pain I caused everybody, and especially John's widow, but He forgives me, and He hears me, and He listens to me. And he is the one all these years that has brought me out of the abyss, not medications or counseling. I've basically had to counsel myself through these years—not that it's non-available here, but I've been very private about this. This is not anything that's easy to live with.

LK: How do you know it isn't a crutch?

MDC: Well, in a way, it's got to be a crutch, because we all need a crutch. Life is not easy, and life for me isn't easy, and, therefore, I think the Lord has a tender spot in His heart for prisoners. He said so. The rest of the Bible says so in many different places. And I've leaned on Him. If it's a crutch, I've been leaning on a crutch, but it's a crutch made out of the cross, because without that I probably wouldn't be alive today, because I was very suicidal, and I certainly wouldn't be in a well state of mind—not without Him.

LK: Did you have, prior to the conversion to the Lord, remorse?

MDC: Well, I converted to the Lord at sixteen, before the shooting. I know a lot of people have a hard time understanding that. "How could someone who's 'born again' shoot someone?" And my answer to that is, after thinking about it deeply, God—if you were God, you wouldn't want a bunch of robots running around. He gives us free will. We are free agents. We can do what we want. He specifically told me—and I don't want to sound like one of those preachers on TV— but He told my heart—let's put it that way—He told my heart, and He let me know, "Don't kill. I don't want you to kill." He doesn't like murder. The first baby born was a murderer. But I chose to kill someone. I went against what He wanted me to do.

[*Commercial break*]

LK: Let's touch a couple of other bases, Mark. Do you expect to get out in eight years?

MDC: No, I don't.

LK: Do not? Do you expect to stay there for life?

MDC: I don't know about that. That's up to the parole division here in the state of New York. I certainly don't think they're going to let me out on the parole date. Because of the nature of the crime, because a man has died, they generally don't let you go right away. . . .

LK: How are you treated at that infamous place? Attica, while maybe it got its rap badly when they had the riots, is known as one of the tough-duty prisons.

MDC: It's a maximum-security prison. It's not the same prison as it was those years ago. I'm treated humanely. I'm eating well, as you can see. I am treated—once the officers get to know me, they see I'm just like everybody else—if that can be imagined—and I'm treated decently. I don't have any problem here in that area. I'm not beaten or tortured.

LK: Are you in a cell alone?

MDC: Every prisoner in Attica has his own cell. That's one of the good things about Attica.

LK: What kind of room are you in now?

MDC: I'm in, probably, a 6-by-8 cell. By the way, I have a job. I'm let out every morning at 6:30, and I work throughout the day.

LK: Doing—?

MDC: My job is called "the kitchen man." I help set up the meals for the inmates that are here in this particular building. And I do other things, too, but basically my job is in the kitchen.

LK: What do you make of all the conspiracy theories that have come up in the last twelve years—CIA, mind control, et cetera?

MDC: Against the death of John Lennon?

LK: Yes.

MDC: Hogwash.

LK: No one asked you to do it? No one prompted you to do it? No cabal, nothing?

MDC: No. They probably wish they would have had me, Larry, but they didn't. This was me doing it. It wasn't them.

LK: This is kind of perverse, I guess. Do you have fans? Do people write to you?

MDC: Well, I don't call them fans, but there are people that write to me. I got a letter yesterday. I guess you wouldn't call the fellow a fan, but he said, "I hereby declare on this date that you will not die a natural death." And then, another fellow sent me a package, a book, a Christian book written by Dr. Henry Cloud, and it's a book on healing, it's a book on looking into your past, and I think I'll read it. So I'm getting both ends of the spectrum—the extreme hate, which I understand, and the compassion, the understanding. People that have read the book have seen, "Hey, you know, this was a monstrous act, but perhaps not done by a typical monster." So I'm getting both—

LK: Do you get romantic letters?

MDC: Everything, Larry, I get—

LK: Yes, girls?

MDC: —every possible thing you could imagine.

LK: The treatment by other prisoners—good?

MDC: I'm upstairs with three other inmates, and they're carefully screened, and most of them are going home very soon. And I don't have any problem.

LK: They're nice to you?

MDC: They're very nice to me.

LK: You haven't had any brawls or anything?

MDC: No.

LK: How about homosexuality attacks?

MDC: None. Zero. That just doesn't happen in this building.

LK: Because it's so tightly secure?

MDC: Tightly secure.

LK: Okay. There was another— I remember the guy who stalked Rebecca Schaeffer, the actress, and killed her, also said he was reading *The Catcher in the Rye*, and there have been other copycats. What are your thoughts about them?

MDC: I regret that the most, because John Lennon wasn't the only person to die because of this. There were suicides after, which I deeply regret—

LK: And there's celebrity stalking.

MDC: And there's celebrity stalking. I'd love to talk about that, Larry. So it didn't end with the death of John Lennon, and that's— You know, you keep paying for this over and over when you hear of a death of a celebrity and maybe they've got *The Catcher in the Rye*, as John Hinckley did.

LK: Yes. Tell me about why you think—

MDC: A copy in his Washington hotel room.

LK: Why do you think people stalk celebrities?

MDC: People stalk celebrities—and this is just my opinion—I haven't studied psychology—because they have nothing inside of themselves. Their esteem is rock-bottom, and they feel that by writing fan letters or actually coming in close contact with the celebrity, they feel important. I know that I did some of those things before the thought of John Lennon—of killing John Lennon—came into my mind. I went to an art gallery and Robert Goulet was there and Leslie Nielsen was there, and I just wanted to be around them. And I had my picture taken with Robert Goulet. I don't think this has ever come out. And I felt important while I was with them. And then, after, you disintegrate again. You become nothing.

So if you have nothing to start with, and your life consists of fantasizing about celebrities or being with them, that can become very dangerous. And that is a phenomenon in this country now that has to be addressed. That's why the Secret Service has been talking with me and other people, to try to find out what was ticking in this thing here [*touches forehead*] on that night and before. I'm meeting with them Friday, by the way.

LK: With the Secret Service? Are they going to talk to you about protecting Clinton?

MDC: They've asked me about presidential candidates: "If there are so many body guards, would that have prevented you?" My answer to that is no. I still would have probably struck out at John Lennon if he had twenty bodyguards. I was that desperate.

LK: The incident with Goulet, which you have not revealed before, taking the pic-
      ture with Goulet and you felt like someone—were you conscious of it at the
      time? Were you conscious while taking the picture, "I felt like someone," and
      then, when removed, felt like less?

MDC: Sure. Yes. I remember I was rude to him, Larry. I touched his shoulder, and he
      kind of turned back to me and said, like, you know, "What's this?" you know,
      "Can't you see I'm trying to have a conversation?" People like me at that
      time—the way I was at that time—they don't think of other people. They're
      not polite. They're just, "Let me have my autograph," or, "Let me have my pic-
      ture taken with you." They don't think of the people as people.

LK: Anyone who gets any attention sees this. Is there anything you could say to a
      celebrity to do about it?

MDC: I couldn't tell them what to do, except don't egg-on anybody. I think that's what
      Rebecca Schaeffer did, if I'm not mistaken. She wrote back to Bardo—not that
      she's to blame for her death—but she wrote back to Bardo, and she said, you
      know, "Thank you. It's the most wonderful fan letter I've ever gotten." I would
      discourage that. I would more likely want to address the stalkers and say, "Look,
      you've got to talk to somebody. If you don't talk to somebody, you're going to
      end up like me."

LK: Have any of them ever contacted you—Bardo or anybody?

MDC: The first time I've ever said this, Larry: Robert Bardo wrote me three letters. I
      don't have them any more. I tore them up. They were very deranged letters.

LK: After he killed her?

MDC: This is before, Larry.

LK: *Before* he killed her?

MDC: Yes. But he did not mention killing anyone, and he did not mention Rebecca
      Schaeffer by name.

LK: Did he leave a return address?

MDC: Yes, he did.

LK: Did you turn it over to authorities?

MDC: Yes, I did. Someone—a Christian worker here—had a Christian group contact
      him and send him some materials. He wrote me back and said, "That's doing
      me no good." You see, we're free agents. We make those choices.

LK: Okay. Why didn't the authorities do something about him?

MDC: Well, again, he wasn't saying he was going to kill anyone. He was just asking me
      questions, "What is it like to be in prison?"—but very, very, deranged letters.
      And, Larry, I got frightened. I tore them up.

LK: Okay.

MDC: When I was watching the news, that news came on, and I went, "My God, that's
      the same fellow that wrote me." I told someone about it, because I couldn't
      contain it, and then tore up the letters, because I don't want any part of either
      being for or against this man for what he did. He'll have to stand alone on that.
      But I did receive mail from him, yes.

LK: One other thing, Mark. If it weren't Lennon, could it have been Goulet? Could
      it have been Goulet, could it have been Sinatra, could it have been Paul
      McCartney?

MDC: Probably not one of the other Beatles. This thing started, Larry, when I got
      angry at Lennon. I found a book in the library that showed him on the roof of

the Dakota. And you're familiar with the Dakota. It's a very nice, sumptuous building. And remember, I'm in a different state of mind, and I'm falling in on myself. I'm angry at seeing him on the Dakota, and I say to myself, "That phony. That bastard." I got that mad. I took the book home to my wife, and I said, "Look. He's a phony." It started with anger. It didn't start with a person walking down the street saying, "Gee, I wish I was famous." This thing, you know, in fairness, wasn't all about becoming a pseudo-celebrity. It was born of anger and rage, and that's what happened. That's where the roots were.

LK: Might it have been anger, then, at a president? Did it have to be—

MDC: It could have been anger at a president.

LK: Or a broadcaster?

MDC: It could have been anger at a broadcaster. It could have happened that way, very easily. But I think, because it was Lennon, because my past—Jack gets into this in the book very deeply. My past was very rooted in Lennon. I believed in the things he was saying, and I believe he did, too, by the way.

LK: Do you listen to his music?

MDC: I don't think he's a phony any more. He's not a phony any more.

LK: Do you listen to his music?

MDC: If it's on the radio, I'll listen to it. I did have some tapes, but recently—let's say, two months ago—I had to get rid of them. I just didn't want them in my cell.

LK: Thanks, Mark. Thanks for giving us this time.

MDC: Thank you very much, Larry. I appreciate it.

Jimmy Carter

James Earl Carter still has a home in the small Georgia town of Plains, where he was born on October 1, 1924. He served in the navy as a nuclear-reactor engineer during the infancy of atomic-powered submarines, and, following the death of his father in 1953, returned home to run the family's peanut farm. Carter served as a state senator from 1962 to 1966 and as governor from 1971 to 1975. After a close 1976 race against republican Gerald Ford, Carter became president, building an administration marked by character and idealism, but also plagued by scandal, double-digit inflation, an energy crisis, and the Iran hostage crisis. Carter was defeated by Ronald Reagan in 1980, but has enjoyed a distinguished post-presidential career as a humanitarian and diplomatic troubleshooter.

"The last three days I was in the White House, I didn't go to bed at all."

LARRY KING: Early reports say the allies did serious damage in Wednesday's raid against Iraq, but Saddam Hussein still talks a good game, and the crisis still dangles. George Bush is not the first president to face a belligerent Middle East leader as he prepares to leave the White House. Jimmy Carter's war of wits against Iran's Ayatollah Khomeini persisted, literally, to his last minutes in office. It is said that only those who have occupied the Oval Office in times like these know what a lonely place it is. At the end of a busy day, and the week before the inauguration of another Democratic president, we are honored to have another return visit with Jimmy Carter here in Washington. And later, we'll be telling you about his new and terrific idea for a book called *Turning Point*.

What's that like—a day like today—for a president? Does it get down to one-man-one-decision?

JIMMY CARTER: Well, it does. The last three days I was in the White House, I didn't go to bed at all. I was staying up trying to get our last fifty-four hostages out of Iran safe and with honor and all alive, and I never even thought about going to bed. And we successfully negotiated their release. They sat there until 12:00 and then, a few minutes afterwards, took off. But it was a very happy day for me when I heard that the hostages were all safe and free.

LK: What do you gather today was like for President Bush?

JC: I think the Iraq war has been going on now for two years with skirmishing back and forth. Everybody knows that American planes can strike Iraq and missiles can strike Iraq with almost total impunity. There's nothing Iraq can do in return except just to make propaganda statements. So I don't think there was any danger to our people. The precision training they have, the superb weapons that we have, make us all powerful in the air, at least without any danger of casualties. But I would guess that now Saddam Hussein has seen from the public statements of Bill Clinton that there won't be any change in American policy, that he has a dedication to carrying out the U.N. Security Council resolutions. And he can't get away with any sort of shenanigans just because we are facing inauguration day. . . .

LK: You never had to make a decision like this, did you? . . . I mean, men never went to their deaths—no one died under you, did they?

JC: No.

LK: And you didn't bomb anybody else?

JC: No.

LK: So what could you imagine that to be like? I mean, that can't be easy.

JC: No, it can't be easy. I was in the navy for eleven years. I was a submarine officer, and when I went out on patrols that I knew to be dangerous, in effect, I said, "Okay, my life is at stake," and I crossed that point, you know, when I became a submarine officer. And any commander in chief who's been in that position dreads the necessity on occasion for exerting our own military might and causing the death of either the enemy or our own people. This is a time, though, when the transition of government is very troubling. I would say that since Harry Truman took over in the midst of the Second World War with Roosevelt's death, no president has inherited such a mess of problems in foreign policy as Clinton will take over next week—just a whole list of things that could go wrong or already have embroiled American troops and American obligations.

LK: Why do you think, Mr. President, in view of all the successes that George Bush had in foreign policy—and certainly, overall, he'd get high grades—all of this suddenly falls into the lap of someone else: Bosnia, we're in Somalia, killing in Iraq, lining up missiles. Why? . . .

JC: I think one of the problems, Larry, is that the United Nations is just now coming of age, since Gorbachev brought an end to the Cold War, and is now able to exert itself in a forceful fashion. I don't think it's yet reached the point where we exert ourselves through the United Nations to prevent Somalias and to prevent Bosnias and to prevent the upcoming crisis that might take place, say, in Liberia, or already takes place in many other countries in Africa—say, Angola and Mozambique, where wars are already going on. The prevention of human rights violations, the prevention of civil wars, the alleviation of suffering as a preemptive thing—not just a reaction when CNN begins to show distended bellies and starving children—is something that we haven't yet arrived at in maturity.

LK: What do you think will happen now with Iraq and Hussein, and what do you see short-range?

JC: My guess is that Saddam Hussein will do what he did after the last war, and that is he'll lick his wounds, he'll try to have as much propaganda as possible, blaming the whole problem on the United States and on the United Nations, and he'll be more cautious for at least a few weeks or a few months. You know, how long we're going to keep all our forces over in the Persian Gulf and monitor every time he places an anti-aircraft battery in the desert somewhere in his own territory, I don't know. But we are monitoring in, like, micro-management what goes on in Iraq. How long are we going to do it? I don't know.

LK: Is he, do you think, based on what you know, a good bet to test Clinton?

JC: I think, in a way, he's already tested Clinton, to see if Clinton would stand staunchly at the side of George Bush as a forthcoming president. I think Clinton has made it very strong, unequivocally, that there will be no change in policy in the United States when we change presidents.

LK: Would you have supported today's action, too?

JC: Yes, I think once the Security Council of the United Nations makes a decision with our full support, that decision has to be carried out. . . .

[*Commercial break*]

LK: President Carter's Mideast crisis was just one of the turning points in his political career. Most Americans first heard of him in 1976, but now he's written the story of his entry into politics. It was 1962. The Supreme Court had issued its landmark one-man-one-vote decision, and a young peanut farmer from Plains, Georgia, ran for the state senate. It's all in the new book *Turning Point: A Candidate, a State, and a Nation Come of Age*, published by Times Books. And we'll talk about this extraordinary work, but there is one other thing we should cover before we move to that, and that's your thoughts on Bosnia. . . .

JC: There again, I think the United Nations has got to do something more to protect Sarajevo, to protect Bosnia and then make sure that supplies at least can get in to these people. And if military action is necessary and the Security Council makes that decision, I think it should be done, but without U.S. troops being in the forefront and without U.S. troops providing the air cover. I think this is a time for the Europeans to assume the responsibility, which they have shirked for too long. The U.S. can provide leadership, and the United Nations we can support, but I think this is a European matter, and they should be in the forefront.

LK: So you would not send troop one?

JC: Not American troops. . . .

LK: Do you think in this matter [Bill Clinton] might be in accord with that?

JC: I would presume so. During the campaign itself, Bill was— I have discussed it with him during the campaign, but not since he was elected. He was basically compatible with what I just said, yes. What he feels now, I don't know. . . .

LK: Why a book about beginnings? Why thirty years ago?

JC: Well, a lot of people don't know, Larry, how the South went about keeping racial segregation in effect one hundred years after the War Between the States, when people were guaranteed equality of opportunity, and why the Supreme Court ruled separate-but-equal when everybody knew that the black and white people were separate, but no one believed it was equal. They did it through the county unit system, which was a subversion of democracy, which all of us took for granted as being okay.

LK: Yes, trees voted.

JC: Well, yes, as a matter of fact, counties voted. And one vote in the county where I had all my trouble equaled ninety-nine votes in Atlanta, and this was completely legal. There were no blacks registered to vote in most of the counties in Georgia, and no Republicans at all—which, you know, might have been a nice thing, but maybe not fair. But I decided to run after the Supreme Court ruling that one man should have a vote, and it should be equal to others. I was a peanut farmer—innocent, believing in democracy and freedom and equality and fairness and justice, and I was on the county school board and wanted to protect the public schools from being destroyed, so I ran for the state senate. I was ahead in six of the counties. But one little tiny county on the Alabama line, across from Eufaula, Alabama, was bossed by a man named Joe Hurst, who totally controlled that county. He was a state legislator. He was the only state legislator who was also a full-time state employee. He was head of the Democratic party, which had the final decision on any election dispute. His wife was the welfare director. This was the only county in the nation where all the welfare checks came to the same mailbox. They personally delivered every welfare check every month. They decided who was on and who was off welfare. All the people had to do to comply with his demand was to vote the way he told them to.

LK: And he didn't want Jimmy Carter in the state senate?

JC: No, he didn't. And the only way you can tell if people vote the way you want to is not to have a secret ballot. So when I went over to Georgetown on election day, there was this man, Joe Hurst, and his associates, standing side-by-side at a little table, telling everyone to vote against me and for my opponent. And he was so powerful in the community that he did not have any fear of the revelation of what he was doing. When I complained, he just ignored what I said or scoffed at it. That evening, when the polls closed, there were 333 people who had voted. There were 421 ballots in the box, 118 of whom voted alphabetically, and a number of whom were dead or in prison or had not voted, as later circumstances came forward. And it took me the next two weeks—which is all the time I had before the general election—to try to get it straightened out. Most people thought I was just a sorehead loser who couldn't take my defeat fairly, but I became— Although I didn't particularly care to be in public office then, I didn't want to be cheated.

LK: And you won the fight?

JC: Eventually won the fight. Went to the state legislature. Although I was not a lawyer, I introduced a new election code for Georgia, along with other people. One of the interesting amendments that was offered to my proposal was by a young senator then named Bobby Rowan—from the interesting-named town of Enigma, Georgia—who proposed that in Georgia no person could vote in a Democratic party or in a general election who had been dead more than three years. And there was quite a debate. Some people claimed in the senate, well, you know, for a few years after, say, a husband dies, the wife and children can accurately ascertain how that husband would have voted if he had lived until the election came along.

Well, this was not only a turning point in my life, obviously, but it was the main vote, I think, that the Supreme Court ever made that really brought an end to racial segregation and made the civil rights effort successful. . . .

[*Commercial break*]

LK: As many have said, we've had lots of former presidents; no one has quite filled those shoes like President Carter, who gets more beloved every day. Must be interesting to see this popularity grow with time and be still young enough to appreciate it. Do you miss office, by the way?

JC: No, not really. . . . I did for a while, but now I've got so many things under way, I don't really miss office.

LK: You've been around the scene so long—southern-born. Are we ever going to see racial peace? Are we ever going to see people just measure people by people, rather than color?

JC: You know, I think in the South the segregation of society is not merely based on race any more, like it was. Take Atlanta, for instance. There's almost perfect harmony among the executives who make decisions in Atlanta—between the mayor and the city council and the county commissioners and so forth, and even the top executives in companies. But I would say that our society now is about as segregated as it was thirty years ago, not based on race, necessarily, certainly not based on legal race. Based on wealth and based on power and the making of decisions that affect a person's life. On the one hand, you've got rich persons, like you and me. I'm not talking about bank account, but a rich person is one that has a home to live in and has a chance of a job and a modicum of education and health care, who lives in a neighborhood where they believe it's reasonably safe to go outdoors, and who thinks the police and the judicial system are on their side. On the other hand are the ones who don't have any of those things, who live side-by-side with us in our major cities, in particular. Atlanta is two cities. Atlanta is a great city—one of the best—but there are two Atlantas; there are two Washingtons; there are two New Yorks; there are two Los Angeles; there are two—

LK: And one doesn't see the other, right?

JC: The one doesn't even—is not even aware of the other. In fact, I think now that the powerful people in our society ignore the suffering people in our society perhaps as much as the white leaders did thirty years ago ignore the blacks.

LK: Why?

JC: We don't want to see it. We have a natural inclination to think that just because somebody doesn't have a house to live in they must be inferior, they must not be ambitious or intelligent or must not care about their family. But as you know, every year Rosalynn and I go somewhere, and we build a house for people—the poorest people in the nation—who work side-by-side with us for a week. And we've found that those people are just as intelligent as I am, just as ambitious, just as hard-working, love their kids just as much. And their lives are literally transformed when they finally move into a decent home that they, themselves, have made, helped to build.

LK: But isn't it also, as you pointed out, beneficial to society for them to do better, economically? . . . Why should we want poor people?

JC: It's a wonderful investment for us. You know, not only are the streets safe and the cities are better, but the employees are better trained. They show up Monday morning, they're not sick as much, they can read and write better, the drug culture is not there to supply drugs to our rich children. You know, all these things are beneficial to us. Rosalynn and I went by the Grady Hospital in Atlanta, which takes care of poor people. We saw a little baby there at the time that was one pound and two ounces. This kid was only—less than a foot long, and it was four-and-a-half months premature. The mother had never had any prenatal care. That child survived. The child weighs thirteen pounds now. The newspapers named the child "Pumpkin," but it cost the taxpayers $300,000 to bring Pumpkin up to normal birth weight. If that mother had had prenatal care, then the taxpayers would not have had to pay that three hundred thousand bucks. It now costs us about $35,000 a year to keep a young person in jail.

LK: When you began in politics, someone could be an avowed segregationist. That does not exist now, right? I mean, you'd be—

JC: No, there are some that maybe in a private way would say things that they used to say about black and white, or African Americans and others. But not publicly. And at that time, when I went through this ordeal with my first election, it was more or less accepted in our society. In fact, the Supreme Court even upheld laws that permitted the continuation of racial segregation.

LK: Were you ever able to examine why you were different?

JC: Well, I had been in the navy for eleven years. You know, on a submarine, you cannot distinguish in a crisis between people because of what color their skin is.

LK: No prejudice. It's stupid to be prejudiced on a submarine.

JC: Well, I wouldn't say that there's no prejudice. It certainly does exist. But you know that you're all in the same boat, you're all on an equal basis, and there's no distinction. And if you remember, in 1948, I believe, Harry Truman issued a strong directive that transformed the military: there will be no racial discrimination in the army, air force, marines, or navy any more. And as commander in chief, his directive was carried out to a substantial degree. Well, you know, this is the way I grew up from an eighteen-year-old until I came home from the navy eleven years later.

LK: When you went to the navy, can you say you thought black people were inferior?

JC: Well, I mean, I had come out of a southern society where it was just an accepted thing. As a matter of fact, it was rarely even questioned. I mean, even the black leaders around Plains and Americus, Georgia, and so forth—they never raised any question about it back in the '40s. I went off to the Naval Academy in 1943. So there was—

LK: So Annapolis changed you, and then the navy changed you?

JC: Annapolis and particularly the navy, on a ship, yes.

LK: Were there any blacks at Annapolis when you went there?

JC: Yes, a few. The first ones came, as a matter of fact, while I was there.

LK: Do you think the country has learned it? Do you know any great people who are still prejudiced?

JC: Well, if I did, I wouldn't name them on this show. [*laughs*]

LK: No, I know, but do you know? Without naming them, do you know people of major prominence who you would consider—

JC: Not really. I know prominent people who are insensitive and who prefer to believe that we Americans, we white Americans, are inherently superior; that God blesses us in a special way with wealth and security and influence and so forth because we are superior. But you know, I wouldn't say that's racism. It's more like ego or somebody that's concentrating on themselves. And I'm guilty of this myself. It's hard for me to realize that people in Sudan, who are dying perhaps much more rapidly than they are in Somalia, are equal in importance to my own grandchildren. You know, I go to Sudan, and I negotiate to try to bring peace to Sudan on occasion, but it's hard for me to equate the suffering that I see with my own grandchildren.

LK: Of course. Do you think this turning point which you write about had the effect to make you what you are now . . . the kind of person who wants to go where problems are?

JC: Yes, I have to tell you that when I ran for that office I did not particularly want to be in public office. I did want to try to save the public school system. But once I saw that I was being cheated, and once the people of that little county came to me and said, you know, "Jimmy, will you stick with it? If you do, for the first time we will demand that this oppression of our voting rights will be lifted," then I made a contract with them, and I stuck it out. But now we hold elections all over the world, as you probably know.

LK: You go and monitor them, right?

JC: We go and monitor them. And I've never seen any election in any foreign country that could have any sort of fraudulent tricks with which I was not personally familiar. . . . I grew up and learned it.

LK: But it also set you a value for human rights, didn't it?

JC: Well, it did.

LK: One-man-one-vote is a concept of yours?

JC: Yes, I don't think anyone could come out of the South into the milieu of the entire American equal system, seeing the benefits that came to white and black citizens from the successful end of the civil rights movement, that wouldn't appreciate the benefits that came to both sides. And I could never have been considered to be the president of the United States had it not been for the successful civil rights movement and what others did.

LK: You still share the view that President Clinton—President-elect Clinton—should sign-off on gays in the military and put that like Truman did with blacks?

JC: Well, he promised to do it. I had a similar question, by the way, when I was first inaugurated, the first day, and that was what to do about the draft-dodgers, so-called, who moved to Canada. And I had promised in my campaign that I would issue a blanket amnesty. It was a highly unpopular act, as you know, right after the Vietnam War. As soon as I took the oath of office and walked backstage, still at the Capitol building, I signed a directive that issued an amnesty for all of our young men who had gone to Canada.

LK: Because you promised it?

JC: Because I promised it, and I wanted to get it over with. I didn't want to spend the first three months arguing about an amnesty for kids in Canada.

LK: So you think Clinton should do the same?

JC: Well, I'm not trying to tell him what to do—

LK: But you would do the same in that position?

JC: Yes, I would. I think it ought to be done once and for all. If he's promised it, if he's going to do it, do it and be done with it. . . .

[*Commercial break*]

LK: The last time you were here, you said there was only one appointment you'd recommend: Warren Christopher, secretary of state. He was appointed. . . . He maybe will be approved. Will he be a great secretary of state?

JC: I think so. I made some other recommendations to the transition team by letter, but not to Bill Clinton. He's the only one that I asked him to appoint. I think he's the finest public servant I've ever known. He's wise, he's courageous, he's a man of great dignity, he has wide experience, and he's—

LK: Do you make anything of these charges that he knew about army spying?

JC: I think that all came up in 1977. It happened twenty-five years ago. I don't think he knew anything about it. He said he didn't.

And he's also gotten to be known quite well with Bill Clinton. I would say that if there's one person that helped Bill Clinton get elected that was unanticipated, not counting his family, it was Al Gore. And the choice of Al Gore was one that was orchestrated by Warren Christopher. So he and Bill Clinton know each other much better than I knew my secretary of state when I went into office, and that's a very beneficial thing, for a secretary of state and a president to already be good friends, to know each other's strengths and weaknesses, and I think it'll be a great benefit to our country. . . .

LK: Onward to phone calls for Jimmy Carter. We go to Newport, Rhode Island. Hello.

CALLER: [*Newport, Rhode Island*] Good evening, sir. I'm from the great state of Georgia, and I'm serving in the navy in Newport, Rhode Island. What I'd like to know, sir, is how do you think history will judge your presidency two hundred years from now? And also, do you ever feel any bitterness toward your contemporary critics?

JC: No, I got over the bitterness about contemporary critics a long time ago. I had critics when I was trying to be governor, and later when I was trying to be president. I got to be governor and president anyway, and reached the highest elective office in the world, in my opinion, so I don't have any bitterness about that.

Well, two hundred years from now, I don't know how history will look back on my administration. I think there will be, maybe, some memories about peace and human rights. There may be an outgrowth from the Camp David accords and the treaty between Israel and Egypt that will pay permanent dividends. I hope it will. I think perhaps that the Alaska lands bill, where we doubled the size of the national park system and tripled the precious areas that are preserved in our country, might be a permanent legacy. But it's too early to say.

LK: The most unpopular president ever to leave office was Harry Truman. . . . A close second may have been, even at his death, Lincoln.

JC: Lincoln—and President Nixon, of course—went out in some disgrace. . . . I was right behind him on unpopularity, so—

LK: But things grow, don't they?

JC: With the passage of time, yes. Even Eisenhower was scorned, as you know, by historians when he first left office, but with the passage of time, grew in stature.

LK: Toronto, hello.

CALLER: [*Toronto, Ontario*] Yes. Hello, President Carter. Like Larry said earlier, it's a real privilege to talk to you. What I wanted to say was, as a Canadian—just comparing our federal politics—whenever we have a federal election here, the whole issue of media scrutiny into the personal past history of the candidates doesn't seem to be as big an issue as it is there. I'm wondering how you would compare the level that that was an issue back when you ran, compared to how it is today? And do you think that is necessarily a good thing or a good trend?

JC: Well, you have to remember that in a parliamentary system like Canada, the leader of the nation is really the leader of the political party; that you kind of grow up as— Something like the speaker of our own House of Representatives would be prime minister of Canada. But in America, of course, the one elected president almost runs on his own. The Democratic party plays a relatively small role in the choice of an American president, if it is a Democrat, and vice-versa in the Republican party. So it's an entirely different system.

I think it's a much more personal, negative campaign than I knew when I ran for president. I would never have dreamed, for instance, of calling President Ford by his own name. It was always "my distinguished opponent," even when I was making critical statements about him. And he would never have said "Jimmy Carter" or "Governor Carter." We always referred to each other as they do in the U.S. Senate, as "my distinguished opponent." And I would never have dreamed of getting on a platform and saying, "these bozos running against me don't know as much about foreign policy as my dog." You know, those are the kinds of things that are now accepted perhaps in some ways in American politics, but they were not then.

LK: How about personal life? How much of a person's personal life should we, as a voter, take into consideration in voting for them in public life?

JC: I think the person's life as a family man—if it is a man—as a husband, as a member of the local community, one's own background, attitude towards crises, ought to be legitimate fodder for the public consumption to make a decision on "This is going to be the leader of my nation." I don't see anything wrong with that. Also, I never have particularly deplored the long and tortuous ordeal that a candidate has to go through to get the nomination and to get the presidency. It does two things. One, it requires the candidate to learn a lot about this nation that they would never know otherwise. And it also lets the people of the country know a lot about the candidates that the people really need to know.

LK: And how about this year's election, with programs like this and candidates conversing with people?

JC: Well, you know, you have been a central figure in deciding the outcome of this election. And even though Ross Perot was not elected president, I think he had a major impact on the consciousness of America, and I think that Bill Clinton and George Bush, who finally survived to be the top two—they learned a lot from Ross Perot, and they had to really pay attention to what he said. And it was on this program, of course, that it was launched.

LK: Do you think politics has changed forever now; presidents will talk to people?

JC: I think so. I think everybody learned that this would be the case. We still have some very serious fallacies in the American political system that we don't even acknowledge or admit. We invited some Latin Americans to come to witness the election in November. They were shocked to find that the way we run a presidential election would be totally out of limits if I was monitoring an election in Latin America.

LK: Like what do you mean?

JC: We're the only country that requires candidates to pay for a right to present our views to the American people, to the people in the public, to decide whether or not we should be holding public office. . . .

[*Commercial break*]

LK: Spartanburg, South Carolina, hello.

CALLER: [*Spartanburg, South Carolina*] Larry King, thank you and CNN. And, Mr. President, it's nice talking to you. And what I want to know is, on the Iran deal, when you was in office I supported you thoroughly, but why didn't we kick some butts over there and pay them back for what they did to us? They did us great harm.

JC: Well, obviously, that was discussed. "Should we bomb Teheran?" I could have destroyed Teheran with one F-15 strike, but in the process I would have killed fifteen thousand innocent Iranians who had nothing to do with the holding of the hostages, and I would also, not coincidentally, have killed all our hostages. So you know, there's a limit to what you can do when they're holding hostages. I think we did the most difficult thing on the hostages, and that was to be patient, and eventually every single hostage came home safe and free. So a lot of people advised me to bomb Teheran, to destroy Iran, to kill as many civilians as we could and punish those Iranians, but it was just a very tiny portion of the Iranians who were doing this crime.

LK: Were there ever moments where your anger at this was so great that you gave thought to that?

JC: Yes, we considered it thoroughly. There was a time when we considered destroying the complete oil refineries in Abadan, for instance. But the ayatollah had already claimed that he was going to put our hostages on trial and execute those that were found guilty of any kind of espionage. I sent him a highly secret message—nobody ever knew about it until after I left office—that if he put a single hostage on trial, we would close off all access of Iran to the outside world, and if he injured or killed a hostage, we would respond militarily. After that warning went to him, which was late in November of '79, he never again mentioned putting one of our hostages on trial.

LK: Fort Lauderdale, Florida, hello.

CALLER: [*Fort Lauderdale, Florida*] Yes. Mr. President, you're one of my heroes because I think you're a good person, I think you're very honest, and I think you have a great wife. Do you think that Washington, which seems so dishonest, has a difficult time dealing with a person with your honesty?

JC: Well, I don't put myself as any more honest than the people that are here now, at all. But I think that the best approach to dealing with very difficult issues is to take those matters to the public. I'll give you a current example—and I'm not saying this in any critical way. During the campaign, for instance, Bill Clinton made some promises about no gasoline tax and about giving the middle class a substantial tax reduction. Now as he approaches inauguration, he discovers, to his surprise, that the budget deficit this year is much greater than President Bush ever revealed to the American people or even knew about during the campaign. So I think the best thing for Bill Clinton to do would be to go to the American people and say, "I'm not trying to be dishonest. I know things now that I didn't know during the campaign. This is what we have to do. It's going to require some sacrifice." And I think in doing that, in being honest, that it'll be a very good political blow. I think it'll be a popular thing for people to see his courage. . . .

LK: Did you ever have to lie?

JC: No.

LK: Never did?

JC: When I was in the White House, no. No.

LK: You could say "no comment."

JC: I often said "no comment," but if I ever made a statement— I think everybody has tried to find that this statement that I'm making now is not true. No, I never had to lie when I was president.

LK: Denver, hello. . . .

CALLER: [*Denver, Colorado*] I'd like to ask the president—I understand you are not going to support the boycott in Colorado as it pertains to [the anti-gay] Amendment 2. And you were speaking earlier of discrimination being as rampant now as it was thirty years ago. And I would like to know how you feel about adding sexual orientation to the 1964 Civil Rights Act? And don't you think that boycotts can have an effect in changing the law, much as they did in the South and in South Africa?

JC: Well, I don't think a boycott of the outside world against the South had anything to do with implementing the civil rights laws.

LK: But boycotts have been effective.

JC: Boycotts have been effective.

LK: And they're American as apple pie, someone once said.

JC: Yes, but he's talking about the boycott against Colorado. You know, we ski in Colorado, and we were out there this past Thanksgiving. The communities that are being punished by the boycotts are the ones that did have very strong protection on gay rights within themselves. Aspen is one of them. They voted three-to-one against the amendment, and they are now trying to marshal financial support and legal support to overthrow, or to prevent the implementation of, this discriminatory amendment. I think it's better for us to try to help those communities overthrow and prevent the implementation of this than just to kill the people that voted against it.

[*Commercial break*]

LK: The second part of the question was, should the Civil Rights Act of 1964 be amended to include people's sexual orientation?

JC: I think so.

LK: Straight answer. New York City, hello.

CALLER: [*New York, New York*] Hi. A friend of mine here in New York City, who works in the United Nations, has told me there's a lot of rumors that you may become the next head of the U.N. Development Program, which is one of the agencies that Bonn is offering to move over to Germany. I was wondering, do you have any comments on that possibility? And secondly, how do you feel about this possible move of U.N. agencies to Germany?

JC: Well, I don't think I'll be offered the job, and if I was offered it, I would not take it. I've got all I can handle at the Carter Center. I don't think it's a bad thing to move some of the U.N. agencies to other countries. You know, concentrating just in New York, I think, gives a very parochial outlook on life, and to have them in different countries I think is very good.

LK: Habitat, that builds homes for the poor: you're going to build your twenty-thousandth?

JC: The first week in April, Rosalynn and I will be working on the twenty-thousandth home that Habitat will have built in sixteen years. We're building now about twenty a day in about eight hundred communities in the United States. We have Habitat organizations in over three hundred universities, for college kids, and about thirty-five foreign countries. It's really a great program.

LK: Was it your idea?

JC: No, it wasn't. It was the idea of a man named Millard Fuller and his wife, Linda, who was a very rich young lawyer from Alabama. He gave away all of his money, started building homes for poor people, lived three years in Zaire, and then came back and started a worldwide program sixteen years ago. So we just, in effect, work for Habitat as volunteers. . . .

LK: Arlington, Virginia, hello.

CALLER: [*Arlington, Virginia*] Mr. President, I would like to ask your opinion on what the United States could—or perhaps should—do about the grave economic situation in the former Soviet Union?

JC: I just came back from the Soviet Union recently and also visited Kazakhstan and Alma-Ata, about two thousand miles further east. The Soviet Union, which is now Russia, of course, is desperately in need of economic assistance, but I would not put it in the category of grants or loans or direct cash payments to them. What we need to do is to implement a very viable program of working with the Russians to modify their laws to make it more receptive to free enterprise. That's what Yeltsin is already committed to do. It's not something that I'm advocating for him. We still don't have very many competent American business leaders who are investing in Russia at a profitable pace to give the people there a clear demonstration of what free enterprise or open markets can do. There's a committee set up that has been set up in the past. The Congress put two provisos on it. It can't go into full operation until Russia first of all promises to stop all trade with Cuba and, second, to withdraw their submarine—one submarine, I think—from the Persian Gulf. You know, we've got a large number of warships in the Persian Gulf. So until these two very embarrassing things, at least from the Russian point of view, are implemented, we can't really help them with American investments. It's a kind of a dopey thing that we do. And I would think that the investments in Russia are better than grants or gifts. . . .

[*Commercial break*]

LK: We're plumb out of time. Your thoughts on the Clinton administration: how are they going to do?

JC: I think they're going to do well. The main thing that Clinton will do, that hasn't been done in the last twelve years, is to bring some harmony between the White House and the Congress, and I hope even between republicans and democrats, and let people see that our government can, indeed, function effectively in dealing with our problems. . . .

April 29, 1992: Trucker Reginald Denny decided to avoid a traffic jam on the Harbor Freeway by taking a short cut on the surface streets of South-central L.A. He found himself in the middle of the worst American urban rioting of the century, sparked by the acquittal of four white Los Angeles police officers on all but one of the charges arising from the videotaped beating of motorist Rodney King. Denny was dragged onto the street and beaten, his head bashed in with a brick while a news helicopter hovered overhead, recording the assault.

Denny sued the city of Los Angeles and was represented by Johnnie Cochran Jr., who later achieved even wider recognition as one of O. J. Simpson's defense attorneys.

"Our information is there were more than 5,000 '911' calls that came in regarding the Denny beating. The police never responded—"

LARRY KING: If he'd come along ten minutes sooner, if he'd taken a different road, Reginald Denny might not be a household name today, but Denny was on the wrong road at the wrong time last spring. Just as the riots began in southeast Los Angeles, with no police around, he was dragged from his truck and beaten almost to death. Now, ninety stitches and several surgeries later, Denny is talking about the beating, his civil suit against the city of Los Angeles, and the still undetermined fate of the four suspects in his case. We welcome to *Larry King Live* Reginald Denny—his first live TV interview—along with his attorney, Johnnie Cochran Jr.

Just so we understand, Johnnie, you were retained right after this occurred?

JOHNNIE COCHRAN JR.: That's correct, Larry.

LK: Why did you pick Johnnie, Reg?

REGINALD DENNY: Well, Mr. Cochran was just recommended through a group of family friends—just somebody who knew somebody who was very familiar with Mr. Cochran's work.

LK: And you're happy with his representation?

RD: Oh, yes, sir. I have no problem with it. In fact, I knew nothing of what Mr. Cochran is capable of doing and his knowledge, but I definitely know now.

LK: And you're suing the city, are you not?

JC: We're bringing an action against the city of Los Angeles.

LK: Asking for a stipulated amount?

JC: No, we've not—it's not an ascertained amount at this point. But what we're saying, essentially, Larry, is that the city failed in their responsibility not only to Reg Denny but to all the citizens of South-central Los Angeles. Basically, they abdicated their responsibility in pulling the police back. They did it only in South-central, not in other areas of the city.

LK: And you're saying that, had the police been there, Reggie would not be as hurt as he was?

JC: Reggie wouldn't have been as hurt, and neither would other people have been as hurt.

LK: Tell us what happened, Reg—I mean, in your words. We've seen it enough, but what were you doing? What were you doing with the truck? Where were you going?

RD: Just my normal route to cut through town to avoid the traffic mess that's on the 10 Freeway in the L.A. area, which is always crazy at that time of the afternoon.

LK: What kind of truck is it? What do you drive?

RD: It's called a bottom-dump. It's a set of doubles, eighteen-wheeler, and two trailers filled with material to make concrete. . . .

LK: Okay. What happened?

RD: And just came off the freeway— You have to— It's an amazing sight to see when something is terribly wrong, but you don't know—I didn't know why or what it was, and it's an amazement.

LK: You hadn't heard that riots had broken out? Didn't have a radio in the truck or anything?

RD: I do, but I listen mostly either to a Christian station in L.A. or to, like, country and western music. And the last thing I really listen to is news, because I know what the traffic situation already is: It's lousy.

LK: So you drive off this freeway, and you're in a war?

RD: Yes, sir, just that quick.

LK: What did you try—? Did you try to get back on? Did you try to get out of there? What did you do?

RD: The thought did cross my mind. I have an older truck with no power steering. If I had power steering, I might would have tried to make a U-turn just to get away from the craziness. It was just—it was such a weird sight.

LK: What did you see?

RD: The broken glass, people taking stuff out of a truck that was in front of me, and cars going every which way—I mean, up and over curbs—and just doing crazy stuff, you know, and lots of glass: People screaming, tires screeching; and just thinking, you know, "What am I going to do to get through this?" and thinking, "I've got an eighteen-wheeler, you know, big enough piece of equipment—the biggest thing on the highway. I'm just going to tiptoe across this intersection and get on down the road."

LK: In other words, you were going to drive through the riot?

RD: Pretty much. Isn't that pretty stupid, to think of that?

LK: What happened?

RD: My right window broke, and that time I was extremely frightened. It's a strange feeling to be—"scared" I guess is another way, just—just, at that point, what do you do? Or "What do I do?" I'm sitting there, you know, turning into a, you know—God, just a—

LK: Sitting pigeon.

RD: Yes, that's basically what happened.

LK: What happened?

RD: From the time my right window broke out from whatever hit it, I knew after that nothing. I woke up—

LK: In other words, you know what you see on film?

RD: That's it.

LK: You have no memory of that?

RD: No. No, sir.

LK: No pain?

RD: Well—

LK: Subsequent pain?

RD: Yes, subsequent pain.

LK: I mean, you woke up in the hospital? Is that it?

RD: Yes, five days later, and I couldn't talk because they had a bunch of tubes going through my throat and everything. And I kind of penciled a note explaining to the people in the hospital to call my dispatcher, Denise—that's the name of the woman who handles the trucks—and tell her where I'm at and what happened, because I thought I was in deep trouble because—

LK: The truck company would be mad at you?

RD: Yes, they're looking for their truck, they're looking for me, and I didn't do what I was supposed to do—get my material, you know, to the batch plant.

LK: All right, now, what happened? What kind of injuries? You had ninety stitches, right?

RD: Quite a few—staples.

LK: Staples? Do you still have a fracture in the head?

RD: Yes, on the side of my head, here.

LK: There's a dent there.

RD: There is. . . . I don't know if you guys can see it, but the dent—[*indicates right temple*]—it's because the skull is missing, parts of the skull. And they can't cast a person's head like they would a bone, so what they can't fix just kind of caves in. And so they want to do a thing called cranioplasty, which is, you know, pull my scalp back—you know, just make another incision, pull the skin back, and put a piece of plastic— It's high-tech stuff.

LK: Do you want that?

RD: I don't want it, but that's a decision of the neurosurgeon. They do CAT scans quite frequently.

LK: They have done a very good job.

RD: Yes, sir.

LK: Boy! Because, you know, looking straight ahead, when the shadow of your hair comes over it—considering the extent of that— Do you have headaches?

RD: No, I take medication for all that stuff. It's controlled medically.

LK: Are you able to work?

RD: Not commercially. I mean, they won't give me back my license, which is what I do for a living.

LK: Why can't you drive?

RD: Because of the stuff that I'm on. I take anti-seizure medication, because I still have— With a major head trauma, seizures are— What can happen, it's like an epileptic fit, is what most people can relate to. The body stops functioning and, you know, no matter what you're doing, you pretty much fall over. I mean, that's exactly— And then, you know, they don't want to risk that—you know, hauling 80,000 pounds going down the freeway.

LK: Do you hate those guys that did this?

RD: No. They're confused.

LK: Don't hate them?

RD: No.

LK: Think they're going to pay a price for it?

RD: I don't know. I almost hope that perhaps the time they've spent they've perhaps learned something, but it's hard to understand—

LK: Because it's weird: You can't testify, right?

RD: No, I don't even have a clue. The only reason I know that there's somebody there is because that's what everyone else has seen. I have no idea.

LK: Now, are you saying, Johnnie, that the city of Los Angeles should have done— what?—to stop that?

JC: The city of Los Angeles should have provided police protection for the entire area. Now, Mr. [William] Webster—your guest who just preceded us—has done a marvelous report called the Webster Report, and what he did was he looked at and analyzed the police response in Los Angeles. What he found was there was really no response. Our information is there were more than 5,000 "911" calls that came in regarding the Denny beating. The police never responded—

LK: People who saw it happen?

JC: Who saw it happening live. In fact, the four Good Samaritans who came and saved this man saw it on television and went down. But yet, the Los Angeles police department never responded. In fact, they had pulled back.

LK: And what did they say to you in response to your questioning as to why they didn't respond? Have they answered?

JC: Not yet. We're in the early stages, but we'll be asking that question. But what basically happened, there's a lieutenant who got into a big fight with then-chief [Daryl] Gates, who said he wanted to return, but his higher-ups would not let him return to the area. And the point is, Larry, if you look at the Webster Report, there were foot patrols in Westwood. There were police in the San Fernando Valley. There were police throughout Los Angeles still doing their job. Only in South-central were they not there. And what we're saying, that's a callous disregard for the rights of the citizens in that area. So their equal protection under the law was violated. . . .

[*Commercial break*]

LK: How do you react to the fact that there's a whole movement in favor of the people who beat you?

RD: It's confusing to me, but I can understand their trying to parallel that with the police officers who beat Rodney King. So in some strange way they're drawing a parallel between, you know, just some bad guys who are just bad guys doing something to just people— And that doesn't give the police a right to do the same thing to an innocent—you know—or to abuse a motorist—

LK: Are you saying, Reggie, you can see their parallel?

RD: I'm beginning to understand it. At first, it's so strange. You have to— It's like anything else. I'm learning things that are going on in L.A. that before were just—it was just "that part of town." And now, I kind of get a feel for how these people must be feeling, but never the way that they feel it, because *they* live it. I don't. And it's just interesting—it's really interesting.

LK: You know, this is very similar to the Pope visiting his would-be assassin. In other words, you— Am I getting the feeling that you wouldn't be terribly upset if they didn't do time?

RD: They have to be— That's the thing that's strange. To make society work, people have to answer for their actions. That's what keeps—what?—America strong. That's what makes the country something that the world looks up to, or at least we'd hope or would like to think—or at least *I* would, anyway. And so, when it becomes—when tyranny becomes the law of the land, there is no self-respect, let alone respect for the country as a whole.

LK: But you're not revenge desirous at all?

RD: Oh—

LK: You understand those who are kind of sticking up for them?

RD: I think they have—oh, gosh, it's hard—I can almost think it, but it's hard for me to say it, only because I'm lost for words. I have no command—

LK: Well, you're someone who's come to understand a part of the community you never understood. You had a violent act perpetrated against you. You're trying to figure out why, and you're giving us some understanding as to why.

RD: Because it wasn't a personal thing.

LK: Yes, they didn't hate you.

RD: No, because they don't know me. In fact, I'm sure if I'd got to know some of these guys independently in a different situation—who knows—we might have been able to at least work for a common cause—I mean, like at a job or something, you know, like a coworker.

LK: Have a beer together.

RD: Yes, you know.

LK: Now, Johnnie, as a black attorney, are you getting any flack for representing Reggie?

JC: No, I'm actually not, because, actually, what we're saying here is that this is a situation that really involves all the community in the South-central area of Los Angeles. It could have been any citizen, but it was Reg Denny, who happened to be white, which is ironic; or it could have been a black citizen. We represent the young man's family who was first killed there in that area, who was black. We represent a gentleman who's also Asian-Pacific. We represent, also, an Hispanic family, as a result of violence in the area.

LK: Will your case be helped or hindered if the charges go well against the would-be assailants or not?

JC: It won't make that much difference. In fact, I think either way we have to persuade— Our burden is to prove that there was a callous disregard for the safety of the citizens of that area.

LK: So you're suing on negligence, and whether they go to jail is immaterial. . . . And you're not overly desirous of them going to jail? You want to see punishment, but you look like someone open to understanding, too.

RD: Yes, we can't— It'd be the same as if I just decided I didn't like somebody, went out and just hammered on him, just for a good day of exercise, and said, "Oops, sorry," and just because someone else did it. Do we do something just because someone else does something? . . . I mean, in school that doesn't work when you're, you know, a kid in school, you know, like—say with my daughter. You always see the people saying, "Just because your friend does it, does that mean you can go ahead and do it?" That doesn't work. It can't.

LK: Let's go to calls for Reggie Denny and Johnnie Cochran Jr. Limestone, Maine, hello.

CALLER: [*Limestone, Maine*] Hello. Good evening, gentlemen. Mr. Denny, you said that you have no recollection of the incident. I was curious to know what your reaction is regarding the suspects accusing you of saying—that you said racial slanders and comments to provoke the attack? And what punishment do you want to see happen?

RD: Actually, that's very old news, only because that was— I think people were just trying to— They were hoping that was the case, or somebody saying that's what they heard. And the fact has come out that is not my nature. And also, some of the people who claimed to have heard someone say it, when asked, you know, just right upfront, "Who said it?" everyone gives one of these shoulder-shrug things. No one knows. That's because it was—it was—God, I want to say a "crock."

LK: You didn't say anything?

RD: No. No, sir. God, I was too scared to say anything. And that's— You know, I don't do that. That's just—

LK: And the last thing you remember is the window broken?

RD: Yes. My right window just shattered. And if you've ever been around a semi, for me to say anything— A running truck is not quiet, and if you ever want to talk to anyone outside a truck or someone wants to talk to you, you have to literally yell—I mean turn and yell—quite loud, to get anyone on a curb to hear. And the finger nonsense—that sign language crud—oh, that's nonsense.

LK: Do you think the city wants to settle?

JC: Well, I think that is interesting. I think they really would like to settle with Mr. Denny. This man is a consummate victim. The problem is we have a number of other people who have also joined in the lawsuit, a number of merchants who suffered damage, and I think their cases are distinguishable, because many of the merchants were outside the area of South-central. But I think that it's going to be difficult because all of our municipalities are short of funds, so it is difficult. . . .

[*Commercial break*]

LK: Reggie was saved by a lot of extraordinary people. In addition to the blacks on the street who saved him, there were black surgeons, right?

RD: Yes. Yes, sir.

LK: Would you tell us, just briefly—you were just doing it off the air and I think the public ought to know—what they had to do with your face? Your eye was in your head?

RD: Yes. What happened was, if I may—it's just a crowbar or a piece of steel, basically, is what it was, and the doctors— We had a joke: we're just glad the curve was out, because if the curve was in, it would have really hurt. You know, crowbars are curved. Anyway, it caught me on the side of the head and fractured—I have a plastic piece underneath my eye now, underneath my skin. My cheek is plastic, and my eye fell down behind my skin because it fractured the little thing that your eye rests on, and they just had to cut open and suck all the bone tissue—

bone material out, because there's nothing left to fix. And so my eye fell down behind my cheek and they thought it was out of my head somewhere, you know, just looking at me, because my eye was behind my cheek. And it was inside my head but I was looking—

LK: What about your teeth?

RD: Oh, fractured my jaw, and when my sinuses were broken it pushed all my upper jaw up behind my nose and they had to—like a fish. You reach up underneath there, and you pull down, you know—those of you who like to fish? Yes, that's the feeling I had. I was like a big fish.

LK: You've got a hell of a sense of humor, Reg.

RD: Oh, it was great.

LK: How many operations did they do?

RD: Quite a few. It took quite a few days. They couldn't do them all in one day. They had to do one one day, and the first operation was to remove the bone—chunks of bone out of my brain. They actually take and they slice the brain. It's like—

LK: Okay.

RD: —if you've ever done liver—

LK: That's enough! [*Denny laughs*] All right!

JC: That's more than he wants to hear.

LK: These were orthopedic surgeons and plastic surgeons together?

RD: All kinds, and neurosurgeons.

LK: Pasadena, California, with Reggie Denny and Johnnie Cochran Jr. Hello.

CALLER: [*Pasadena, California*] Hi. Mr. Denny, I wanted to say, first of all, that I'm very sorry for what you've been through, but my family and I can really relate. My father-in-law was shot the first night of the riots in the head, and he's permanently blinded because of it, and he, you know, has kind of the same thing that you have, as having to take anti-seizure medication, that type of thing. And I just wonder how you feel about being such a celebrity from this because, you know, your event was caught on camera, and just that the news has focused on you solely, you know, to the exclusion of everyone else?

LK: Do you feel your father-in-law has been kind of left out in this?

CALLER: [*Pasadena, California*] Yes, completely.

LK: All right. Her father-in-law got shot—same kind of situation.

RD: Yes, and I'm sorry to hear about that. And, you know, that is the strangest thing. If we can just remove the light from my situation— How many motorists have been hammered on by the police? How many people have went through enormous situations and, just because it was not captured on live TV, it doesn't, almost, exist? And also, the strange thing about movies or anything like that— Isn't it something how, once it's on tape and it's happened live, even if you're just watching anything, it's so— It's incredible to me. You ought to be on this side of the camera for a change and just know how incredible it is—and it's really something.

LK: You don't like it?

RD: It's incredibly different. I've come to just have a sort of a strange compassion for the folks who have to do this for a living, much like yourself, because it is—it is different.

JC: Larry, one of the things I'd like to say to the caller from Pasadena is this: that what Reginald Denny has become is really a victim. He's a spokesperson for all victims who are similarly situated, so that I think his case becomes important for everyone who was injured in South-central Los Angeles, to give you a look at it from that standpoint. Certainly, the media has highlighted his case, but he's never asked for the attention that's been focused upon him.

[*Commercial break*]

LK: Back to the calls—Lexington, Kentucky, hello.

CALLER: [*Lexington, Kentucky*] Yes. Reginald, I'm glad to see that you're doing fine. I just have two quick comments. First of all, I am amazed at your attorney—I have to be honest—not because of skin color, but just because of what has happened. It amazes me. Second of all, I think it's a shame that the media puts you in light with Rodney King. It seems like every time they show your picture, they show Rodney King. I think he was a criminal. I think you were an innocent victim.

LK: Why are you shocked at his attorney?

CALLER: [*Lexington, Kentucky*] Well, it would seem to me—well, this goes into my statement that I was going to make. It seems that injustice is always white and that inequality is always black, and I think that we should blame those directly responsible and not— You can't always run to the police department just because—now I'm not saying this will happen, but just because you'll get more money out of it. I think we should blame those that are responsible. They should be "responsible" for their own sins.

LK: So you think the police officers should be responsible, and the blacks who beat up Mr. Denny should be responsible?

CALLER: [*Lexington, Kentucky*] Absolutely.

LK: Okay, thank you. Want to comment?

JC: I'd like to respond to that just briefly, to the caller. Certainly, the people who did the act certainly have a great amount of responsibility. But where you have a whole system that breaks down and causes tyranny and chaos in the second-largest city in America, where the police don't do their job and all the citizens are put at risk there, that's a responsibility of government, and they should be responsible. And they bear that burden as they share the benefits, and I think that's only reasonable.

LK: Aiken, South Carolina, hello.

CALLER: [*Aiken, South Carolina*] Hi. Larry, glad to get on. Mr. Denny, I watched your thing in horror. I want to ask you a question. Were your doors locked, and did you happen to have your CB on so you kind of knew maybe what was going on beforehand?

RD: I don't run a CB as—you know, just to talk to other drivers. That's just more electronic equipment that I prefer not to carry.

LK: And were your doors locked?

RD: You know, I honestly don't know—probably not. My right one is always locked because there's no passengers allowed, and when you're driving around town, you always get somebody wanting to come up and open your right door and say, "Hey, can I get a ride?" So my right door is always locked. My left door is not.

LK: Has this matured you, changed your outlook? Are you a different person?

RD: You know, not to be goofy about this, but I used to just drive through a bad part of town and not—I mean, my part of that town was this side of my truck, and that was all I cared about. Now, I know what L.A.'s starting to be about.

LK: You know more about you, too, don't you?

RD: Yes. It's an enlightenment.

[Commercial break]

CALLER: [*Fairbanks, Alaska*] Yes. Curious as to the estimate on the total cost of Mr. Denny's expenses for medical treatment and any insurance involved in this. Thank you.

JC: Clearly, in the several hundreds of thousands of dollars—amazing kind of care that he's received. You can't really put a value on it, but certainly in the hundreds of thousands of dollars.

LK: You were telling us also, he's an amazing client. Like, the White Citizens Council—prejudiced groups—will send him money. He sends it back.

JC: Absolutely. He is an amazing client. From the standpoint of the man, what you see is what you get here. Here's a man who received letters from all over the world—more that 25,000 letters. When he received letters that preached hate, preached intolerance, he sent those letters back.

LK: I know you're divorced.

RD: Yes.

LK: You're here with your daughter. Your ex-wife was wonderful through all this.

RD: Yes.

LK: How's your daughter handling it?

RD: She sees counseling, you know, because—I can't imagine what it's like. She used to always wonder if someone was going to beat me up again, and for a long time she didn't want to touch me because she didn't want to hurt me, you know, when I was home and still kind of bandaged up and everything. It was a weird moment for her and—

LK: How's she doing now? She seems fine.

RD: She's doing better. She's doing a lot better.

LK: Thank you both very much. Good luck, Reg.

RD: Thank you. Thank you, Larry.

"The thing that has surprised me most is how difficult it is . . . to really keep communicating exactly what you're about to the American people."

He was born William Jefferson Blythe in Hope, Arkansas, on August 19, 1946, six months after the accidental death of his natural father. Bill Clinton took his step-father's name when he was seven. He was educated in the public schools of Hot Springs and at Georgetown University (1964–68), also attending Oxford as a Rhodes Scholar (1968–79). After graduating from Yale Law School (1970–73), he returned to Arkansas as a law professor, entered politics, and in 1976 was elected state attorney general. Two years later, he became the youngest governor in the history of the state. While serving his fourth term, Clinton secured his party's nomination for president, calling for a new generation to assume national leadership.

At the outset of his term, Clinton promised to appear on Larry King Live *every six months. What follows is his second interview, from the White House. In the course of the interview, President Clinton suggested extending the show to ninety minutes, but had to cut the interview short when he received word of the suicide of Vincent Foster, the friend and lawyer who had helped arrange the Clintons' investment in the ill-fated Whitewater real-estate venture.*

LARRY KING: Back in Louisville, about three days before the election, President Clinton said on this program, "I'll come on every six months." This is the sixth-month anniversary. The timing is perfect. Tonight is six months in office for Clinton-Gore. Before we get into some issues, what we'll do is cover some current issues, talk about the budget, take calls, okay? But first, there's no way you could plan for this job, so what about it surprises you the most?

BILL CLINTON: That's hard to say. I've learned a lot in the last six month, and as much as I have followed this over twenty years, I think there are some things that you cannot have anticipated. I think the thing that has surprised me most is how difficult it is, even for the president, if you're going to take on big changes and try to make big things happen, to really keep communicating exactly what you're about to the American people.

LK: And why is that hard?

BC: I think because there's so much else in the atmosphere, first. And, secondly, because when you do something like this big economic plan we're pushing, only the controversy is newsworthy at a time when there's so much else to cover. So I'm trying always to remind people, look, we've got as many spending cuts or more than tax increases; that the upper-income people, people over $200,000 are paying 70 percent of the burden; that the middle class is paying very little, the working poor are paying nothing. And all of the details I try to get into, but it's very difficult. And we find that the American people knew the most on February seventeenth, the night I announced the plan and went through it point by point, and that since then—this sort of yelling and rhetoric and screaming and back and forth—that I have lost the ability to make sure everybody knows the things I want them to know, and I feel very badly about that.

LK: And is that everybody's fault? I mean, is it your fault, the media's fault?

BC: Oh, I think certainly so. I mean, I'm not trying to shift responsibility away from myself. But you ask me— That's been a real surprise to me, because when I was a governor in a smaller place, where lots of people knew me, even if I were doing something that was quite unpopular with the media, say, and they were criticizing me, I could always get my side out there, my points. The essential facts would be out there. And that, to me, has been the most frustrating thing. And also, when you're president, you have to make a lot of tough decisions. You just have to keep lining them up and making them—whether it's, you know, base closings, or the very difficult problems in the Pacific Northwest with the forests, or the whole litany of things that we've done here: the POW/MIA issue and how we're going to deal with Vietnam, the FBI, the gays in the military, you name it. And they keep coming in quick succession. You can't just say, "Okay, stop the world. I'm going to just work on this. I'm not going to make these other decisions." You have to keep going.

LK: We were talking before we went on . . . about Elvis Presley and isolation, and I was saying that I thought he had a more isolated life than you do, but this is an isolated life in here, isn't it?

BC: It can be very isolating.

LK: Do you have to fight it?

BC: I fight it all the time. And it can be isolating for two reasons. One is, there's so much to do that you have to be very disciplined about your time. And I think the more I've been in this office, the more conscious I've become of it, and, I think, the more disciplined I've become about my time. But discipline means deciding things you won't do, people you won't see, calls you won't make. The second problem is, frankly, the security problem.

LK: How so?

BC: Well, because I think the Secret Service do a very, very good job, but if your job is to keep the president from being harmed in a world full of people who may have some reason to do it, may have the means to do it, obviously the best thing would be if you put him in a bullet-proof room, you know, and walked out—if you see what I mean.

LK: Yes. You couldn't stand that.

BC: No. No, I couldn't stand that. So they do a terrific job, but we worked out our accommodations so that I can at least, you know, run every day. I run different routes, and we do different things, and I try to get out and see the people when I can.

LK: Is it hard for you to understand their job?

BC: It's much easier now. I really respect them. They've got a very tough job, and I make it harder because I'm a real people person, you know. I like to be out there. I think it's an important job. But if you don't spend some time with just ordinary people, who tell you what they think, hey, you almost forget how to hear and how to listen and how to speak in the way that most people live.

LK: By the way, have you seen *In the Line of Fire*?

BC: I watched it last night.

LK: What do you think?

BC: I thought Eastwood was terrific. I thought he was good in *Unforgiven*; I think he's good in this. I think he's making the best movies he's ever made.

LK: Did you like the movie?

BC: I liked the movie very much.

LK: Was it realistic?

BC: I think it was as realistic as it could be and still be a real rip-roaring thriller.

LK: All right. We helped their business a lot. Let's touch some other bases. Okay. First, today, Aspin—Secretary of Defense [Les] Aspin—appears with—it looked like the entire military in the world—before Senator [Sam] Nunn's committee, and Senator Nunn finished by saying he still wants to go to Congress, but he's inclined to support it [the administration's liberal policy on gays in the military]. Is this a plus for you today?

BC: I think it is a plus. The Joint Chiefs came a long way on this policy from where they were back in January when we talked.

LK: When they were almost totally against it, period.

BC: Completely against changing it at all; grudgingly said, "Well, we'll stop asking"— none of the things that were in this policy, except for that. And I commend them. They really tried hard to come to grips with this, and they know that there are, and always have been, homosexuals in the service who served with real distinction. They and the secretary of defense deserve a lot of credit. But also, frankly, the people who argued for an even broader policy deserve a lot of credit. The Campaign for Military Service, Congressman Studds, Congressman Franks— they worked hard to try to come to grips with this. I don't think anyone was fully satisfied with the result, but I believe it's the best we can do right now.

LK: Were you in a no-win?

BC: Well, I don't know—I don't view it that way. It depends on what the standard is. I was in a no-win if the only way I win is to do exactly what I think is right and—

LK: Which would have been sign them and let them in, right?

BC: Yes, but even I never— What I said was that I thought that status should *not* be the judge. It ought to be conduct, not your orientation. . . . That's what the policy is now. I further said that I thought a person ought to be able to say, "I'm gay," and, as long as they didn't do anything that violated the rules, they should be able to stay.

LK: That's now true?

BC: That's only true in a restricted way. Now, if you say it, it creates a presumption that you're going to do something wrong while you're in the military, but you are given the opportunity to present evidence that you won't—to convince, in effect, your commander that you will observe the rules. But I never promised to change the rules of conduct. That's in the Uniform Code of Military Justice. That's the way it is. Now, to be fair to the Joint Chiefs, they agreed to go further on matters of privacy and association than I ever discussed in the campaign. So this provides dramatically increased protection and a range of privacy for present and future soldiers who happen to be homosexuals but happen to be good military people.

LK: So in other words, you filled your promise?

BC: I did, except for the fact that we were not able to do precisely what I wanted, which was to give people the freedom to acknowledge their sexual orientation, as long as they were following the rules of conduct. Today if you do that, it can get you in trouble, but you have the option to convince your commander that you really are following the rules. So I don't think it goes quite as far as I wanted on statements. On the other hand, it goes quite a bit farther to protect private conduct on the rules of investigation than I anticipated. . . .

LK: How do you take . . . bashing? You know, the heat that a president takes—and you've been taking a lot of it. How do you deal with that?

BC: Well, it's all part of it.

LK: You mean it rolls off you?

BC: Most of it rolls off of me; not all of it, if I think something is particularly unfair. The only thing that really bothers me, if you want to know the truth, is when I think that the bashing is in some area that prevents the American people from focusing on what we're doing about the things they care about that are most important, or if it undermines my ability to get things done. The criticism is a part of the job and frankly, you know, Benjamin Franklin said a long time ago, "Our critics can be our friends; for they show us our faults." Sometimes our critics show us our faults, and I try to listen and learn from my critics; but if I think they're diverting the attention of the American people from the real issues, or the whole thing is undermining my ability to do what I was elected to do, that bothers me. But just to be criticized, shoot, that's part of it. . . .

[Commercial break]

LK: Was it hard to fire Mr. [William] Sessions, director of the FBI?

BC: It was not hard, but it was sad for me. I admire the FBI greatly. I've had a lot of contact with former FBI officers—had several of them in my administration. My criminal justice adviser was once the number-two man of the FBI. My chief of staff for some time was a retired FBI agent. I love the FBI, and I hated to be the first president ever to have to fire a director, but he said that that's the way he wanted it. He refused to resign, and I felt I had no choice. I do think that Louis Freeh, the federal judge whom I appointed today, will be a sterling FBI director.

LK: The word is this guy—where's he been? This guy's, like, flawless.

BC: Well, he's an amazing man. I mean, he grew up in a working-class family in Jersey City. He married a wonderful girl from Pittsburgh, whose dad was a steel worker. He worked his way through law school. He's my kind of guy, you know—just from the heartland.

LK: That "flawless" is the quote from the guy who did the investigation.

BC: Absolutely . . . And then he was a great FBI agent, and then he was a prosecutor. He did the "Pizza Connection" case, which was then the biggest heroin ring ever broken in the United States. He investigated sea-front corruption and brought indictments against 125 people. And then that awful mail bombing, two murders in the South—the federal judge, the civil rights leader—he broke that case when people thought it could never be broken, and then he prosecuted it himself. He has really been an amazing success. And as you know, President Bush made him a federal judge, and I think it's really a testimony to his character that he was willing to leave a lifetime job to be director of the FBI, because he knew the agency needed him.

LK: He's also very big in the area of civil rights, is he not?

BC: That's right. That was a big thing with me. I wanted somebody who was tough on crime, but who knew the FBI had to bring in more women and minorities. They've been behind on that, and they're moving, and I want to give Judge Sessions credit for that. He did a good job on that, trying to open the Bureau, and Judge Freeh said he'd continue it.

LK: Do you expect [Supreme Court nominee] Judge [Ruth] Ginsburg to be approved easily?

BC: Yes. I'm very proud of her, and she did real well today, I think. She's an extraordinary woman. She is a real pioneer in women's rights, but also has, I think, been a judge in the best sense. She's very hard to categorize as liberal or conservative, but she'll take a tough decision when she thinks it's right.

LK: On your key issue, though—which you said in the campaign—of freedom of choice, do you think she'll come through?

BC: Yes, well, she's got a real record, a statement there. I didn't give her any kind of litmus test in the interview.

LK: You didn't?

BC: I didn't think it was right, no. But I was familiar enough with her rulings and her speeches and her statements to know how she felt about that issue.

LK: And [Surgeon General nominee] Dr. Joycelyn Elders: standing with her?

BC: Absolutely.

LK: Were you at all dismayed by some of the things she said—"enemy of the fetus" and—

BC: Well, she's a very passionate woman. But I think you have to understand where she came from. I mean, Joycelyn Elders grew up as one of seven children in a cotton field in south Arkansas. She came from nowhere—economically, anyway. Her brothers and sisters worked hard to help her get through medical school. She married a man who later became the most successful high school basketball coach in our state—very much a beloved man. And she was a doctor, a professor in the medical school, when I finally—after three times—talked her into becoming the health department director. And she said, "What do you want me to do?" I said, "I want you to fight teen pregnancy, I want you to fight AIDS, I want you to do something about environmental health, and I want us to get infant mortality down." And she just—she found that her passion, in effect, drove her. I mean, she's a very passionate woman, and sometimes she says things in stark and blunt terms that make people draw up, but I think it's fair to say that in our state, which is a pretty old-fashioned, conservative place, she was very popular, because people believed she was fighting for children, she was fighting to reduce infant mortality, she was fighting to reduce teen pregnancy. She was not pro-abortion and, as a matter of fact, in many years I was governor, the number of abortions performed dropped over the previous years.

LK: So, are you surprised that the far right has kind of taken off on her?

BC: No, because she is a lightning rod. They sort of took off on her in Arkansas for a while, but in the end she prevailed because people believed she cared about people. She was trying to save these kids from having babies, she was trying to reduce the infant mortality rate, she was trying to force people to do things to change their behavior, so AIDS wouldn't be communicated.

LK: Will she prevail here, too? Will she be confirmed?

BC: I think she's an extraordinary woman, and I'll be very surprised if she's not confirmed.

LK: [Illinois Representative] Dan Rostenkowski gets into trouble on the eve of maybe the most important time for him in your administration, because he's spear-carrier for the House side of the economic bill. How do you feel about that? What happens if he isn't— That's a fair question, because there's a possibility he could be indicted.

BC: Well, first, about that, of course, I can't comment. I'm not involved, and I shouldn't be, and I can't comment. I can only tell you that I've worked very closely with him and with Senator [Daniel Patrick] Moynihan, and he was here today continuing to work. I think, like every other American, he should be given the presumption of innocence.

LK: Well, what happens if this team—?

BC: But all I can tell you is he has been—his backbone has been a mile wide and awful stiff in this whole thing. He's been a major force in pushing for changes that will finally get this deficit under control and help us to turn our economy around, and I'm going to keep working with him as long as he's—

LK: Have you asked him about this incident with the postal—

BC: No.

LK: If something were to happen, do you have another point man in mind? I mean, will this hurt the chances of a compromise, if Rostenkowski's stature is limited?

BC: Well, I don't even know how to comment on that. All I can tell you is that if he keeps working at it like he has, he's going to make a positive difference. . . .

[Commercial break]

LK: We're at the White House. Our guest is President Clinton. We're in the library. We're ready to go to your phone calls . . . Orlando, Florida, hello.

CALLER: [*Orlando, Florida*] Yes, good evening, Mr. King. And good evening, President Clinton. It's a pleasure to talk to you both. I would like to ask you first, President Clinton, why that the Orlando training center is going to close, when it is one of the newest, the largest—we have a lot of land here that we can expand. There's a lot of old people who have served their country well, and they're retired. They cannot drive or go to other places, and a lot of them do not have the money to go to the hospitals and the doctors because of the insurance. And this is known to be one of the biggest and nicest training centers here. They train women here. They do not train—

LK: We got the gist.

BC: Let me say, first of all, I think it is a good training center. For all of our listeners, the Orlando training center in Florida was one of the bases recommended by the Joint Chiefs of Staff and by the secretary of defense for the base closing, and the commission voted to do that, to close the Orlando center. One of the biggest problems when you close a big military base is that many military bases have people retired around them who used to be in the military, who use the medical facilities. And therefore, in the aftermath, that's often one of the toughest issues.

Let me answer those two things separately, if I might. First of all, I can't answer why the Orlando training center was picked by the Joint Chiefs. That process began before I became president. They sent the recommendation to the secretary of defense, who sent it to the base-closing commission. They thought that it should be closed, and they approved it. They sent the whole list to me, and I either had to sign on or off, and I concluded that I had no basis to reject the whole package, so I approved it and it went on to the Congress.

Now, let me make just one important point about that. It's very tough when you close these bases. I know it. But we have taken the military down from about two-and-a-half million people, going down toward 1.6, then 1.5, then 1.4. You can't reduce the military by 40 percent and only reduce the base structure by nine. Most of the bases that are recommended for closure are in Europe, some in the United States. But we have to reduce the base structure because, otherwise, we won't have enough money to train the personnel and to keep developing the smart weapons and the important technology to keep our people the best fighting force in the world and keep them safe. Now, secondly, let me just say on the health issue, when the First Lady agreed to take up the health issue, and her task force began to work, one of the things I asked her to do is to look into health care for military retirees around military bases and look into those facilities. That is one of the things that that task force has done. They are looking at those facilities, asking, "Can they be opened? Can they be reopened? Should they be reopened? Should they be military facilities? Should they be available for military and civilian personnel? What's going to happen in terms of the availability of health care?" So that's something that the commission is looking into, and I expect that I'll get some recommendations on that that we'll know about pretty soon when we announce the health care plan.

LK: To St. Louis, Missouri, with President Clinton. Hello.

CALLER: [*St. Louis, Missouri*] Hello, Mr. President. It's a pleasure to speak to you. I was wondering, have you considered a national lottery to reduce the deficit? . . .

BC: Yes. Let me say, it has been proposed, a national lottery to reduce the deficit, and every time I have seen anybody talk about it, the conclusion has been that we probably shouldn't do it, for two reasons. Number one, it would probably not raise an enormous amount of money. And number two, it might dramatically eat into the proceeds that are now going to the states who have lotteries. Most states have lotteries now, and that money generally goes to the education of our children or, in the case of Pennsylvania, the care of elderly citizens. And the federal government, I think, would get a lot of opposition from the states if it appeared that we were going to take away their efforts to educate people, to pay down the debt.

I have to say, finally, I, personally, have always had some reservation about the lotteries because, disproportionately, the people who play them tend to be on the lower-income scale. But even if you put that to the side, for the other two reasons, I think it is probably not a very good idea.

LK: It is voluntary taxation, though, isn't it?

BC: It is absolutely voluntary, and that's the best argument for it. The best argument for it is it's absolutely voluntary, and if it raised a billion dollars a year, it's a billion we wouldn't have otherwise. So there are some arguments for it, but the two I mentioned are the reasons I think that it's never been adopted.

LK: We have to take a break, but, quickly, why did you have to change your mind on the tax rates for middle income?

BC: Because after the election was over, the government of the previous administration revised upward the deficit by—oh, about $50 billion a year in each of the next three years.

LK: So you had no idea of that when you were running?

BC: No. I didn't know it would be revised upward. So the decision I had to make was, "Well, are you going to live with a bigger deficit and less deficit reduction, or should you ask the middle class to pay a little?" I also, frankly, did something else I didn't like. I revised upward the tax burden on the wealthiest Americans. And I think there's a limit beyond which you don't want to go on them, either. . .

[*Commercial break*]

LK: Before we take our next call, we want to pick up where we left off, because he's taken a lot of shots on this, and it will be interesting to hear, in this setting, the other side.

BC: Yes, I just wanted to say that when I became president and the deficit had been estimated upward since the election quite a bit—over $125 billion, $130 billion— I decided that we were going to have to cut more spending and raise more revenues than I had thought, to get the deficit down to a point that it was manageable and to keep long-term interest rates coming down. I think that it's very important to hammer home that there's a real connection between an effort to reduce the deficit and getting these long-term interest rates down. Before the election, basically, you had short-term interest rates brought way down by the Federal Reserve Board, but a big gap between them and the long-term rates. And that's what determines mortgage rates, business loans, and a lot of other things. So we decided that it would be worth it to really take a tough stand, to raise some more money—most of it from upper-income people, but a modest amount from middle-class people—and cut more spending. . . .

LK: Copenhagen, Denmark, hello.

CALLER: [*Copenhagen, Denmark*] Yes, hello. Hello, Mr. King. Hello, President Clinton. My question to President Clinton is about the United States' attitude towards the crisis in the former Yugoslavia. Such a small country as Denmark has sent more than one thousand troops to Bosnia and Croatia. There are about only three hundred American peacekeepers down there in Macedonia. President Clinton, do you think it's fair?

BC: Well, let me remind you, sir, that we have had several thousand troops in Somalia, we have contributed hundreds of millions of dollars in humanitarian aid to the former Yugoslavia, we have done air drops of supplies. We have always been committed to use our air power to protect your troops and any other troops. We have not wanted to get the United States involved in the conflict there unless there was a settlement. I have always said that we would send appropriate military personnel to be part of a United Nations enforcement of the settlement. Let me also say that the closest we ever were to settling that was when the Serbs and Croats thought that the Europeans were going to go along with my proposal to lift the arms embargo and to make available standby air power to enforce no use of the Serbian artillery against the government—the Moslem, the Bosnian government there—while the arms embargo was being lifted. When it became obvious that I could not prevail in the United Nations because of the opposition of some of the European nations, that's when things began to deteriorate again instead of move toward peace. So I had a policy. I am disappointed that it was rejected by some of the European countries. I am grateful that the Germans and some others supported it, but we are prepared to do our part to try to resolve this. We are working weekly on it. I feel terrible about it, but I do not believe the United States needs to send a lot of troops there, which might get involved in a civil war on the ground, when we had a plan which would have led, I'm convinced, to a settlement, which was not accepted. If we get a settlement, as we might now under other conditions, we are prepared to do our part through the U.N. to help to enforce it. . . .

[*Commercial break*]

LK: [*laughs*] This is funny, folks—what happens behind the scenes. But it's all right, we'll make it public for you. We had arranged with President Clinton's staff that we would finish at 10:00 Eastern Time, in one hour, and the staff had arranged it with our producers, and then President Clinton just said to me, "Can we go a little longer?" and I said, "Sure, if you want to go a little longer, we can go another half-hour," and he said he'd be happy to. So *we* didn't do it, and I just want the staff to know that *we* didn't do it. *You* would like to do it. *We* would be happy to accommodate.

BC: You offered us the opportunity this afternoon, and I think at that time we didn't know whether we could or not, but I'd like to do it.

LK: You're feeling refreshed.

BC: Yes, and I like answering the questions. I think that's important.

LK: By the way, before we take our next call—he did give credit to Mr. Eastwood. He did add on the break that he also wanted to give credit to John Malkovich in *In the Line of Fire*.

BC: He's a great villain, isn't he? I mean, he was fabulous.

LK: I haven't seen it yet, but they tell me it's unbelievable.

BC: Unbelievable. I like—Renée Russo was good, too, and I'd only seen her in that Mel Gibson movie.

LK: You are a movie buff, right?

BC: I love the movies. I love the movies.

LK: What's it like when you order them here in the White House?

BC: Well, you know, they send in movies on a regular basis, so I get to see a lot of movies here. Normally, what we do is on Friday night—I normally work pretty late on Friday night, till 7:00, 7:30. Last Friday, I worked till 8:30. And then we gather up whoever is still working late in the White House, and Hillary and I and, when Chelsea is here, Chelsea would come down and watch the movie. We like that.

LK: All right, we're ready to go back to more phone calls for President Clinton. . . .

LK: Montreal, Quebec, Canada, hello.

CALLER: [*Montreal, Quebec*] Mr. President, I'm an American citizen, and my question to you is that, as you are well aware, President Truman decided that the military had to be desegregated. [Segregation] was unconstitutional and, as commander in chief, he felt he could [desegregate]. There was a lot of flak by the military against what he decided but, notwithstanding, he went ahead, because he was their commander in chief. Now, may I ask why you did not act in a similar circumstance as he did, being the military chief?

BC: Well, first of all, let's talk about what I did do, then I'll tell you why the argument you made is not analogous. What I did do was to give instructions to the secretary of defense to promulgate a policy which permits gays to serve for the first time and judges them like other servicemen and women, on their conduct, not their sexual orientation. That is a big change. They are not going to be asked about their sexual orientation. Their privacy, including their rights of association, are going to be protected—that is, if they're seen going into a gay bar, that will not lead to an investigation of their sexual orientation. The laws against sexual misconduct will be enforced clearly and unambiguously in an evenhanded way against heterosexuals and homosexuals, and if a gay person says that he or she is homosexual, while that can create a presumption that they're doing something that's prohibited and lead to their separation from the service, they will be given an explicit opportunity to argue that they are honoring the code of conduct. Now, that is a big change.

Now, how is that different from the situation with President Truman? The real thing you ought to ask is, how long did it take before African Americans, in this case, were treated fully equally in the service? It didn't just happen, snap, with Truman's order. It didn't happen after Truman's order. And it developed a long time before Truman's order. There was an explicit, open involvement of the military culture with blacks in a segregated way for a very long time before this order was issued. The same thing happened with women. If you notice, one of the things that's received almost no notice is that during my administration the Pentagon has voted to dramatically expand the role of women in the military services, making available far more roles for them than were available before. But it didn't happen overnight. It happened over a period of years, as the military culture adapted to it.

Now, if I had done what you suggest, if I had just said that gays can serve and whatever they do in private is their own business—which I never committed to do in the campaign—I'll tell you exactly what would have happened. Congress would have overturned it immediately, and have done it on the Defense bill, and in ways that would have been difficult, if not impossible, for me to veto. So the situations simply aren't analogous. Congress had no intention of overturning President Truman's position, and it is something that had built up over a long period of time, not something that just entered the public debate, in effect, about a year ago.

LK: Saint Thomas, the Virgin Islands, hello.

CALLER: [*Saint Thomas, Virgin Islands*] Hello. . . . My question is this: Myself and several million other neighbors of ours—the Commonwealth of Puerto Rico—are not given the opportunity to vote for the president, and yet any tax packages or tax increases that your budget planned would require us to pay. What possibly can be done that would permit us to express our right to vote for the president of the United States?

BC: Well, it would take a legal change. I'm embarrassed to tell you, I don't know if it would take a change in the Constitution. I'd like to invite you to write me about it and, I'll commit to you, I'll look into it. I know that, in the case of Puerto Rico, they did have a presidential primary, which I was very active in, and the people there were very good to me, and I'm grateful for that. I have strongly supported in the case of Puerto Rico self-determination; that is, if they have a referendum there and they vote to continue their commonwealth status or to become independent or to become a state, whatever they decide I will support.

LK: You also support statehood for Washington, D.C.?

BC: I do. And I didn't until—frankly, until about a year and a half ago, when a number of people, including Jesse Jackson, who is one of the shadow senators for D.C., pointed out to me that this community, which was once a federal preserve entirely, now has more people than five states, pays more taxes than ten, and sent more soldiers into harm's way in the Persian Gulf than twenty. So I think there are ways you can carve out a federal enclave here that's still separate and apart, and let the rest of those folks become a state. There are some complicated issues there. I think there's a lot of worry if you had the first city-state, they'd try to tax people from other states, and we'd have to work through all that, but I think—

LK: And if Puerto Rico wants statehood, you'd be happy to welcome them?

BC: If that's what they vote for. I think the people of Puerto Rico should decide. . . .

[*Commercial break*]

LK: We're back on *Larry King Live*. Now, you would think these are two pretty powerful— The President of the United States. We're doing all right. The President had another commitment he didn't know about, right? So there's a schedule. So he'll be with us till the top of the hour. However, every six months we have a kind of rotating date—right?—as promised during the campaign.

BC: I owe you a half-an-hour now.

LK: And he'll owe us a half-an-hour. So the next appearance will be ninety minutes—

BC: You bet.

LK: —in six months. Or two hours—as pointed out by Atlanta. They never stop! Two hours—okay. But there was another appointment which he was unaware of and we were unaware of. So we'll get to some calls quickly, and he will be returning every six months. He promised it during the campaign, and this is the six-month anniversary. Arlington, Virginia, with President Clinton. Hello.

CALLER: [*Arlington, Virginia*] Good evening, President Clinton. This is Cheryl Dunsy. It's an honor. In the past six months, the media has really been focusing on such issues as gays in the military, [controversial attorney general nominee] Lani Guinier, and sort of drawing attention away from some of the, perhaps, more important issues. And if you had three or four things or issues that you'd like to be your legacy, what would they be?

LK: Or is it too early to have a legacy?

BC: No, I'd be happy to tell that. Number one, I'd like to get this economy moving again, get the deficit down, and start creating jobs and seeing working Americans have their incomes go up.

Number two, I'd like to provide health security for all Americans. I'd like for us to join all the other advanced countries in the world and provide a system of affordable health care to all of our people.

Number three, I want my national service plan to pass. It will open the doors of college education to millions of Americans for lower-interest loans and give many, many of them the chance to work those loans off through service with their communities.

Number four, I strongly want to pass a welfare reform bill that will move people from welfare to work and end welfare as we know it.

And five, I want to reform the political system. We have already passed the motor-voter bill that makes it easier for people to register and vote.

Three other bills that I care very deeply about have passed one house of Congress, but not both: one, a campaign finance reform bill to lower the cost of political campaigns, reduce the influence of PACs, and open the airwaves for debate; two, a bill to drastically open up lobbying behavior, restricting some lobbying behavior and requiring them to report what they spend on members of Congress; and three, the modified line-item veto, which I think will help discipline spending. So those are the things that— I would like those things to be my legacy.

LK: Do you want NAFTA passed, too?

BC: Very much. I strongly support it. I think it means more jobs, not less. Let me just make one—

LK: You disagree with Mr. Perot?

BC: I do because, keep in mind, anybody who wants to go to Mexico because they have low wages and send the products back here can do that today. Mexican tariffs on American products, on average, are higher than American tariffs on Mexican. Because of what President Salinas has done in lowering those tariffs in the last few years, we've gone from a $5 billion trade deficit to a $6 billion trade surplus with Mexico. They now have displaced Japan as the second-biggest purchaser of American manufactured products. So I think a wealthier Mexico means more products going down there, and more jobs for America.

LK: Quick call—last call—Paris, France, hello.

CALLER: [*Paris, France*] Good evening, Mr. President. I have a question on your policy toward Iran. During Rafsanjani's four-year tenure in Iran, his regime's hit squads have assassinated representatives of the *Mujaheddin*, the main Iranian resistance movement, in Europe and elsewhere, and suppression of the citizenry has been stepped up inside the country. My question is, why do you not take some practical and specific measures to pressure and impose sanctions, such as comprehensive—

LK: All right, I have to cut you there, only because we only have about thirty seconds.

BC: The answer is, we are doing everything we can to impose restrictions on trade with Iran. We are pressuring our allies and friends all the time not to support any government, including Iran, that supports terrorism and assassination. I'm glad you brought it up. I think it's a very significant problem. I hope you will press as hard in Paris as you are pressing Washington, because that is something that all the West should be sensitive to. We must not allow Iraq, Iran, and other agents of terrorism and assassination to dominate the world politically and to terrorize innocent people. I think you're absolutely right.

LK: Thanks very much, Mr. President.

BC: Thank you.

LK: Okay, now, we've got a date—six months?

BC: We've got a date.

LK: And longer time. He did have an appointment. We're sorry about that. And we thank President Clinton for giving us his time in this house. We have been broadcasting from the library at the White House, and we appreciate all of your calls.

Once called "the most admired, hated, fascinating, boring, radical and conservative leader in the Western world," she is the only woman ever to be prime minister of Great Britain.

She was born October 13, 1925, in Grantham, England, entered Oxford at seventeen, and, after graduation in 1947, took a job as a research chemist. In 1961, she was elected to Parliament. Prime Minister Edward Heath appointed her Secretary of Education and Science, and Thatcher succeeded him in 1975. Reelected in May 1979, she successfully faced an international crisis in early 1982, when Argentina seized the British Falkland Islands. Thatcher was elected to an unprecedented third term in 1987, but was brought down by a rebellion within her own party.

"No matter what happens, all of the patriotism and affection goes to the monarch. . . . The prime minister takes all the flak. That's absolutely right."

LARRY KING: When we look back on this twentieth century—and we'll do that in a few years—our guest tonight will rank as one of our most influential figures. In eleven years as British Prime Minister, Margaret Thatcher dealt with the Soviet invasion of Afghanistan, the Falkland Islands War, assassination attempts by the IRA, and the collapse of communism in the Soviet Union and Eastern Europe. She was "The Iron Lady," an icon of Western resolve. And then—astonishingly, to onlookers—Mrs. Thatcher was ousted by rebels in her own Conservative Party. Her own account of her remarkable political life has just been published by HarperCollins. It's the bestselling book in Europe. It's on its way to the top here. It is called *The Downing Street Years*. It's the first volume of a two-volume memoir, and we're very honored to welcome to Washington Margaret, the Lady Thatcher.

MARGARET THATCHER: Good evening.

LK: Together, you and I were watching Bill Clinton, President Clinton, a couple of minutes ago talk to the people in California about the fires. And I wonder, as a prime minister, as a leader of the country, if that, when tragedy is occurring and you have to address the folks—if that's one of the hardest parts of that job?

MT: Always, when there was a tragedy, I had a rule to go to it—not immediately, because they're so busy getting people in ambulances or getting them out of their homes into safety. The following day, I always went. And if there was any great need for finance, then the state simply must provide it. These disasters can't be coped with by normal means, and people need some reassurance, and they're desperately in need of help. The voluntary spirit is marvelous. The heights of heroism that you see from ordinary people are quite remarkable, and everyone gathers around. Nevertheless, they have got to know that the great losses will somehow be met by the state.

LK: Is the talk important—the leader's talk to the people—do you think?

MT: Oh, yes. As the leader represents the people, it is the whole nation pulling together behind those who have suffered, because everyone is thinking, "Look, it might have been me."

LK: And then, going there puts the leader at the scene, right?

MT: It shows the concern, very much. You also want to go because you want to see what has happened, you want to see the people. And I found sometimes, if there were many hospital cases, I would say to the doctors, "Look, is it all right if I talk to them? Would it be better if they didn't relive the disaster?" And the doctors would say, "No, it's better for them to talk. Let them talk if they want to," and mostly they did. And the stories they told were quite horrific.

LK: . . . Why did you write this?

MT: I wrote it because I felt that no one else could tell the story but me. A historian might look at all of the documents, all of the papers, and so on, but he wouldn't have known the agonies one went through, he wouldn't have known the difficulty of making some decisions. He wouldn't be able to get that from the papers. And he wouldn't have known—because in our cabinet papers we give all the arguments, but not the people who put them—he wouldn't have known who said what.

LK: So, "number one said this," "number two said that"?

MT: No, no: "The argument was put—this argument was put for, that argument was put against, the conclusion was—" So, only I really could have told it as it was lived.

LK: And how much of "all" is told? When they say, "Tell it all," Lady Thatcher, how much have you told?

MT: I've told quite a lot, because I had to tell it to make it live. I had to say who said what and the kinds of arguments we had between heads of government and heads of state. Things which concern security, of course, are never told.

LK: When, along the route to your own rise, did you say to yourself, "I want to be prime minister—"

MT: Oh, never.

LK: "—I want to lead the country"?

MT: Never.

LK: How did it happen?

MT: I can tell you exactly how it happened. I became an ordinary member or Parliament. I went and saw some of those scenes in Parliament, the debates. You know how noisy they are. I thought, "Thank goodness, I'm on the back benches, an ordinary member and not a minister. I don't think I could take this, some of the cat-calling they have." And then, I became a junior minister, and it seemed all right—"I can deal with it." Then, I became a cabinet minister, and that seemed all right. And then we lost that election, and we had lost several, and so

Keith Joseph and I decided to go right back to the drawing board on principles, followed by policy, followed by detailed decisions. And I had expected, when Ted Heath put up again as leader of the party, that Keith Joseph, as the leader of this particular group, would stand. And he came into my study one day and said, "Margaret, I just can't stand. I don't think I can take that kind of criticism and that kind of pressure." And almost immediately, I said, "Look, Keith, if you won't stand, I will. Someone who holds our views has got to stand, so that we have a chance of putting them into action."

LK: So, had he stood that day and said so, you wouldn't have—

MT: I would have been his most loyal lieutenant, and I wouldn't have been prime minister. We still had to go through, of course, a general election.

LK: Of course. Would you say that it was worth it? All the ups, all the downs, the travails. Was it worth it?

MT: Of course, every minute of the time. It was the most fascinating time of my life, and they were gripping years. We sorted out the economy. People came to have a higher standard of living, a real enterprise economy. We then saw the end of the Cold War. We had all the suddenness of things like the Falklands, and then the Gulf. Then, I had a sudden telephone call from Ronald Reagan: what about the Libyan raid, could his bases be used? They were fascinating: event after event after event.

LK: But what does that take out of you? I mean, certainly there's— With every good there's a bad, they say; up, there's a down.

MT: What does it take out of you? If you put yourself in the front line in politics, you're going to be shot at with all the criticisms. You're going to be criticized in the media. Of course, you are. You must expect that, and I don't know how you'd get through it if you didn't really believe in what you were doing and know why you were doing it. And I knew full well—and indeed, I said to Mr. Gorbachev many years later—that when you're doing a great reform, when you're really changing things, all the difficult things will happen first, and it'll quite a time before the benefits begin to show. That was so with me, and it was so with him.

LK: He'll be here this Saturday night.

MT: I know. Give him my warmest regards.

LK: I will. What is special about him? Because Mr. Reagan said it, you said it. What is it?

MT: I had never met before a person from the Soviet Union who could get into argument, answer debates, be very ebullient in all of his actions. Normally, you know, they were so dull. They had great sheaves of paper. They looked in the sheaves of paper and the briefing for the replies. Not Mikhail Gorbachev. He didn't have sheaves of paper—just all in his head. He was willing to admit that some things were wrong in the Soviet union, which was very unusual, and he would tell you what they were. And also, when he got into power, he deliberately tried to make changes, to try to get them right. It was difficult if you were turning from a totally controlled economy, which had been controlled for seventy years, to try to say to people, "Look, you must be enterprising." He didn't quite know how to do that. But what he did was to give people what you and I would regard as our birthright: freedom of worship—they'd never had it before—freedom of speech; freedom of movement; freedom of association; freedom of election. Marvelous.

LK: His life is a success?

MT: His life was not only a success, it was a great factor in the history of our time.

LK: Is it hard after the cheering. Is it hard to be the *former* prime minister?

MT: No, it isn't. You just have to accept it. You must accept exactly what's happened and start to build a new life. If ever you look back and live an "if-only" life, you'll do nothing constructive in the future. And I thought I was very lucky to have been prime minister of my country for eleven and one-half years during the years that were the most gripping of this century.

[*Commercial break*]

RONALD REAGAN: [*videotape, November 17, 1988*] She is a leader with vision and the courage to stay the course until the battles are won, and on occasion she has borne the added burden of having criticism incurred on America's behalf. I've been fortunate over these eight years, and for several years before that, to enjoy such a close professional and personal rapport and a genuine friendship with Margaret Thatcher.

LK: That's Ronald Reagan's picture. What's your picture of him?

MT: It was just very providential that he and I were in power together. He had the same beliefs as I did. He had something else. He had the most marvelous voice and communication talents, and he could get everything across—not only what he wanted to do, but the reason why. And also, we had something else in common. He never deflected from his purpose. He kept straight on towards his goal, and so did I.

LK: But you can have the same opinions and the same goals, but that doesn't mean you have to like someone. And the two of you had genuine affection.

MT: Oh, but I did like him. Yes. . . . We just got on very easy together. Sometimes, you know, the chemistry works, and you just click into action with— But I knew him before I was prime minister, and also before he was president.

LK: And it was instant? You knew him, you liked him, when you first met him?

MT: I knew his views, and I knew his capacity for communication. I'd seen him speak, and he can grip people with his total belief and sincerity. And I saw it again in action. You know, there were some people among other heads of state and government when we met in the G-7 who didn't think that he could make speeches off his own bat. I think they thought speechmakers made up all the speeches. And once in Paris he was asked really about what he thought and about the economy and how it should come right. And he just sat and gave a fifteen minute belief in free enterprise and why it worked and low taxation and how marvelous the people were who could create the jobs. And after that, President Mitterrand was in the chair. Even he said, "Well, you just have to know that President Reagan really believes every word, and it's very compelling."

LK: You do not, according to advance reads of this book, have the same feelings about President Bush. Correct?

MT: I like President Bush very much. You couldn't have a more decent, honorable man than President Bush. I felt that he inherited these principles. And it's one thing to inherit them; it's another thing to have fashioned them and believed in them and to have had an absolute yen to achieve your goal.

LK: He didn't have that?

MT: I don't think so. I think President Bush was absolutely first-class with all of his experience on foreign affairs, and we were very grateful for that. That was his experience. I think that he felt that the kind of regime that Ron Reagan had put in place—cutting the regulations, cutting the taxes—the enterprise would come up again. And of course it did, but it wasn't showing at the time of the last election.

LK: Do you know President Clinton?

MT: No, I don't know President Clinton.

LK: What are your impressions thus far from across the Atlantic?

MT: It is very early to say. He's obviously trying very hard, indeed. He obviously can put an argument extremely well, and the rhetoric is excellent. I noticed that during the election campaign. He's very anxious to please and very anxious to do as much as he possibly can for people. The ways he chooses would not be the ways I'd choose, but that's a difference of political view. I was, however, extremely pleased when he showed sympathy towards the Bosnian Moslems and tried to do something about their plight. Indeed, he went to the Security Council and asked for the arms embargo to be lifted. Quite right. Everyone has a right to defend themselves. It's quite crazy that the United Nations said, "Yes, you have a right to defend yourselves, but we'll deny you the weapons to do so." President Clinton tried to do something about it. Unfortunately, others did not help and, therefore, those people are no better off. And it should be a blot on the conscience of the whole Western world.

LK: And President Clinton could not go it alone in that kind of task, could he?

MT: He couldn't in supplying arms, because a mandatory resolution passes into the law of every land.

LK: What would Lady Thatcher, were she prime minister, have done?

MT: I did put it in writing about eighteen months ago when I was very, very deeply concerned that nothing was being done. And Vice President Ganic came out of Sarajevo to see me, and I said at that time two things should happen. That embargo on arms should be lifted so that the Moslems can be trained to use weapons and can defend themselves. I've never believed in putting troops in on the ground. The local people know their terrain. Give them the weapons, train them, they will fight better than anyone else. It was not done.

Added to that, I thought the lesson of this century was *Never appease an aggressor*. If he goes into someone else's land, he has to be thrown out. And I then said, "We must give an ultimatum to Serbia: 'Two, three, or four days. You have to get out of the lands you've taken. And if you do not, then with our highly technical aircraft and highly technical missiles we will bomb all military installations and the supply lines and the bridges.'"

LK: Did you convey those views to Prime Minister Major?

MT: They were published all over the papers and all over television.

LK: Did you speak with him?

MT: No, I didn't. I knew that his views were very different from mine, and so were the views of the foreign secretary.

LK: Does he disappoint you, or can you say you're not surprised?

MT: I am disappointed. Worse than disappointed, I'm appalled that the scenes we've seen on television haven't inspired and instigated some action greater that just trying to get aid to the people until they are mortar-bombed and shot at.

LK: Why do you think, Lady Thatcher, it hasn't? Why hasn't the world pounded its fist?

MT: They now aren't so ready to go it alone, as I was, and so was George Bush at the time of the Gulf. They seem to want to get together, either in the Community, the Twelve—"We must go and discuss it"—or get together in the United Nations—"We must discuss it." And do you know what happens under those circumstances? There's always someone who can find an argument for doing nothing: "Oh, let's not get involved." And so, the act of consensus is the negation of leadership, and it comes to the lowest common denominator.

LK: So, you don't go to the meeting, or you go, but still take independent action?

MT: Look, when the Gulf came up suddenly, I saw President Bush, because we were both at the same conference, and we got together very, very quickly and said straightaway, an aggressor must not be appeased. He must be thrown out. So, either he gets out, or we make him get out. And secondly, in that particular case of the Gulf, if he's left to go on, he can go over the border into Saudi Arabia. He can get, within a matter of days, 60 percent of the world's oil reserves. So President Bush and I decided, when Saddam Hussein did not go out, we decided that we would send our aircraft, and I contacted my leading ministers, and the aircraft were sent. They were sent within a week—within less than a week. But we didn't go and seek someone else's view. We said, "This must be done—now. Follow us."

LK: And they did.

MT: And France did, and others did. That's the difference. Give a lead, always, and then try to get other people to follow you.

[*Commercial break*]

LK: We go to Minneapolis, Minnesota. Hello.

CALLER: [*Minneapolis, Minnesota*] Having run the British health system, what advice would you give to President Clinton on how to control the long-term costs of the nationalized health care system that he's proposing in the United States?

MT: Well, I can only give advice as to the kind of health care system that we have. It is financed not by employers; it's financed by general taxation. It's free at the point of use. It works now very well, and we keep it down to 6 percent of the gross national product—slightly less. I say we keep it down. We've been able to provide a very efficient service at 6 percent of the gross national product. So, everyone is registered with a family doctor and, also, that family doctor will advise as to which hospital or which consultant to go to if hospital treatment is needed. It has one advantage: you don't pile costs onto the employer and tend to make the price of his goods noncompetitive.

LK: Do you recommend some sort of national health program for this country?

MT: I think you simply must have people who need medical care having access to it. I mean, anything else is utterly repugnant. But I've always understood in this country that a hospital could not turn away, by law, someone who needed medical care, and I've been around so many cities in this country, helping to raise money for people who couldn't have access to the best health care for any length of time, and the combination of the law and the voluntary aspect I think has perhaps been ignored.

LK: The royalty aspect of that job—something you have to deal with; something you like, dislike? What are your thoughts on Lady Di and the queen?

MT: I think the monarchy is the best possible system. No matter what happens, all of the patriotism and affection goes to the monarch. The queen's been on the throne since 1952. Every day of her life she's had to do the red boxes, the documents, receive ambassadors, go around the world—indeed, she probably has more experience than any other head of state of seeing other heads of state and of knowing at firsthand the problems of other countries—every day for more than forty years, and until she dies. She can't get out of it. Her very name spells duty. And then, the prime minister takes all the flak. That's absolutely right.

LK: You *like* that? Does a prime minister ever talk to a queen about things material?

MT: Oh, indeed. Usually, every Tuesday evening there is an audience with the queen when she's in London. It may be at Balmoral, if she's at Balmoral, or elsewhere. There's a regular weekly audience between prime minister and queen, prime minister and monarch, and the prime minister reporting to the queen, telling her all the things which are going on and which are expected to come up.

LK: When the tabloids get onto something, or you have a "Charles and Di," does it bring you down?

MT: I think these things happened in the past, but it wasn't dealt with in the front pages of the newspaper. I think it would be better if it were wholly private, but that's not the world we live in. But the important thing is that the monarchy must continue. It is a monarch and prime minister, and the prime minister is elected, and the continuity is in the monarch. . . .

[*Commercial break*]

LK: We go to Londonderry, New Hampshire. Hello.

CALLER: [*Londonderry, New Hampshire*] I have a question for you, which is based on the fact that I emigrated here in 1989. You were still in power at that time. And after you were ousted, I felt as though the press coverage was rather inadequate. . . . What went wrong with the problems in the Parliament?

MT: What happened was that there is a system of reelecting the leader of our party which can be operated every year. Normally, it's not during the time a prime minister is in office, but it can be. And it was operated that particular year, 1990. And Michael Hesseltine, who had great ambitions—and no one blames anyone for that—who wanted to be leader—I came through the first ballot with a majority of the MPs in my party. Only MPs can vote. So, I'd got the majority, but not quite a big enough majority for the rules—just two short. I was away. I was negotiating and, indeed, signing one of the treaties we'd worked so hard with Mr. Gorbachev on, a reduction in conventional weapons. And all the thirty-five heads of government and state were assembled in Paris to sign it. And so, of course, I stayed there and, of course, we stayed for two days, debating the issues of the future. I remember the ballot coming through and thinking, "Oh, I'll have to go to a second round. I do wish it would have been sorted out in the first round." It wasn't, but I was away. And that night my fellow MPs and my fellow cabinet ministers just lost their nerve. That's the only way I can explain it.

LK: Nerve to do what—hang tough?

MT: The nerve to say, "Right, we must go out and get a few more votes for Margaret, and then all will be well." And those who were very much against my policies—there are always those in your own party—got working. And I'm afraid, by the time I got back, the whole thing had fallen apart.

LK: Do you have bitterness?

MT: No point in being bitter.

LK: Anger?

MT: I saw every cabinet minister separately, and what they said is full recorded, because there were two other people in the room with me. And what slowly dawned on me, as they came in one after another, is, "Now, look, I'm a friend of yours, and I must tell you, as a candid friend, that I will support you if you go on, but I don't think you can win, and I think that you should stand down and let someone else who's more likely to beat Michael Hesseltine—" And then, the next one came in, "You know I'm your friend and I will support you, but I must be candid—" et cetera. It was the strangest thing. And then one came in, a marvelous man came in and said, "Look, I support you, and if you go on I will fight for you, and you can do it if all the guns blaze and go out fighting," but I was beginning to doubt whether any of the guns would blaze. And that, in fact, after I had seen them all, just really decided me. You can't—even generals must have good officers.

LK: Leiden, Holland, for Lady Thatcher. Hello.

CALLER: [*Leiden, the Netherlands*] Good evening, Lady Margaret Thatcher. My question is, what is your current opinion about the British Falklands? And do you still believe you made the right decision when you decided to defend the Falklands by military means instead of diplomatic ones?

MT: Most certainly. The Falkland Islands were invaded by an aggressor. At the time, there were no Argentinian people on the islands, except those who were running the air service from the Falklands to the mainland. British people had been there for 149 years. It was a plain, straightforward invasion of the Queen's lands and taking captive British people. Just our people at home simply wouldn't have had it. We had to go back and get those islands from [Argentine President Leopoldo] Galtieri, and he had to be seen to be defeated. And he was defeated.

Whatever makes you think that diplomatic activity could have got those Falkland Islands back? When you read the book, you'll see there were negotiations after negotiations. [U.S. Secretary of State] Al Haig did some. There were the Peru proposals. There were one lot of proposals after another—all designed to say, "Keep on negotiating," all designed— I'd be negotiating now, and the people would have still been under a military junta and not under democracy.

LK: Isn't it the hardest thing to send people into battle, though?

MT: Look, there is this remarkable thing. A prime minister never expects to send people into battle. I was agonized over it, but you couldn't leave our people captive of a military junta of the Argentine. Yes, it seemed militarily impossible to go 8,000 miles into the south Atlantic Ocean, where it was bitter winter; to have to fight with your aircraft bouncing upon the deck of aircraft carriers in the cruel seas. What had I got to stand us in good stead? We had got all the weaponry, we'd got all the ships, we had the best-trained professional men—as you do, also, have in the United States. And I had great faith in them. I had marvelous admirals, marvelous officers, marvelous men, wonderful fighting men, marvelous sense of humor—and they knew they had a task to do, to free British people.

LK: And like Harry Truman, I guess, once you make a decision like that—no qualms?

MT: No. It is done. But you go through agony every day when things go wrong. Can I tell you one thing, the first thing that happened? And it caused me great grief and alarm. We were going to get South Georgia back first, because that, too, had been taken, and we had to put a reconnaissance team on the *Fortuna Glacia*—an excellent reconnaissance team, crack troops, landed by helicopter. Very soon, the weather worsened, a terrible blizzard, and they radioed to be taken off. There was no cover. And the helicopter went to try to rescue them and could not take them up. They just couldn't get out. At that stage, the admiral came in to tell me what had happened—and my secretary of state for defense—that here we had these troops in a blizzard, two helicopters, two helicopter crews, and we couldn't get them off. And I had to go out to a dinner in the City of London that night, and I was agonizing, and I said to Admiral Llewyn, "Oh, does this mean we should never have gone?" And he, with all his experience, said to me, "No, don't be dismayed yet. Sometimes the best of battles start very badly."

And I went upstairs and changed to go to the City of London to speak; came down with a heavy heart—nothing in my mind except what was happening on that *Glacia*. I didn't know what I was going to do about the speech. Suddenly, at the bottom of the stairs—it was the prime minister's staircase—out dashed my principal private secretary from his office. He said, "It's all right! A third helicopter has gone in, and it's taken up all the troops and the other two crews, and it's due to land on *HMS Antwin* very shortly," and it did. It was impossible, again. We specialized in making the impossible happen during that campaign. And I walked out of Number 10 Downing Street to do the dinner, absolutely on air. I've never in my life felt so relieved. . . .

[*Commercial break*]

LK: Before we take the next call for Lady Thatcher—Hong Kong: what's going to happen in '97?

MT: In 1997, the lease which we were given [for] 99 years will [expire,] mean[ing] that the land and the people have to revert to China. I knew this, and thought that if I didn't try to negotiate with Deng Xiaoping, then we would have no confidence in the financial aspect of the colony, because you couldn't get a mortgage because you'd be coming up to the end of the lease. And Deng Xiaoping—who, after all, has started free enterprise in China—said, "All right, you can keep your capitalist system in Hong Kong. It produces prosperity. And you can keep your own law and your own rules of administration. And you'll have to negotiate on these things in detail," which we did. So, we should have those things. But Deng Xiaoping is very anti having full democracy, so we only have about one-third of the legislature elected.

LK: Are you optimistic?

MT: I am optimistic that it will turn out right. There are enormous changes happening in China, as you know full well. The annual growth rate is terrific. Steadily, Deng Xiaoping, although he didn't want democracy, said, "Right, I want an enterprising society, and I'm going to give the people powers to create one," and they're doing it.

LK: What do you think of the governor?

MT: The governor I have great confidence in. He knows the feeling and spirit of the people. He's very popular. When I was last there, I went around on a three-hour tour with him and saw the popularity. And the people wanted a little more democracy, and so he tried to fashion some solutions which wouldn't go against the agreement we had with China.

LK: And he angered some Chinese.

MT: China doesn't like it, and we've been trying to negotiate, and we haven't quite got an answer yet.

LK: But he'd be your governor there, too?

MT: Well, he was sent there. I think he's a very good governor. . . .

LK: Windsor, Connecticut, hello.

CALLER: [*Windsor, Connecticut*] Good evening. A great honor and privilege to speak to you both. . . . Mrs. Thatcher, would you have any recommendations to our President Clinton concerning the NAFTA treaty—any recommendations or cautions?

LK: We're voting in two weeks on NAFTA.

MT: Yes, I would have great recommendations, which I think he agrees with. The whole of the postwar prosperity has been built on increasing free trade. Contrast the '30s, when we all went protectionist and got into a depression. This is the lesson of our times. There's a second lesson. Mexico wants to pull up her standard of living by her own efforts. That's how we, all of us, started—building a better standard of living by our own efforts and selling our goods to other people who would buy them. It's not for us to deny other people the right to do that. And as they become more prosperous, so, indeed, they'll be the first to come and buy the more sophisticated goods of the United States.

Don't fear employers going to set up with cheaper wages in Mexico. If they were going to do it, they'd have done it already. The wages have been cheaper for a much longer time, and the tariffs aren't that high. Just think of the much bigger two-way trade you'll have as Mexico becomes more prosperous; her people wish to stay there because they're building prosperity; and her people will have more income with which to buy American goods. That will work, and it'll be in keeping with the whole of the postwar idea of freer trade among all peoples. . . .

[*Commercial break*]

LK: Our next caller for Lady Thatcher is from London, England. Hello.

CALLER: [*London, England*] How do you do, Lady Thatcher. Do you think that John Major will lead the conservative party into the next general election?

MT: I hope and believe so, and I hope and believe he'll win.

LK: So, you put personal things aside, here?

MT: Good heavens, yes. John Major is now prime minister. He's leader of our party. I hope he'll never have to go through the kind of leadership election I went through. I don't believe it's very constitutional, because the leader of a party is one thing, a prime minister answerable to Parliament is another, and the two should be separated.

LK: But you support him?

MT: I support him, and I believe we shall come out of recession sooner that the rest of Europe—firstly, because we reconstructed our industries and dealt with trade-union law and privatized things; and secondly, because we came out of the exchange-rate mechanism quicker than anyone else.

LK: Columbus, Ohio, for Lady Thatcher. Hello.

CALLER: [*Columbus, Ohio*] Yes, good evening, Lady Thatcher. . . . My question is, can you explain briefly the causes of this terrible world recession—and particularly, in the United Kingdom, as you know, and in Europe? And secondly, were you in power, how would you fix it?

MT: I can't give you a long answer. I'll give you one as brief as I can. I think we've got a recession, and I think it's longer because I think we had an excess of credit offered to people—whether it was people who were constructing great big property projects, or people who were constructing new things in industry, or people borrowing far more than they should have done in order to buy consumer goods. This in the end meant that we had a surplus of property, and people took on far too much debt. All of a sudden, they've realized that they've got too much debt, and they will not start spending again until two things have happened. They've lost capital on their houses, because the prices have fallen; therefore, they feel the loss of capital. And also, they've still got too much debt. So, until the price of houses starts to rise again, and until they feel comfortable with the debt they have got, any money they have got at the moment will go to repay that debt, and not to increase the expenditure. And because there are more and more people who own their own houses now than there used to be, this will be a longer recession than usual. But we shall come out of it—as we are coming out of it—but more slowly than used to be the case.

LK: I just wanted to ask you, what is your opinion of our former First Ladies, and what was your rapport with them?

MT: With Nancy and Barbara, I got on very well with both of them. They are completely different. Everyone has their own style. Nancy was a great support to Ronald Reagan. And you know when he had that terrible assassination attempt and then had cancer, Nancy just had to carry on, and she did it with great quiet courage. Barbara had her own life. She had her own great pet charities. She did wonderful things to help people who were illiterate or found it difficult to read. She was a totally different person—a tremendous person, who I think the whole of America and the whole of Britain loved. And she, too, was a great asset to George Bush. Each played their own role, in their own way, in their own style.

LK: By the way, would you like to meet the Clintons?

MT: Yes, indeed. I hope I will do so one day . . .

[*Commercial break*]

LK: Do you miss being prime minister?

MT: Yes, I did miss it. I missed it very much at first, because it was the whole structure of my life. I knew that on Tuesdays and Thursdays I was answering questions; I had cabinets on Thursdays; on Mondays I saw some of the party officials; on Wednesdays I was out and about in the country; on Fridays I was in my constituency. It's the whole structure of life, and you have to build a new structure. But that happens to many people, and fortunately—

LK: You've obviously done it.

MT: Yes, very successfully.

LK: Thank you so much.

MT: Thank you.

Michael Durant

America's humanitarian mission in Somalia turned ugly when fire fights broke out between warlord Mohammed Farrah Aideed and U.S. forces. One particularly brutal incident followed the downing of an Army helicopter piloted by Chief Warrant Officer Michael Durant on October 3, 1993. Badly injured, Durant was taken captive. Millions of Americans saw etched in his battered face the terror, pain, and bewilderment of modern warfare.

Eleven days after his capture, in what warlord Aideed called a gesture of goodwill, CWO Durant was released and a few weeks later gave his first primetime interview on Larry King Live.

"I knew . . . if they discovered that I was here . . . they would come in and kill me."

LARRY KING: It was the 101st that jumped on D-Day at Normandy, led by General Maxwell Taylor. We're at this famed base [Fort Campbell, Kentucky] tonight with one of its genuine heroes, according to its general, Jack Keane. He is Chief Warrant Officer Michael Durant, back from Somalia. . . . I thank you very much for joining us, Michael. I really appreciate it.

MICHAEL DURANT: It's a pleasure to be here.

LK: General Keane told us before that not only are you a great, great pilot, but you're a genuine American hero. Do you feel that way?

MD: It's taken me a while to really understand the scope of that term. As you know, I was just released from the hospital today, so I've kind of been isolated. And I'll try to live up to that name. I basically did my job as best as I could.

LK: Are you enjoying the attention, the people around, the status you're being given here at the fort, the way the people are toward you, the photographers and the like? Are you liking that?

MD: Well, it's fantastic to see the American people come together and show so much support. I like that portion of it. But to be honest . . . I'll be glad when all this is over and my life gets back to normal.

LK: Do you want to fly again?

MD: I really haven't made a firm decision. I'm considering taking a break after this, possibly going back to school and get a degree, but I think I'll be back in the cockpit eventually.

LK: Why are you making a career of the service?

MD: Well, it didn't start out that way. Actually, my intentions were to fly helicopters. A friend of my father owned one, and I went for a ride when I was about fourteen years old—had so much fun, I thought that would be a great way to make a living. And the Army was really the best way to go ahead and achieve that goal, so I joined the Army in hopes to fly some day.

LK: And if you don't fly again, the schooling will be in what? What do you want to do?

MD: Well, as an Army officer, it's a goal by your fifteenth year to have a degree, and I don't have one yet and I'm at fourteen, so I'm a little bit behind. But really, I haven't made a decision. I'd like to pursue something that I can use after I retire—possibly a different career.

LK: Did you know while you were being held—and that picture was shown all around the world, taken by our man in Somalia for CNN—did you know what people were saying? Did you have any idea what reaction you were getting?

MD: Absolutely no idea. They had told me that the video had aired, but I did not realize the magnitude or the scope or the impact of the video. . . . Really, the first time it hit me was in Germany, when Lorrie brought in the three magazines—*Time*, *Newsweek*, and *U.S. News*—and they all had my picture on the cover. And I accused her of going through the carnival and having my face put on the cover.

LK: Phony magazines.

MD: Yes. That really took me by surprise. That's really when it hit me.

LK: And there is your lovely wife, right here. [*Mrs. Lorrie Durant is seated to the side.*] . . . All right, what happened that day? First when you were going to Somalia, how did you feel about going to Somalia? . . . You got the job. You're in. You can tell us honestly how you felt.

MD: Yes. [*laughs*] There were some reservations. I mean, any time you go somewhere where there's a conflict, I think thoughts cross your mind that you may not come back. And I recall the last drive in the United States, looking at the trees, just wondering, you know, "Will I see this scene again?" It just—it just crosses your mind.

LK: So, you thought that you might not come back?

MD: Well, and I think everybody does, you know. Some people may not, but, you know, your mind wanders, and there's always the possibility anything can happen.

LK: What happened that October day?

MD: Well, it started out as a normal day. It was a Sunday, and we were doing some planning for some training the following day, when some intelligence sources reported possible—or a potential mission. So we began to plan, based on the location that we were given, and things became a little more firm, and it got to the point where we were pretty confident that the individuals that we were trying to go after were at that location, and the word was given to launch.

LK: It was after Aideed?

MD: No, not that day.

LK: Other individuals. . . . And so "launch" means "Off we go"?

MD: Yes.

LK: How soon after that did what happened to you happen?

MD: Really, for the first forty-five minutes to an hour of the mission, it went as briefed. That was our seventh mission. Things had gone smooth up to that point, and, again, things were going fairly smooth.

LK: Were you feeling confident?

MD: Really, we were. The plan was for us to put the Rangers in on the ground using the helicopters, and then for them to return to the air base via ground transportation. So, actually, my perception was, "My job is over. The Rangers are in. I'm basically on standby for a contingency." And I thought, basically, my part in the mission was over.

LK: So, you're whirling around with how many men in the plane?

MD: None—just the crew, four.

LK: Four, and you? . . . Then what?

MD: Then it began to escalate. There was a lot more resistance down there than I think we anticipated. There was a lot of RPGs being fired.

LK: That's what?

MD: Rocket-propelled grenade, which is what we assume knocked down the first aircraft, which was over the target area, another Blackhawk.

LK: Did you see it go down?

MD: I did not. I heard the radio transmission from one of the pilots, that they were hit and they were going down. We had a contingency plan for that. We had an aircraft with a load of Rangers onboard, and their mission was to go in and secure that site in the event an aircraft did go down. And we executed that contingency. That group of Rangers went in, secured the site, treated the wounded—and it basically went as planned.

LK: And then, what hit you? What happened?

MD: Well, I was called forward to replace the aircraft that was hit. And again, as I say, there was a lot more resistance down there. The Rangers were really engaged in a pretty heavy firefight at this point.

LK: At this point, were you a little nervous?

MD: I certainly was, and I know the whole crew was. And I recall, as we went in there, I said, you know, "This may get a little hairy. We need to keep our heads in the game." And it makes me proud to say that not a word was spoken. Nobody said, "Hey, do you really think we should go in there?" They all knew what their job was, and went in there without a word.

LK: What was the first— When you get hit, what does that feel like?

MD: I had made some notes later on in my captivity to try to remind me of what had happened, and I wrote down "a speed bump."

LK: Speed bump?

MD: It's really what it felt like. A Blackhawk is a fairly large helicopter, and the RPG hit the tail, and it felt like a speed bump. We knew we had been hit, but had no idea where. And really, at first the aircraft flew normally, so I still felt fairly comfortable—thought that I could make it to the airfield. But that changed rather quickly. What had happened was it hit a small transmission, which drives the tail rotor and because—

LK: Down you went.

MD: And down we went.

LK: How high up were you?

MD: We were at about seventy-five to one hundred feet when the tail—about three feet of the tail came off, including the tail rotor.

LK: Michael, do you remember what it was like, those seventy-five feet?

MD: It was pretty terrifying. What happens is the aircraft starts to spin, because the tail rotor is on there to counter the torque effect of the engines. And the aircraft was spinning so fast that the only thing I could see was a blur of the land and the horizon in contrast.

LK: Does the conscious thought enter your mind, like, "I've bought it"?

MD: No, not really. What I was thinking was, "If I can get the aircraft on the wheels, then we've got a chance of surviving," because helicopters are designed to absorb fairly—

LK: So you were thinking that while spinning?

MD: Right. I've been flying for over ten years, and it just— You know what you've got to do and, really, your priority at that point is to try to save your life and the lives of the crew.

LK: All right, when it hit, where did it hit? How did it hit?

MD: It landed on the wheels. And that's the only reason—

LK: So, you're okay? . . . Were you jarred?

MD: Yes, severely. We landed very hard. I believe I was unconscious for possibly two to three minutes. My first recollection on the ground is a sense of being confused, not really realizing what had happened. And then things began to clear up, and I realized that we had crashed. I started to clear— There was debris in the cockpit, a piece of tin from a roof, and the windshield was broken. I started trying to clear that stuff out, and I began to assess my injuries.

LK: Which were—?

MD: I realized at that point I had broken my right femur, because my leg was gone off at a strange angle. My back—I actually had more pain in my back at the time. I thought I had broken my back. I really couldn't move very well without a lot of pain. And that was it. I don't believe at the time that I had a compound fracture. I don't think the bone had broken the skin.

LK: What about the other men?

MD: I looked over at Ray, who was to my left—the other pilot. I asked if he was okay, and he— It appeared to me that he had suffered the same sense of confusion as I did. He began to really— Things began to clear up for him, and he said that his back was injured, also. And then he began to try to get out of the cockpit, and he succeeded. He was able to get out on his own power. I could not, because of the fact that I had the combination of the back and the leg.

LK: And the other two?

MD: Tommy Fields, one of the crew chiefs on the left, I did not hear speak, and I did not see. Bill Cleveland, on the right, was talking, but I could tell that he was injured pretty badly.

LK: They both died?

MD: Yes.

LK: Did you see them die?

MD: No.

LK: Who took you then? How were you taken?

MD: Well, it's a series of events that lasted about twenty to thirty minutes. Another aircraft came down to assist. This aircraft had the only ground forces remaining airborne onboard. There were three guys. And they tried to land near the site. There was too much debris. They had to shift to the south about one hundred meters. And they got down to about a two-foot hover, and two of the individuals jumped out of the aircraft and made their way to the crash site to try to assist us and secure the site. I did not know this was taking place until they actually showed up at the cockpit.

LK: Did you feel relieved?

MD: Very. I really felt confident at that point—knew we had assistance. We were about a mile away from the main battle, and I thought we really had a good chance of getting out of there without being captured.

LK: And what happened?

MD: I explained my injuries. They helped me out of the cockpit and set me to the right side of the aircraft about fifteen feet, and then I'm pretty sure they went to assist the other members of the crew. Bill Cleveland, one of the crew chiefs, was placed about ten feet to my left, face-down. And again, he was still talking, but I could tell he was hurt pretty bad. They gave me my weapon and then—I'm assuming this—it appeared that they began to look for ways out of the immediate area to a potential pick-up zone large enough for a helicopter to land.

LK: And what happened?

MD: Well, the Somalis were trying to come into the site. At first, everyone ran away because of the violence of the crash, but then they began to try to come back into the site. And where I was, access was pretty limited. We were right there up next to a tree and a building, and the tail blocked access to the rear. The left side was pretty wide open. So, I was able, really, to cover the whole right side, even though I was injured. They placed me where I had fields of fire to keep the Somalis away, and I fired two magazines' worth of ammunition and was successfully keeping them away from the site.

In the meantime, one of the guys who had been dropped off by the other helicopter was hit. I heard him cry out that he had been hit, and he went down. So, at this point, there's me and then the one other guy that came into the site. And he came back around the aircraft, explained to me that he was also running out of ammunition. I was out at the time. He asked if there were any more weapons. I told him that the crew chiefs had some M-16s in the aircraft. He went, searched the aircraft, found them. When he came back, he gave me another weapon with a full magazine. He made a radio call to any aircraft in the area asking what the status was of any ground force, and we were told that a ground reaction force was en route. And again, I felt comfortable knowing somebody was coming to try to get us . . .

[Commercial break]

LK: All right, now, you're on the ground. You're feeling up, you're feeling down, you're feeling confident, less confident, the Ranger is there with you. What happened?

MD: The next significant event: somebody throws some type of hand grenade into the site. The other individual is on the other side of the aircraft at this time, and it lands—I don't know how far away, but fairly close to me. I pretty much panicked—flailed my weapon around in an attempt to knock it away, and then turned, and it exploded. And I don't know what it was, but nothing hit me—whether it went into a hole or just rolled away. So, now I'm back to—

LK: Feeling better?

MD: —not feeling so confident any more.

LK: All this is happening in quick transformations of ups and downs, right?

MD: Right. And Somalis are continuing to try to come into the site. Some have weapons, some don't—but treating them all as hostile. And once again, I run out of ammunition. Then things got quiet, and I thought, "Either that ground reaction force is getting close and they're backing away, or they're just giving up."

Unfortunately, what I think they were doing at this point now is regrouping and coming up with a plan to attack the site.

What happened next was, the guys on the left side of the aircraft were trying to keep them away over there, and there is a huge volume of fire from the left side. So, I'm assuming either the militia showed up and attacked, or the people that were trying to come in individually decided to consolidate and make an attack.

LK: But now you know you're in big trouble?

MD: This firing went on for about thirty seconds, and then I heard him cry out that he was hit also, and he went down.

LK: He died, too?

MD: He did die.

LK: Do you have any idea why they didn't shoot you?

MD: They tried. I think the reason I never was hit was because I was lying flat on my back with my leg propped up and I was firing, basically, from the hip, and I just happened to be in the right spot where no rounds hit me.

LK: But eventually, They did take you prisoner. They could have killed you then. . . . Were you shocked? What is it like to be taken? I mean, you know people are dead around you, the mission's gone—something's gone amok. And here you are taken by what might be termed fanatics, or you don't know what they are. How do you deal with that?

MD: I was terrified. There's no doubt about it. I was sure they were going to kill me. When they came on the site, it was a crazed mob. They were yelling and screaming and throwing stuff out of the way. And again, I had no ammunition left, and I just placed that weapon across my chest and put my hands on it and looked up at the sky and—

LK: And—?

MD: It was out of my hands at that point. And the first guy came around. I think it took him by surprise that I was laying there. He backed up, and then he came again, and then the rest of the mob came. And as far as how many there were, I have no idea. There was enough around me that I could not see past my immediate area. And they were pretty much divided between those that were hitting me and those that were stealing my stuff. I still had all my flight gear on and my boots, and they immediately started—

LK: Were you saying anything or just—

MD: I tried to be as non-aggressive as possible. I knew there was no chance of winning that fight, and I felt like if I just remained passive, there was a chance that they might feel I was more valuable as a prisoner. My only consideration at that point was staying alive.

LK: And who made the decision—*prisoner*? How did you know you would be taken prisoner?

MD: I didn't. And again, they were hitting me, and I thought they were just going to beat me. And then, I have to assume that somebody there took control of the situation and tried to stop the beating and say that I was more valuable as a prisoner, because when people would hit me, others would push them away. So, it became evident at that point they wanted to keep me alive.

LK: And they took you where?

MD: They wrapped—well, one guy threw dirt in my eyes and in my mouth, and then they wrapped a rag around my head, and they hoisted me up in the air, and they

carried me out into the street and they were parading me around for a few minutes. And again, people would come out of the crowd and hit me, and they'd get
pushed away. And I really don't know how long this went on. That was— Of the
entire experience, that particular phase was absolutely the worst. My leg was being
manipulated all over the place, my back was really, really hurting me bad and,
again, I thought there was a pretty good chance they'd still end up killing me.

LK: So, you're at a constant pitch of fear?

MD: Yes.

LK: Did you ever get calm? Did you ever say—

MD: Not until they threw me in a room and—I really started thinking then, "Okay,
they're going to take me prisoner." And although that's an unpleasant experience—

LK: It's living.

MD: —it's better than death. And I just started— You know, I did calm down once
that happened.

LK: Did you realize— You had no idea that a picture of you was circulating, taken by
a CNN— You had no idea?

MD: No idea.

LK: And you were held twelve days?

MD: Eleven.

LK: Eleven. Treated?

MD: Medical treatment? The doctor first came just before they filmed the video. He
didn't have anything. He had sterile 4-by-4s and Betadine and—

LK: So you had no treatment on a broken leg?

MD: No

LK: Nothing on the back?

MD: He cleaned the open wound and, obviously, that helped, because I have not had
an infection. And he gave me antibiotics . . .

[*Commercial break*]

[*From videotaped interview made in Somalia, October 4, 1993*]

SOMALIAN INTERROGATOR: What— How do you think of this operation?

MD: I'm a soldier. I have to do what I'm told.

SOMALIAN INTERROGATOR: Killing—killing the people—innocent?

MD: Innocent people being killed is not good.

LK: All right, now, when you look at that, that horror: what was that like?

MD: I guess the worst part was the pain. I had asked them to film it with me lying
down, and they insisted that I sit up, and that's why I'm supporting my weight
with my hands.

LK: They forced you to film it, right?

MD: Yes.

LK: So you're in constant pain there?

MD: Yes.

LK: And scared, too. You look scared. Was this the time you thought that maybe they
wouldn't let you go?

MD: Well, that was about thirty hours after the capture, when they filmed that, and I
still really didn't feel like I was going to get out of there alive. I knew that the
people in the neighborhood, if they discovered that I was there—I had been told

they would come in and kill me. And again, I really didn't feel like I'd make it out of there at that point.

LK: . . . A couple of other things I want to cover before we break and then go to calls. There was a drive-by shooting, right?

MD: Well, that's the term I use for it. It was the morning before the video, so I'd been in captivity about twelve hours at this point. I was chained up and—

LK: *Chained?*

MD: Yes. In the corner of a room. The room had one door.

LK: No treatment for the leg?

MD: None. None yet. And I could hear the guards when they'd come. They'd come every hour or so to check on me. And someone walked towards the door. I was awake. I looked over, the door opened and some type of weapon was stuck in the door, and then somebody fired a round. And the bullet hit the floor somewhere between me and the door and then ended up in my left arm. And any thoughts I had of surviving the situation were pretty well gone at that point.

LK: So, obviously, you now know that some people want to keep you alive, but there are potential assassins out there who want to cut you down?

MD: Right.

LK: I don't want to breeze through anything, and the next eleven days had to go by. Did you hear from anyone? Were you aware of anything from the other side at all?

MD: No. I asked a lot of questions. I asked what the status was of the rest of the guys at the site, and they said they didn't know anything. They claimed that they had no one else in captivity other that the Nigerian soldier who had been captured on a previous—

LK: Was anyone kind to you?

MD: Yes.

LK: Many?

MD: People are people, even in that situation. And there were some who would come in there to check on me that it looked to me like, if they were in charge, I would be dead. And yet there were others who would come in there, try to almost comfort me and, you know, say—they're all Moslem—say, you know, "If Allah wills it, you'll go home." It was— And that helped, you know.

LK: Did they feed you okay?

MD: Yes. And that's when I began to realize, "Okay, they want to keep me alive." They asked me what I wanted to eat, and I tried not to be too demanding, so I said, "Well, how about spaghetti?" That happens to be my favorite food, anyway.

LK: Did they have it?

MD: Yes. They went out and made me—

LK: Was it good?

MD: It was pretty good.

LK: Tomato sauce?

MD: No. I guess they don't eat it with tomato sauce. I'm not sure what it had on it, but it was good.

LK: How did you find out you were going home?

MD: Well, there was an individual named Mr. Abdi, who was General Aideed's minister of internal affairs, and he had been coming almost every day to talk to me. No question the guy was in charge—well educated.

LK: Talk to you about what?

MD: He'd come and explain what was going on and explain the developments, check on how I was doing. And he certainly was reporting back to General Aideed. And forty-eight hours before my release, he told me that I would be released within the next twenty-four to forty-eight hours.

LK: You believed him?

MD: And I believed him. Everything he had told me prior to that—

LK: Boy, that time must have been terrific.

MD: Well, the thing was, as anyone who's ever been in captivity— It's a psychological battle. And I tried not to get my hopes up too high because—

LK: Even though you believed him?

MD: Well, I believed him, but anything can happen. And I really tried not to get focused too much on that forty-eight hours, because if that went by, and I wasn't released, I really felt like I'd be so down that I'd kind of defeat myself. So I said, "Okay, if it happens, that's great, but let's prepare for the long haul," and I tried to really almost assume it wouldn't happen.

LK: And when they took you out, did they just come and say, "You're going home"?

MD: Well, he came back the next day and, you know, he had said twenty-four to forty-eight, so I said, "Well, is today the day?" And he said no, that the following day General Aideed would do a press conference, and once he announced that I would be released unconditionally, then the Red Cross would be notified, and they'd come get me. And that is what happened. He had the press conference at 11:00 local time, and at about 12:15 the Nigerian soldier was brought to my room, and it became evident right there that we were going to, for sure, be released.

LK: Lorrie Durant is here. Did you see the press conference of General Aideed?

LORRIE DURANT: Yes, I did.

LK: So, you knew then. Where were you?

LD: Well, someone from the military called me at 4:00 in the morning, and I was in bed—[*laughs*]—but I got up quickly and turned the television on and—it was pretty unbelievable.

LK: Did you have faith he'd come home?

LD: To be honest, no.

LK: You thought he'd be killed?

LD: Well, when I was notified that he was shot down and missing in action, that's not a good sign, you know. And I had initially thought that he was dead. I didn't want to set myself up for a large disappointment.

LK: What did you see when you saw the picture and that hostage video?

LD: Fear. I saw my husband looking with the look of fear in his eyes, and that terrified me, because he's always the strong one.

LK: Now, you grew up here at Fort Campbell, right?

LD: Yes, I did.

LK: Your parents— You're a military brat, is what you call it, right?

LD: Yes.

LK: But nothing could prepare you for this, right?

LD: Absolutely nothing.

LK: How do you hold up for eleven days?

LD: I had tremendous support from my friends and my family and the community and the letters from the United States. There were letters from Germany. I mean, the whole world was behind us, and that's really what helped.

LK: And that was important to you?

LD: Very important.

LK: And, of course, you had no idea of that?

MD: Right.

LK: Someone wrote a letter and said, "What's your birthday?" because there are people all over America who are making— They became your adopted mother. What *is* your birthday?

MD: It's July 23rd . . . They've got a long ways to go.

LK: Long ways to go to knit you stuff, right? . . .

[*Commercial break*]

LK: All right, as they say: Only in America. We're going to go to your phone calls for Chief Warrant Officer Michael Durant. A month ago, we were worried if he'd be alive or dead; tonight, we're at Fort Campbell, Kentucky, and taking your calls. And we go to Boulder, Colorado. Hello.

CALLER: [*Boulder, Colorado*] Hello. The first thing I'd like to say is, Michael and Lorrie, you're an inspiration to all America, and we back you all the way. I get tears in my eyes when I see that video. You know, that's just how I feel. But one thing we found out while you were in captivity is the fact that the secretary of defense turned down, you know, sending a couple of tanks and armored personnel carriers to back our quick reaction force on the ground, like about a month or two before this event happened. And I'm wondering what you think about that?

MD: Well, that kind of falls into the category of foreign policy, and I answered this question before by saying anybody can armchair-quarterback events that have already taken place. And I really can't criticize that decision. But I would say that any commander in the field has a better chance of mission success with additional assets.

LK: But you hold no brief against Les Aspin?

MD: No.

LK: To Columbus, Georgia. Hello.

CALLER: [*Columbus, Georgia*] Hey, how're you doing? Good to have you back, Chief. I've got a two-part question for you real quick. The two Delta operators that came in after you guys, do you think you would have survived if they hadn't showed up at the crash site? And, part two, do you think SPECTRE would have made a big difference in your specific situation if it had been on station?

MD: Well, the members of the Ranger task force that came in there—there is absolutely no doubt in my mind, had they not come into the site, that I would have been killed. I was sitting in that cockpit and an easy target for anybody who wanted to come into that site.

LK: The second question?

MD: And on the SPECTRE, it could have possible helped. Again, the more assets you have, your chances of success increase.

LK: Do you ever have that feeling when others died around you that, "Why me? Why am I alive, and they didn't make it?"

MD: All the time. To me, the experience is kind of like a series of miracles. There were so many times when I was sure that I was going to die, and then somehow I didn't.

LK: To Cairo, Egypt, for Michael Durant. Hello.

CALLER: [*Cairo, Egypt*] Hello, Michael. Well, first of all we want you to know that we all were supporting you during your capture in Somalia. Congratulations for your freedom. The first question I would like to ask you is, do you have any bad feeling against the Somalian peoples? We know that you went for a good mission and you received the bad treatment from them.

MD: Well, I think that the Somali people have survived a lot of hardship. They lived under the dictator, then they had the civil war and the famine, and then a lot of innocent people have been killed during this conflict. General Aideed's and the Ali Mahdi forces continue to fight to this day. And I think they just took out their aggressions on us.

LK: You have no bitterness toward them?

MD: There's bitterness. They—

LK: But not as a group?

MD: Well, again, they're not all General Aideed's supporters. Some of them are still pro-U.S. I mean, they killed my—

LK: They killed your friends.

MD: —friends, so there is some bitterness. But they've had a pretty hard road.

LK: By the way, today the Red Cross declared that the famine in Somalia is over. Present circumstances aside, did we do the right thing in going?

MD: Well, I think we did some good. The pictures that we see today of Somalia are certainly different than a year ago, so obviously some good was accomplished. If somebody else could have done it, I don't know. For that aspect, the mission was successful.

LK: As a member of the armed forces—and we are the only superpower left now— do you think we have a mission to help where help is needed and go where we must go?

MD: I think there's going to be cases where that is true. However, there's others where we have no business there. . . . And that's not for me to decide. That's certainly a decision to be made in Washington.

LK: This "go where you're sent," is that easy to— I mean, you're a New Hampshire boy of French background, right?

MD: Right.

LK: That's independent. If you know anything about the French in New Hampshire, they're independent. Is it hard to, when they say "go," go?

MD: It isn't for me. A military force would be ineffective if you allowed the members of it to choose what they wanted to do. You have to follow the orders of your superiors.

LK: To Camp Rucker, Alabama. Hello.

CALLER: [*Camp Rucker, Alabama*] Hello, Mr. Durant. Say, I'm the class leader of a flight class currently attending flight school, and I was wondering if you could pass along some advice that might help these future aviators prepare themselves for an experience such as you endured?

MD: That's a tough question. I guess, stay with the books and, once you get out there and start flying, apply for as many schools as possible, because the more training you receive the better prepared you'll be for any situation.

LK: Do you like flying?

MD: I love it.

LK: Still like it?

MD: Well, I didn't like it on October 3rd, but I really love it. There are certain missions that we've flown that—there's just no feeling like it afterwards. It's like winning the Superbowl sometimes, when things go real well.

LK: Is a helicopter more fun than a plane?

MD: You could argue that. It is a lot of fun.

LK: Amsterdam, Holland, hello.

CALLER: [*Amsterdam, the Netherlands*] Hi, Larry, Michael. My question to Michael is, how does it feel like to serve as an American abroad? I'm calling from Holland, a country that hasn't sent any soldiers abroad for about forty-five years, so it's a main issue over here how people deal with it.

MD: Well, I think there's a feeling of pride, knowing that the United States has a leading role in world affairs. There's no one else that can say that. And our intentions are always good.

LK: So, you're proud of that.

MD: I am.

LK: Could you tell us quickly—and we'll take a break—what they did medically to you? Now, on the leg, you broke the leg where?

MD: Basically, right in the middle of the femur [*indicates on right leg*].

LK: What do they put in?

MD: It's absolutely incredible. I didn't know anything about this procedure until it was done. But two weeks ago today, they made an incision at the top and drilled a hole in the top of the bone and actually hammered a steel rod all the way down through the center of the bone, and I guess it's about eighteen inches long. And they lined it up, drilled across here, put in two screws across here, put in two more screws. And they told me an interesting story—if we have about thirty seconds. They say that the Germans were the first ones to use this procedure, and they did it on someone they had captured, and the guy had just broken his leg, and when he woke up on the operating table he jumped off and ran away. . . .

LK: Now, what did they do to your face?

MD: That was in Germany. They made an incision up underneath my lip and used a tool to go up in there—it almost looked like a spoon—and lifted the bones back into place, put some packing in there to hold them there. And the packing is all removed, and everything feels fine.

LK: How's the back?

MD: That's really where I've got the only pain now. We're treating that with a brace [*taps on brace around waist*]. It's kind of like a "Ninja Turtle" shell. . . .

LK: Let's go back to calls. Halmstad, Sweden, hello.

CALLER: [*Halmstad, Sweden*] My name is Rolf Kantof, and I was wondering what has been the toughest adjustment since you came back to your family in the States?

MD: I think dealing with the attention. . . .

LK: And you've been telling this story, then, to people in the Army—officers? Did psychologists talk to you, too?

MD: Yes.

LK: First moments with your wife—difficult, awkward?

MD: Fantastic. I mean, that's one of the things that I was looking forward to, and it was really well orchestrated. We were alone, and we had plenty of time. As you can imagine, very emotional, but—

LK: Were you able to hold each other a little?

MD: Yes.

LK: Lorrie, where did you first see Michael?

LD: In Landstuhl.

LK: In a hospital room?

LD: Yes. They put him in the bed and got—

LK: You walked in alone?

LD: Yes.

LK: That was very nice that they were that thoughtful to do that.

LD: Very thoughtful. We had our own wing.

LK: We've only got a minute left. Recovery time: what do you do now, Michael? You're out of the hospital.

MD: I've got some physical therapy that I have to do every day, and making progress every day, getting stronger.

LK: Any vacation?

MD: Yes.

LK: Where are you going?

MD: Well, right now, again, as I said earlier, it's the simple things that are important, and just staying around the house and playing with Joey.

Mikhail Gorbachev

Mikhail Sergeyevich Gorbachev was born March 2, 1931, into a family of farmers. Admitted to Moscow State University law school in 1950, he joined the Communist party in 1952 and, by 1980, was a member of the Politburo. In 1982 his mentor, Yuri Andropov, became general secretary of the party—the most powerful position in Russia—with Gorbachev as his aide. Andropov died soon after and was succeeded by Konstantin Chernenko. When Chernenko died in 1985, Gorbachev became general secretary and embarked on a program of reform called perestroika *("restructuring"), while assuring peaceful relations with the West, in part through a policy of* glasnost *("openness"). Thwarted by growing nationalist unrest among the Soviet republics, Gorbachev soon found himself presiding over the elimination of communism as a major force in world affairs. Communist hardliners seized control of the government in 1991 and held the Gorbachevs prisoner for several days. The coup was crushed by Boris Yeltsin, but it left Gorbachev bereft of power, and on Christmas Day 1991, he resigned. Today Gorbachev, a Nobel laureate, is a private citizen who devotes his time to lecturing and writing.*

"Over the years, I became angry . . . about what was happening in the country, how we were treating our people, our citizens."

LARRY KING: In the West, a hero, the Soviet leader credited with helping to end the Cold War. In Mikhail Gorbachev's homeland, often portrayed as a failure, blamed sometimes for national collapse. And today conventional wisdom says he'd have trouble being elected—but not in the United States. A Russian court has even ordered him to apologize for insulting Moscow's mayor.

But political tides often turn. After all, in his seven years in office, this man opened a society closed since 1917, nurtured freedom of expression and religion, encouraged his people to be something new: enterprising. On Christmas Day 1991, Mikhail Gorbachev resigned, as the USSR crumbled away. He's here tonight to talk about the past, the future, and, for the first time, to take your phone calls. We are honored to welcome the former Soviet president, Mikhail Gorbachev, to *Larry King Weekend*.

I thank you very much for coming. Do you, Mr. President, miss holding office? Do you miss being president of your country?

[Throughout this interview, Mikhail Gorbachev speaks through an interpreter.]

MIKHAIL GORBACHEV: Well, I regret the fact that I was not able totally to implement my plans, fully to implement my plans. But I think that one could hardly have expected that the plans to reform such a vast country as my country is—the Soviet Union, and now Russia—that this could be done by a reformer within one or two terms. . . . But I was not able to do certain things.

LK: I know, but do you personally miss not being the head of the country?

MG: Well, if I said to you that I am pleased with my role today completely, that would not be quite true. But at the same time, I will tell you that I am working on the same problems as before within my foundation, and also within the International Green Cross I am doing the same—working on the same problems. We are working on the problems of reforming Russia. The foundation also works on CIS problems, and also on problems of the new thinking and rebuilding international relations. So, in a way, I am doing the same things but, of course, with less effectiveness than at the time when I had power. So, in that sense, yes, I feel the difference.

LK: Mr. President, do you miss the world stage? Do you miss meeting with the president of the United States and the prime minister of England, and that kind of life that you had?

MG: Well, I still meet them. I meet them. This is quite routine. In all my travels I have meetings with members of Parliament, presidents, prime ministers, scientists, political figures, and with many people representing the public. I would say I'm meeting more people now. But, so far as meetings with your president, I have not yet met with your incumbent president, even though there was a chance that we could meet when I was still president, and maybe we intended to meet later, but this did not happen. Yesterday, I answered a similar question from your press. I said perhaps when a meeting between us was suggested and we discussed the possibility, probably the horoscopes were against us. But maybe it is yet ahead. Maybe it will still happen, I think . . .

[Commercial break]

LK: What do you think of Margaret Thatcher?

MG: Well, I've just recently completed the chapter of my memoirs about our cooperation with my counterparts at the time when we were exploring ways of getting together and of trying to change the world for the better and to avoid the dangers. I have to tell you that she was one of the first political figures of that time who began to work with us, and did that in a far-sighted way. She was not an easy counterpart to deal with, but we were able to work together, even though sometimes we had very lively debates—two people who had their convictions, who had their positions, and who were committed to different values. But at the same time, we were consistently working on changing the atmosphere and improving dialogue, on improving trust. And within that trust and a better personal relationship, we were able to find keys to the most difficult issues. So, I hold Mrs. Thatcher in very high regard, as a politician, as a person, as a woman.

LK: It also sounds like you like her. . . . You genuinely like her as a person.

MG: Oh, yes. . . . I'll tell you that that also helped us to work together. Our families knew each other, and we met between our two families. It was not just political discussions and meetings, but as human beings.

LK: The same with President Reagan, right?

MG: Yes, that is true. That is true.

LK: Okay, let's discuss some current things. There were reports in Moscow today that your successor, Mr. Yeltsin, is going to put off the early presidential elections that he promised, and he'll serve through 1996. That's sort of sketchy. I mean, we're not sure he said that, but pretty sure he said it. Your thoughts?

MG: Well, after he said that, I understand that in the evening there was an interpretation, a spin, given to that by his chief of staff—Mr. Valadov, the chief of staff of the Russian president. He said that the president was perhaps misunderstood; that he may, perhaps—he might, perhaps, decide that it is for the parliament, for the new parliament—the state *Duma*—to decide that question. So, I still don't know what's the latest. I have those two reports. Anyway, my viewpoint—

LK: What do you think?

MG: My viewpoint is that he should do as promised. I think he would only win as a result of keeping his promise.

LK: Will he win the election if he runs in June?

MG: Well, this depends on how things evolve and what kind of policy will be followed by the government after the parliamentary elections. A lot will hinge on that. If the government continues reforms in the form, in the style, in the spirit that they have been doing it when reforms resulted in a kind of implosion, when people found themselves in a kind of trap, when people were not ready to accept the kinds of reforms, to understand the kinds of reforms that were happening, when two-thirds of the population were below the poverty line—people did not accept it, and people were angry. So, if the government changes course and readjusts its policies, then this will have an impact, and so people will have a certain view of the president, too. So, it depends on the policies. The results depend on policies.

LK: Too early to tell now? It's too early?

MG: Yes. Yes, I think so.

LK: Okay. You: what changed you? You grew up in an atmosphere of communism, your grandfather was a famed communist, your people were very involved in the communist movement, you grew up in a traditional Russian household. What changed Mikhail Gorbachev? What made you able to turn a place that didn't have freedom into freedom? What did it to you?

MG: Well, life changes us. Efforts, attempts to reform the country, to reform our society, were made several times after Stalin's death, because what we inherited after Stalin—a totalitarian regime; repression; the domination of one party, of one ideology; the suppression of freedom—that did not give our society, our country, enough fresh air; and, therefore, the country was suffocating, and it needed second wind. And, therefore, every people who were concerned about our country tried to do something. They wanted to try some reforms. Khrushchev tried it, Kosygin tried an economic reform, but all of those were defeated because the *nomenklatura* always acted in a way to prevent reforms from succeeding.

So, we had to give a lot of thought to how we safeguard reforms. During the first years of reforms, I acted just like my predecessors, mostly focusing on economic reforms, on industry, agriculture, et cetera. But then, we saw that when we really wanted to push the reforms forward, the system, the *nomenklatura*, began to resist, began to sabotage that process—and not just the party *nomenklatura*, but also the management *nomenklatura*. And I decided, I concluded as a result of that,

that we would lose just like the previous reformers, like Kosygin and Khrushchev, if we don't implement democratic changes, if we don't have free elections.

LK: But you decided to do what they didn't do. You took them on. You didn't have to take them on. You could have lived the life of a typical Soviet president. Why did you take them on?

MG: Well, no, this I think would be someone other than Gorbachev if I did not take them on. My experience, my convictions, my education, my pain, and my feeling about my country and my people—all of this was growing in me. And over the years, I became angry. I became unhappy about what was happening in the country, how we were treating our people, our citizens. . . . But initially, I thought that the system could be improved, and I began by trying to improve the existing system. And then I thought that we have to change the system, to replace the system; it cannot be improved.

LK: Was it difficult to open doors to the United States? Because you had to be raised with feelings about the United States like we were raised with feelings about the Soviets. Was that hard, to open that door?

MG: Very difficult. I think maybe that was the hardest thing. And if we, in moving from Geneva to Reykjavik to Washington to Moscow, in trying to understand the positions of each other, in studying each other—if we had not believed each other, then I think, if we had not established human rapport, then we wouldn't have been able, I think, to develop real cooperation, real work together.

It was hard. When President Reagan and I first began to talk, we were together, just like you and I today, at a small table, and President Reagan began to accuse me, you know, of human rights violations. He said, "You have no democracy." He said, "You need to make these changes in foreign policies, and these changes, et cetera, et cetera." And my answer, when our dialogue began to go that way, was, "Mr. President, you are not a prosecutor, and I am not an accused. Let us not lecture each other. We represent big countries. Let us speak as equals. I think that then we will be able to find keys to any problem." So it was difficult, but still it became possible. Without changes in Soviet-American relations, nothing would have changed in the world.

LK: Yes. So, it became possible because humans talked to humans and got along, right? Mutual survivability.

MG: Absolutely. Mr. Reagan was initially no less ideologized that Mr. Gorbachev, than President Gorbachev, so we had to rise above those ideological fences and obstacles that were dividing us. Those divisions were a little like religious wars. If you really throw away those ideological dogmas and think about how people live, how this country lives and our country lives, whether they can cooperate; if you ask, "Does Moscow really think about how to destroy the United States?" or, "Does the White House in Washington think about destroying the Soviet Union?"— But that was what the people thought. . . . So, we had to really overcome many things in ourselves.

LK: Secretary of State Warren Christopher, in a story that will come out Monday in *U.S. News and World Report*, says there could be an impending nuclear catastrophe in the Ukraine with the buildup. Are you worried about that?

MG: Well, I think that if he made that statement, such a conclusion—I have not heard that statement in that kind of way. Maybe it's an exaggeration. Perhaps it's some kind of political pressure. Politicians do that sometimes when they engage in dialogue. They want to make the other side think and make the other side respond to that. But I don't think that this is really happening in the Ukraine. I know Ukrainian political leaders, I know that republic, I know the people. I really don't think, really, that there are such irresponsible leaders in that country who would be acting in a way that a nuclear catastrophe, a nuclear disaster, could happen. I think you should seek implementation of the Lisbon agreements and, also, then to think about how to work together in implementing START II. I hope— I think that the Ukrainians are basically engaged in political bargaining, political tradeoffs. It's normal. I am not dramatizing this. I was doing that, too. Your presidents were doing that, too. That's normal. I don't think that in the Ukraine something is being conceived of that kind in an irresponsible way. Let us just continue dialogue. Let us look for a solution. . . .

[*Commercial break*]

LK: We will begin to include your calls now for President Gorbachev on this live edition of *Larry King Weekend*. We begin with Taipei, Taiwan. Hello.

CALLER: [*Taipei, Taiwan*] Mr. President, it's an honor to speak with you. My question is, simply, have you ever had the opportunity to speak with Fidel Castro, or the powers that be in Mainland China—Deng Xiaoping, Li Peng—and candidly had a conversation about the fact that their days might be numbered under communism?

MG: I had many meetings with Fidel Castro; fewer meetings, but some, with the Chinese leaders. We discussed all problems, including problems of socialism. And my viewpoint, as I expressed it to them, was this: What we are doing, what we were doing as a part of *perestroika*, is our choice, is what we want to do, what we need to do to change our society, to make it free and to make it possible for people to realize their potential and their talents. But I also thought that what China needed, what Cuba needed, is for them to decide, and for the Chinese and for the Cubans to do. So this was my approach. This was my concept when I talked to them.

LK: You didn't tell them to do what you were doing?

MG: No. No. My position was that if they need to take advantage of our experience, we were ready to share, but we were not imposing it, just like the Soviet Union used to impose its model on Eastern Europe and other countries. We want every nation to choose.

LK: Are you, Mikhail Gorbachev, still philosophically a communist?

MG: No, I don't think that that would be the right description, the right reflection of my thinking today.

LK: How would you describe it?

MG: It is quite clear that the communist model as was imposed on our country, the Soviet Union, Russia, then Eastern European countries—that that model was defeated; that that model was based on dictatorship, on a totalitarian system. It rejected democratic principles of states and social functioning, and that model inevitably had to lead the country into a dead end, and this happened. But that model also had certain aspects that our state and other states were able to use, particularly enforced ways of addressing certain problems, quick ways of addressing certain problems. But for a good life for citizens, that model was not good. It did not create the right conditions. I rejected that. I have abandoned that. But that doesn't mean that I, as a matter of principle, have abandoned any kind of link with the past, that I have no interest toward problems of social justice. No, I do have interest. . . .

[*Commercial break*]

LK: Before we take the next call, I mentioned NAFTA. What do you think of NAFTA and our debate over this, and Gore— You don't know Mr. Perot, do you?

MG: Well, I'm a little familiar with him. Last year, April of last year, when I was on a tour of the United States, someone suggested to me that I could agree to become his vice presidential running mate. I said to that, "I can't agree, because that's too little for me; I used to be president, after all."

LK: What do you think of NAFTA?

MG: Well, a short answer, of course, is that this is your problem, and it's for you to decide, and that would be the right answer. But I still think that this is not just the only regional market that is evolving. There is also the European Community. There is the Asian community. Here you have North America. I believe that regional cooperation agreements are necessary. This is a need. There is a need for that. It's not something that someone invented. This is the requirement in the world today. Neighboring countries that have a lot in common need to regulate their cooperation, need to make that cooperation effective, efficient. They need ground rules. And if one is to look, for example, at the European Community, the European Community has gained a great deal as a result of such ground rules and working together, and they now would like to close the gap between them and others by cooperating. So, in principle I think this is probably what you need— what you need—what life needs.

LK: Lancaster, California—back to the phones. Hello.

CALLER: [*Lancaster, California*] I would like to ask Mr. Gorbachev if he—during the siege on the [Russian] White House, was he in contact with Mr. Boris Yeltsin during that event? Thank you.

MG: Unfortunately, I was not in contact with him, but I explained my position, and I appealed to him at that time. I asked him to do everything possible to avoid a military clash and to make sure that the aggravation should not result in bloodshed. But first, Rutskoi and Kasbulatov—they appealed to people who were at the White House to storm the TV tower and then even the Kremlin. There were very few people there who were armed militants. Most of the others were just citizens of Moscow, demonstrators who were normal and basically quiet people who just wanted to lift the siege of parliament. And when that mob began what I would call a *pogrom*, certain steps had to be taken, and it was right that emergency measures were taken. But then, when during the night that ended, the pogrom ended, and when we saw, you know, on CNN and our TV, we saw that the situation was put under control. And then, suddenly, in the morning of the next day, I was in my office, I was watching TV, and then I saw tanks. On a sunny day in Moscow, the situation was basically under control. There were some snipers, and they could be taken care of in a different way. But then, suddenly, before our very eyes, they started to shell the White House, and that, I think, is not the way to address political problems. Even if you don't like those opponents, and you can't find a political solution, it has to be taken care of differently. There were more than two thousand people in the White House, and shelling them from tank cannons—no, I can't accept that.

LK: Did you ever have to use your military in a violent manner?

MG: Well, you know, the situation—when it began to become grave and acute during *perestroika*—sometimes required us to take certain measures and to use the help of the armed units in order to separate the two sides in hostilities. For example, in Karabakh, we wanted to separate them so as to make sure that it doesn't become worse. There was the state of emergency in Baku, and there was, unfortunately, a lot of bloodshed, and the republic was being destroyed. We were at that time discussing what to do. We wanted to avoid the use of force. We did use force and, as a result, there was loss of life. I have to admit that. But in every situation, in all the other situations, I tried to avoid the use of force. My approach was not to use force. Gradual reform without bloodshed.

In our history in our country, there was a lot of bloodshed. We went through a lot. So, if we say that we want democracy, that we're democrats, that we want democratic change for the people, with the people, it means that we have to avoid the use of force.

LK: Champaign, Illinois. . . .

CALLER: [*Champaign, Illinois*] President Gorbachev, I'm honored to talk to you. Do you believe that communism as a political philosophy and a system has still something to offer to the world?

MG: I think that in principle—in principle—as a system, as a philosophy, as a model of organizing society, of reforming society, it has to be rejected, based on our experience—the experience of our country and of Eastern European countries. As regards the use of certain methods to achieve greater social justice, greater regulation by the state of certain processes, there were certain useful aspects that could be used in the future, as well. That's why I'm speaking of socialist values.

By the way, I believe also that socialists who are in power in some countries, they also use liberal theories, not just socialist theories. It's not really a choice of capitalism versus socialism. I believe that, based on our experience and on the Western experience, Western values and other values, we have to conclude that what we need is a new society, a new civilization that will take advantage of all that is best, and would reject all that is worst, and take advantage of the good things for the new civilization, together. So, let us not just try to stamp out everything. We have to reject what did not work in our country. . . .

[*Commercial break*]

LK: Rotterdam, Holland, hello.

CALLER: [*Rotterdam, Holland*] My question is, if Mr. Gorbachev had known that *perestroika* would lead to the disintegration of the Soviet Union, would he still have supported it the way he did?

MG: No, I don't think that this was our plan, and it was not fatalistically inevitable. I think that it could have been avoided. The collapse of the—the breakup of the Soviet Union could have been avoided. I believe it was one of my big mistakes that I was not able to explain my policies, to conduct the kind of policies, more vigorous policies, that would have made it impossible for the coup plotters in 1991 to have that coup that made it impossible to sign the new union treaty. We had the treaty, we had even the scenario of how we will be signing the treaty, where we will be sitting, and how we would be signing the treaty. And that treaty would have opened, I think, a very fruitful chapter in a new federation, in a new country. It would have been a real federation, rather than the unitary state that we used to have, a totalitarian state.

LK: New York City, hello.

CALLER: [*New York, New York; speaks in Russian*] President Gorbachev, during the past fifty years, apart from the time of the Cuban missile crisis, do you know if the Soviet Union or the USA seriously considered dropping nuclear weapons on any country—for example, on Afghanistan, Vietnam, or Korea?

LK: Well, he wouldn't know about the United States. But did the Soviet Union ever intend, to your knowledge—ever come close to using them?

MG: You know, I think that at a certain point the policy makers understood that the use of nuclear weapons would be a disaster, and it was not an accident that when we met with Mrs. Thatcher in 1984 at Chequers and also in the British Parliament, we said even at that time that nuclear war must not be fought. With President Reagan in Geneva, we recorded, and I'll communicate, that nuclear war cannot be won and must not be fought. So, this was the result of an analysis, of the analysis and of the understanding that nuclear weapons simply should not be used. So, this is true. But at the same time, we have to say that since those weapons existed, since they were targeted on both sides, it means that those weapons perhaps could have been used, and that would have been a disaster. And I believe that it is an extremely important turn in the development of international relations that cooperation between the Soviet Union and the U.S. made it possible for us to begin disarmament and end nuclear weapons, the nuclear arms race.

LK: But other than the Soviet missile crisis in Cuba, to your knowledge, was there ever a time when it was close to being used?

MG: No, no, I would say that—I simply cannot state that. I don't think there was this kind of intention that we can record, well, there was a decision. There was a lot of loose talk about local nuclear wars. This kind of loose talk and theories existed. But, you know, in this kind of super-armed world there can be no local nuclear war. It would have been a global war. And policy makers understood that. So maybe certain statements were made but, basically, policy makers understood. They had the information. And they were able to know what the consequences would be. . . .

[*Commercial break*]

LK: Boca Raton, Florida, hello.

CALLER: [*Boca Raton, Florida*] Good evening, Larry. It's a pleasure to talk to you, Mr. Gorbachev. My question is, I'm Jewish, and I go to Moscow a lot, and I love the country a lot, but the Jewish community, Mr. Gorbachev, is— I heard a lot of people tell me anti-Semitism is still bad over there, people are trying to leave to go to Israel, different parts of the world. Do you think the conditions are getting better?

LK: Anti-Semitism in Russia?

MG: There was a period when, indeed, things were changing very quickly for the better in our country as regards that question. I don't think that anti-Semitism has profound, deep roots in our country. I don't think there will be roots for anti-Semitism. But when the situation deteriorates, when certain right wing radicals, radical movements, begin to emerge, and a certain kind of people begin to emerge who even support—almost support—fascism, all kinds of things can be heard from those people, and not just against the Jews. They want to hang those who began the process of reform in our country, they say. It's not just the Jews that they hate. So, the country is in a very tense state, and certain people, certain reactionaries, are trying to exploit that, but I am sure that it will not come to the worst. I am sure that in our country it will not result in new *pogroms*, in the suppression of the Jews. I think that we have come a long way. We are different.

LK: Would you like to go to Israel?

MG: I would be pleased, yes. I visited that country last year, and I like the country. I saw how that country, too, is over-burdened with all kinds of problems because it's very tense. It's kind of—always kind of military readiness. Even in a kindergarten, in a school, teachers have automatic weapons all the time. And I have a lot of sympathy for that kind of problem, for the problems of that nation, and for the problems of all the other nations involved in the Middle East conflict. So I'm very proud that President Bush and I opened that Middle East peace conference in Madrid in 1991.

LK: You *should* be very proud. Helsinki, Finland, hello.

CALLER: [*Helsinki, Finland*] Hello. Mr. Gorbachev, do you not agree that Yeltsin should immediately withdraw Russian troops from Estonia, Latvia, and the border of Finland?

MG: I think that we should be engaged in a dialogue, active dialogue, in order to find the right kind of solution, exactly as planned, with respect for the sovereignty of those countries, and also with some regard for the interests of Russia. Russia has gone through a great deal; had to make a number of important decisions regarding the reductions of nuclear weapons, conventional weapons; to reorganize in a major way its armed forces. It has had to withdraw its weapons from Eastern European countries, from Germany. So there are certain problems, but I think that dialogue is necessary in order to complete that in a quiet way, because we will be living—we will continue to live together and will have to cooperate, so we have to retain, to preserve, respect between the people, and we should not taint this situation with mistakes and political blunders.

So, of course, these troops have to be withdrawn. But at the same time, let me take advantage of this situation. I would like to wish all our friends in the Baltic States—that they should pay more regard for the Russians, they have more consideration of the Russians, the Poles, and others who live in those Baltic States. Sometimes they don't keep the promises, those Baltic people do not keep the promises that they were giving, and that could be a problem for the withdrawal process and for the negotiations. . . .

[*Commercial break*]

LK: We're running short on time. A couple of quick things: tomorrow is the seventy-sixth anniversary of the Bolshevik revolution, and Russian police are preparing for riots. Are you expecting bad things tomorrow in Moscow?

MG: Well, I would be really taking a different kind of action. I would have allowed those who would like to demonstrate on that day to do so, on certain conditions, that would have eased the tensions. . . . The prohibitions, the bans only aggravate the situation.

LK: You would have let the parades go on?

MG: Not the military parades. That was government sponsored. But demonstrations, manifestations? Why not?

LK: What do you think so far of President Clinton?

MG: I was asked this question yesterday, in Richmond, Virginia, the same question, and I said then and let me quickly repeat what I said—that the accession of

President Clinton is because the people here want change, and, therefore, he has a crucial mission, a lot of responsibility. It's one thing when a country is, so to say, on a roll, and all you do is to shift gears. That's one status of things. But when a society is ripe for change—for serious change that affects the economy, the social sphere, and politics, of course—the burden of responsibility on your president is enormous, and I very much would like your president to be up to it, and your country to be up to it.

LK: Would you like to meet with him when he comes to Russia?

MG: I am always at his disposal. No problem.

LK: One other thing. Will you return to politics?

MG: Well, I'm not hiding in the woods. I am involved in a different political role, but I am in politics in a way.

LK: In other words, you're never out of politics, are you?

MG: Absolutely. Absolutely.

LK: Last call, quickly: Edmonton, Canada—quickly. Hello.

CALLER: [*Edmonton, Alberta*] Mr. Gorbachev, how would you like history to judge you?

LK: All right, we only have thirty seconds. How would you like history to judge you? What should it say?

MG: Well, this is what history—this is history's privilege. History is a capricious lady, but I hope that it will judge me fairly. . . .

NAFTA Debate

The North American Free Trade Agreement (NAFTA) is a treaty among Canada, the United States, and Mexico to eliminate all barriers to trade in North America over a fifteen-year period. Negotiations on NAFTA began in 1990 on the heels of a comparable free trade treaty signed between the United States and Canada in 1988. After years of talks, the treaty was concluded in August 1992 but had to be ratified by the legislative bodies of each country. Many felt that the extraordinary live debate that follows influenced the ultimate Congressional vote approving NAFTA.

PEROT: "Give me your whole mind."

GORE: "Yeah, I'm listening. I haven't heard the answer, but go ahead."

LARRY KING: . . . When President Bush signed NAFTA in San Antonio, he was on our show, and then a few nights later I was with you and then-governor Clinton, [who said], "Well, I'm basically for it. I want to see the side agreements and I want to hear what the unions object to, and then I'll come back and sort of let you know." But it was not a definitive yes. What changed?

AL GORE: Well, we negotiated two side agreements that protect labor and protect the environment. And not until the two side agreements were completed did we agree to support NAFTA. Now, this is a good deal for our country, Larry, and let me explain why.

LK: But you were hedging earlier?

AG: Well, we said from the very beginning that we wanted to improve the basic arrangement, which we did with the side agreements. And the reason why this is so important can be illustrated by the story of a good friend of mine that I grew up with, named Gordon Thompson, who lives in Elmwood, Tennessee, with his wife, Sue, and his son, Randy. He makes tires for a living. He's a member of the United Rubber Workers, and he's for this because he's taken the time to look at how it affects his job and his family. We make the best tires in the world, but we have a hard time selling them in Mexico, because they have a 20 percent tax collected at the border on all of the tires that we try to sell. Now, when they make tires and sell them into the United States, the tax at the border is zero. So it's a one-way street. NAFTA changes that. It makes it even-steven.

LK: So he'll make more tires.

AG: Well, his job will be more secure, they'll make more tires; they'll be able to sell more tires. His son will have a better chance of going into that line of work, if that's what he should decide he wants to do, and, remember this—I mean, people think, "Well, they don't buy tires." Mexico bought 750,000 new cars last year. The Big Three sold them only 1,000, because they have the same barriers against our cars. Those barriers will be eliminated by NAFTA. We'll sell 60,000, not 1,000, in the first year after NAFTA. Every one of those cars has four new tires and one spare. We'll create more jobs with NAFTA.

LK: Weren't you a free-trader always, Ross?

ROSS PEROT: I am a free-trader now.

LK: Do you favor some sort of NAFTA?

RP: Absolutely.

LK: Then what's your rub?

RP: The problem is that this is not good for the people of either country. . . . Yes. I think the important thing for everybody watching this show tonight to remember, this is not an athletic contest. This is not a question of who wins, whether I win or the vice president wins. This is a question of do the people of the United States and the people of Mexico win? Now, that's the important issue, and I'm sure we're in agreement on that. My concern is very simple. I look at many years experience in *maquiladora* programs, and here is what I see. We have a lot of experience in Mexico. I've been accused of looking in the rear-view mirror. That's right. I'm looking back at reality, and here is what I see after many years. Mexican workers' life, standard of living, and pay have gone down, not up. After many years of having U.S. companies in Mexico, this is the way Mexican workers live all around big new U.S. plants. Now, just think if you owned a big U.S. company and you went down to see your new plant, and you found slums all around it, your first reaction would be, "Why did you build a plant in the middle of slums?" And your plant manager would say, "Oh, there were no slums here when we built the plant." And you say, "Well, why are they here now?" They say, "This is where the workers work."

LK: Your agreement would have been a different NAFTA, right?

AG: And I would suggest—

RP: This would be a NAFTA that gives the people—now, what are the rules here? Do I answer his questions or yours?

LK: Well, mine, or both. This is freewheeling now.

RP: Okay, but the point being, this is—there it is. Here it is on a more personal basis. Livestock in this country and animals have a better life than good, decent, hard-working Mexicans working for major U.S. companies. And here's one just to look at [*shows photo*].

LK: Now, all this—

RP: Now, here's a good, decent man working his heart out, making his cardboard shack. And the cardboard came from boxes that were used to ship the goods down there.

AG: Can I say something about this picture?

RP: This— I didn't interrupt you.

LK: Okay, now, guys.

RP: Now, maybe it just—

LK: Now, your concept would have been what, Ross? If this was a bad deal, what would you—

RP: All I'm saying is if after ten active years—this has been in effect since the '60s, but let's say ten active years, you would think the standard of living of the Mexican worker would begin to come up. Instead, it continues to go down, by design. Thirty-six families own over half the country. . . . Eighty-five million people work for them in poverty. U.S. companies, because it is so difficult to do business in this country, can't wait to get out of this country and go somewhere else, and, if possible, get labor that costs one-seventh of what it costs the United States.

AG: How would you change it? How would you change it?

RP: Very simply. I would go back and study—first, we look at this. It doesn't work.

AG: Well, what specific changes would you make in it?

RP: I can't— Unless you let me finish, I can't answer your question. Now, you asked me, and I'm trying to tell you.

AG: Right. Well, you brought your charts tonight, so I want to know what specific changes you would like to make in the treaty.

LK: That's a fair question. Let him respond, okay?

RP: How can I answer if you keep interrupting me?

AG: Go ahead. Go ahead.

RP: Okay. Now, first, study the things that work. The European Community has had a similar experience. They got to Spain, Portugal, countries like that, where the wages were different, people didn't have rights, so on and so forth, and they made them come up the economic scale. In 1904, Theodore Roosevelt wrote a beautiful, simple statement. And basically, he said something very similar to what Congressman Gephardt recently said. He said, "Under no circumstances can we lower the standard of living of the working American." Therefore, any trade agreement we enter into must require a social tariff, I would say, that makes it an even playing field, that gives Mexico an incentive to raise the standard of living with those people, which it does not have now.

AG: Okay, can I respond now?

RP: They have lowered the standard of living for those people.

AG: Okay. Now, so, your basic response is you would change it by raising tariffs—

RP: Now, I just started, but you interrupted.

AG: —on Mexico—

RP: That's the first thing I would do.

LK: Well, let's do it one by one.

RP: That's the first thing I would do.

AG: Okay, now, I've heard Mr. Perot say in the past, as the carpenter says, "Measure twice and cut once." We've measured twice on this. We have had a test of our theory, and we've had a test of this theory. Over the last five years, Mexico's tariffs have begun to come down because they've made a unilateral decision to bring them down some, and, as a result, there has been a surge of exports from the United States into Mexico, creating an additional 400,000 jobs, and we can create hundreds of thousands more if we continue this trend. We know this works. If it doesn't work, you know, we give six month's notice and we're out of it. But, we've also had a test of his theory.

LK: When?

AG: In 1930, when the proposal by Mr. Smoot and Mr. Hawley was to raise tariffs across the board to protect our workers. And, I brought some pictures, too. This is a picture of Mr. Smoot and Mr. Hawley. They look like pretty good fellas. They sounded reasonable at the time. A lot of people believed them. The Congress passed the Smoot-Hawley Protection Bill. He wants to raise tariffs on Mexico. They raised tariffs, and it was one of the principal causes—many economists say *the* principal cause—of the Great Depression in this country and around the world. Now, I framed this so you can put it on your wall if you want to.

RP: Thank you. Thank you. Thank you. . . . You're talking two totally different unrelated situations. Now, you do need to measure twice and cut once, but, then, if you have a program that is failing, you should not institutionalize it. See, the Mexican program has failed. It's failed the people of Mexico, it's failed the people of the United States. These numbers they give of exports from the United States are not realistic numbers. For example, they count in the government figures automobile parts going into Mexico to be put into cars made by U.S. car companies in Mexico and shipped back to the United States to be sold as if Mexican consumers bought those parts. But it didn't happen.

Then, if you take a— Let's just say you have a piece of glass crystal, that you spend $100 making it in this country. You're going to send it to Mexico to have $10 of additional work done to it. They count it as a $100 export, and you come into Mexico from the U.S., then they count it as $110 import back in the United States. Now, then, when you look at how they count, the real export figures to Mexican consumers are tiny. The used factory equipment coming from U.S. factories going into Mexico, new factories going to Mexico—

LK: Are not bought?

RP: No. No, no. Zenith moves equipment from the U.S. into Mexico. That's used equipment. Then we count that as if the Mexican consumers bought it. Nobody bought anything. Old equipment just came to Mexico.

AG: Let me respond to that if I can, because, unfortunately, there's a grain of truth to that, but it's so tiny that it's— I mean, it's not a half-truth, it doesn't quite rise to that level. There are a few things in that category, but the vast majority, 80 to 90 percent, are exports that stay in Mexico and are bought there. Here's what happened to our trade surplus, and these figures are net figures. It takes into account everything that he's talking about in that small category.

In 1987, before Mexico started lowering its taxes at the border, its tariffs, we had a $5.7 billion trade deficit with Mexico. After five years, the goods we make and sell into Mexico, the volume has been growing twice as fast as the goods they make and sell in the United States. So, last year we had a $5.4 billion trade surplus. Now, if that trend continued for another two years—and NAFTA will, by removing those barriers, greatly accelerate it—we will have a larger trade surplus with Mexico than with any country in the entire world.

LK: Why are trade unions so opposed to it, then? . . . I mean, it's your friend who makes the tire, and he's a union member, he's going to benefit from this. Why are the unions aligned with Ross Perot? Why do we have this alignment of Ross Perot, unions, Jesse Jackson, Pat Buchanan, and Ralph Nader?

AG: Because some of them make the mistake that, with all due respect, Mr. Perot makes. They confuse the bad trade deals in the past with this one, which is the first time we've been able to get one that's even-steven with zero taxes on both sides. You know, I told you about my friend Gordon Thompson. The international president of his union opposes NAFTA. Gordon Thompson has taken the time to look at the facts, and he supports NAFTA. Let me tell you who else has taken the time: every living former president of the United States, in both parties, the two-termers and the one-termers; every former secretary of state, every former secretary of defense, secretary of treasury; every living Nobel Prize winner in economics; conservatives, liberals, everyone in between. They'd never agreed on anything, and distinguished Americans from Colin Powell to Tip O'Neil to Rush Limbaugh, Ross Perot Jr.; the head of his business, Mort Meyerson; Orville Swindle, the head of United We Stand, the last time; and Ross Perot, Sr. supported it until he started running for president and attempting to bring out the politics of fear.

LK: Ross?

RP: Will I be able to speak for a second or two? From time to time?

LK: You may, you—you're on.

RP: Because there's a lot of inaccuracies here. Let's go to the big picture and skip the personal stuff. People who don't make anything can't buy anything. Let's start with that. We are 85 percent of the market. Canada is 11 percent of the buying power. . . . And Mexico is only 4 percent. People who don't make anything cannot buy anything. Never forget that. Now then, let's look at these exports. [*exhibits charts*] See, here's Mexico, 4 percent; Canada, 11 percent; the United States, 85 percent. We're the biggest buyer of goods and services in the world. Please remember that tonight; that's one of our aces. Now, then, here's the real export story. You get down here, these are the phony exports down here. Here are the real exports here, about $7.7 billion. You take this thing into pieces. You take this big number here and take it right down to here, and that's what you're really talking about. And, just remember this. If you want to trade, you trade with people who make money. You don't trade with people who oppress their workers and they don't have any money.

Now, a good deal will sell itself, folks, just plain talk. Four former presidents came out for it and couldn't sell it. All the secretaries of state came out for it and couldn't sell it. We had satellite going across two hundred auditoriums across the country. That didn't sell it. Got Lee Iacocca for it. That didn't sell it. Thirty million dollars coming out of Mexico, and that is rotten and that is wrong, and that didn't sell it. Thirty, thirty-five million dollars coming out of corporate America to try to get out of this country, go south of the border and hire that cheap labor, and that didn't sell it. . . . This dog just didn't hunt. Now, today they don't have the votes in the House of Representatives. We're in the third quarter. They can get them because they're buying them big-time with your tax money. We're working the halls night and day to make sure it doesn't happen. You can play a key role in it. But, sure, they all tried to sell it to you, and the fact that they couldn't demonstrates that this deal is not good for our country.

LK: . . . It doesn't impress you that every former president supports this?

RP: It impresses me that they couldn't do it.

AG: But it's not over with yet.

RP: Those are the guys that cut the worst trade deal in history. He's already talked about it.

AG: It's not—it's not over.

RP: Wait just a minute, now! They did the Japanese deals, they did the Chinese deals that cost you two million jobs.

AG: Do you think they fooled Colin Powell? Do you think they fooled Colin Powell?

RP: He's a great soldier. Doesn't know anything about business.

LK: We'll have the vice president respond—

AG: Do you think they fooled Lee Iacocca?

RP: They must have.

[*Commercial break*]

LK: We're back on *Larry King Live*. . . . I want the vice president to respond to Mr. Perot, who's made some charges here that this is being bought.

AG: Well, there's been more money spent against the NAFTA than for it, for sure. You can just look at the commercials. Every dollar that has been spent lobbying for it has been publicly disclosed. That is not true of the other side, and I would like to suggest to Mr. Perot—

LK: You say they're hiding the—

AG: Well, I think it would be a good idea, seriously, if you would publicly disclose the finances of your organization lobbying against it. They have not released the money spent, the contributors, where it's coming from, how much of it is Mr. Perot's, where the rest of it is coming from. But there was another statement I wanted to respond to also. And that is that Mexico doesn't buy a lot of products, that they're too poor to buy a lot of products. There's a big misunderstanding in the minds of some people about that. They are buying a lot of products. In fact, they're our second largest customer for manufacturing goods. They will be one of the largest customers overall if the trends continue. They already are. Seventy percent of everything that they buy from a foreign country comes from the United States because we're so close to them and because they prefer our products.

LK: And this treaty would increase jobs here?

AG: Oh, no question about it—

LK: Because there was an announcement today that it would be minimal either way.

AG: There have been twenty-three studies of the impact of NAFTA on jobs in the United States. Twenty-two of them have shown that it will cause an increase in jobs in the United States. The one that didn't showed that there would be a decline in illegal immigration, and they counted all of the illegal immigrants as holding jobs. And when they were taken out of the picture, they said that was a decline. Everybody else says it increases jobs in the United States.

RP: Okay. Government studies are kind of like weather forecasters before balloons, even, and certainly before radar.

LK: You don't trust them.

RP: Let me give you three. Let me give you three. Now we're back down to common sense. Number one: You remember in the tax and budget summit when they said, "Watch my lips, no new taxes"? Then they gave you a big tax increase, and they told you if you would pay it they would balance the budget, pay off the debt, and we'd live happily ever after. See? Now then, the new president had to raise taxes again because that one didn't work. And you picked up the difference. Now, let's go to Medicare. When Medicare was first conceived in 1965—

AG: Are we talking about NAFTA, or—

RP: I'm talking about government forecasts.

AG: Well, can we talk about NAFTA?

RP: Excuse me, Larry, I don't interrupt. May I finish? . . . Could I finish?

LK: Yeah, but of course.

RP: I'm saying all government forecasts— How come the facts are—

AG: Well, I don't want to sit here and listen to you just take shots at President Clinton on other subjects.

RP: Well, excuse me, I haven't taken a shot at it. He wasn't here in 1965. I'm saying—

AG: Well, no, but you talked about—

RP: No, the, the—

AG: We tried to reverse trickle-down economics, and we're proud that we did.

RP: The, the tax and budget summit occurred before he became president.

AG: Yeah, you went on from that, though. Why don't we talk about NAFTA?

RP: Excuse me. All I said was he had to raise taxes again. That's hardly a cheap shot.

AG: Well, on the wealthy, on the wealthy.

RP: Oh, my goodness!

LK: Back to the point.

RP: That's the campaign promise.

LK: Let's try to stay on the point. He says: are you spending more money than the other side?

RP: Larry, I would really like to finish. I don't interrupt him, and if I could finish— Let me give these two examples. We've talked about the inability to forecast the debt—right?—and the fact that we have to keep paying more taxes. Then when Medicare came along in 1965, they said it would cost us $9 billion in 1990. It cost us $109 billion. Then, when Medicaid came along, they said it would cost $1 billion in 1990. It cost $76 billion in 1990.

LK: Meaning that you don't trust any government forecast?

RP: I'm saying they basically come out with phony numbers. He's talking about exports—

AG: Can I respond?

LK: Hold it. You're saying the forecasts on NAFTA are phony?

RP: Yes. Then, let's take the next one. We say that we're spending more money against NAFTA than they're spending for it? That is not even close to truth. It is a matter of record how much Mexico has spent. It is a matter of record how much USA/NAFTA has spent. You take—

AG: Why isn't it a matter of record how much you all spent? Can that be a matter of public record? Can you release those numbers?

RP: I really would appreciate being able to speak.

LK: All right, go ahead, it was a question he raised before—

RP: I really would—

AG: It's a fair question, isn't it?

RP: Excuse me—

AG: I raised it earlier.

RP: It was my understanding tonight we'd have a format where you would ask the questions. . . . I would be able— I am not able to finish.

LK: But if he makes a statement— I'm just trying to balance so that he answers yours—

RP: Well, excuse me, I would like— I would like to finish a sentence, just once before the program's over. Now, we are not able to buy time. If you are anti-NAFTA, you cannot buy time on the networks. We have had to go buy local station time. We cannot buy network time because the networks won't sell it. . . . We didn't run ten-page supplements in the *New York Times*, et cetera, et cetera.

AG: Okay, now, I'd like to respond to that, okay?

LK: Let him finish, he's got one more thing.

AG: All right, go ahead. I do want to respond.

LK: For the benefit of both of you, our time is equal. You both have spoken equally tonight in time. We're keeping time in the control room so that we're fair.

RP: All right. And on the manufacturing goods, second largest manufacturing goods—second largest manufacturing goods, they send all this phony turn-around stuff and count it as though we sold it to Mexican citizens. Now, people who don't make any money can't buy anything. When you look at the Mexican worker, and you go to the *Miami Herald*, and you look at the man who works for Zenith in Mexico, and you compare him to his counterpart who works for Zenith in the United States, this poor man makes $8.50 a day. You know what his dream is? To some day have an outhouse. You know what his *big* dream is? To some day have running water. You know why these people are desperate for running water? Because Mexico ignores their pollution and environmental laws—

LK: But this is all without NAFTA.

AG: Yeah, that's all happening now—

RP: Excuse me, excuse me, but this is the prelude to NAFTA. They have strong environmental laws that they don't enforce— Now, just one second—

AG: Let me respond to that—

LK: Let him respond to that, and then we'll have—

AG: Okay. First of all, you will notice, and the audience will notice, that he does not want to publicly release how much money he's spending, how much money he's received from other sources to campaign against NAFTA. I would like to see those public releases that other side has made. Now, let me come to the point. He talked about accuracy of forecasts and numbers. I watched on this program, right here at this desk, when the war against Iraq was about to take place, and you told Larry King, "This is a terrible mistake because it will lead to the death of 40,000 American troops." You said you had talked to the person who had "ordered the caskets." You were wrong about that. You said on *Larry King* just before the election that after Election Day, there would be one hundred banks that would fail, costing the taxpayers $100 billion. You were wrong about that. Now, the politics of negativism and fear only go so far.

[*Commercial break*]

LK [*in progress*]: —president finish his statement and Mr. Perot respond, and then we'll get to some specifics and your phone calls.

AG: Well, you're getting to the key issue there because Bill Clinton and I were elected to do something about what's happening to working men and women in this country. . . . They've been losing their jobs. There has been unfair competition from foreign countries that don't let our products in, even though we buy their products. This will help to stop that. Some people want to stay with the status quo, just keep things the way they are. We want to open up these barriers. And let me give you a specific example. Valmont Electric Company in Danville, Illinois, less than a year ago was trying to sell products into Mexico. They've got a 13 percent tax at the border. We have a zero tax coming the other way. They closed down in Danville, four hundred jobs lost. They opened up in Mexico with one hundred jobs down there, and now they ship their products duty-free back into the United States through the Alliance Airport, which is the free trade zone that Mr. Perot's company has set up for— It's kind of a private free trade zone outside of Dallas. . . . And they take Valmont Electric's products and distribute them through the United States duty free. Now, if we passed NAFTA, that 13 percent tax that they have at their border would be gone, and companies like Valmont could stay here in the United States, sell their products in Mexico, and not have to go down there to get over the barrier.

LK: Are you saying that Mr. Perot is personally benefiting by attacking NAFTA?

AG: I think he has set it up so that he will benefit financially either way. But if NAFTA is defeated, this family business that has a free trade zone outside of Dallas will continue to distribute products coming from Mexico into the rest of the United States. What is the deal with Alliance?

RP: I'll explain it, but we see here tonight why our country is four trillion dollars in debt, going a billion dollars in debt every working day. Nobody focuses on the real problems. Now, I'm going to try to say this as simply as I can. Alliance Airport is in Fort Worth, Texas, not in Mexico. Alliance Airport is owned by the city of Fort Worth, not my son. Do you shake your head on that?

AG: No, the—

RP: Alliance Airport—check the FAA—is owned by the city of Forth Worth.

AG: You don't have ownership of Alliance Carter Incorporated?

RP: The airport. Now, I'm going to—please.

LK: Let him finish.

RP: Let's have an unnatural event and try not to interrupt me. Now, my son owns land adjoining the airport. Now, the purpose of that land is to build factories and warehouses so that industrial goods can be moved by rail and by air. Just—now, watch my lips: the jobs will be created in Texas. Texas is in the United States. The workers will be United States citizens. They will be paid U.S. wages. It is a job creator in the United States of America. And all of this other Silly Putty throw up— For example, the free trade zone concept goes back to the 1930s. It is nothing new about the free trade zone concept. You have to apply to the U.S. government to get it, and if it didn't make sense, I guess they wouldn't have given it to him. But it is not aimed at doing business with Mexico.

AG: You're not involved in it?

RP: Mexico will be a tiny little pipe of this whole operation. I am putting my country's interest far ahead of my business interest.

LK: You would do better with NAFTA?

RP: I would—no. When I'm in a room with corporate America, the first thing they say is, "Perot, why don't you keep your mouth shut. You could with your resources make more money than anybody else." Here is the NAFTA game. Buy U.S. manufacturing companies cheap—right after NAFTA passes—that are labor intensive, that make good products, that have marginal profits, close the factories in the U.S., move the factories to Mexico, take advantage of the cheap labor, run your profits through the roof, sell the company stock at a profit, go get another one.

AG: That's what they do now. That's what they're doing right now. . . . And they're using Alliance Carter Incorporated in part to do it.

RP: Oh, come on, come on. You're talking about something like a trickle of water coming over Niagara Falls as opposed to the gusher. You know it.

AG: Now, you say it's your son's business, but isn't—

RP: Now, do you guys never do anything but propaganda?

AG: Isn't your business also—

RP: Would you even know the truth if you saw it?

AG: Oh, yes.

RP: I don't believe you would. We've been up here too long.

AG: Let me ask you a question.

RP: Please let me finish. This is not *Crossfire*, is it, Larry? . . . May I finish?

AG: And then I'd like to ask a question.

RP: All right, I have tried to explain with countless interruptions that this creates jobs in the United States. I am extremely proud of what my son is doing. I want to answer the question that he jumped in to ask. I own a minority interest in the airport. Everything I'm doing makes it next to impossible for my family to ever do anything south of the border, and I could care less, okay?

LK: You do no business in Mexico or are going to?

RP: Look, I will put my country's interest in front of making money.

AG: Let me know when I can respond.

RP: And I don't ever want to make money at the expense of other people. Now, I got interrupted a minute ago when you shifted it back—

LK: One other thing we could finish with.

AG: No, I'd like to respond on this.

LK: The financing of the anti-NAFTA campaign, it has not been answered, and he asked it.

RP: Okay, fine, I'll answer it. See, again, he throws up propaganda. He throws up gorilla dust that makes no sense.

LK: What is it, then?

RP: May I finish?

LK: Yeah.

RP: Okay. Most of the television time I bought during the campaign. That is a matter of public record. I have had two television shows since the campaign in the spring. They cost about $400,000 apiece. Those were network shows. Then we just did a NAFTA show, but we have to buy the time locally. I don't have the figures yet on what that cost me or I'd be glad to tell you. . . I had to buy—no, I buy the television time because I don't want to take the members' money for that. They understand that. They approve of that.

AG: It's not all his money, and we don't know because they do not—

RP: No, but television time— I just told you.

AG: Well, but—see, they do not release the records, but I accept your response because you have said that now—

RP: If it makes you feel better to see the checks and the bills from the network—

AG: It's okay for you to interrupt, but not me? . . . Now, hold on. You just said that you would—

LK: Let's go back to jobs.

AG: You just said that you would release the records, and I appreciate that. Now, this—

RP: It has nothing to do with what's going to happen to our country.

AG: Well, we need to know who's trying to influence it.

RP: I am paying for it. It's that simple.

LK: We got the answer.

AG: Now, on this—this Alliance business is connected to the jobs issue.

LK: Why is it important?

AG: Well, because right now we've got these barriers that we cannot surmount to sell into Mexico. We have been trying for years to get an even relationship so that their tariffs, their barriers, their taxes at the border will be eliminated. A lot of companies now have an incentive to leave the United States and locate down there. We heard about auto parts. Right now there is 13 percent tax at the border collected by Mexico on U.S. auto parts. . . . And there is less than one half of one percent tariff the other way. That big growing market down there, in a few years they're going to buy a million cars a year. In order to sell into that market, these companies now have an incentive to pull up stakes and move down there. This business, which is not just his son's business, and there's nothing dishonorable about it all, but here is the brochure for it, and here is the prospectus. And here are the two principal, what look like the principal investors there, Mr. Perot and the American eagle. And in the prospectus it says—okay, see it there. And in the prospectus it says that this is an ideal national distribution center for products coming out of Mexico. Plus, they have—he has lobbied the taxpayers to spend more than 200 million dollars in taxpayer funds in this project—

RP: Who is he?

AG: That takes in you and your business.

RP: No, I'm not lobbying anybody.

AG: There's nothing illegal about it.

RP: I haven't done it. I don't—I haven't lobbied anybody.

AG: You've never hired a lobbyist?

RP: I—in my life? You mean on the airport?

AG: Both.

LK: No, on the airport

AG: On the airport.

RP: I don't hire lobbyists. This is my son's project. I went to the airshow and haven't been out there—oh, probably been eighteen months since I've been out there.

LK: What's the relevance?

AG: Well, the relevance is that if the free trade—if NAFTA is defeated then—

LK: What?

AG: —then this free trade zone that he has is still in business. If it's good enough for him, why isn't it good enough for the rest of the country?

LK: Do you say he's doing this for personal profit?

AG: I said before that I think he is in a position to benefit either way. And he was in favor of NAFTA. Again, he made speeches in favor of it, wrote in favor of it in your book before you started running for president. You started getting a response from people—

LK: Let's ask this, then: what turned you against it if you were in favor of it?

RP: Well, conceptually I am for free trade. I am, if we ever get back to the subject, for a good agreement with Mexico. I am deeply concerned about the 85 million people who live in poverty and don't have any rights. I am deeply concerned about workers who, when they go on strike, U.S. companies call in goons, bring in the state police, shoot several workers, kill one, injure dozens, put the workers back to work, and cut wages 45 percent. Those are things that are wrong. We can do this right. I am not in favor of a one political party country. The PRI runs the country. President Salinas will pick his successor. President Salinas went to the thirty-six families who own over 54 percent of the gross domestic product and asked them for twenty-five million dollars apiece. Fortunately for their families, one of them leaked it to the *New York Times*, and they didn't have to pay. That's Mexico. He will pick his successor, not the Mexican people. Read the State Department's annual report on human rights: a journalist being killed, people in the opposing political parties being put in prison and killed and tortured. This is not a free society, and yet for some reason the same people who are willing to put our troops at risk around the world to make sure people are protected, once we get to Mexico, ignore all of that.

LK: Are you not anyone that supports a fascist kind of state?

RP: I'm concerned any agreement we do should give the Mexican people a decent life and over a period of time should give them some purchasing power. If I'm going to do business with somebody—let's just say if the U.S. is going to do business with another country, let's do business with a country whose people can buy things. Let's go—

LK: You don't think President Salinas is a progressive.

RP: President Salinas is almost out of office. I'm worried to death about who follows him.

AG: Can I respond to that?

RP: When you treat people the way they treat people, it's a matter of time until they lose power. And they've had it for a lot of years, and they keep it by force. But whether it's labor and management or countries and people, you oppress people long enough and you got to change, and that will happen.

AG: Let me respond to this because some of what he is saying here is true. Mexico is not yet a full democracy. They do not yet have full protection for human rights. They do not yet have the kind of living standard and labor standards and environmental protection standards that we would like them to see, but they've been making tremendous progress. And the progress has been associated with this new relationship to the United States. The decisions in Mexico will ultimately be made by the people in Mexico. The question is whether or not we will have the ability to influence what they and their government decide. The best way to eliminate our influence down there is to defeat NAFTA. The best way to preserve it is to enter into this bargain, continue the lowering of the barriers. We've got a commitment that they're going to raise their minimum wage with productivity. We've got an agreement for the first time in history to use trade sanctions to compel the enforcement of their environmental standards. As they begin to develop and locate better jobs farther south, we cut down on illegal immigration. Now, one of the reasons why all of the living former presidents and the other folks that I mentioned are supporting this is because this is the kind of choice that comes along only once every forty or fifty years. This is a major choice for our country of historic proportions. Sometimes we do something right; the creation of NATO, the Louisiana Purchase, Thomas Jefferson did the right thing there, the purchase of Alaska. These were all extremely controversial choices, but they made a difference for our country. This is such a choice. If we should happen to give into the politics of fear and make the wrong choice, the consequences would be catastrophic. If we make the right choice, we have a chance to encourage Mexico to continue on the path they have been traveling.

LK: Ross is not saying he wants the status quo. He wants a different treaty, am I correct?

AG: He wants to raise tariffs on Mexico.

RP: Just a second. Let's look at reality—

LK: And then we'll take our first call. Go ahead.

RP: Let's look at reality instead of theory. There's a major U.S. chemical plant in Mexico that digs holes in the ground, dumps the chemical waste in those holes, bulldozes over those holes, and contaminates the water supply for the people in that area. A disproportionate number of the babies born in the shantytown around that plant are born without a brain. Now, I don't care if you're poor or rich. If your baby is born without a brain because a U.S. company is willing to take advantage of workers to that extent, that's wrong. Now, if there's any question about it, the xylene, the chemical xylene, in the water content in a ditch coming out of that plant is 53,000 times the amount permitted in the United States. This outfit, big democratic group—backing the Democratic Party—here's the videotape that shows them digging the holes, putting the chemicals in the ground. It shows one child whose foot is horribly burned from chemicals, and it shows the classic worker abuse—

AG: Can I respond? Can I respond?

RP: Because I know he cares, and I'm not—I'm not trying to play doctor . . .

AG: I agree with you on this, I agree with you on this.

RP: I know you care deeply about these things.

AG: Yeah, can I answer?

RP: I know you're a good man, but the laws are on the books. They're not enforced.

LK: NAFTA would what? Change them? Not change them?

RP: Well, they have this little side agreement, but the facts are Mexico is so sensitive about its sovereignty they're not about to let us go down there and get into the middle of their— The Rio Grande River, all right, folks, the Rio Grande River is the most polluted river in the Western Hemisphere—

AG: Wait a minute. Can I respond to this first?

LK: Yeah, let him respond—

RP: The Tijuana River is the most— They've had to close it—

LK: But all of this is without NAFTA, right?

AG: Yeah, and let me respond to this, if I could, would you—

RP: Larry, Larry, this is after years of U.S. companies going to Mexico, living free—

LK: But they could do that without NAFTA.

RP: But we can stop that *without* NAFTA, and we can stop that with a *good* NAFTA.

AG: How do you stop that without NAFTA?

RP: Just make— Just cut that out. Pass a few simple laws on this. Make it very, very clear—

AG: Pass a few simple laws on Mexico?

RP: No.

AG: How do you stop it without NAFTA?

RP: Give me your whole mind.

AG: Yeah, I'm listening. I haven't heard the answer, but go ahead.

RP: That's because you haven't quit talking.

AG: Well, I'm listening. How do you stop it without NAFTA?

RP: Okay, are you going to listen? Work on it. Now, very simple: Just tell every company south of the border if they operate that way, they cannot ship their goods into the U.S. at any price, period, and they will become choir boys overnight. See, Mexico is a country that can't buy anything. Japan, everybody else in the world is going to flood into Mexico if NAFTA is passed, so that they can get cheap labor. . . .

[*Commercial break*]

AG: [*off-mike*] Are you going to give me a chance to respond to this?

LK: Okay— [*on-mike*] Okay, if we keep responding and responding, we're never going to get some calls, but I'll have the vice president respond, and then quickly to calls. Quick.

AG: Oh, thank you. Well, if we defeat NAFTA, we'll lose all leverage over the enforcement of Mexico's environmental laws.

LK: Ross says we just pass a law to—

AG: That wouldn't affect Mexican companies or the investments from other countries. But the problem has been not so much their laws, but the *enforcement* of their laws. We can probably agree on that. This side agreement that we negotiated gives us the ability to use trade sanctions to compel the enforcement of their environmental laws.

LK: Let me get some calls in . . . We go to Washington, D.C.

CALLER: [*Washington, D.C.*] Hello. My question is for Mr. Perot. How can the United States expect to compete on a long-term basis in an increasingly interdependent economic world, while Europe and the Pac Rim nations unite through their own respective trade alignments?

RP: Very simple: we've got the most productive work force in the world. We're the biggest buyer of goods and services in the world. We're the market everybody wants to sell to. Our problem is we do the world's dumbest trade agreements. You go back to the agreements we've done all over the world, you'd be amazed that adults did them. We're about to do another one, but the American people have stopped it, and it's dead in the House of Representatives. It's time we draw a line in the sand, and we've done it. Now, here's the key: you want to buy and sell with people who have money. You want to trade with partners who have money, but then if you make a one-sided deal with Japan, they get all the benefits, we get all the problems. Then you come to Mexico. It's an emerging nation. You want to help it. You put in this tariff that as they raise the standard of living of their people, the tariff goes away. If anybody wants to do things like destroy people's life by dumping chemicals and all that and polluting the Rio Grande River and destroying the Tijuana River and the beaches in San Diego—and the life in San Diego, pretty soon—you just say you can't ship your goods to the U.S.

LK: Ross, his question was—

RP: You can help Mexico and do it—

LK: Ross—

RP: No— You can't compete. Go put your primary effort with people who have money to spend. Then, because we want to help emerging nations, help nations like Mexico. But your primary effort has to be—and believe me, you say, does everybody want to do business with us? More than anything else in the world, because we buy a lot.

LK: Please try to limit answers, so we can get our calls in.

AG: I'd like to respond to that quickly. Could I?

LK: Yeah.

AG: Let me give you a quick example. Mattel just announced that if NAFTA is passed, it will move a plastics factory from Asia to Mexico. Instead of getting the plastic from China, it will get the plastic from the United States. With NAFTA, we will enlarge what is already the largest consumer market in the world with the addition of a country that buys 70 percent of all of its foreign products from the United States of America. It will position us to compete effectively with the rest of the world. That's why a lot of these other countries are a little nervous about it. One of the trade officials in Japan described this as "sneak protectionism" and raised a lot of questions about it. It will benefit us in our trading relationship with Asia and Europe, and we're right now in the middle of the negotiations with the GATT—that's the larger world trade agreement. If we pass NAFTA, we will be able to use the leverage to drop the barriers against our products in other countries.

LK: Fairview Heights, Illinois, hello.

CALLER: [*Fairview Heights, Illinois*] Hello, Larry. Vice President Gore, I understand the United States will spend $7 billion to clean up the pollution left by multi-national companies in Mexico, much of it polluting our rivers. I would like to know why we're going to spend that money, and couldn't it be better spent here at home?

AG: Well, Mexico will join in, so will the Inter-American Bank, and so will the polluters who have caused the problem. And we should clean up that pollution that Mr. Perot was talking about so eloquently earlier, whether we have NAFTA or not. With NAFTA, we will have the cooperation of Mexico and other countries in this hemisphere in doing that.

RP: May I cut in briefly?

LK: Yeah, sorry.

RP: It will cost us several billion dollars in tariff losses. It will cost us at least $15 billion and probably more to build infrastructure. And we will have a $20 to $40 billion bill on pollution alone. Now, guess who's going to pay that? All you hard-working taxpayers that still have jobs, go look in the mirror and ask yourselves why the government's policies have caused four out of five of you to have to lower your standard of living. Ask yourselves why your government sent two million jobs to Asia alone, manufacturing jobs, in the 1980s. [*to Gore*] Now, you agree with that number?

AG: All of that happened before NAFTA—

RP: You agree with two million, or not?

AG: —and before we took office.

RP: That's not the point. Is it a good number?

AG: Oh, we've lost a lot of jobs to lousy trade deals in the past, because they weren't fair. They weren't fair.

RP: Well, we agree that we've made—

AG: Let me finish, now—

RP: Excuse me, excuse me.

AG: Thank you very much. I'll let you finish. I like that line. I appreciate that. The fact is that we have the opportunity with NAFTA to stop this kind of stuff. All of the problems that Mr. Perot talks about will be made worse if NAFTA is defeated. We have an opportunity to make all of them better if we pass NAFTA. Listen, Larry, the whole world is poised, waiting for America's response to Mexico's decision to say "yes." We have knocked on their door for twenty years, trying to get them to stop being protectionist—

LK: Are you saying this embarrasses us if we—

AG: Well, of course it does, but it's far more important than just embarrassment. It diminishes our ability—it would diminish our ability to open other markets overseas. The GATT round would probably not be completed if NAFTA were defeated.

[*Commercial break*]

LK: Nanimo, British Columbia. Hello.

CALLER: [*Nanimo, British Columbia*] I'd like to know what Mr. Perot and Mr. Gore have both learned from the previous free trade agreements between Canada and the U.S.

RP: Well, just by watchin' it. First thing, thousands of people joined United We Stand America, out of Canada. I couldn't figure out why, so I checked: they were mad at NAFTA. Then I watched the election. The Conservative Party had 155 seats and the prime minister. There's a message here for both political parties in the United States. After the dust cleared, they had two seats in parliament, no prime minister. The reason—

LK: NAFTA?

RP: Reason: NAFTA. Why? Huge numbers of manufacturing jobs left Canada, came into the United States because of a 15 percent wage differential. We pay our workers less than Canada. Now, when you've got a seven-to-one wage differential between the United States and Mexico, you will hear the giant sucking sound—

AG: Now, wait—

RP: There's a political lesson, there's a business lesson . . .

AG: But this is an important question, and it's important to realize that only one of the parties in that election campaigned against the basic NAFTA treaty. That was the socialists. They *lost* seats. They only got nine seats out of 258, and now the person who won has been talking with President Clinton. This has been a good deal for both Canada and the United States. Both have gained jobs; both have gained trade flows; both have become more competitive in the world marketplace as a result.

RP: And there is a Tooth Fairy, and there is an Easter Bunny.

LK: Bethesda, Maryland, hello.

CALLER: [*Bethesda, Maryland*] Good evening, Larry. I'd like to ask the vice president specifically to answer, in terms of a time limit, how long—how many years—five, eight, ten years—will it be before we see these new jobs in America that are supposed to be out there?

AG: Well, we're already seeing a great many new jobs. We have seen 400,000 new jobs just in the last five years, because of Mexico's unilateral decision to lower the barriers to U.S. products. We'll see 200,000 jobs, it is estimated, over the next several years—

LK: But there'll be a dip first, right?

AG: —in the wake of NAFTA. No, no, no. We think, absolutely not.

LK: Unions are wrong?

AG: Oh yes. I think they're wrong. . . . Absolutely. Now, there is always, in our econ-
       omy, a churning of the economy. With or without NAFTA, that is the case. But
       the net change is positive with NAFTA. Now, there are all kinds of estimates: vir-
       tually all of them show job gains, as I've said before. Some of them show very
       large job gains, but the importance of NAFTA goes beyond that because, again,
       it gives us the ability to open up markets in the rest of the world, because other
       countries— Let me give you a specific example to illustrate this. Computers in
       the United States will sell into Mexico. They have a 20 percent tariff on our com-
       puters. After NAFTA, they will have a zero percent tariff on our computers, but
       the 20 percent will still apply to Asia and to Europe, so with the transportation
       advantage and a 20 percent price advantage, who are they going to buy their com-
       puters from? They're going to buy lots of them from us. Now, that gives us an
       advantage, and when you sell more products, you make more products. When you
       make more products, you hire more people.

RP: Quickly. If you believe that, I've got a lot of stuff in the attic I can sell you.
       Second, if this is all true, why is corporate America downsizing? If this is all true,
       why do we have the largest number of college graduates this year unable to find
       jobs since at any time in the '40s? If this is all true, why is that everywhere I go
       in a hotel, I've got a college graduate comin' up to the room, bringin' food, carry-
       ing bags, so on and so forth, waiting till they get their job? If this is all true, why
       isn't our economy booming? You see, it just doesn't fit, folks. Just go look at
       reality.

AG: I'd like to answer the question, if I could. . . . No, because, see while we have a
       $5.6 billion trade surplus with Mexico, we have a $49 billion deficit with Japan, a
       $19 billion deficit with China, a $9 billion deficit with Taiwan. Those are trade
       problems, Mexico is a trade opportunity. If we use the opportunity to pry open
       the markets in the rest of the world, we'll change this. All of the problems that he
       talks about? That's what we want to change. We don't accept the status quo. We
       want to fight for working men and women, and NAFTA is part of it.

LK: Zagreb, Croatia, hello.

CALLER: [*Zagreb, Croatia*] Good evening. My question is this. Mr. Perot, since you
       obviously have many, many criticisms about the NAFTA agreement, can you
       give us specific answers as to an alternative to it? If you don't like it, tell us what,
       really, we should be doing?

RP: Yes, I will do it again. First, we've got to have a clear understanding with Mexico
       that we can only do business with a country that gives its people a decent stan-
       dard of living and respects human rights. Because we are all humans. Every
       human life is precious.

LK: And that would be the first part of it?

RP: Every human life is precious. If you don't treat your workers fairly, and if you
       don't treat your people fairly, history teaches us that that produces stress that will
       take maybe a century to cure. It's in Mexico's interest to do that. Then, their
       workers will come up the economic scale. We'll put in a social tariff that drops as
       they bring their workers' pay and benefits up. If we pass NAFTA and we pass
       health care, and your competitor goes to Mexico, you will either have to go to
       Mexico or go out of business. I can give you a whole list of things like that.

LK: You would have a tariff that swings?

RP: No, it's a social tariff: As they bring their people up, we drop the tariff. When it's head-to-head competition, and their people have equal pay and benefits as ours—

LK: What's wrong with that?

RP: —there is no tariff, and we've brains and wits, and off we go. That's good for Mexico, and it protects our people.

LK: Why is that bad?

AG: Well, it kind of goes back to the Smoot-Hawley idea—

RP: Oh, come on—

AG: —seriously, for this reason: The idea that we can isolate ourselves from the rest of the world and only do business with "perfect" countries that do everything the way we want them to do is pretty unrealistic. His proposal, as I understand it, is to raise tariffs and call it a social tariff and use that to keep products out from any country that doesn't meet our standards in all things.

RP: I said Mexico—

AG: Now, let me finish, please. Now, you take—

RP: —tiny little market—

AG: —that kind of approach to Mexico and you defeat NAFTA, you've lost the partnership we've been building with Mexico for a generation and more. But beyond that, here's the central point. We have to realize that we, unilaterally, cannot change the entire world. We can't force every country in the world that we want to trade with to meet our standards in everything that we would like to see them meet. Now, the guts of this whole thing is the reason why some people listen to what he's saying, is that they think if a country has wages lower than we have, then it's fundamentally unfair to trade with them, even when it's totally even in all other respects. If that were the case—if low wages were the determinant of where you locate businesses, then Haiti would be an economic powerhouse; Bangladesh would be a powerhouse. We have problems—trade problems—with countries that have wages higher than we have, like Germany and they have fewer barriers than we do and higher wages because, Larry, the secret is productivity. Our working men and women are the most productive of any nation on the face of the earth. You give us the opportunity to sell our products unimpeded, without these trade barriers and we'll knock the socks off the workers of any other country in this world.

LK: Why doesn't that make sense to you?

RP: Well, it wouldn't make sense to most people over six years old.

LK: Why?

RP: If I have to explain it to the audience, they'd probably— I don't think I will. Bangladesh and Haiti? They all got that. Well, I won't waste your time on that one. You understand that that—

AG: No, but they have the lowest wages.

RP: That's not the point. Everybody out there understands why Bangladesh and Haiti are not like Mexico, so I won't waste my time. Secondly—

AG: But tell me, I mean, humor me if you would and—

RP: No, I won't. I don't think I can. Now, next thing. It's pretty simple stuff. We've been out-traded by everybody. All we've got to do is explain very nicely to Mexico that they out-traded us on this deal. We've got to make a fair deal with them. They'll huff and puff for a few days. They'll be back. We'll make a good deal. For a very simple reason. They need us. We don't need them. Now then, we go to Japan. Send a horse trader over to Japan. Send somebody that knows how to negotiate and just explain to them that they have the most one-sided trade deals in the world. We've got to reopen 'em. We've got to make 'em fair, and they'd say "What do you mean?" I say, "We'll just take the same deal we gave you." They would look at you like, "Good gracious sakes alive! You mean, you want the same deal *we've* had for years?" That's fair. Then you start to negotiate and say, well, a fall-back position—"We'll just take the deals that ya'll made with Europe because they're a whole lot better than the ones you made with the U.S."

You know what the problem is, folks? It's foreign lobbyists—are wreckin' this whole thing. Right here, *Time* magazine just says it all. It says, "In spite of Clinton's protests, the influence-peddling machine in Washington is back in high gear." The headline, *Time* magazine: "A Lobbyist's Paradise."

AG: I'd like to respond to that.

LK: Okay.

RP: We are being sold out by foreign lobbyists. We've got thirty-three of them working on this in the biggest lobbying effort in the history of our country, to ram NAFTA down your throat. . . . The good news is it ain't working. . . . I'll turn it over to the others.

AG: Okay, thank you. . . . One of President Clinton's first acts in office was to put limits on the lobbyists and new ethics laws, and we're working for lobby law reform right now. But, you know, we had a little conversation about this earlier, but every dollar that's been spent for NAFTA has been publicly disclosed. . . . Tomorrow, perhaps tomorrow we'll see, but the reason why, and I say this respectfully, because I served in the Congress and I don't know of any single individual who lobbied the Congress more than you did, or people in your behalf did, to get tax breaks for your companies. And it's legal.

RP: You're lying. You're lying now.

AG: You didn't lobby the Ways and Means Committee for tax breaks for yourself and your companies?

RP: What do you have in mind? What are you talking about?

AG: Well, it's been written about extensively, and, again, there's nothing illegal about it.

RP: Well that's not the point. I mean, what are you talking about?

AG: Lobbying the Congress. You know a lot about it.

RP: I mean, spell it out, spell it out.

AG: You didn't lobby the Ways and Means Committee? You didn't have people lobbying the Ways and Means Committee for tax breaks?

RP: What are you talking about?

AG: In the 1970s.

RP: Well, keep going.

AG: Well, did you or did you not? I mean, it's not—

RP: Well, you're so general, I can't pin it down. I mean, 1970—

AG: I'm not charging anything illegal. It's this blunderbuss attack on all lobbyists.

RP: Wait just a minute. Wait just a minute. Let's talk about the lobbying reforms. That's the biggest sham in history. All you had to do was take a pledge. The pledge is like a pledge to quit drinking. We don't have lobbying reform under Clinton. We will get it, but we don't have it yet. And this stuff they've come up with is nothing, and if you look at who's running all these economic negotiations, it's a Who's Who of former foreign lobbyists now in the Clinton administration.

LK: McLean, Virginia, hello.

CALLER: [*McLean, Virginia*] Sir, this is for Mr. Perot. Sir, over the past five years, and I think you probably know this, the U.S. has nearly tripled its electronics exports to Mexico, worth about $6 billion. Now that's produced a lot of high-tech, good-paying jobs in America. Now if Congress does the right thing and passes NAFTA and removes the tariffs on these products, how can you believe that this wouldn't increase our exports, create more jobs, create more exports for America?

RP: Well I think you're seeing, counted in that figure, every piece of electronics that goes to Mexico, does a turn-around in an assembly plant, and comes back to the United States. I am certain you're seeing all the radios that go down and get put in cars that come back to the United States. If we strip it down to the real electric products that the Mexican people buy that stay in Mexico, it would be a fraction of that sum.

AG: Did you see the Wal-Mart that opened in Mexico City on the news? . . . Largest one in the world, if I understand it. They have seventy-two cash registers ringing constantly with people in Mexico, taking American products out of that store. We have this image of them being so poor that they can't possibly buy any electronic equipment or anything else that we make. They *are* poorer than we are. But you know what? They spend more per person on American products than any other country except— Let me finish, let me finish, because this is very important. Japan, if you take everything that Japan buys, only 2 percent of it comes from the United States. If you take everything that Mexico buys, it's 800 percent larger, and if you take what they buy from foreign countries, 70 percent of everything they buy from other countries comes from us. They prefer American products. If we lower those trade barriers and get rid of them altogether, we will have an export surge into Mexico, and we'll have a partnership with Mexico that will help us remove the trade barriers in the rest of the world.

LK: Fairfax, Virginia, hello.

CALLER: [*Fairfax, Virginia*] Companies can come into Mexico by, you know, thousands and set up manufacturing of products using the cheap Mexican labor, and I think that that is the biggest threat to the loss of U.S. jobs. Is this correct?

AG: No, it's not correct, because American workers are more than five times more productive than their counterparts in Mexico, because they have better tools, they have better training, they have a better infrastructure. There are lots and lots of companies that moved down to Mexico and decided that they would rather move back to the United States. I've got a whole long list of them. General Motors is one of them, that moved down while Mr. Perot was on the board. He may have voted against that, but they have— I don't know, but they now moved, started moving jobs back from Mexico, back to the United States. Let me give you another example. Norm Cohen in Charlotte, North Carolina, is in the textile business. Fifteen years ago, he tried to sell his products in Mexico. He had the price, he had the quality, he couldn't sell. Why not? He went in and investigated. His Mexican counterparts got a little mail-out from the Mexican government every month with a listing of all the foreign companies, including American companies, that wanted to sell in competition into Mexico. They were given an opportunity to put an "X" beside the name of any company they didn't want to compete with. He got some investors and opened up a company in Mexico. Now NAFTA not only eliminates the taxes at the border, it eliminates practices like that "X marks the spot," and if NAFTA passes, Norm Cohen has plans right now to shut that factory in Mexico down and move 150 jobs back to Charlotte, North Carolina.

LK: Want to respond?

RP: If I have to.

LK: Don't have to.

RP: First off, the whole textile thing is a joke. Talk to anybody in the textile business, and they will tell you if their competitors go to Mexico, they will have to go to Mexico. They will also tell you that the Mexicans have spent a fortune building textile plants and are building them now in Cuba, where labor is next to nothing. Next, the GM bringing back jobs into this country is a sham used in the union negotiation. Next, the U.S. worker is five times more productive than the Mexican worker: big joke of the century. The Mexican worker is a good worker. He is an industrious worker. He quickly gets up to 70 percent as productive, and after three to five years, is 90 percent as productive, and only makes one-seventh as much. You cannot compete with that in the good ol' USA, particularly with our benefits, retirement, and so on and so forth. It's just that simple. It's a tilted deck.

LK: Mexico City, hello.

AG: It's not just that simple.

CALLER: [*Mexico City, Mexico*] Hi. The subject has come up about the possibility of Japanese taking over if NAFTA doesn't go through. I'm American. I've been living in Mexico City for many years. There are thousands of Japanese here. They are waiting. They are lurking. What are you people doing? Why [*call cuts off*]

AG: Let me answer that.

LK: What's the finish of it, ma'am? All right, I didn't hear the end of it.

AG: Yeah, she said, What are you doing? Why don't you wake up?

RP: Does he get to answer first every time?

LK: I think the question was for him.

AG: You go ahead and answer.

RP: No, *you* go ahead.

AG: I'd like to answer it, but you go first.

RP: Let him go ahead, he can have it. I know—as long as I get a brief follow-up.

LK: Well, I think the question was for you.

RP: It will only take a minute to kill *this* snake. Go ahead.

LK: Go ahead, kill it.

AG: You're talking about the question, not me, right?

RP: No, the question. Absolutely. Excuse me.

LK: Go ahead, it's for you.

RP: It's just this basic. There's a constant in the Clinton administration. Any time they get cornered, they go into what I call "the sky is falling routine"—the presidency is at stake, the Japanese are coming.

LK: No, the question was— She says there are Japanese—

RP: Next thing we'll have is "The British are coming." You know, the ghosts are coming. Look, the Japanese cannot just wander into Mexico, do anything they want to do, dump across our border, unless we're stupid enough to let them. Now, if our foreign lobbyists stay wired in the way they are now, we'll probably say, "Ooh, this is wonderful." I can tell you about the Japanese deals that have been cut through out foreign lobbyist. I can tell you a deal that's buried in this agreement that gives $17 million benefit to Honda. It's buried. I can show it to you in print. It's there big time. I can show you a deal—

LK: Benefits a single company?

RP: You bet. I can show you a deal on Tennessee whiskey that'll make you just wonder what the heck is going on. The sky is not falling. The Japanese are our friends—

AG: Well, let me respond—

RP: They're not a threat.

AG: Let me respond. Both automobile manufacturers, including Honda in Marysville, Ohio, Nissan in Tennessee, Saturn in Tennessee, all of the companies in Detroit: they benefit because that Mexican tariff is brought down to zero. Every other American from Tennessee—whiskey benefits—every American business potentially benefits, if they want to sell in Mexico—

RP: And they—

AG: Hold on, hold on, because I want to respond to her question. This is extremely important. President Salinas has a trade mission to Japan the month after the vote on NAFTA. If we don't take this deal, you can bet that Japan will try to take this deal. They'll be in there in a New York minute. Europe will try to get this deal. They are concerned about us taking this deal. Listen, we— Larry, we ought to thank our lucky stars that the Mexican people have had the vision and courage to strike out on the American path toward the ideas of Thomas Jefferson, toward democracy, toward free markets, and now they just want to know "Can we take 'yes' for an answer?"

LK: In the interest of time, Ross, is there—are there things about this treaty you like?

RP: Oh, sure, but here's the Honda deal—

LK: Are there any—is there anything about it—

RP: Here it is, folks. As they say, it's in the book. There's the Honda deal. Here is the Tennessee whiskey deal.

LK: Al, is there anything about the deal you *don't* like?

RP: Now, stay with me one second. Here is the deal on Tennessee whiskey. Only in the state of Tennessee, authorized to produce only in the state of Tennessee—

AG: No—

RP: —this is foreign lobbying big-time. This is what's wrong with our country. This is what you and I will clear up through government reform.

LK: That's protection of a brand name. I mean, that's protection of a brand name. One of the things about this treaty is it protects intellectual property.

RP: Why just that brand name?

AG: Well, it's not just that brand name. If you'll look at the line above it, it says "Bourbon Whiskey." That doesn't have— That's not a brand name.

RP: Stay with me. Tennessee whiskey—

AG: —and Tennessee whiskey—

RP: —authorized to produce only in the state of Tennessee—

AG: No, but that refers to the other one. It recognizes— It deals with all bourbon—

LK: Bourbon is only from Kentucky, right?

RP: Caught in the middle of the act, folks. No place to run, no place to hide.

LK: I think bourbon is only—

AG: It's two different brand names.

LK: Is there anything about—

AG: Excuse me. Just so you're clear about that. Those are brand names, and one of the things we've been trying to get in our trade dealings with other countries is protection for what's called intellectual property. And it's a good thing, too, because Mexicans now prefer U.S. brand-name products. That's why they're going in and out of Wal-Mart so fast.

LK: All right, there's a six-month out if it's turned down, right?

AG: Yeah. Now, let's talk about that for a minute. If I'm wrong and he's right, then you give six months notice, and you're out of it.

LK: Ross, what's wrong with that?

RP: Now, here's the way we get out of it. If the House of Representatives lets this go through, the whole House of Representatives is running in 1994 and a third of the Senate. We've got a little song we sing, "We'll Remember in November," when we step into that little booth. If we have to, we the people, the owners of this country, we'll clean this mess up in Washington in '94.

LK: Are you saying you will—

RP: —and, and we'll make sure that we put the six-month tail on this thing in 1995, and if you think these guys will, you believe in the Tooth Fairy.

AG: Well—

LK: Ross, are you saying that you're going to work against congressmen who vote for it?

RP: I'm not. Our people are really angry about this. Working people all across the United States are extremely angry. There is no way to stop 'em. They are not going to tolerate having their jobs continued to be shipped all over the world—

AG: I'd like to say something about that.

RP: —we've got to have a climate in this country where we can create jobs in the good old U.S.A.—that is one thing that the president and vice president should do for us, and they're not.

AG: Excuse me. I'd like to say something about that. Because that's a direct political threat against anybody who votes for this. This is a choice between the politics of fear and the politics of hope. It's a choice between the past and the future. It's a choice between pessimism and optimism. It's a choice between the status quo— leave things as they are—enact new tariffs on Mexico and I don't know who else—or move forward into the future with confidence. We're not scared. We're not a nation of quitters. We're not a nation that is afraid to compete in the world marketplace. And when we face a choice as important as this one, it is extremely important that we make the right decision. This is a fork in the road. The whole world is watching.

LK: What's going to happen in eight days?

RP: I love the way these guys turn around on a dime. They've been out making speeches that everybody ought to get a depression check every time they get their eyes checked, and the president's made a stream of speeches telling us how insecure we are. Now, suddenly, they figure out that we are a strong, proud people, and we are not going to let this trade agreement go through and create further damage to this great country. Let me make sure I say this before we go off the air tonight. I'll give you one reason that will just stick, why we can't continue to do these agreements.

LK: Thirty seconds for each.

RP: If we keep shifting our manufacturing jobs across the border and around the world and deindustrializing our country, we will not be able to defend this great country, and that is a risk we will never take.

AG: He started off as head of United We Stand. I'm afraid he's going to end up as head of Divided We Fall. Everything that he is worried about will get worse if NAFTA is defeated. We want jobs for America's working men and women. We want to get rid of the barriers that have prevented us from selling what we make in other countries. This is an historic opportunity to do that.

LK: Thank you both for this historic evening. The vote in Congress is eight days away. You'll be hearing lots more about it. Thanks to Ross Perot and Vice President Al Gore. For everyone here at *Larry King Live* and for the superb staff that put this all together, the best in the business. Thanks for joining us and good night.

Roseanne Arnold

Roseanne Barr was born in Salt Lake City, Utah, on November 3, 1952, a Jewish girl in the predominantly Mormon community. Through sheer persistence and extraordinary talent, she carved out a career as a stand-up comic with biting humor that skewered marriage, husbands, and life in general. She parlayed this success into an offbeat but on-target television series that now earns her an estimated $450,000 per episode. Meanwhile, the private life of Roseanne and her second husband, actor Tom Arnold, has been notable for not being private. After a number of tabloid-trumpeted disputes, they divorced, and Roseanne married her former bodyguard, Ben Thomas, on Valentine's Day 1995.

In this interview, she discusses her memoir, My Lives, as well as the multiple-personality disorder that afflicts her.

> **" 'Cause, you know, a normal person, you'll be driving down the highway, you know, you're listening to a song on the radio. You'll miss your turnoff because you left yourself for a minute in your consciousness. You dissociated. But then you wake up and you go, 'Oh, I missed my turn.' Well, for people like me, the only difference is that sometimes missing that turn will be months or years before you wake up again."**

LARRY KING: Good evening. In the '50s, it was Lucy, in the '70s, Mary Tyler Moore. In the '90s, the woman at the top of American television is Roseanne. Her show is one living, breathing portrait of real life in these uphill times, but Roseanne Conner's fictional troubles are sometimes overshadowed by those of the woman who plays her. Her painful past, her fights with ABC, her joyous marriage to Tom Arnold—all out front. And Roseanne is brutally honest in a terrific new book, *My Lives*, from Ballantine. She's funny for a living, but ... *My Lives* is not a funny story. We're honored to have her with us—more than just a star, a real person. Roseanne Arnold joins us in Washington. When she walked in, I said, "Roseanne Barr," and you got—you said, "I hate that name."

ROSEANNE ARNOLD: Yeah.

LK: Why?

RA: Well, because it belongs to the family I'm no longer a part of.

LK: So you don't even like the fact that you were once a Barr?

RA: Well, I can't change it, but I have a new family now.

LK: Why the book, Roseanne? Why'd you do this?

RA: Well, I wrote it for a lot of reasons, I guess. Sometimes I asked myself that, too, but I know that there—I know that my sister wrote a book and it's coming out, and there's two other people that wrote—*are* writing or *have* written books about me.

LK: Tell-all kind of thing?

RA: Yeah, due out this year, so I felt like I had—wanted to tell, you know, my story in my own words, before they—

LK: Certainly you didn't do it for financial reasons. The money you didn't need from this book.

RA: No, and also it was therapeutic for me and 'cause I thought it would help a lot of other people, too.

LK: What was the toughest thing about doing it?

RA: It was all really tough. I had a hard time putting things together and remembering things and—

LK: Was there anything, now that it's done, you left out you should have put in?

RA: Yeah. I wish I had put in this prayer that I was going to put in and then I don't know why I took it out.

LK: What prayer?

RA: I had written a prayer of thanks to, you know, God, and I don't know why I didn't put it in. I can't figure out why I didn't. I wish I had left that in.

LK: Why don't you have it published?

RA: Well, I guess I will, 'cause I want to do a book of poetry, too, some time.

LK: You know, when a person lays everything out, the hard part is the doing. Once it's done, though, there's a kind of freedom about it. Do you feel that way?

RA: No, it's—

LK: It's still bothering you?

RA: It's bothering me more and more that—

LK: Why? That's not supposed to happen in a catharsis.

RA: Well, when I go and I talk about it, it's still really painful to me, and you know, there has been a period of probably three or four years where I—people always used to wonder why, you know, Tom went on all these shows with me. Because I could not keep myself together unless he went on with me. And it's hard to do it. I've broken out with hives and have been covered with hives all over. It's scary to—it's still scary, at forty-one, to remember the things that happened to me.

LK: Do you remember more things all the time? The more you remember, the more you remember?

RA: No. I basically still have the same—I basically remember the same things I have for the last three to four years, but wave after wave of remembering the feelings that came with it is what's happening now, and that's really— It was okay to remember certain things—

LK: Intellectually—

RA: Yeah, but then when you get the feelings that you had then, that's very hard. And when I talk about the stuff, I can feel it again.

LK: But don't they also say that that's the road through to total recovery?

RA: Yeah, they do. I guess they do. I know I have to go that way, but I wish there was an easier way, but I guess there isn't.

LK: Explain the title, *My Lives*. Why not "My Life"?

RA: Well, you know, I originally wanted to call it "Kiss My Ass," and they wouldn't let me, so then I thought . . .

LK: Not going to get promoted easily.

RA: Yeah, a lot of bookstores didn't want to carry it with that name, although they carried Howard Stern's *Private Parts*—

LK: Well—

RA: But I guess you could double-entendre that. But "ass" isn't even dirty, is it?

LK: They say it on network television.

RA: I know, but— What did you ask me? I got lost.

LK: Why *My Lives*, instead of "My Life"?

RA: Oh, because I feel I've lived many. I feel I've lived many lives.

LK: You mean there was the Barr life and the Arnold, early life, middle life, now life?

RA: There are a lot of—well, yeah, there's that, and then there's also a lot of different people inside of me who have all lived their own life.

LK: The multifaceted personality. Have you been—

RA: It's not really called multifaceted. It's called multiple personality disorder or dissociative identity disorder.

LK: Do a lot of people have it?

RA: Well, a lot more people than they ever thought. Now they say perhaps one percent of the population. . . .

LK: How long have you known you had it?

RA: For three years.

LK: Which one is here now?

RA: Well, we're all here all the time, but—

LK: But one of them's talking now.

RA: Yeah, yeah. We all do—

LK: The others are here, though?

RA: Yes, we're all here, and we all do—we all do and say different things, and I can't really explain it better than that. Mostly the difference between me and people who have it and normal people—'cause everybody can dissociate—is that we lose track of time for a long period time. And that's really what—the only difference, really, is about. 'Cause, you know, a normal person, you'll be driving down the highway, you know, you're listening to a song on the radio. You'll miss your turnoff because you left yourself for a minute in your consciousness. You dissociated. But then you wake up and you go, "Oh, I missed my turn." Well, for people like me, the only difference is that sometimes missing that turn will be months or years before you wake up again.

LK: There is, I assume, a principal personality, right? The upfront, most-at-a-time Roseanne Arnold.

RA: No.

LK: There is not?

RA: No.

LK: So therefore, we can't say that it drives anyone crazy?

RA: Well, it drives *me* kind of crazy. 'Cause I forget a lot of things, you know, and then—

LK: How then does it affect performance?

RA: I have one person does all the work, and it does not affect, but that's all that that person does.

LK: The show.

RA: And the work and the performing and action and writing.

LK: So that person on stage—stand-up or doing the TV show—that's a personality?

RA: Well, it's at least one. I don't really know how many. It might be four people that do some of it.

LK: But doesn't affect performance?

RA: But no, they're not the mother, and they're not the, you know, the other parts of me.

LK: That person remembers lines, right?

RA: Yes, I have—I have total recall, photogenic memory—what do they call it? Photographic memory?

LK: Yeah. . . . How do you explain your own clout? What's happened to you? How do you explain it to yourself?

RA: Well, in the book somewhere, I said I think it's because I dissociate—that people kept telling me I can't do it and I can't do it, and I keep forgetting that they said I could not do that, and I keep doing it.

LK: But everyone has wishes. They want to be a fireman, a doctor, they want to be a success in what they do. There's no way you could have dreamt you would be what you are.

RA: No, I always knew I would be what I am.

LK: You really did?

RA: I have always known it since I was three, yeah.

LK: That you'd be a star of—

RA: I always knew I would have my own TV show and be a comic.

LK: Okay. You didn't know you'd be this big.

RA: I thought I was going to be pretty big.

LK: Therefore, none of this is a surprise to you.

RA: Yes, it's all a total surprise.

LK: But you knew you were going to be big.

RA: I know, but you know how when you're a kid and you think, "Oh, I'm going to be a famous rock star"? I mean, it usually doesn't happen, you know, but this time it did. So that is surprising still.

LK: Can you take a step back—since you also write for the show and as exec producer, and your husband is producer, you have to judge—judge why we like that show. Why does the public like that show so much?

RA: Oh, I think they like the characters in the family, and they like that it attempts— The show attempts to say something different than other shows say, and it's fresh.

LK: But they don't necessarily—do they associate with that family?

RA: I think—yeah, a lot do, but for different reasons. A lot see a family that they consider not as healthy as theirs, and a lot see a family that is exactly like theirs. And a lot see a family they wish they had. So there's a lot of different perceptions of it. . . .

LK: What was the big deal in two women kissing on television in 1994?

RA: Well, I sort of think that— Well, some of me thinks that the people at the network just wanted to make a great big case out of it, so more people would watch.

LK: A little PR here.

RA: I think— Well, you know, I think that that was probably some of it. And then the rest of it was so ridiculous that I wouldn't even go into it, but there's a lot of homophobia and because it was me. They said it wasn't right—

LK: 'Cause people of the same sex have kissed on network television before, right?

RA: Yeah, but I think it's 'cause it's me, and I'm the main character in the show, and— you know, but I mean, I'm always the one that does the things on my show.

LK: When you saw this script, did you feel any way about it? Did you feel—

RA: Yeah, my husband came to me with the idea—he's the one that wanted to do it—and I said, "No, I do not want to do that, because it's going to be nothing but controversy and a big pain in the butt." And he went ahead and wrote the script anyway and then brought it back to me and said, "Read it." And I read it, and then I really liked it, because I saw that what it was about was questioning yourself. And I thought that that was a good thing for a main character to do, is question themselves. . . .

LK: Anyone at the company, Carsey-Werner, have a problem?

RA: Well, I never talk to them, so I don't know what they think.

LK: You don't talk to your own company?

RA: No, no. But it was the network that had the big problem. The president of the network said it was a lawyer above them who—

LK: A lawyer above the—

RA: A lawyer for Capital Cities that wasn't even—isn't even involved in TV at all. . . . He said if children saw two women kissing, they would think it was okay.

LK: Why did they finally decide to go with it?

RA: Well, my husband handled all the politics of that, and he did not give them the show until he got a written agreement that they would show it unedited or we were not going to give them the show at all. So I guess they figured, like, well they should show it.

LK: If it was a publicity stunt—

RA: But they said they lost $2 million of advertising money.

LK: Oh.

RA: Nabisco pulled out and a couple of other things, for a totally ridiculous—

LK: If it was a publicity stunt, it worked. It probably got super numbers, right?

RA: It did get good numbers against the Grammys. . . . I don't think it was anything disgusting or anything that America has not seen or heard of or does. You know, most people know gay people, have them in their families. You just kind of get sick of that real provincial, stodgy attitude that's just so quasi-violent against gay people.

LK: Has it soured you about your network?

RA: No. In fact, it kind of made me feel good about my network, because I know that Robert Eiger—who I have had a bad time with for a time—he put his own job on the line for this show to go on, and I really appreciate that. And so did Ted Harberd, both presidents of ABC, and I appreciate that. I think it was a groundbreaking night, and I'm proud that they did that. I'm real happy.

LK: Let's say all things being equal and all dollars are the same, you'd stay with ABC.

RA: Well, it's more than money.

LK: Like?

RA: Well, it's respect for my work.

LK: And ABC gives you that?

RA: Well, they did this week, very much behind me, and I really appreciate that.

LK: Why don't you speak to the people at Carsey-Werner?

RA: They're never there. They're in Cape Cod.

LK: They own the—who owns the show?

RA: They do.

LK: They own the show. Are you going to try to break that relationship?

RA: No, not at all.

LK: 'Cause they just don't bother you.

RA: No, they've been— We *like* that they don't get involved or come down there ever, 'cause that gives us total creative freedom.

[*Commercial break*]

LK: We're back on *Larry King Live* with Roseanne Arnold. This is your program as well, so we're going to start to intersperse your phone calls amidst the questions for Roseanne. We go to Sarasota, Florida. Hello.

CALLER: [*Sarasota, Florida*] Hi, Roseanne. My name's Kathleen. I just really want to commend you for coming out about your multiplicity. I'm sorry I didn't get to see you on "Oprah Winfrey." And I'm a survivor of incest. I wrote you a letter. In fact, Heather Terry received the letter, so I hope to hear back from you, and I took the courage to write Clinton a letter, too. My name's Kathleen.

LK: Do you have a question?

CALLER: [*Sarasota, Florida*] Well, the question was, I just wanted to make a comment that I commend her for being real honest about this stuff, that this is what happens to people that are abused. I was abused starting at six month old, and I really—

LK: You think multiple personality is the product of abuse?

RA: Oh, absolutely it is, especially of sexual abuse.

LK: Because you're hiding in different people?

RA: Well, no, because you have no place in your head to fit this stuff. It doesn't go along with parents who take care of you and then also hurt you, so you have to— You split more every single time.

LK: Did you feel an association with the Menendez brothers?

RA: Yeah, I do. . . . I understand how someone could come to that point. I'm not saying that, you know, it's right or that people should necessarily kill their parents, but I can understand how you reach that point.

LK: To Vienna, Austria, with Roseanne Arnold. Hello.

CALLER: [*Vienna, Austria*] Hi, Roseanne. I just wanted to say how much women here in Europe love you and admire your work, and I wanted to ask if there was something like a special event that made you come out with the child abuse. . . .

RA: Yeah, there was kind of an event. For one year, I had been writing the people in my family—the parents, the brother and the sisters—letters saying what I remembered and, you know, that I wanted to speak to them about, that I wanted them to address these things. I wanted them to talk to me about these things. And for one year they never, ever answered any of my letters. And I got— you know, I sent them all certified mail, so I have the slips that showed they signed them. And it was a year later that I met Marilyn Vanderbur Attler, and I was telling her about me, and she suggested I come to Denver and speak to the same group of people that she speaks to. It was an all-survivor group. And that was a great—

LK: And that was an incredible day.

RA: —great day for me. It was a very great day for me.

LK: Had your parents responded to that initial letter and talked to you about it, might we have never learned of this?

RA: No, you would never have learned of it.

LK: To Germantown, Maryland. Hello.

CALLER: [*Germantown, Maryland*] Yeah, hi, Roseanne. My name is Francine. I just want to say I admire you really so much, and I missed your book signing yesterday. I was sick with the flu. More than anything I wanted to meet you. And to change the subject a little, I just wanted to say I heard you in the beginning where you said that you left out the prayer in your book.

RA: Yes.

CALLER: [*Germantown, Maryland*] And if there is anything else that you might have left out, could we be expecting another book in the future?

RA: I think I will write a third book when I'm—the therapy I'm in takes ten years, and I have about five more years of it to go, and I think after that I will write another book, yeah.

LK: They know that it takes ten years?

RA: On the average it does, yeah.

LK: How often do you go?

RA: Three times a week for four years.

LK: Is it helping?

RA: It's helping, yes.

LK: To Arlington, Texas. Hello.

CALLER: [*Arlington, Texas*] Yes. Roseanne, do you ever have a guilty conscience over the actions and the trashy mouth that you use and the negative influence over young children and the potential positive influence you could have if you changed?

RA: Well, I think that that's all in the way you look at it so— I don't agree with what you said, and I think that, you know, most human beings do positive and negative things. I'm not a saint, so I really can't speak like one.

LK: You don't think of negative-positive. Do you think you are a role model in any way?

RA: For some things and not for others.

LK: I mean, do you think, like, young women—obviously a lot of people love you, some people get angered by you.

RA: Yeah, some people don't like me, some people do, but—

LK: You don't think about it, though.

RA: No, because I know that whatever is inside you is what you see in me, so you have to deal with that, not me.

LK: Oh, in other words, the problem, dear sir, is with the viewer?

RA: It's not a problem so much as— But any art that anybody looks at or any artist, what you perceive of that art and that artist is because of what's inside you— what you know, what you perceive. So—I mean, a million people could perceive me in a million different ways. I don't think that I have a uniform impact on any group.

LK: With all you've been through, how do you explain how funny you are? I mean, really. You are funny.

RA: Well, I think that comics are people who have gone through a lot, and you have to start looking at things funny to get through them. I think that that's probably very common for all of us comics, and I'm funny 'cause I look at things skewed. I can't help it. It's like everything seems skewed.

LK: Walking-around dyslexia.

RA: Yeah, like being from another planet.

LK: So you see things funny.

RA: I see things like from such an outside vantage point that I do feel that I come from another planet a lot.

LK: Want to name it, Roseanne?

RA: I said it was Saturn, because it's the biggest planet and has the most interesting rings, but I forget to wear my diamonds. . . .

[*Commercial break*]

LK: We're back with Roseanne Arnold. We were talking during the break about her being Jewish—so many comics are Jewish—and how proud you are of it. It's a faith you, therefore, live with, right? You carry it with you.

RA: Yes. Yes, it's a comforting faith, very much so.

LK: Los Angeles for Roseanne Arnold. Hello

CALLER: [*Los Angeles, California*] My name is Lee, and I was wondering what regrets you have, if you have any regrets, from going into show business, and also if you belong to any of the anonymous recovery programs here in Los Angeles.

LK: Well, if she was in an anonymous recovery program, she couldn't tell you, right? 'Cause you—

RA: Well, I'm not in any anonymous thing.

LK: Any regrets?

RA: Any regrets? No, not really.

LK: None?

RA: I can't remember any of them.

LK: Anything you worry you didn't do? Did you ever turn down something you regretted professionally?

RA: No—well, I've turned down a lot of really good movies, but I don't regret it 'cause I got really cool vacations in the summer, and I needed them.

LK: Mechanicsville, Maryland. Hello.

CALLER: [*Mechanicsville, Maryland*] Hello, Larry. In the first place, you need to have an 800 number. Roseanne, we made eye contact last night when you signed my book, and I told you how very happy your work makes me and my family. Thank you so much for many, many wonderful hours. You relieved pressure and tension. And also, I saw you in the early '80s on *Northwest Afternoon*. You were very happy and very bubbly, and since that time—since those many years—I've noticed that perhaps maybe you've become a little sadder when you've been on talk shows. Can I ask you if you are a happy person, or is it perhaps that the things going on in your life have truly made you a very sad person?

RA: Well, I think I'm a very—not very, but I think I'm mostly positive and happy, but you know, I can't be like that all the time, like most people. I have bad days and bad times, you know, like you do and everybody else—

LK: Was life at times more fun the less you knew?

RA: There was a time when I was very drugged and, you know, that made me probably appear happier, but I like being without the drugs now.

LK: Columbia, Maryland, hello.

CALLER: [*Columbia, Maryland*] Hello, Roseanne. I'm honored to talk to you. My family says hi. We have a question. We watched the show once where everybody in the cast wore—

RA: Had the chicken shirt.

CALLER: [*Columbia, Maryland*] The chicken shirt. What is the significance of the chicken?

LK: How did you know she was going to say that?

RA: That's because everybody—that's the number-one question out of this book tour that people want to know about, so this is good that I get to tell it here. . . . It's because it was the ugliest shirt I ever saw in my whole life, and so I wore it, and then my husband, Tom, you know, he's the producer, and he says, "Stop wearing that shirt, it's ugly." And I said, "Well, I'm going to wear it in every scene, then," you know, 'cause I think we were having a fight or something. And he said, "You're not going to wear it in every scene," so then I gave it to every other actor. And so in that one show, every scene, another actor is wearing it.

LK: Just to—

RA: Just to bug Tom. And then I gave the whole cast and crew a chicken shirt for Christmas, because it's like it got so popular, people called from all over the country: "Where'd you get that shirt? It's fantastic."

LK: Was it ugly?

RA: It's really ugly. It's got eggs and chickens on it. . . .

LK: How's John Goodman going to do with the Flintstone movie?

RA: Oh, I hope it's just great. I hope it's a huge success for him.

LK: There's Flintstone dolls, right?

RA: Yeah, and they look like John. I thought how cool that would be, you know. You grew up with this cartoon your whole life, and you—then it looks like you. I mean, that'd be great.

LK: What is he like to work with?

RA: He is the funniest human being I've ever, ever seen or met. He can go right off the top of his head for hours. It's unbelievable and frightening. He can do character after character after character.

LK: 'Cause he can also be shy.

RA: Oh, he's very shy, too. Yeah, he's very shy, but because we've been working so closely together for six years now, he kind of got over his shyness. We all kind of got over our shyness. But John is an improvisational genius, just a— I never call anybody a genius, but he is. And he's a great actor, and he's really fun to work with.

LK: You won all the awards, but just one Emmy, huh?

RA: Yeah. Yeah, I won an Emmy, and Laurie won an Emmy, but John—John didn't get one yet, but I hope he does this year. The show's never even been nominated for an Emmy. . . . Never been nominated, six years.

LK: I'll make you feel good. Gleason never won one.

RA: I know. I always think of that. I always think of that. . . .

[*Commercial break*]

LK: Are you definitely committed to staying with *Roseanne*? Will *Roseanne* stay on the air?

RA: Well, I hope so. I hope people will continue to watch it. . . .

LK: Houston, Texas, with Roseanne Arnold. Hello.

CALLER: [*Houston, Texas*] I just wanted you to know that I think you're a terrific role model for open-minded people who don't judge other human beings. My question is, do you ever plan to do any stand-up comedy tours, specifically to—you know—just the comedy clubs or bigger theaters?

RA: I have done that in the past, but it doesn't look like I'm going to be doing that for a while.

LK: Because?

RA: Well, you know, the show takes so much of my time. It's hard to put an act together.

LK: Isn't that the biggest high, though, to stand alone on a stage and make people laugh?

RA: Yeah, it's the greatest. It's just the greatest.

LK: So you got to miss that when you're—

RA: I do miss it sometimes, but I've found that now I've been going places and reading from my book, and that's a big high, too, when I'm reading stuff that—

LK: Oh, you appear and do readings from the book.

RA: Yeah.

LK: Are you enjoying all the book signings and everything?

RA: Oh yeah, I love the book signings. I love to meet my fans eye-to-eye.

LK: Boy, you packed them in here yesterday. . . . Signing books. . . . Wooster, Ohio. Hello.

CALLER: [*Wooster, Ohio*] I'm just wondering if you see that there is or should be a line between an entertainer and being an activist and, if so, where would that be?

RA: Well, yeah, I think that there's a line between it, and I think it's a thin line, and I think it's a line that you can go over if you get too arrogant. And that's what usually happens to people. They get real arrogant and then that kind of makes me sick, too.

LK: You don't get politically involved?

RA: I do get politically involved, but I don't talk about it in public. I give money and stuff like that, or, you know, give support.

LK: And you don't talk about it, why?

RA: Because I think that voting and that stuff is, you know, a private thing. I think it's a private thing, and you know, although I guess I have publicly said things about George Bush and stuff—well, I didn't like him too much.

LK: You can't hold it back, can you, Roseanne? Orlando, Florida. Hello.

CALLER: [*Orlando, Florida*] Hey, Roseanne. I am so excited that I'm actually talking to you. I love your show, and I tell you I have a really stressful job, and I can count on seeing you on Fox every day and plus once a month on your non-rerun show, and I get a laugh every time. If you leave after a couple of years—I can't make it without your show. What would you do then?

RA: Well, I think I'll try to do something funny always, you know, but I don't really know.

LK: You'll not leave television, right?

RA: I don't really know. I don't really know what I'll do.

LK: You would not leave television, would you?

RA: Well, I might take some time off or something—go to Spain and live on the beach, nude. I don't know.

LK: Haven't heard much lately about you being tough. Have you fired anyone lately?

RA: No, I haven't fired anybody in a long, long time. I finally got the people together that I work well with and that, you know, I have good collaboration and good relationship with, so—you know, that takes a long time, to assemble your people.

LK: We've had people on who worked with you who didn't think you were tough at all—

RA: I'm not.

LK: —who thought you were just totally professional—

RA: I am.

LK: —that if you come across with less than 100 percent, you're gone.

RA: That's right, because I give that, and I believe that the audience deserves that, because I think when they tune in to my show, the way that I feel about it is that they're giving us a half hour of their life a week—not just watching a crappy show, but their life—and so I try to do the best work I can every week, and if people are taking it lightly, I don't want them around me, 'cause I don't like people like that.

[*Commercial break*]

LK: Worcester, Massachusetts. Hello.

CALLER: [*Worcester, Massachusetts*] Oh, hello. This is Sally. And I wanted to say that I'm very glad to know more about Roseanne and that I certainly appreciate your very positive attitude toward her. What I'd like to know is what part you feel Tom has played in your life. Since you've come from a dysfunctional family, where do you think you might be today if you hadn't met him?

RA: Well, I don't think I'd be anywhere, 'cause I don't think I would be here at all. And he— I was looking at the cover of my book. . . . It was like this romance-novel thing, but I was looking at it yesterday, and I thought, "Gee, that's really how I feel about him." He kind of was the guy on the white horse or whatever that childhood fantasy a lot of us girls have.

LK: Are you saying you might have been not here, like dead?

RA: I know I wouldn't have been here, yes.

LK: How do you handle the tabloids? You're always in the tabloids. I mean, you had a good run for a while, 'cause you sued one and won.

RA: Yeah, I sued two and won. But I have to admit that I'm like a total tabloid junkie.

LK: You read them?

RA: And I'm like such a hypocrite that I would go out and say, "The tabloids this and that," 'cause like I'm there every Monday morning and reading about everybody else—

LK: And do you believe them?

RA: Some— I don't *want* to. I don't want to.

LK: But wait a minute. You know they lie, 'cause they lied about you.

RA: I know they lie. I know they lie.

LK: But you read about—

RA: Well, they have some part of the truth in them, though. Everything has a little kernel of truth, and then a lot of—

LK: Even with you.

RA: Yeah, and then a lot of blown-up— Whenever it doesn't name the person, then you know that's a lie. When they say an insider, that's a lie. But if they do name the person, that's the truth. . . . And I do believe that an alien shook hands with George Bush and Clinton. And *Weekly World News*, which is my favorite tabloid of all, I do believe that's true.

LK: That an alien shook hands with—

RA: You saw it right on the cover, and they were the only newspaper that had the guts to cover that.

LK: That's right. *The New York Times* never ran that.

RA: No, never.

LK: *The Washington Post* ducked it.

RA: That's right.

LK: And that alien was right there.

RA: Right there for the world to see.

LK: Toronto, hello.

CALLER: [*Toronto, Ontario*] I just wanted to know where you get such great ideas to deal in such human ways in everything that you say on your show, especially the show about when your father died. I really think they really touch a core.

LK: How are ideas formed? Is it a group thing?

RA: It's me and Tom, usually—me and Tom, usually, for those kind of shows. Tom's mother had just died last year, and he had not spoken to her for a few years because, you know, she was kind of a negative person in his life. And he went to her grave, and he read this thing to her after she died. And that's where we got the idea for me to do it with my father, because it was a very healing thing for Tom and—and I wanted—I guess I—whenever something seems like it's healing, I really want to put it on the show, 'cause I know how many people out there need something, some idea of something to hold onto so badly. People are spiritually thirsty and thirsty for positive things that you don't generally get just on TV or, you know, wherever. And so I try—I try to have that in every show, something real positive. . . .

[*Commercial break*]

LK: I guess one of the things you had to be proudest of—I know we were—was winning the Peabody, right?

RA: Oh yeah, absolutely.

LK: I mean, when a sitcom wins a Peabody, that's saying a lot.

RA: Yeah, that was a great honor, yeah.

LK: You're not a sitcom. What are you?

RA: Well, I like to think of it that way, 'cause it gets serious sometimes, you know, but we do above all try to make it funny.

LK: If John Goodman says, "Rosie, I'm not happy with this line," can he change it?

RA: Oh, he does, all the time. We all ad lib a lot, and if it's funny, we put it in immediately, which is one of the things that they didn't like before and I wanted. 'Cause Laurie Metcalf is extremely funny, too. . . .

LK: Thanks, Rosie. As always—

RA: Thank you very much.

LK: —great having you with us.

RA: Great to be here. Thank you.

Whoopi Goldberg

We know her publicly as Whoopi Goldberg. Her given name she guards closely and declines to reveal. Born in New York in 1950, she was raised in a public housing project. In the 1960s she dropped out of school, performed in the Broadway choruses of Hair, Jesus Christ Superstar, *and* Pippin, *then created a stand-up comedy routine while working as a licensed mortuary cosmetician. Producer Mike Nichols caught her act and produced it as a one-woman Broadway show. Her film career took off from there with* The Color Purple, Ghost, Sister Act, Corrina Corrina, *and others.*

"Don't let anybody ever tell you there's anything wrong with not looking like everybody else. It did me pretty well."

LARRY KING: Good evening. We might as well call it the Year of the Whoopi. Listen to this roll. She is in— she is in seven movies in 1994, *seven*. In the first, she was back in the habit with the smash-hit *Sister Act II*. Later this year, she'll send her voice up and lend it to two animated movies for kids. Coming this August, from New Line Cinema, *Corrina Corrina*, a love story starring you-know-who as a housekeeper in love with Ray Liotta, to name just a few. That's not all. She's got a lot of other things going for her. Last month she made Academy Award history as the first woman to solo host the show. It wound up being one of the highest-rated Oscar shows ever. And, along with her pals Robin [Williams] and Billy [Crystal], she put on the cable comedy show *Comic Relief*, the most successful one yet. They raised $28 million to help the homeless. We're out of time, so goodnight.

    With us here in Los Angeles, the lady of the year, the Whoop herself.

WHOOPI GOLDBERG: I'm exhausted. . . .

LK: Why are you doing so much?

WG: I have no idea. I had no idea I was doing seven things. I truly didn't.

LK: And now that you hear it, you're worried.

WG: A little bit, you know.

LK: First, how do you choose what you do? What's your —when you say, "Yes, I will do that?"

WG: It has to interest me. It has to spark something in me. If it doesn't do that, then there's no point.

LK: And it doesn't have to be the lead, right?

WG: No, no. I just like working. I like acting. It's fun.

LK: Why?

WG: I don't know. The idea that you could go and play somebody else. It's an extension of childhood, you know, this idea of pretending. Because I can be anything. I can be a princess, I can be a king, I can be a knight. I can do anything when I'm in the movies or on a stage.

LK: But it's you in it, right? I mean, you never lose yourself totally. . . . It's Whoopi's—

WG: No, it's still me, but it's them. I sort of feel like I channel people.

LK: You were discovered by Mike Nichols, and, you were a stand-up in New York. It was a come-see-Whoopi-stand-on-a-stage-and-talk.

WG: Yeah, I was a monologist. I did monologues. Yeah. . . .

LK: What took you to acting?

WG: Well, I was always an actor. And one of the reasons I started doing the monologues was because I couldn't get any work, because people sort of look at you and decide what you can do and what you can't do, and what they think you can do. So I thought, if I did these monologues—and, of course, if you write them yourself, you can, you know, put anything you want out there.

LK: Now how did Mike find you?

WG: Judith Ivy took him to see my show. And she hadn't seen me, she just read about it. And they were taking each other to different performances. And so—

LK: And what did he do? Because I remember, it was, like—you were regarded as his discovery. . . . Did he then produce you on Broadway?

WG: Yeah. He wrote me a letter and then called me up. Said, "I would like to produce you anywhere, any time." I said, "Oh, okay, right." And he was serious. . . . And from that, [director] Steven [Spielberg] found me, through—through lots of different folks.

LK: And cast you in a very serious role. . . . Did he ever tell you why he saw you in a serious role?

WG: Well, I think it's because [novelist] Alice [Walker] had seen my work in San Francisco and knew that what Celie needed was not just one note. She needed to be able to ride this wonderful wave. And so he just sort of trusted me to do this, because I was in a panic, because, you know, you don't want to mess up a Steven Spielberg movie.

LK: But he also cast Oprah, who was not an actress, right? . . . I mean, there were some risks in that movie.

WG: Well, he's a risk-taking kind of guy, you know.

LK: And that was the start of it, right? That was Boonsville?

WG: Yeah.

LK: Now, you like all kinds of roles. . . . Let's run down some. . . . *Corrina Corrina*, this is for New Line. Is this your first film for New Line?

WG: I think so.

LK: Well, you don't know. You work so much, you don't know who you're working for, right?

WG: Yeah, no, no. . . .

LK: Okay. In *Corrina Corrina* you play a housewife in love with the man you're working for?

WG: No.

LK: No.

WG: I'm a writer, actually, who is black, in the '50s, and a female who can't get the gig that she wants. She wants to write liner notes, because she's a jazz fanatic. And—

LK: And who is Ray Liotta?

WG: Ray Liotta is a guy whose wife has passed away, and his daughter stopped talking. And so, because it is the only way that she can make a living, she finally goes and applies for this job as the housekeeper.

LK: But she really is a writer. . . . And Liotta is a what?

WG: He's a jingle man. He's an advertising cat.

LK: This is a comedy?

WG: In places. I don't know quite what it is. I know it's different.

LK: Are you Corrina, or is the daughter Corrina?

WG: Yes. No, I'm Corrina.

LK: Had fun doing it?

WG: Yeah.

LK: You like working with Ray?

WG: Yeah.

LK: Is that important, by the way, that you like who you work with?

WG: Well, it helps. You know, if you really detest the person—

LK: Not necessary, though, right?

WG: No. I've been lucky enough not to detest anybody I've worked with, and vice-versa, I hope. But maybe we'll get a call. I don't know.

LK: You haven't worked with anyone yet who you would say, "I don't like?"

WG: No.

LK: Okay. The only minus mark was the talk show you did. I mean minus in the sense that it didn't succeed.

WG: Well, you know, but it did. It did succeed. It succeeded for me because it got done, and I got to talk to all these really strange and wonderful people. I mean, when else am I going to talk to Alexander Haig? I mean, come on. I said to him, "What should I call you?" He said, "Call me Big Al." You know, where else can I get that?

LK: So, for you it was fun?

WG: Oh, it was heaven. It was heaven.

LK: Are you always someone who wants to try things new?

WG: Yeah.

LK: Okay, so, like I'd guess Broadway theater. . . .

WG: You mean, do I want to do a play?

LK: Would you like to do a play?

WG: If there was something interesting out there, yeah. But I've done a lot of theater. That's what I came from. So that would be all right. Broadway is, you know, another story.

LK: What haven't you done you'd like to do?

WG: I haven't ruled a country.

LK: That could be next. You could announce on this show.

WG: Maybe. . . .

[*Commercial break*]

LK: Okay, some other things. What do you do in *The Lion King*?

WG: I'm a hyena. Cheech Marin and I are bad guys, which is wonderful.

LK: How did you find the voice for a hyena? Just do your own voice, or did you give it a voice?

WG: No, we just—she's really sort of rude and obnoxious. . . .

LK: Is it fun to do that kind of thing?

WG: Yeah, it is. It's a little time-consuming, but it's all right, because they draw to you. So you do stuff, and then they draw, and then you do more stuff, and then they draw, and then you do more stuff. So it's an ongoing process.

LK: Okay. You're in the *Little Rascals*. . . . What part do you play?

WG: I'm Mrs. Wheat.

LK: Mrs. Wheat?

WG: Yes. Mother of Buck.

LK: Mother of Buck.

WG: Yes. Did you know that Buckwheat's full name is Buckminster? Buckminster Wheat.

LK: I did not know that.

WG: There you are.

LK: Who is Mr. Wheat?

WG: Well, I can't tell all the secrets.

LK: There's a lot about the *Little Rascals*. It's like people are hiding.

WG: Yes.

LK: Why?

WG: Well, for the same reason we don't know who is the father of Olive Oyl's baby.

LK: Okay. I'm going to leave that alone.

WG: Yes. You know what I'm talking about.

LK: Yeah, I know.

WG: You know.

LK: I know.

WG: Who is he? Nobody asks, because it would be pressing.

LK: *Pagemaster*. . . . What is that?

WG: I play a book called "Fantasy."

LK: Your agent must have a riot, right? He calls you up—"Whoopi, I got a part for you. You're a truck."

WG: I call *him*. I call *him*. I say, "I'm doing this." He says, "Fine."

LK: Okay. Now, you just finished shooting the *Gone with the Wind* remake. [*Goldberg shakes head*] No. Okay, *Boys on the Side* . . . with Drew Barrymore . . . which you shot in Arizona.

WG: And Pittsburgh and New York and New Jersey.

LK: And what's that about?

WG: Three women. One is ill and dying. One is gay and a rock 'n' roller looking for her life. And one is just sort of a young innocent who gets involved with strange stuff. And it's about family, how people come together as family.

LK: Was Drew Barrymore fun to work with?

WG: Yeah, she's a sweetie. And Mary Louise Parker, another sweetie.

LK: And who do you play?

WG: I'm the lesbian. I'm the lesbian rock 'n' roller.

LK: How did you find that role?

WG: Well, you know, I think being a lesbian or being gay is like being black. It's just something you are. So it's not something you put a lot of thought into. It's just what is.

LK: Couple other things, Whoop, and then we're going to devote a lot of time to people calling in. . . . Were you annoyed when the tabloids played up so much when
you and Ted [Danson] were going together?

WG: Yeah, I was.

LK: Why?

WG: Because it was new, and I didn't understand what the fascination was. And it was
mean. It was mean-spirited. You know, it's great if people sort of put out positive
stuff, but it was really all kind of nasty. And people hanging from trees, going
through your drawers. I mean—

LK: They really hide outside your—

WG: Yeah, they do.

LK: They look at your garbage?

WG: Yeah, yeah.

LK: Why, do you think?

WG: Because I think people are fascinated by it. We've become a society, in many
ways, that thrives on dirt. That's why there are so many of these shows around,
where, you know, people come from under the gutter to take your picture. I
mean, it's amazing.

LK: Tabloid heaven. . . . Now, you hadn't had it before the relationship with Ted—

WG: Actually, they sort of did it with my daughter when she was young, and she got
pregnant. And they did it for a little bit. And then they stopped. And then this
sort of popped out. You know, the Friar's Club [at which Danson appeared in
blackface], I'm sure, fed the—

LK: What did you make of that, on reflection now?

WG: I had a great time. I thought the material was funny. And for the Friar's Club,
that's what it was. You know, that's what it was.

LK: Why do you think they overreacted like that? Montel [Williams] walked out.

WG: Well, Montel is brainless. Come on.

LK: Brainless?

WG: I think so. I think so.

LK: You watch his show, then?

WG: No. I have on occasion. I just think he wasn't thinking. I don't know what people thought they were coming to. This was not, you know, the cinema ball's trib-
ute to— It was the Friar's Club.

LK: Ted was shocked, wasn't he?

WG: Yeah, this really hurt him, I think.

LK: Was the break-up amicable, by the way?

WG: Yeah. You know, it had to happen, like, five months before we did the Friar's Club.

LK: Oh, you weren't—

WG: No, no. And we were—and it was great because it was something that happened
between him and I. It was about us separating. And then, you know, it sort of got
really ugly, but I have a great boyfriend now.

LK: Who is he?

WG: I'm engaged.

LK: Who is it, Whoop? This is news. Is this your engagement ring or a Band-Aid?

WG: No, this is a Band-Aid. That's the—

LK: Is this the engagement ring?

WG: Yeah, isn't that pretty?

LK: Hey, this is a first, Whoop.

WG: Yeah. I've actually not said it publicly before, so—

LK: You are engaged?

WG: I'm engaged.

LK: And who— That's a beautiful ring. . . . Who is the lucky man?

WG: Well, I don't know how lucky he is.

LK: *Is* it a man? Based on your parts, we never know—

WG: Yes, it is a man. It's definitely—

LK: Taking a risk.

WG: He's a union organizer.

LK: Oh-oh. Don't leave him. . . . Don't leave him, Whoop. These guys don't know from no. How did you meet?

WG: He came to organize a movie I was on.

LK: And you quickly joined?

WG: Actually, I'm real pro-union, because I think it's the only way we can sort of monitor—

LK: What's his name?

WG: Lyle Trachtenberg.

LK: And when are you getting married?

WG: Soon. No, *soon*. Down the line soon.

LK: Ninety-four soon?

WG: Maybe ninety-five.

LK: How do you feel about Ted and his current woman? Ted Danson is going with Mary Steenburgen.

WG: I don't pay any attention.

LK: Do you wish him luck?

WG: Oh, always.

LK: Yeah. I mean, you're friends, aren't you?

WG: Yeah.

LK: Does he know Trachtenberg?

WG: No.

LK: When are we going to see Trachtenberg? When are you going to reveal him to the world? You know, union organizers don't go out smiling on *This Is Your Life*.

WG: Well, he's been around. There have been pictures of him.

LK: But this is official. You are engaged?

WG: Yeah.

LK: All right. Now, there's one other thing I'm going to ask you. . . . Why do you do your hair like that?

WG: Because it's comfortable, and I like it.

LK: How long have you been doing it like that?

WG: About twenty years.

LK: You were ahead of your time. . . . Were you the first?

WG: No, lots of people did it.

LK: It's off the Rastafarian look, right? . . . From Jamaica.

WG: But you know, Rosalyn Cash, wonderful actress, they always made her put wigs over her dreads. But now, of course, you know, because of—of the tenacity of people like Rosalyn and myself, this is the natural state of women, you know.

LK: Who does this?

WG: Me. I don't touch it.

LK: Every day?

WG: No, no. You just leave it. It just does its thing. . . .

LK: You don't have to go to anyone. . . .

WG: I have someone who massages my head periodically.

LK: Yeah, but you just get up, and that's the way it is.

WG: That's the way it is. . . .

[*Commercial break*]

LK: Okay, let's go to calls for Whoopi. Prairie View, Texas. Hello.

CALLER: [*Prairie View, Texas*] This is Sue Orzoff, and I wanted to tell you, Whoopi, that I thought you were great on the Academy Awards. And Guinan, your character on *Star Trek: Next Generation*, are you going to be in the last, two-hour episode, and in the following movies? Because I love—I just love your character.

WG: I won't be in the two-hour episode, but I will be in the movie. And thanks for liking the Academy Awards. A lot of people had a hard time, I think. But—

LK: Why?

WG: I don't know. I don't know.

LK: Did you accept right away?

WG: Yeah.

LK: Were you surprised they called?

WG: Shocked.

LK: Because?

WG: Because I would have thought they were going to go to Gary Shandling or something.

LK: You mean, not great comic, but conventional.

WG: No, Gary is fun, you know. He's fun.

LK: He's terrific.

WG: And he's—you know, he's got that groove, and I just sort of thought they were going to go in that direction. So it floored me.

LK: Did they control anything you said?

WG: No. They just asked me not to say, you know, a couple of specific words. And I didn't. . . .

LK: Carmel, California, with Whoopi Goldberg. Hello.

CALLER: [*Carmel, California*] Hi, Whoopi. I just want to tell you how proud I am of you and how far you have come. And I want to tell you that, you know your movie *Ghost*? . . . This movie was all about you. I mean, with respect to the others, it was *you*. And I want to know if you plan on doing another one. And you're absolutely fantastic. And I'm very proud of you.

WG: Thank you.

LK: *Ghost II*? . . .

WG: No. I think sometimes it's better to leave a good thing alone.

LK: Did you have any idea that movie would do what it did?

WG: No. Clueless.

LK: In fact, no one associated with it did, right?

WG: No, no. It was a shock to everybody. I spend a lot of time in shock.

LK: Because, when you think about it, that's an off-beat film.

WG: Yeah, but it's a film that talks to everybody, because everybody wants that moment, that last moment, you know.

LK: And you won the Academy Award for that.

WG: Why, yes, I did, Larry.

LK: And you won a Grammy.

WG: Yes, I have.

LK: You won an NAACP Image Award, a Golden Globe, a People's Choice, a Drama Desk.

WG: Yes.

LK: So, you've got to come back to Broadway just to get a Tony.

WG: The Tony, yes. . . .

[*Commercial break*]

LK: We go to Amsterdam, Holland. Hello.

CALLER: [*Amsterdam, the Netherlands*] Hello. Thank you for your good work, Whoopi. I'd like to know, now that you've attained professional and, say, financial, commercial, success, how does your family feel about the mark you've made in the business?

WG: They're actually really excited, because it's— I'm sort of the—the reality of the American dream, you know. I sort of encompass that. And so, they're really proud. There have been a lot of firsts. And you know, somewhere, somehow, all those people who make up my family know that their lives push towards something. And that's what I've been able to accomplish so far.

LK: Who is the family?

WG: My mom and my brother, you know, and my daughter and my granddaughter.

LK: Does your mom flip over this?

WG: She's actually very cool, but she's really excited.

LK: Oh, I mean, come on.

WG: You know, she was knocked out that I did the Oscars. Because, of course, as kids we used to watch it, you know. And it's really something.

LK: You're a grandmother?

WG: Yeah.

LK: What do you have, a grandson?

WG: Granddaughter.

LK: How old?

WG: Four.

LK: Richmond, Virginia, hello.

CALLER: [*Richmond, Virginia*] Hi, this is Cheryl. Whoopi, how you doing?

WG: How you doing, Cheryl?

CALLER: [*Richmond, Virginia*] Oh, pretty good. And I'd like to congratulate you first on your engagement.

LK: You're not kidding about this, right? We're not going to put this guy on, and he's going to deny it?

WG: No, it's real. . . .

CALLER: [*Richmond, Virginia*] I'd also like to repeat what other people said, you did a great job with the Oscars. I really enjoyed it. . . . I really did and also, I'd like to make a comment, too. There was a special where you took a portrait with all of the actors who had won in the past, the Best Actor, Best Actress award. And I was really honored to see you sitting there, among all those legends. And that really meant a lot.

LK: Do you have a question?

CALLER: [*Richmond, Virginia*] Yes. Are you planning on doing it again next year, the Oscars?

LK: Oh, did they tell you anything?

WG: They haven't said a word. You know, I think they're hedging their bets.

LK: If asked, you would?

WG: Oh, I think so. I think I would. It's really great. You get to see all of those actors. I'm still really star-struck, so I'm really happy to be, you know, rubbing elbows with people. . . .

LK: Orlando, Florida, with Whoopi Goldberg. Hello.

CALLER: [*Orlando, Florida*] Hello. Yes, Whoopi, I hope you do the Oscars next year. What I wanted to say is, I love your *Sister Act*, and I love *Ghost*, but when are you going to do another great classic with deep meaning, like *The Color Purple*? You were great. You're a great dramatic actress.

WG: Thank you. As soon as you write it, darling, I will do it.

LK: That's the hardest thing, right, the script?

WG: Yeah, finding somebody to put together a great script is—is not easy.

LK: Have you turned down anything you regretted?

WG: No.

LK: You haven't had that happen with, "Oh, I should have taken that role?"

WG: No, no. So far so good.

LK: To Antioch, California. Hello.

CALLER: [*Antioch, California*] First of all, I would like to say that I really enjoyed you on the Academy Awards. It was tremendous. And congratulations on your engagement, and I was wondering—actually, it's kind of a two-and-a-half-part question: What was your favorite movie to make, and which one would you—well, not really which one was your favorite, but which one did you have the most fun making, and which one was your favorite? Maybe they're the same. And also were there ever any plans to maybe do the *Comic Relief* maybe up here in the Bay Area some time?

WG: Last question first; not that I know of. I think *Comic Relief* is sort of done with its wandering. We did New York, and it was really way too much work, so we came back to L.A.

LK: Favorite movie?

WG: Favorite movie—I don't have one. But I had a great deal of fun working on *Ghost* and *The Player* and—most of them. Most of them I have a good time on, because I like what I do.

LK: All right, *Sister Act* you had to expect would go through the roof.

WG: No.

LK: You didn't?

WG: No.

LK: No. See I would have guessed it. There's a great script.

WG: No. We thought we had a big old thing—plop—on the table.

LK: No kidding? Why?

WG: Because that's the way we're trained. That's the way we're trained. If you liked it, it's going to be terrible.

LK: Los Angeles, hello.

CALLER: [*Los Angeles, California*] Congratulations.

WG: Thank you, girl.

CALLER: [*Los Angeles, California*] And I wanted to ask you about *Sister Act II*. Wasn't it really based on a particular lady, Iris Stevenson? Was that based on her life, or did she just assist you in, like, the directing and all the stuff that you did? . . .

WG: *Sister Act II*, I think, is loosely based on Iris. Iris is a friend of mine. She's a wonderful lady. . . . She's a music teacher . . . in South Central [Los Angeles] who has changed the lives of dozens, *thousands* of kids, really. And her story, I guess, was owned by Disney. I knew her prior to that. And I guess they sort of mixed it up or put it together.

LK: Shawnee, Kansas, hello.

CALLER: [*Shawnee, Kansas*] I have a little girl that's seven years old that's staying up past her bedtime to watch you. And one of the things that has so impressed her is the one-man show you did about looking different than the rest of the kids. We're Cajun: black eyes, black hair, very fair skin. She doesn't look like all the little kids in Shawnee. And that has just thrilled her to the bone, that there are other people that feel like that. And she has watched every movie. We've rented them, we've gone to see them. She loves you to death.

WG: What's her name?

CALLER: [*Shawnee, Kansas*] Danielle Elizabeth.

LK: Is she there?

CALLER: [*Shawnee, Kansas*] Yes, she is.

LK: Put her on.

CALLER: [*Shawnee, Kansas*] Hang on a minute. Danielle, Ms. Whoopi would like to talk to you, darling.

LK: Cajun girl.

CALLER: [*Shawnee, Kansas*] Hi.

WG: Hi.

CALLER: [*Shawnee, Kansas*] How you doing?

WG: I'm pretty good. How *you* doing?

CALLER: [*Shawnee, Kansas*] I'm fine.

WG: You're up a little late, aren't you?

CALLER: [*Shawnee, Kansas*] Yes.

WG: Oh, well, all right.

CALLER: [*Shawnee, Kansas*] Well, I wanted to tell you that my favorite show of yours is *Sister Act*.

WG: Oh, well, I'm glad. I'm glad. And you know what, don't let anybody ever tell you there's anything wrong with not looking like everybody else. It did me pretty well.

CALLER: [*Shawnee, Kansas*] Okay.

WG: Okay.

LK: You're going to do okay, kid. Thanks for joining us. Never know what's going to happen. That kid, it made her life. We'll be back. And don't forget, we're going to meet Lyle. Don't go away.

[*Commercial break*]

LK: Los Angeles, Hello.

CALLER: [*Los Angeles, California*] Hello. My name is Felicia. Way to go, Whoop.

WG: Thank, Felicia.

CALLER: [*Los Angeles, California*] Listen, I want to know, how do you get started when you're not "what they're looking for?"

LK: Are you an actress? Is that it?

CALLER: [*Los Angeles, California*] No. I would like to get into writing music and singing, but I'm overweight and uneducated, and I live in "the wrong neighborhood," and every door that I go to, it gets slammed in my face.

LK: Well, there is prejudice against the overweight.

WG: There's a lot of prejudice, against women and overweight people and black people and all kinds of stuff, but the only thing I could say to you is to find those little clubs, you know, and talk to somebody, and tell them you really want to do this. Get on those amateur nights. Get out there. Start sending out fliers to people, and let them know that you're singing. Just send the head shot, let them find out whatever else they need to know once they get there. You've got to stay in it. It's just, you have to be tenacious, because everything—I mean, you know, basically, if you don't look like, I don't know—Cindy Crawford—these days, it's kind of tough to get stuff going. But if you stay with it—and, you know, it's a lot of hungry days. It's a lot of hungry days and hungry nights, and a lot of frustration. But if it's your heart and your soul and that's what you want to do, then that's what you have to put into it.

LK: Pensacola, Florida, hello.

CALLER: [*Pensacola, Florida*] Hi. First of all, I have a great admiration for you, Whoopi. I feel you're a wonderful actress and comedienne. I've seen your movies, *Comic Relief*, some of your older comedy specials, with Fontaine and such. You make a good role model for the general public. You're very outspoken. You don't hide your feelings. And I think that's very important, with everybody trying to be in this politically correct society that we have nowadays. And I was wondering, with all the other famous people going into government, do you have any aspirations for—

LK: Do we have another announcement here, Whoopi?

WG: No, no, no, no, no, no. I'd rather fight those battles from here, because it's a lot simpler to fight them from here. You know, I don't envy Bill Clinton at all. It's a tough gig. It's a tough gig. I don't envy hardly any politicians, because what your beliefs are and what you're able to do are often two different things.

LK: Is *Star Trek* fun to do?

WG: I love it. I love *Star Trek*.

LK: And you still play it, right? I mean, you play it as if it's today. I mean, you can't think, "This is *Star Trek*, it's somewhere in the future. I'm not going to—" you know, you can't— You've got to play it. Science fiction is fiction.

WG: Well, science fiction is the present, at another time. It's someone else's present time. But I love it.

LK: What are you going to do when the last movie hits—you're in, what, *Generations*?

WG: Yes.

LK: Who do you play?

WG: I'm playing Guinan. . . .

LK: You're always Guinan.

WG: Yeah. . . .

LK: Do you like wearing those clothes?

WG: I do. My hats drive me berserk. I love them. I have a good time. I mean, how can I complain? I love it. I get to go into the future. I get to go into the past. I'm just a blessed little girl.

LK: Life ain't bad, Whoop.

WG: Not bad at all. . . .

[*Commercial break*]

LK: Attention, tabloids, here it comes. Whoopi is already feeling it. Are you regretting that you did this, Whoopi?

WG: Yes, yes.

LK: Okay, why? Because you feel you—

WG: Just because I suddenly feel like this poor man's life is going to—

LK: Okay. This is Whoopi's fiancé. He is Lyle Trachtenberg. International representative for IATSE, which is what union?

LYLE TRACHTENBERG: It handles all the technical crafts for the motion picture and television stage, across the United States and Canada.

LK: And you organize, right?

LT: Amongst other things, yeah, we organize, we represent, we rewrite contracts.

LK: Aren't most people who work on movies in the union?

LT: Most are, Larry. However, in certain cases, there are producers who sometimes want to circumvent our agreement. And that's where we come in. Absolutely.

LK: Now, you got great earrings that sort of match the engagement ring. Did they go together, or did you have them when you met Whoopi?

LT: No, no.

WG: They went together.

LT: They went together.

LK: Was that your gift to him?

WG: No, I'm not saying anything. I'm not saying anything.

LK: I mean, you bought it to match?

LT: Yeah. Actually, there's a little story behind it, but—

LK: What is it, Lyle?

LT: It actually has to match the car that I drive, the color of it, and I wanted to match it as close as possible.

LK: In other words, Lyle, you love this car. Right, you don't like this car, you love this car?

LT: I love this car. But I love this woman also, so I wanted to get—

LK: How did you two meet?

LT: Actually, it was on a movie, *Corrina Corrina*.

LK: You came to organize the people.

LT: Precisely, yeah.

LK: Did you succeed?

LT: Yes, we did, actually, because of Whoopi herself.

LK: Oh, she helped you?

LT: Beyond help, yes, absolutely.

LK: Was it, like, right away? Were there sparks?

LT: Whoopi, you answer that.

WG: I don't know if there were sparks, but he definitely had my attention.

LK: So this is just, like, six months you know each other?

LT: It's going on seven months, yes, yeah.

LK: Seven months. He had your attention. How did you ask her out? How did this begin?

LT: Well, I said that the I.A. and Lyle would take her out to dinner, and then it eventually narrowed down to just me taking her out to dinner.

LK: Where did you go?

LT: We went to a little restaurant in Santa Monica.

LK: When, along the way in these past seven months, did you realize this was it, Whoop?

WG: I don't know. It just—it just felt like it was right. You know, he's a real normal guy. He's, like, 9-to-5.

LK: Normal guy in love with his car, with a blue earring. But a normal guy.

WG: Yeah, you know. But he—you know, he works at a normal job, and he does normal stuff. And it doesn't seem to phase him what I am and who I am.

LK: Do you have children?

LT: No, no.

LK: This is your first marriage?

LT: No, I've actually been married once before.

LK: You've been married twice.

WG: Twice, yeah. He's got a bird. . . .

LK: Well, how do you feel now, about all— I mean, it's going to happen fairly soon, right? I mean, not immediate, but fairly soon. You're engaged.

LT: Yeah. I actually feel a little more relaxed, I think, than Whoopi, really. If you really get to know her, you know that she's very relaxed, and it's—

LK: What attracted you to her? Other than the hair or the rings on her fingers, what was—

LT: Well, actually it's two-fold. I mean, you get to be with someone like Whoopi, who everyone knows, the world knows, and then, you also get to know someone who is—I mean, really real and calm and really peaceful.

LK: And it doesn't bug you, like, when you go into a restaurant that you're, like, Mr. Goldberg?

LT: I've been called that before, already. But—

LK: Does it bug you?

LT: No, it does not.

WG: Secure.

LK: He's well within himself.

WG: You know, it's really interesting, because it's kind of a first, where, actually, someone has their own life, and I'm allowed to have my life, too, and it's okay, you know? And he's fun. He's just fun. We go to bed at nine o'clock.

LT: Sometimes 9:15.

WG: Sometimes we splurge.

LK: Big excitement, huh? Do you travel a lot?

LT: Yeah. My job sometimes takes me on the road.

LK: And Whoopi, too, right?

WG: Yeah.

LK: Is that okay?

WG: Well, you know, what's funny is that I'll probably be home a lot more, because his job also requires that he be there. You know, he's got a 9-to-5 five days a week.

LK: We'll be back with our remaining moments with the future Trachtenbergs. Hey—

WG: He's a present Trachtenberg. I'm the future—

LK: You're the future Mrs. Trachtenberg.

WG: We'll be Berg and Berg.

LK: Goldberg-Trachtenberg merger. You never know what's going to happen on this—this is a good job . . .

[*Commercial break*]

LK: Quick call, Los Angeles. Hello.

CALLER: [*Los Angeles, California*] Whoopi, I thought your speech on political correctness at *Comic Relief* was fantastic. Do you feel emotionally extra nervous being on the line like that? And did you get a lot of response for that?

WG: Yeah, we got a lot of response for that, but I felt absolutely justified in what I was saying, because I think it's gotten ridiculous, you know. I don't like the idea of monitoring. I just think it's wrong. And political correctness is a bug, to me. It's a pain.

LK: Good luck, man. We're out of time.

LT: Thank you very much. Thank you.

LK: Excited, Lyle?

LT: Oh, absolutely. Absolutely.

LK: The lovers. Thank you both.

Mike Tyson

Tyson was born in a dismal section of Brooklyn, on June 30, 1966. He became a street tough who ended up in the state reformatory, where he was introduced to Cus D'Amato, one of the best fight trainers in America. D'Amato agreed to take custody of Tyson and molded him into a champion.

Tyson defeated all challengers, earning huge purses and living the high life with the likes of actress Robin Givens, whom he married in 1988. The union ended in divorce amid revelations of Tyson's violent nature. Soon after this, "Iron Mike" was convicted of raping a beauty queen and was sentenced a prison term. This interview took place from the Indiana State Penitentiary. Tyson was released on March 25, 1995.

"I'm not bitter, but, you know, this is one time I would like to have a little revenge."

ANNOUNCER: Welcome to *Larry King Live*. Tonight, Mike Tyson. A true rags-to-riches story, but the saddest of endings. From heavyweight champion of the world to prisoner number 922335. We talked with the former fighter from his prison in Indiana. . . .

LARRY KING: With the former heavyweight champion Mike Tyson. How do you adjust to this kind of life?

MIKE TYSON: You never adjust to this. You never adjust. That's—that's what it's designed to do. I believe—and I've seen this—prison is designed to have you adjust, have you adjust to being an animal, . . . I mean, this is a form of a circus, an animal-taming-like environment. And we say we have to adjust in order to survive. But, in any kind of environment that you're in, even though you're outside, anybody that actually obeys authority is not actually free.

LK: So is it designed, then, to keep you in place?

MT: More so, yeah.

LK: Okay. It's supposed to produce a citizen who comes out better than when he went in. Will it do that?

MT: Not in my opinion. . . . It doesn't rehabilitate you, more so *de*habilitates you, because I find myself—

LK: Dehabilitates.

MT: —because I find myself doing things that I never dreamed I'm capable of doing.

LK: Like?

MT: Or saying things I never think I'd be capable of saying.

LK: Like?

MT: Well, you know, you just basically respond to somebody in a way that's not as pleasant as it would normally be, say, outside . . .

LK: In other words, you're treated less than a human?

MT: Yeah, we have those days. We have those not-to-be-human-treated days.

LK: And is that at the whim of people?

MT: You know, maybe you want to evaluate, since you've never been n this predicament.

LK: Never.

MT: Just say you have somebody . . . humiliate you. Say somebody grabbed you and just put you on the ground, and held you there, and just— You can't get up when you want to get up.

LK: And that can happen any time?

MT: Basically, yeah.

LK: So that's—well, this is a twenty-four hour—

MT: Yeah, but you have to understand that. Do you do any writing?

LK: Sure.

MT: Sometimes you could be in your room writing. You want peace. And someone can come—an absolute stranger can come in, open your door, and start checking through your things, as you're writing. And going under your bunk and checking for—

LK: What are they looking for?

MT: I don't know, contraband, drugs, and—worse than that. It comes to a state where you act as if they're not even there, and you just continue to write.

LK: In other words, you tune it out?

MT: Yeah. I never tune it out, though. I always—for some reason, I have to rebel some kind of way. I only do that to keep my state of mind, make myself believe I'm still human. I just have to rebel. Sometimes there's repercussions from it, but I just have to.

LK: Is there any, Mike, self-blame? Is there any time you say, "I caused what happened. Even though I may be innocent, there's a part of me that caused me to be here"?

MT: There's no doubt about it. We write our own story in life. Whatever we do, whatever good we do in life, we get good in return. Whatever ill we do, we get ill in return. There's no doubt about it.

LK: So you think you're paying for something now?

MT: Well, I think I used bad judgment, and I mean, I had to deal with the circumstances, that I don't believe was normally fair circumstances. But, regardless of the circumstances, that I have to deal with.

LK: So there's no bitterness? Or is there?

MT: I'm not bitter, but, you know, this is one time I would like to have a little revenge. You know, I mean, I always go from this perspective. Whatever happens, you know what I mean, and sometimes you hit me with your best shot, and we see how to handle it. But when the same thing happens to you, you must always remember never to take it personal. I never take this personal. And that's how I look at my life. I just never take it personal, because eventually, one day, we'll grow old and we die, and then we won't have to worry about what anyone thinks or says about us any longer.

LK: How about the anger at the—the woman?

MT: That's— I'm not angry. I'm not angry at her, just— I just despise her actions.

LK: But not angry?

MT: No.

LK: In other words, you don't want to see her harmed?

MT: No, not at all. You know, I mean, it wouldn't bring me any benefit to see her harmed or hurt, but it just . . . And just the fact—you know, I mean, for somebody to take someone's life, you know, you really never know until you actually spend the amount of time in prison. This is only two years for me. And you realize there are vicious people. We use the word *vicious*, like a vicious person, but vicious is malice. And it just obliviates someone's life and their family's life.

LK: The thought outside would be that Mike Tyson, even in here, is king of the hill. He's former heavyweight champ. The correctional office must respect him. The warden must, I mean, respect the athletic ability. There must be a sense of admiration here.

MT: Well, because I'm Mike Tyson, former heavyweight champion of the world, that gives them more reason to despise me. You must understand, we're not in New York City, where I've roamed, and Los Angeles or Paris, where I used to roam the streets, buying everyone champagne and going in the clubs and living a gay life. I'm just saying we're in a very lethargic type of atmosphere, where there's a great deal of people that are confused, because they don't—they've never been around someone like me. They've never hardly experienced being around minorities in general. So you know, I mean, they look at me kind of funny, but they also despise me.

LK: Despise?

MT: Exactly.

LK: No one holds you in awe?

MT: No.

LK: How old are you now?

MT: Twenty-seven.

LK: That's very young. Very young. You feel very young?

MT: I feel great.

LK: You do?

MT: Yeah.

LK: Before we talk about the champ . . . Give me the schedule. Like, what time they get you up here.

MT: I go to school at eight o'clock, and after eight o'clock, we come back at three-fifteen, and we go to rec. And it's just very—I mean—

LK: Same thing every day?

MT: —mundane type situation every day.

LK: What time do you go to bed?

MT: Eleven o'clock, eleven-thirty.

LK: Do they let you—? If you want to wake up in the middle of the night and read, can you?

MT: Yeah, we do that. You have to read in a very dark, dim light. I guess that's the torture chamber, like, you know, in old Spain, in the— They used to have those lights stay on all night, and I guess it was designed to make you go crazy.

LK: You have gotten a lot into reading, right?

MT: Yeah.

LK: Why?

MT: I don't know. Know what? I used to read only boxing, I mean, boxing magazines. And then, from reading the boxing magazines, you may read about—someone— a great writer may have quoted a fighter, and he may have been very friendly. Because George Bernard Shaw, believe it or not, was very friendly with Gene Tunney. You know what I mean? And then that—that just made—

LK: Great writers are attracted to fighters. Always have been.

MT: I never knew that. I never knew that.

LK: Norman Mailer was intrigued with boxing.

MT: I knew that. . . . But I read a guy by the name of Homer, and he wrote about a guy, Achilles, and Hector, and he wrote about that war. Even though it was so many years ahead of his time, it's been passed down, and he's told the story. And I'm sure that things have been exchanged from all those years, but the story he says is, like, as if he was there. And I just like reading. I like reading about the writers and the boxers, how they have so much in common.

LK: I think Pete Hamill wrote in *Esquire* that you were reading the classics.

MT: Yeah.

LK: Like, you mentioned Homer. Are you reading others?

MT: Yeah, I read quite a few of them.

LK: And modern novels, too?

MT: Not too many. Not too many. If someone—a modern author sends me his book, then I'll read it.

LK: What do you do with your mind, in a place of confinement? You know, they confine everything but your mind. You can't confine someone's mind.

MT: And I think that's the only state of you that's actually free at all. Even when you're out in the streets, it's the only thing, because, as we know, we have neutrons in our brain. And our brain's—our body's only purpose is to carry our brain. It's just to carry our brain. And from that perspective, I believe that we live for our brain to absorb knowledge, because there's really no wise men in this world, because, as you know, knowledge is just everlasting. The only wise man is God. So I believe we have to look for God within ourselves, and it's just common sense.

LK: Have you found a new faith out of this?

MT: Meaning what?

LK: Did you change faiths? Did you change your opinion of faith?

MT: No. I just always had a great deal of belief. I was very confused with God, because I was in—I was in a world where everything was material to me. So if I didn't see God, I couldn't believe—how could I actually believe God? I was almost in the same mentality of the drug dealer. His god was money. His god was what he believed in—the bullet, the gun. Not that I believed in killing or shooting, but I believed more like finance, and what the finance could bring you. But then again, you have to just use something that's very simple, like you look at an eagle, he could be three hundred feet in the air, and he could see a field mouse. And we can't see a field mouse if he's ten feet away from us. So, if he could see a field mouse from up here, our eyes are not properly programmed for us to see God. Maybe God is not meant for us to see, but he's there. . . .

[*Commercial break*]

LK: We left the subject of religion during the break and started to talk about Joe
Louis being buried in Arlington Cemetery. And you are a great admirer, I know,
of Joe Louis, whose son wrote a book about him. And then you mentioned some
fighter whose grave you'd like to visit.

MT: Yeah, it was a fighter by the name of Jack Blackburn. He was Joe Louis's trainer.
And he was a great fighter also. He never won a title, and the reason why is
because another fighter at that time, who was named Joe Ganes, was just magnificent. No one could touch him. He was impossible to beat.

LK: All right, so you have faith in a god, right?

MT: Allah, yes.

LK: Allah. Now, you were raised Catholic.

MT: Yes.

LK: That's been a switch, hasn't it?

MT: Yes.

LK: How did that happen? Did that happen here?

MT: Yeah. You know what, let's go back to Catholic. I was raised Catholic, basically, in
my home in Brooklyn. But at that particular time, I was running the streets.
Religion never had no impact on me. Then I met Don King. Then he basically
put me in a situation, a state of religion he thought would be good. But I was—I
was—I was champ of the world. I was in another state.

LK: You didn't need that jazz.

MT: I didn't need that stuff. And, plus, I didn't understand it. So being in here put me
in a confinement, put me in a situation to understand Islam, to become a
Muslim, and be proud of becoming a Muslim, and to know the situation of the
Muslims in this world, that we're becoming extinct, and because other Muslims
are allowing it to happen. But you must understand, there's always—there's religion, but there's always a contradiction in religion, where you look at one set of
people who are supposed to have the same belief as another set, but they preach
totally different. Well, who are we to say who is wrong? Who are we to doubt
someone else's faith?

LK: What do you think of what's going on out there in the world, with the Farrakhans
and the like?

MT: I—personally, as a personal man, you know what I mean, people differ with me—
I absolutely love Farrakhan. I don't know the gentleman by the name of Khalid
Muhammad. But Farrakhan, as a person, I love Farrakhan. And it's very easy for
a person to judge someone for what they say, but a real wise man—a real wise
man would never have ill feelings of the speaker, but they take in heed what he
says. If what he said is true, you know what I mean, you must correct yourself.
And if it's not true, you must prevent it from happening.

LK: But if he's wrong, you should correct him.

MT: If the man is wrong, then what he says has no significance.

LK: You don't carry around harsh feelings based on race, do you?

MT: No.

LK: Did you ever?

MT: Out of ignorance, yes.

LK: So, out of ignorance, you were once, like, anti-white, or anti-Jew, or anti—

MT: No, no, never that, because I wouldn't know—by looking at a white person, I
wouldn't know if anyone in here is Jewish or Irish, Catholic, or Italian. You know

what I mean? It's just that we don't know. We don't know. And we're influenced. And that's why I believe that people are so much—have to differ with Mr. Farrakhan because the Minister—they're afraid that the Minister can control somebody's thinking. Just like some people in the media control the thinking of people. They feel now they have to compete with somebody for the minds of these people. And he, perhaps, is giving them a run for their money, without the sophistication that they have, using the television, using the cameras.

LK: So, you think he frightens them?

MT: He makes them uneasy, yeah. I believe that.

LK: Yourself, what do you—what do you miss the most?

MT: Oh, man, you just asked me. I don't know. I never think about anything.

LK: You don't think about women?

MT: I had a problem with that at one time, when I first came here. . . .

LK: Do you miss bonding? Do you miss other people, touching, holding, things people miss?

MT: Every time I was in that situation where I would bond with somebody, it had no other significance but to bond. And after that, it was emptiness. So, what is the purpose of really thinking about it? Because it would be the same as being in prison, if there's no actual feelings there, because then again, we go on a subject really we don't know. What is love? Who knows what is love? You know what I mean, I'm not in a position to say what is love.

LK: But, you've experienced love, attention—you had that wonderful lady that helped raise you, right?

MT: Yeah, but we're talking about love from a different perspective. You said women. You didn't say family.

LK: All right, romantic love. Do you miss romantic love?

MT: Maybe. But what is love? Love is—love is like a game. Love is competition. It's competition. Most people— Who is gorgeous? A guy, or a woman, maybe, love comes to them all the time, because they attract love. But they never fought for love. What are they prepared to do for love? You know what I mean? Love is a situation where you must be prepared to do something, because you have something that lovely, somebody could want to challenge you for it. And if you've never been competitive enough—the slightest struggle—you're going to give in.

LK: Obviously, you're gaining better control of your own total environment here. What about food? Do you miss certain foods? Do you miss certain—no? I'm trying to put the audience into what would it be like not to have the things they have every day.

MT: You're in the situation, and there's people out on the street who have been to prison, and perhaps a lot worse than the situation I'm in. But you just—you become so much attached to you. It's very much attached to you. . . . There's somebody, a writer by the name—he's a playwriter [*sic*] named Tennessee Williams—said, "You must distrust one another," because that's the only way we could protect each other from betrayal. And I'm a great believer in that. I believe everyone that's involved in my life, one day or other, will betray me. I believe that. I totally believe that. I just totally and all am believing that. And other people say, "No, no, no," but that's what I believe.

LK: If you believe that, you must be unhappy.

MT: No, I'm not unhappy. I'm just aware of my circumstances.

LK: Not unhappy about the fact that you don't have ultimate faith in other people?

MT: But Allah. Allah is the only faith. Because, you must understand, from someone being in prison—maybe I wasn't astute enough to learn it outside. But being in prison, I know human beings are capable of anything. That's why, when a cop arrests one of his friends, he said, "Bill, you've got to be kidding." Bill said—well—he doesn't even call him Bill, Mr. Johnson—he doesn't even call him Dave no more, it's Mr. Johnson, because he knows—he's taught that human beings are capable of doing anything, because we have no control over ourselves. We don't have no simple control of our feelings or emotions.

[*Commercial break*]

LK: On June 13th, Alan Dershowitz, friend of mine, says we got another hearing coming for you, in Indiana. They're going to hear the appeal. I think—let's get this right—that you claim that the prosecutors knew the woman who accused you was also considering suing you. Are you hopeful of this hearing?

MT: Hey, I don't hold my breath for this, okay? I don't hold my breath for this.

LK: Have you been disappointed? Did you think you'd be overturned?

MT: Listen. Can I tell you something? . . . I accept the good, expect the worst, okay? When the good happens, it happens. You know what I mean? But . . . if someone puts me in here, and the more polite I am to them and the kinder, the more I lay back, that's not going to make them take their foot off [my] neck, it's going to make you want to crush them more. If you're in a fight with somebody and you hurt him, the objective of the fight is not to back off and let him recoup. The objective is to smash him to oblivion.

LK: But the law says, if you made a mistake, you—

MT: Whose law says that? The law of the United States?

LK: Yeah.

MT: Well, who controls the law of the United States?

LK: Legislatures—

MT: Yeah, legislatures that have their own agenda. Laws mean nothing. You give me the currency of a country, and you can have—you can make all the rules in the world. And that's all that matters, who is in control.

LK: So, then, you will be surprised if this hearing comes out in your favor?

MT: Absolutely.

LK: Even though you have a very upbeat lawyer. You know, Mr. Dershowitz is—

MT: He's something else, isn't he?

LK: Got to like him, right?

MT: Hey, you know what I mean, he's a good man. He does his job very well. But we're dealing with a circumstance way beyond him doing his job. We're going beyond the facts. When you go with the facts—the facts is something that's evidence. But you go beyond the facts, and what makes it evidence? What makes it evidence that I'm in here is bull shenanigans. I should not be in here.

LK: Do you remain close to Don King?

MT: Don has to know—my only alliance and my true honesty is to Allah. And not to no other Muslim, not to no set of Muslims that come—he's a Muslim now. He's with—you know, my loyalty is with other individuals who are loyal to me. My first loyalty, my first obligation, is to Allah, not to anyone else that have anything—not black, white, anything. You know what I mean? It's Allah.

LK: When Ali fought for Allah—he said he fought for Allah—right?—when he converted. I knew Malcolm X when Malcolm X was part of the conversion of Muhammad Ali. Does this have any bearing on your fighting again?

MT: I'm in a state now where, you know, I love fighting. It's not that I can't do anything else, it's just that fighting is all I wanted to ever do. I never wanted to do anything else.

LK: So, you'll do it again?

MT: I would love to do it. And there's nothing wrong with it.

LK: So you will fight again?

MT: Exactly. But my situations of my life have to be conducted totally different than it was before.

LK: Like?

MT: Just, basically, before, the Mike Tyson that was out there before, conducting business, was just a child. I won a title. I was just twenty, just turned twenty. I won a title. I was just a child, and I had no chance to cultivate myself, because if I did cultivate, I didn't cultivate in a proper direction, because everything was chaos. I was fighting with a wife, with managers, you know what I mean, with promoters and managers fighting. I was torn between everybody, because I wanted to be loyal to everyone. I never had a chance to be loyal to myself.

LK: All right. Therefore, you will fight again, but it will be a different head, a different person, in that sense. Certainly, we're fighting with a different concept now.

MT: There has to be. If we don't, there's no way we can survive.

LK: But you're an athlete, and an athlete still wants to win. Do you think you still have that determination? Do you think you still have that get-off-the-floor-and-get-up? Sometimes that can change.

MT: Are you talking about my skills?

LK: Yeah.

MT: Let me explain something, too, that you may not even know about me, okay, because I'm sure that we—this is our first time. You see, there's some people that do things very well, you know what I mean? Like yourself, and like others—doctors, lawyers. I'm a specialist in what I do. . . . What I do, I'm a specialist, you know what I mean? There's people that's specialists in Islam, Christianity. But in this field, what I do, I'm a specialist in it. I'm just a specialist. There's no doubt about it. And, allow—forgive me for being vain—but I'm just expressing the fact: I'm the best in what I do. I'm just the total best. There are other guys out there that are great. They are great fighters. But they could do anything else. This is *all* I want to do.

LK: All right. But you can't do it forever.

MT: No.

LK: So is your goal to be heavyweight champion again?

MT: If the time is probably right—who knows? I may die tomorrow. Some one of these guys may hit me over the head with a weight. You know what I mean? We can't predict what we're going to do in the future, you know? I would just like to take one day at a time.

LK: Riddick Bowe said to me—Riddick Bowe's manager said to me that when you get out of prison—and he expects that to be, with time off, probably within a year—he expects that you will fight, and that if you eventually get into a fight with whoever is heavyweight champion, it will be the largest Pay-Per-View, the

MT: biggest draw, the biggest-attended fight—whether it's Michael Moorer, Holyfield, Bowe—ever. Would you agree with that, financially?

MT: I don't know. I don't need much, you know what I mean? Less—less is more to me. I've been through that before. I've been through the big—big, super—super mega-bucks before. Maybe—you know, people say it's the state I am now, but I'm just more conscious of my security within myself. You know what I mean? You know what I mean?

LK: So that doesn't intrigue you, the thought of a big—big—biggest money fight ever?

MT: No. It would intrigue me more than that just to win. Intrigue me more than just the—I would just like to win. And I think that's probably why I am the way I am. It's against everything Allah believes.

[*Commercial break*]

LK: Since you're a fan, let's look at the division a little. Are you surprised that Moorer beat Holyfield?

MT: I haven't seen the fight, but I was surprised, yeah. Because, from what I remember of Michael Moorer, and I remember Evander Holyfield, if I was to put the two fighters in my mind and let them fight, I would think Holyfield would win.

LK: There are thoughts Moorer said he may quit. . . . He said that he doesn't need it, either. He said there's other things in his life.

MT: Well, then, it's a decision—do what he wants. But I'm sure there's people that have his ear that won't allow that to happen.

LK: He will fight?

MT: That's only on him. I'm just giving you my opinion on the issue.

LK: Who is the best of those out there?

MT: Man, there are so many good fighters now. There's this new gentleman from Detroit, Jerry McClullen—I believe the name, McLean, I've seen some tapes of him, it's from highlights, and he seemed like a dynamo.

LK: —Lewis?

MT: Leonard [Lenox] Lewis, yeah, he seemed like he was doing well also.

LK: Do you like Riddick Bowe?

MT: I love Riddick Bowe.

LK: You're friends.

MT: Yeah.

LK: Did you grow up together?

MT: We went to school together.

LK: In Brooklyn?

MT: Yeah.

LK: What a story! Two heavyweight champs in the same school.

MT: Yeah, but it was like that before. Like, in the '20s, guys grew up together, like, in the same neighborhood, like Benny Leonard and Sammy Mendel used to fight against—they're from the same—you know—

LK: New York club fights.

MT: Yeah. They all knew each other.

LK: Would you fight Bowe?

MT: I don't know. Can I tell you something? That's one thing that I would take different. I'd probably, at this stage of my life, and being as conscious as I am, I don't think I would. I don't think I would.

LK: Because you like him?

MT: There's a lot of respect, see? And people wouldn't understand that.

LK: So, the purpose is to hurt him, and you would have to hurt Riddick Bowe in order to beat him, and you don't want to hurt him?

MT: He would have to try to hurt me.

LK: So why should two friends hurt each other?

MT: That's what I'm trying to say now. It's just too disrespectful. The only reason you put your hand on somebody, even in a street fight, if you're conscious, is because you have no respect for him. Like, kids fight because we don't know any better. But if grown men fight, and if they're conscious, the only reason I'll put my hand on you is because I have no respect for you, if we have a fight. And I feel that's the same way in—and it goes between personal and business. Before, I used to say it's only business. But I think it's personal, when two people who admire one another like that fight.

LK: Do you want to hate your opponent?

MT: No, because it's discipline. Listen, how could you be upset with a person, you don't know me from a can of paint?

LK: So we're fighting. How could I be mad at you?

MT: That's why you have to be a highly disciplined athlete, to understand this is a *job*. I mean, regardless of who it was, this is a job. We have to fight. But I just find it—you know, I mean, people may say it's unprofessional. I just can't picture myself fighting Riddick Bowe. He's been more than a gentleman to me, and I have done things that was out of gentleman character in the past to him. And he's just—

LK: But fighting—fighting Moorer or Lewis or Holyfield: no problem?

MT: No, no problem at all.

LK: When do you expect to get out? Let's say appeals don't work.

MT: Hey, next year.

LK: Next year?

MT: June, perhaps.

LK: With time off, right?

MT: No, with June. I will leave with June. This next June coming up, or March. I believe that's the end of my sentence.

LK: So, what is the first thing you're going to do?

MT: I want to take a bath.

LK: You don't take a bath here?

MT: No, we take showers.

LK: Oh, you're a bath-taker?

MT: Yeah.

LK: There's two kinds of people in the world, bath-takers or shower-takers.

MT: I'm a bath-taker.

LK: First thing is take a bath. And go where? Where do you want to go?

MT: Hey, man, I would lie to you if I tell you anything after that. I would lie to you.

LK: Because you don't know?

MT: Yeah, because I'd have a totally different perception of even sex, you know what I mean? I feel that sex is with somebody that accomplished, so you have to earn—you have to reach a pinnacle for sex. You have to work for something— something has to be accomplished, in order— I always look at that as something as a reward. You know what I mean? I don't look at sex as just, you just have sex out of the blue.

LK: I wasn't thinking of that. I was thinking of—

MT: But *I* was. I was.

LK: You're not going to live in Los Angeles, or New York?

MT: No. No.

LK: Do you miss anything about that lifestyle?

MT: No. Know why? At first, come in here, but once you're in here and you're under the circumstances that you are, you find out what that life thought about you, and what the people that are involved with that life, that was with you at one time, thought about you. And you learn to lose—I don't know—maybe love, or you become disappointed in the lifestyle and people that were involved in that lifestyle. So you don't want to go back to it.

LK: Do you keep in touch with people all the time?

MT: Very few.

LK: Very few. You can make collect calls out of here, right?

MT: Yeah.

LK: You can't receive any calls.

MT: No. But some— One day, someone calls me back. One day, I put the phone down, and somebody—I don't know who it is—they called me back, and I picked up the phone. Everybody looked and thought I was crazy.

LK: You broke the system.

MT: No, I didn't break the system. They asked the operator to break the system.

LK: How often can you see visitors?

MT: Usually every day, or once every fourteen days for the same visitor. Like, if you were to visit me now—

LK: I can't come back for fourteen days.

MT: Fourteen days, yeah.

LK: Do you stay in shape? Obviously, you look in shape. Do you work out?

MT: Yeah, I do basic shadow boxing and running, because I—I love it, man.

LK: There's no boxing in here, is there?

MT: No. I just love—I love to work out.

LK: There's a new crime bill, and one of the things being proposed is stopping gymnasiums in prison—that exercise equipment and the like is a plus. It shouldn't be given to a convict.

MT: Listen, you must understand . . . for instance, I have a class that I go to. I go to— it's economics class, all right? And in this class— Is it economics or is it government? Well, regardless. And it shows the three systems. It shows the Japanese system, it shows the German system, and it shows the American system, and talks about pre-school kids. When kids get out of high school, and they look for a job, they have a contract—Japanese people—with the government. They have a contract with—Mitsubishi and Toyota and Honda have contracts with the school. The smartest students are guaranteed jobs. And sometimes they come to the principal and say, "Come on, we need more students." And he's negotiating students for jobs. And this is like a deal: "Well, no, you can't get him. No, we're not going to give—we don't have that many students. Unless you guarantee more jobs, and then we can skip some up." And in Japan, the parents are involved with the education, what school they go to, what job they get. And it's just an involved environment. In America, big business is prisons. They make rules for prisoners. Of course they're not going to let us—now they're trying to stop, I believe, education in prison, as well. So, they're going to get a prisoner here, they're going to get him adapted to this circumstance, then when he go back to society, he won't be able to cope. So, he has to come back. It's a revolving-door situation.

LK: And you think they want him to come back?

MT: Oh, it's finance: $40,000 a year, $30,000 a year, do you think you would like—say someone has thirty years, and you get $30,000 a year [to keep him in jail]. And that's over a million dollars: $1.4–$1.5 million, so to speak. And, what do you think? Do you think that the government is going to give that up?

LK: Wouldn't you say a gym is necessary, though? I mean, just basic health?

MT: There is nothing necessary but God. You know, I mean, we—they may think *they* need it, from time to time. But, there's nothing necessary. There's nothing that you need [other] than [a] fine body and a free mind, the most powerful element in the world, because you could be what you want to be all day long.

LK: You read Arthur Ashe's *Days of Grace*, right? . . . In fact, I think you were so moved, you—it's one of the most important books in your life.

MT: Only thing . . . he didn't like confrontation.

LK: That surprised you, because he was a great competitor.

MT: Yeah. And I'm different. I go right for your throat.

LK: Oh, I know that.

MT: I just go right for your—not only in fighting, but just in life. I just go right for your throat, especially if there's a point where you violated somebody else's feelings, or mine. You know what I mean? And that's why I like him, because he—he was human. You know what I mean? He was a human. He went through life with a human outlook on life.

LK: I'll give you a human thing you must miss: cheering.

MT: People cheering for me?

LK: You must miss that.

MT: Can I tell you something, though? I cheer for myself a hundred million times a day, in my mind. To me, I'm my biggest fan. There's nothing in the world better than me. So, I don't think about that. Those guys really don't know what they're cheering for. I know the total me. And I know why—why they should be cheering, but they don't know. They cheer for the knockout. That's all. They cheer for the knockout and the performance. I cheer because I know who I am in here.

LK: They're not cheering you, the man; they're cheering you, the punch. . . . One other thing. Will you go right into training?

MT: I don't even make that assessment yet. I don't even conceive leaving this place yet.

LK: Okay, but twenty-eight, twenty-nine, you're going to be in your prime, right? That's an athlete's prime, when you get out of here. I mean, you should be at ripe prime of your fighting ability.

MT: I'm in the prime, as far as my thinking capacity. And sometimes I shadow box and say, "God, I didn't know that much. I didn't know this." And I think—and it falls into place naturally, doesn't it? And I don't know, I would love to fight, under the proper circumstances. But, like I said, I've been robbed and abused and taken advantage of all my life, and lied to. I'm not going back into that same predicament again. You know what I mean? Eventually, I might have a family, and I might have children. And I have to set an example for that.

LK: And what do you want to do when the greatest skill you have, to box, goes away?

MT: We'll deal with that when that happens. You know what I mean? Eventually, something is going to be dealt with about that. But the main objective is to take care of what happens. And that's just to make sure the people that I care about are loved dearly and taken care of.

LK: Thanks, Mike.

MT: Thank you, sir.

Jean Harris

"This was the only man in my life I ever loved, and I think of him every day. I wake up thinking about him."

In 1966, Jean Harris was a forty-three-year-old divorcée and the director of the Middle School near Philadelphia when she met cardiologist Herman Tarnower. He pursued her, they became inseparable, and they were engaged. When Tarnower abruptly broke off the engagement, Harris continued to see him even after he had taken up with another woman. She moved to Washington, D.C., in 1976 as Headmistress of the Madeira School. Two years later, Tarnower published his bestselling Complete Scarsdale Medical Diet, *and he and Harris continued to date, although he repeatedly humiliated her by flaunting affairs with others.*

On March 10, 1980, Harris armed herself with a handgun, confronted Tarnower, and shot him—inadvertently, she maintains. Harris was sentenced to fifteen years to life imprisonment. She was paroled for health reasons after serving twelve years.

This interview took place just as the O. J. Simpson trial was getting under way in Los Angeles.

LARRY KING: The latest piece of evidence seized upon by O. J. Simpson's lawyers is, believe it or not, ice cream. We've learned that Nicole Simpson stopped by a Ben & Jerry's on her way home and, hours later, partially melted ice cream was found near the body. That discovery could affect estimates of when the two murders took place. Hard to believe that the fate of a public figure might hang on such tiny, ironic details.

Our guest tonight knows what it's like to go from a position of great respect to the world of evidence, lawyers, and suspicion all around. Jean Harris was headmistress of the prestigious Madeira School. Her trial for the 1980 murder of her lover, "Scarsdale Diet" doctor Herman Tarnower, caused a national sensation.

Jean Harris, however, stayed productive during twelve years in prison, teaching parenting classes to inmates. She was paroled last year and now she campaigns for the rights of inmates with children. She joins us in Washington to talk about the O. J. Simpson case and, of course, a lot more.

You were paroled, and for a sickness reason?

JEAN HARRIS: I think so. Yeah.

LK: How long was your sentence, Jean?

JH: Fifteen to life.

LK: So did you expect, by the way, to get out sooner?

JH: No, indeed, I didn't. Never did. But I always kept trying. I mean, you know, I tried. I applied for clemency four times and got it on the fourth try, but I think my health had a great deal to do with it.

LK: How is your health?

JH: Great. I have a dog that takes very good care of me, takes me walking.

LK: What was the matter? Did you have heart surgery?

JH: Quadrilateral bypass.

LK: Know it well.

JH: Do you?

LK: Oh, yeah. Came through it well. Did you come through it?

JH: Well, we're both in good shape, yeah.

LK: In the club.

JH: It's amazing that they can slit you open like that and have you come out feeling as well as I do.

LK: Would you describe yourself as empathetic with O. J. Simpson, as you look at all that's going on? I mean, you went through similar things—different circumstances, but how do you feel?

JH: Well, I don't envy him what he's about to go through. I can't say that I feel empathy, because I have a strong feeling he may be the one who did it, but I think he's going to have a very rough trial, because the people trying him are so sure that he's guilty that they will stop at nothing to prove it. And I think that was true of my case, too. You know, not to the extent that his is, but they manufactured some things. I mean, I—

LK: You even had a thing with a glove, right?

JH: They found a black glove. My dog—my dog, Cider—when we were walking, had found an old black glove about a month before, and she was very proud of it, and she kept it with her all the time. And she spent a lot of time driving with me every time I went out. She loved the car. So the black glove got into the back seat of my car. It was filthy dirty. It was covered with dried saliva of the dog, and half of the thumb was ripped away. And when they searched my car, they said to me, "Where is the gun?" and I said, "It's either up in the bathtub or in the car." I couldn't remember, at that point, what I'd done. So they rushed out and found it in the car and took it, and I guess because they didn't have a search warrant for the car, they were told by the judge, "That is all you can take. Nothing else can be removed from the car." Well, there wasn't anything in the car that had anything to do with the trial, anyway. So part way through the trial, suddenly, the district attorney began saying, "She walked up the dark, winding staircase, wearing a black glove." And I said to Joel, "I wasn't wearing a black glove. I wasn't wearing any gloves at all."

LK: Joel is your lawyer.

JH: Yeah.

LK: They're charging you with premeditated murder.

JH: Premeditated murder. And to begin with, all you have to do is look at it and know if you're going to be trying to keep your fingerprints off of a gun, you wouldn't wear a glove that had the thumb missing.

LK: So this glove was introduced in evidence?

JH: It was in the back of my car, and it was introduced in evidence. They said it was up in the doctor's room. It was never in the room. I never wore it, and it had nothing to do with the thing. The district attorney knew where it had been found, knew that it had been found in my car, after a court order that nothing was to be taken, knew I wasn't wearing it, and knew it was never up in the doctor's room, but he repeated it again and again and again.

LK: So when O. J.'s lawyer said that it's possible that a glove was dropped somewhere, while you're not saying it was, you're not shocked.

JH: I said to my son that night, "David, I'd feel a lot better about that glove if it'd been found before the police got there," because I have no way of knowing, but I suspect everybody that has anything to do with prosecuting that case, because trials are a game of winners and losers. They are not a search for the truth. That becomes almost incidental, especially in a high-profile case like this.

LK: In other words, the district attorney doesn't want someone else to be guilty.

JH: He doesn't want to lose, or she doesn't want to lose that case. She's out to win.

LK: So in your case, while it was acknowledged that you were the one that did the shooting, any other circumstances relating to it, they were uninterested in.

JH: That's right.

LK: They were interested in getting a conviction.

JH: You know, Larry, in his final summing up—whatever you call it, I can't remember right now—he kept saying to the jury, "She was so mad. She threw clothes. She was knocking over the furniture. She was throwing. She was tossing." And the pictures that they took that night in Hy's dressing room—I had thrown a box of curlers, and there was a picture there of just a blank floor and a box of curlers. Up on a shelf were a lot of clothes, carefully folded, ready to be packed to go away. They were sitting there. Three months into the trial, we discovered quite by accident, because of a slip of one their witnesses' tongue, that they had two hundred pictures that they had never shown us that were taken in that room. And one of the pictures was one that they were obviously planning to use. It was taken back in the dressing room, and they had taken all the clothes that were folded the night they took that other picture and thrown them all over the floor. But what they didn't know when they took it—until they developed it—was that a man who had never come to the house until three weeks after Hy's death was just walking into the room as they took it, so you could see part of his face and you could identify him. So they couldn't produce that for the jury, and it was never shown.

LK: So if you were saying something to Mr. Shapiro [O. J. Simpson's attorney], you would say, "The prosecution will do anything," in your opinion.

JH: Well, Mr. Shapiro already knows that probably as well as I do, but not with the same emotional feeling that I do.

LK: But, in other words, you would put nothing past—

JH: No, I wouldn't.

LK: —someone who wants to win a case. But defense lawyers do the same, right? They want to win.

JH: They do, but I know that Joel didn't make up stuff and try to put stuff in places that it wasn't.

LK: How do you feel, though, Jean, knowing that you did take a life? I mean, I've never—

JH: Oh, I feel—it's a tragedy to me. This was the only man in my life I ever loved, and I think of him every day. I wake up thinking about him. Of course, I feel terrible about it. It was a struggle, and I—you know, I don't want to go through that again.

LK: You still love him.

JH: Some days, I say it out loud, and other days, I don't love him. There are days when I think, "Damn it, Hy, you could have—you could have saved both of us."

LK: Do you have remorse?

JH: Of course I have remorse! How could you not have remorse? I've lived with it. I live with it all my life. There isn't a day that I don't think about how—and feel the loss.

[*Commercial break*]

LK: What did you think when you saw Detective [Mark] Fuhrman testifying?

JH: When Fuhrman said that those four policemen went to O. J. Simpson's house because they were worried about hostages and was asked directly, "Did you consider him a suspect?" and he said "No," that was the end of Mr. Fuhrman, as far as I was concerned, because you know and I know anyone with the brains of a house plant knew that O. J. Simpson was a suspect when they went there. My son watched that and called me that night and said, "Mother, does it all look familiar?" And I said, "It certainly does." Those policemen have been told exactly what to say, and they were told, "Whatever you say, you can say anything you want, you were afraid your grandmother was in there, but don't, for God's sakes, say that he was a suspect because—"

LK: Help us through a trial. You're on trial. Were you worried that you'd be convicted? What went on in your— How long did the trial last?

JH: It started in October, and I was found guilty the twenty-eighth of February, so that was a long time.

LK: Did you have up and down feelings throughout?

JH: No, they were all down. I was so depressed then. I had been deeply depressed for two years. I had been given some strong drugs that I shouldn't have had by Dr. Tarnower for almost ten years, and I didn't know what they were, and I was too dumb to—I just was trusting, and I took them and—

LK: Tranquilizers?

JH: Uppers and downers. He had me on Desoxin once a day, which is sold on the street as Speed. I was told that by my lawyer when I—after Hy was gone. But I was really in such a state that I didn't think about what was going to happen. I was in a state of shock over what was being done and things that were being said in that trial that were patently untrue, that I know the district attorney knew were patently untrue, but he kept saying them anyway. I sometimes wonder if he doesn't really know in his heart that I didn't murder Hy.

LK: All right. You didn't *murder* him, but you *killed* him.

JH: Yes, well, it was—

LK: Can you explain the difference?

JH: —my gun and we—and—well, we were struggling for a gun. I had it, raised it to my head—

LK: You were going to kill yourself.

JH: —to shoot myself. Hy grabbed it. A bullet went through his hand. And then he—he—oh, it's awful to go through this all again. Eventually, he got the gun away from me, and then I went and tried to get it back, and in the back-and-forth and fighting for this gun, he was—he was mortally wounded.

LK: Okay. Now, you know this happened. In your heart, you know it.

JH: Sure, I do.

LK: No one else was there.

JH: That's right.

LK: You know it.

JH: That's right.

LK: When they say "guilty," and you know you're not—

JH: It made very—well, I *felt* guilty. I knew that I had been responsible for his death. If I hadn't gone there with the gun, he would be alive. So I think I felt so much guilt and so depressed that I really didn't give a damn. It was hell to be alive inside or outside of prison, and for the first couple of years I was in there, I was on large quantities of Elavil, which I read the other day is maybe the reason I can't remember anything anymore. I don't know.

LK: Yeah, that's right. You do have memory loss.

JH: Oh, boy!

LK: But on the other hand, had Prozac been around then, you might have done a lot better, right?

JH: I don't know. I don't know. I've been told by a psychiatrist that putting me on the stand for eight days when I was— They tried to take the Desoxin away from me, and each time they did, I became so suicidal, they had to put me back on it. So all the time I was on the stand, I was taking a very strong drug.

LK: How did you lick addiction?

JH: I didn't know I was addicted. I never took any more than was prescribed to me.

LK: Yeah, but when you went to prison, they didn't give you any, right?

JH: No, they certainly didn't, but they gave me an awful lot of Elavil, and I slept half the time, and I never had a feeling that I couldn't cope without having it. As a matter of fact, as soon as I walked in—there'd been so much talk about this old druggie, that a prisoner approached me and said, "Now, just name the drug you want, and we'll get it for you for a price." Scared me to death. That more than anything, I think, probably got me off of wanting—even thinking about it. The last thing I want to do is start dealing drugs in prison.

LK: We all imagine captivity, but very few of us are ever faced with it. How do you—?

JH: More than you think. An awful lot of Americans have been in prison at some time or another, or in jail.

LK: How do you cope?

JH: Well, I was lucky, Larry, in many ways. For one thing, I like to be alone. I'm very much of a loner. But I've done so much talking publicly since I was arrested, you wouldn't know that I was a loner, but I was. I enjoy reading, and I like being away from people. I enjoy people, too, but I've spent a lot of time alone in my life, in my adult lifetime. And I was fortunate in that I could get books. I could get paper and pencil. And then I was fortunate that Sister Elaine Roulette has worked there for twenty-four years, and she made it possible for me to do something useful.

LK: You became kind of a leader in the prison, didn't you.

JH: No, no. Not in any sense of the word.

LK: We were reading that you were counseling other prisoners and—

JH: Well, you know, the papers do—

LK: Not true.

JH: No. When I first went in, I was the Bitch of Buchenwald, and then they decided that was kind of a boring story, and I became Florence Nightingale, and neither one of them was the case. I was a prisoner. I had a number, just like everybody else. And, boy, don't think they didn't remind me. "You ain't—you ain't shit. You got a number, just like me." And I was reminded of that each day. I was permitted to do some things, but it was in teaching. It wasn't in telling anybody what they were supposed to do, as far as the prison was concerned.

LK: Does the "celebrity prisoner" have an edge?

JH: No, I think a celebrity—you're suspect. Everybody is suspicious of you. I mean, the women took a long time before I could get their trust so that they would even listen to what was going on in the parenting class. And the C.O.'s, I think, got a particular amount of pleasure out of putting me down and letting me know that I was 81G98, and I think they all had a picture of me that was totally false.

[*Commercial break*]

LK: Now, you'll be on parole the rest of your life, do you think?

JH: That's what I've been told. That's what I've been told. It's kind of a silly waste of people's time, I think, but that's what I—

LK: You had to get permission to come here, right? Because you had to leave the state.

JH: Uh-huh.

LK: Did prison teach you anything? Did prison help you in any way?

JH: Well, you know, I would hate for anybody to be left with the idea that going to prison makes you a better person. In fact, it drives me crazy when anyone even suggests that. But my life is much richer for having been there, because I know a side of life that I would never have known.

LK: You didn't know from this when you were headmistress at Madeira, did you?

JH: Not only that, I didn't know it when I was growing up in Cleveland and going to a girls' college preparatory school. I went to a school where chewing gum and running in the halls were pretty big, important things for demerits, and now I hear people say, "We must give condoms to these kids in the high school," and it breaks my heart, but I think they're right. I think the number of illegitimate— well, there aren't illegitimate babies, but there are certainly a lot of mothers having babies that they can't take care of. I think the number of single parents in this country is one of the biggest problems we face, and I don't think we're doing half enough about it. I don't know all the things we can do, but certainly—

LK: How do they deal with sexual difficulties in a women's prison? How do they deal with lesbianism—and there's no conjugal visits, are there?

JH: Oh, yeah. There are conjugal visits. The only problem is you have to be married to get a conjugal visit, and about 9 percent of the women who go to prison are married.

LK: So 90 percent can't get a conjugal visit.

JH: That's right. You can't have a common-law husband come. It's got to be all written down and official. The visits that they have are visits with their children. We have— I keep talking about "we" as though I were still part of Bedford. I will be part of Bedford all my life, as far as my brain is concerned, and I still talk to the women.

LK: Do you ever go back?

JH: I haven't yet. I haven't gone back. I was going to at Christmastime, and then when I got there, I was told I didn't have enough signed permissions to get in. But anyway, I do talk to some of the women. They call me. I gave them my phone—

LK: If it happens to O. J., will it be triply difficult for him?

JH: Oh, I think so, yes.

LK: He'll be hassled a lot?

JH: I don't know. He's a big guy, and— I don't know that Tyson has been hassled, has he?

LK: No, but Tyson broods. I was in that prison and—

JH: Well, I'm sure— I don't think for a minute he won't brood, but, I mean, nobody's going to try to rape him, and that's what happens to a lot of the young kids that go to prison.

LK: When you're on trial is different than after you're convicted, right?

JH: Oh, yes.

LK: On trial, you have hope every day, and you were on bail, weren't you?

JH: Yeah, I was on bail.

[*Commercial break*]

LK: Our guest is Jean Harris. We're going to go to your phone calls. A place familiar to her—McLean, Virginia. Hello.

CALLER: [*McLean, Virginia*] Yes. I'd like to know Ms. Harris's thoughts on the death penalty. And has that changed after she was convicted of murder?

JH: Oh, I think it would have to have changed because I've met too many people who I think didn't belong in prison, for whom—who might have been guilty of something, but not guilty enough to have one of these mandated sentences where they stay there for fifteen years.

LK: And therefore, we can assume that innocent people have been executed.

JH: I don't see how we could have avoided— We're humans, and we can make mistakes.

LK: Bloomington, Minnesota, for Jean Harris. Hello.

CALLER: [*Bloomington, Minnesota*] Hi. Yes. Ms. Harris, first of all, I'm glad you're recovering well. And second of all, do you find the public response towards your ordeal that you went through is more positive or negative?

JH: It was so positive, it was overwhelming. I would say that in twelve years in prison, I can count on one hand the ugly letters that I received, and they were never signed. They were anonymous and counted for nothing. I think the fact that I had such a positive response is the reason I'm sitting here now instead of sitting in a cell tonight, because thousands and thousands and thousands of letters went in my behalf to the governor.

LK: You became a cause, a feminist cause, did you not?

JH: Actually, I don't know that. I only remember that Betty Friedan was asked what she thought of Jean Harris right after I went to prison, and she said, "I think she's a damn fool," and I said, "I think she can make a very strong case for that."

LK: Shana Alexander fought the good fight for you.

JH: Oh, Shana—Shana was—but Shana isn't a great feminist. She's not an active feminist. She does the deed, but she doesn't do all that talking.

LK: Did you expect, being Governor Cuomo and liberal and certainly a passionate liberal and an anti-execution man, certainly strong against the death penalty, would have been—did you expect to be commuted earlier?

JH: No, indeed, I didn't. And now, it was not half as traumatic for me to lose those petitions as it was for my kids, because they were sure I was going to win. They couldn't see how anyone could keep dear old Mom in prison, but—

LK: You weren't angry at the governor?

JH: No, I'm angry at him because he refuses—not from a personal standpoint—but there are 67,000 people in prison in New York state, and for him to give two people clemency—and one year, he didn't give any, and one year, a couple of years, he gave it to one person. You know that there has to be—the law of averages tells you that there have to be more than one or two people out of 67,000 that had a legitimate plea.

LK: Naples, Florida, for Jean Harris.

CALLER: [*Naples, Florida*] Yes. I'm sick and tired of hearing about the prosecution's tactics. I've watched Mr. Shapiro rubbing O. J.'s back over and over. I'm convinced that he would rub Adolf Eichmann's back if he were defending him.

LK: Why do you say that? How do you know that? How do you know that, sir?

CALLER: [*Naples, Florida*] How do I know it?

LK: Yeah. I mean, how do you know he would rub Adolf Eichmann's back?

CALLER: [*Naples, Florida*] Because that's my impression.

LK: Oh.

CALLER: [*Naples, Florida*] That's my impression.

LK: Well, wouldn't you want a defense—

CALLER: [*Naples, Florida*] Watching his tactics.

LK: If you were on trial, would you want a defense lawyer to be supportive of you, sir?

CALLER: [*Naples, Florida*] To a point.

LK: Just to a point? Other than that, you wouldn't want him to be supportive?

JH: Don't like to have your back rubbed?

LK: And you won't want to have your back tapped. All right, what do you read of that? Was your lawyer very supportive with you?

JH: Yes, he was. He was trying very hard. He wasn't very effective, but he was trying very hard. He was very kind to me, really.

LK: Halmstad, Sweden, hello.

CALLER: [*Halmstad, Sweden*] Hello to you, Larry. Mrs. Harris, during your trial, how did your friends react? Did they support you or turn their backs on you?

JH: They supported me. Within two weeks after Dr. Tarnower's death and I was indicted, over four hundred people had written or wired or called to ask to come and be character witnesses for me. This is one of the lucky things, though, for me. I think being old made it much easier for me to be in prison than to be young.

LK: You think it's going to be harder—let's say if O. J. had to go to prison, it would be harder for someone forty than someone fifty?

JH: Maybe not forty, because by forty, you've pretty well made your friends, and you know who your friends are. But I was fifty-seven when I went to prison, and I'd known people for thirty and forty years, and they weren't about to turn their backs on me. They knew me and loved me and trusted me.

LK: What would you say to someone going to prison?

JH: I would say, "Don't let them make you waste the time. Find a way to use it. Find a way. If you look around in that prison, you're going to find some place that you can be useful, so that when you wake up in the morning, you have a reason to get up and you know at the end of the day you didn't throw away a day of your life."

LK: So you can keep hope going.

JH: You don't even have to stop and hope. I didn't think about getting out all the time.

LK: You didn't keep a calendar on the wall or—

JH: Oh, no. I was aggravated as I could be by the guards. They drove me crazy, and I reacted very badly to them and got a lot of demerits and charge sheets, but I didn't sit in there thinking, "How many more days before"— That's what you can't do. You've got to find something more interesting than that.

LK: The guards gave you a lot of trouble?

JH: I don't know that it was a lot. They asked me to do stupid things, and I don't like stupid people, and I don't like to be asked to do stupid things by people who have power to make me do it. I'm writing a fourth book right now, and the first chapter is about my getting out. And that last month as a prisoner in the hospital, I had twenty-four-hour-a-day armed guards in my room, and they drove me right up the wall.

LK: They thought you were going to bust out from heart surgery?

JH: Beats the hell out of me. I don't know what they thought. One of them, when I was being operated on, stood outside the door, and the other one prepped with the doctors and stood four feet from the operating table. Now, come on. . . . The taxpayers of New York had to foot that bill.

LK: Boy, if you would have escaped, man—

JH: Yeah, I didn't—

LK: Well, they'd have picked you up because not many people are running around with open chests.

[*Commercial break*]

LK: We're back with Jean Harris, and we go to Stockton, California. Hello.

CALLER: [*Stockton, California*] Hello. I would like to make a statement and then I have a question for Ms. Harris. My statement is, I really commend you, and I think you're one heck of a woman, and good things will happen to you. And my question is, have you thought, or Mr. King thought, about the time factor involved in the O. J. Simpson case? No one has brought up the time factor between the time that she was on the phone and by the time he was supposed to have left. It's virtually impossible—

LK: We don't know—what time was he on the phone, ma'am? We don't know that.

CALLER: [*Stockton, California*] I guess he said, what, 10:17?

LK: How do you know?

CALLER: [*Stockton, California*] Well, that's what they said on the news and everywhere else.

LK: All right, with the news. But we haven't had a trial yet.

JH: That's a question we don't know anything about, so we can't really answer it. I think this is one of the problems of these high-profile trials, is everybody has an opinion, and there's so much garbage being written about it that nobody— Like mentioning the ice cream. They said on the news tonight there was ice cream out there next to the bodies. Well, then they retracted that, and they said the ice cream was in the refrigerator.

LK: How do you feel when you watch it, though?

JH: It drives me crazy, so I don't watch it. Watching Fuhrman drove me crazy, and when the district attorney argued that she couldn't share any of the blood because if she did, they might miss the chance to find some exculpatory material, I thought, "There's a snowball's chance in hell if you find any exculpatory material that anybody's ever going to see it." So I thought, "Oh, boy. That's too much for me. I don't want to watch it."

LK: But you tend to root for the defendant?

JH: I don't root for the defendant. I root for justice, for somebody being really wedded to the truth at these things. This is one of the problems with televising all this stuff, because the public, by and large, has never been through it, so they look at these things the way I walked into my trial, that justice is always done and that a trial is a search for the truth. They do not understand some of the egos that are involved. They don't know what goes on at the sidelines. They have no idea. One person really knows what the truth is, and that's the defendant—if the defendant is guilty. So you sit there, and everybody's got an opinion, and they haven't a right to an opinion, really.

LK: If the defendant is not guilty, then someone out there knows the truth.

JH: That's right. That's right.

LK: Do you favor the crime bill?

JH: No. I think it's an absolute disaster. I guess we need some more policemen, but the idea that $10 billion worth of more prisons is going to help solve anything as far as crime is concerned I think is so naive. . . . What did I read the other day? Cervantes called the public "the honorable legislators." They really determine what the laws are. This "three strikes and you're in" is ridiculous. You know, Pennsylvania, the state of Pennsylvania, already has that, only they have "one strike and you're in." Life in Pennsylvania means you never get out. No parole.

LK: Metairie, Louisiana, with Jean Harris. Hello.

CALLER: [*Metairie, Louisiana*] Yes. Ms. Harris? What I wanted to ask you is, you were apparently very determined to kill yourself, is that true?

JH: I was at one time, yes.

CALLER: [*Metairie, Louisiana*] But, I mean—I mean the night of this tragic accident—

JH: That was the whole purpose of being there, yes.

CALLER: [*Metairie, Louisiana*] Yeah, well, I mean, I'm just—my point is that that's the lowest depression anybody could be in, and you were so determined to kill yourself, it seems to me that once the tragic accident happened with Mr. Tarnower's death, that that would have been even more reason to kill yourself. I was wondering what gave you the will to go on and live.

LK: Good question.

JH: It is a good question, and I was asked that in the trial, too. "If you were so eager to kill yourself, why didn't you do it?" I didn't have a gun, for one thing, and at that point, I was taken right to a psychiatric ward for ten days and—first I was in jail, then I went to a psychiatric ward.

LK: Well, I guess she means right in the room. Tarnower falls. Why didn't you just—?

JH: Because I couldn't get the gun, because Hy got it away from me and that's what—that's when he was killed. I was trying to get it from him. You know, it's too bad to talk about this because this happened a long time ago, and there's so many people in prison or about to go to prison whose cases are just as important as that, and those are the people we should be concerned about.

LK: Did you want to kill yourself, though, after?

JH: Oh, of course I did. Yeah.

[Commercial break]

LK: Placentia, California, with Jean Harris. Hello.

CALLER: *[Placentia, California]* Hello, Larry. I wanted to ask Jean Harris, considering everything you've been through for twelve years, if there was some way that you knew that O. J. was guilty, would you advise him to admit it now and perhaps that would save him and maybe a lot of people a lot of trouble and a lot of stress?

JH: To tell the truth, I would. I think it would be easier for his kids. I think it would be easier for everyone. Besides which, I think he's going to go through all of the money that his children were going to need for their education by paying all these lawyers of his.

[Commercial break]

LK: We only have a minute left, Jean. What's life like in a log cabin?

JH: Oh, it's marvelous. I love it. I really do. There's such peace there. It's really lovely, and my children love it up there because it's a good place to, it's a good pad to have right next to the ski country, so I see quite a bit of them.

LK: How often do you have to report to your parole office?

JH: About once a month. They've been very decent about letting me travel. I've traveled all over the United States, and they even told me I could go to Canada, but then Canada said I couldn't come.

LK: They wouldn't take you in because you're a convicted felon?

JH: They said if I apply in another five years, if they think I'm rehabilitated, they'll reconsider.

LK: It's been a great pleasure having you with us tonight.

JH: Thank you, Larry.

Marlon Brando

Born in Omaha on April 3, 1924, Marlon Brando got into show business as a trap drummer and modern dancer, but went on to become the most important of the so-called "method actors," having made a sensational Broadway debut as Stanley Kowalski in A Streetcar Named Desire *(1947). He repeated the role in the movie version and went on to bring his brooding, introspective male presence to a series of major films.*

Except for increasingly infrequent film appearances, Brando has shunned public attention, but in 1994 his autobiography, Songs My Mother Taught Me, *was published and occasioned this interview—one of the wildest ever to take place on* Larry King Live.

"The idea of being successful and having a lot of money and having all your dreams come true is completely crazy. I've had so much misery in my life, being famous and wealthy."

LARRY KING: We're honored to be here in the beautiful home of Marlon Brando in Beverly Hills, California. His book, *Songs My Mother Taught Me: Brando, the Autobiography*, has been published by Random House. We're going to spend an hour and a half with him. We're going to be taking your phone calls. He's lived in this house how many years?

MARLON BRANDO: Ninety-seven.

LK: Ninety-seven years.

MB: Ninety-seven years.

LK: Explain what you did—don't put me on, Marlon. You put your own makeup on today.

MB: I did, because I wanted to look exactly like you. And—

LK: This was your goal?

MB: This was my goal. I wore some red suspenders in your honor.

LK: Oh, my God.

MB: I did everything I could. And then, now I—I've received some criticism from these people.

LK: They wanted to do you themselves. Well, I'm honored. Do you see my eyebrows that dark, in that way, that dark look?

MB: Yes, yes, a little of the, what do you call it? Who was that guy, that famous Italian guy? Not Ramon Novarro, but the other guy? Oh, the big lover. What was his name? Played the Sheik.

LK: Oh, Valentino.

MB: Yeah.

LK: That's the look you have.

MB: That's right.

LK: Why—I want to touch a lot of bases with you. It's not easy to get—why don't you like interviews?

MB: Well, primarily because the interest is in money. That's the principal guiding feature of all interviews today, is money.

LK: What do you mean?

MB: Well, you know perfectly well what I mean. You know that a story has—that one story is more valuable than another because of the readership. For instance, O. J. Simpson has taken over the airways. You're sweating a little. O. J. Simpson has taken over the—what are you smiling at?

LK: I'm smiling because you just pointed out that I was sweating. I'm Jewish. I sweat. You're part Yiddish. You understand. Okay, and that's money, so you say that—

MB: No. It's been forced, because market forces determine that. . . .

LK: But the question was, why don't you like being interviewed?

MB: Because I don't like the idea of selling yourself for money.

LK: So you don't like selling a book, right? You don't like to go on to sell a book or to sell a movie?

MB: I don't. I don't. I've never sold a movie, and this is the first time I've ever been on, beating the drum for some product. In this case, it's Random House's book.

LK: Because you promised them you would do one?

MB: It was—unbeknownst to me, it was part of the contract. And, if I didn't, I would be in breach of contract. But, aside from that, I have had pleasure talking to you. I'm fascinated with people, especially the kind of people—I wouldn't lump you with others, because you are exceptional.

LK: Thank you.

MB: Because there are many people who have asked me to be on programs, and I've refused. But you—without flattery—I have nothing to gain—you have impressed, I think, all people, and certainly me, as being very forthright, sincere, and direct, and unexploitative.

LK: And now, the subject is you.

MB: No, not necessarily.

LK: Yeah, but in this—

MB: Because the audience really would like to know what it is that makes Larry King tick.

LK: Okay. Well, one night we'll have *Marlon Brando Live*. You'll host it. I'll guest.

MB: That's this night.

LK: No, this night, *you're* the guest. Why did you choose acting as a career? Why did you choose to be other people?

MB: It's useful to make an observation about that, that everybody here in this room is an actor. You're an actor. And the best performances that I've ever seen is when the director says, "Cut," and the director says, "That was great. That was wonderful. That was good, except there was a few—we had a little lighting problem. Let's do it again." What's he's *thinking* is, "Jesus Christ, that's so fucking—" Excuse me. "It's—that's—it wasn't done well, so we've got to do it over." But, everybody tries to handle—When you say, "How do you do? How are you? You look fine," you're doing two things at once. You're reading the person's real intention, you're trying to feel who he is, and making an assessment, and trying to—to—

LK: So the director—

MB: —ignore the mythology.

LK: So, when the director says, "Cut, but I didn't like the lighting," he's acting?

MB: I'm not talking about that. I'm talking about going to the office and saying, "Good morning, Mr. Harrison."

LK: I know, but we're all acting.

MB: And—we're all acting.

LK: You chose it as a profession.

MB: Because there isn't anything that pays you as much money as acting while you are deciding what the hell you are going to do with—

LK: So, wait a minute, are you saying you're still deciding?

MB: It took me a long time to decide. You know, people have never decided. I mean, most people have never decided. I mean, most people, if you ask them what their dreams are—give this guy a Kleenex.

LK: I'll get a tissue in a while. Go ahead. I sweat. We've got hot lights here.

MB: No, we don't. I'm not sweating.

LK: Well, you're Marlon Brando, I'm Larry King. I sweat.

MB: You're a darling man. I don't know. Why do you sweat and I don't?

LK: No, let's get—I don't want to get off—

MB: Why do you escape trying to make one-to-one contact?

LK: I—

MB: Because I'm the product?

LK: Yeah, you're the product. Right.

MB: Okay. Then you answered my first—you answered—

LK: But this is about money, then?

MB: This is about money.

LK: Okay. But it's also about interest and learning.

MB: If I was Joe Schlep, I don't think I'd be sitting here. Even though you might like me, even though we went for a taxi ride, and I was a very interesting guy, I don't know that I would appear on your program.

LK: You are correct. But, you've attained something.

MB: Because of market values.

LK: But you've attained something that people are interested in. That's why there's a market value. That's why they pay you the money to do the film. Okay. So, when Brando goes up on the screen or on the marquee, people will come to see the movie. That's money, and brings money to you.

MB: It's market forces. That's the way it works. If you don't carry demand, you don't get—

LK: Did it come easily to you? So, in other words, you could make money this way.

MB: Acting comes easily to everybody. All I've done is just, simply through the extra-ordinary talents of Stella Adler, who is my teacher and mentor, learned how to be aware of the process. And some people are never, never aware of it. . . .

LK: She taught you how to, what, impersonate?

MB: No. How to be aware of my own feelings. And how to access my own feelings. Many actors can do that. I'm sure you've seen pictures of actors that—I mean, you've seen a performance of an actor who really gave his all, and he was—he was very effective, but he was ugly. He was ugly in the expression of his emotions. Or he was truly being himself, but what he was was boring, or was dull, or was—

LK: All right. So she taught you to take that inner self of you and bring it to a *Waterfront*, or a *Godfather*, or whatever?

MB: I'm not sure of what she taught me. We'd all like to be certain of what we know. But I think the most important question is to ask yourself, do you really know what you know?

LK: Okay. Help me with something, because it's fascinating. Let's say you get a role, it's *The Godfather*. You're not a Mafia kingpin.

MB: Yes, I am. Who are you?

LK: No, no, you're not a Mafia—

MB: Yeah. Well, as a matter of fact, I'm not.

LK: Okay.

MB: There isn't anything that you are, or that you feel, or that you have, that I don't feel, or that I don't have. And so—

LK: But you can bring it into someone.

MB: You can ask an actor, or they will hear, "This is what you get. You get hit with a crowbar in the head, and you get a brain concussion. You're lying there, and you're mumbling." Well, I mumble, anyway.

LK: Okay. So you're saying anyone could do that? No?

MB: Nobody can die. So you have to pretend you're dying.

LK: Okay. Are you saying that when you are the Godfather, you're pretending?

MB: Sure, I'm pretending. . . . I mean, we're going to get lost in vocabulary here, very quickly.

LK: No, we're not. We're learning what you're doing. What do you do? Do you read? You read the script, you like it. By the way, how do you—?

MB: I usually read the script and hate it.

LK: You usually hate it. But you didn't hate *The Godfather*, right?

MB: No, I liked—I wasn't sure that I could do it. And Francis Ford Coppola, fortunately, asked me if I would do a—

LK: Test?

MB: Yeah, a test. I would never play a part that I couldn't do. And if somebody asked me to play Hamlet tomorrow, with Jesus Christ playing Mary Magdalene, I wouldn't do it.

LK: Have you turned down anything you regretted?

MB: That I've regretted? No. No.

LK: Ever taken anything you regretted?

MB: Oh God, taken anything—? You mean swiped stuff?

LK: No, no, no, played a role—"God, I'm sorry I—"

MB: Oh, yes, of course.

LK: Lots of them?

MB: No. Regretted, no. I think to regret is useless in life. It belongs in the past. The only moment we have is right now, sitting here, and talking with each other. You can't see my feet, can you? I forgot to put my shoes on.

LK: It's okay. That's allowed. It's your house. This—that's—this is the moment. We'll come back with more of these moments, okay? I'll take a break.

MB: Okay.

LK: To make money.

MB: All right.

LK: We'll be back with Marlon Brando. The book, by the way is—and he said I don't have to mention it, but I will—*Brando: Songs My Mother Taught Me*, from Random House.

MB: Wait a minute, you *have* to mention—I *have* to mention the book.

LK: You *have* to mention the book?

MB: Yeah, he made an error.

LK: Okay. We have to mention the book. We'll be right back. Don't go away.

[*Commercial break*]

LK: Marlon built half this house, this vista overlooking the entire San Fernando Valley. In fact, if you stand on the roof, you can overlook—

MB: A third. A third.

LK: A third—well, you can see a lot. If you stand on the roof, you get a 360-degree view there. . . . Okay. Back to movies, then we'll touch a lot of bases. I want to talk about the environment, Tahiti, the causes you get involved in—

MB: I'm glad you said that, so we can get off of movies.

LK: I know, but there's certain things I want to—

MB: —most fascinating topic in the world. Oh, there are my shoes.

LK: Do you ever miss theater?

MB: Only when I'm going around 47th Street about eighty miles an hour in a cab, and I—

LK: You say you'd like to be inside—

MB: No, I pass by the Alvin and almost hit it. That's the only time I miss it.

LK: You do not miss being on a stage?

MB: No. God, no.

LK: Why not?

MB: Because it's three hours of blood, sweat, and tears every night. There's nothing to do but, "Blah, blah, blah, blah, blah."

LK: Oh, don't diminish that. . . .

MB: I don't diminish Shakespeare. I can recite Shakespeare from morning until night, until I put you to sleep. I love Shakespeare. But I don't like—I'm not much about going to the theater. It's so awful. In the past, I've gone to the theater and been so bored.

LK: How about working in it, though? I mean, first of all, you get applause. . . .

MB: Who cares about applause? If I get applause from my dog, if I get applause from my children, that's enough. God, do I have to turn into an applause junkie in order to feel good about myself? . . . What about you? Do you need applause? "Larry, that was a great show."

LK: Yeah, I need acceptance.

MB: "Oh, God, I've never seen you so stimulated and so inspired in asking the questions of this person." And you say, "Oh God, *oy, veh ist mir*!"

LK: This Yiddish thing, you got a lot of that in New York, right? You're part Jewish?

MB: Well, technically, I'm not a Jew, but culturally, I am. I spent ten years in New York, and New York—it was when New York was New York, *The Jewish Daily Forward*, and—and Stella very kindly invited me into her home. And my employers, my teachers—I went to the New School of Social Research, which is an extraordinary institution of learning. . . . And it was at a time when all the people were coming out of this extraordinary academia of Germany. And, like Hannah Arendt and—the list is endless.

LK: You read them all?

MB: I did. I never had a chance to take her class. She taught at the New School of Social Research. It was sort of a clearinghouse, until they went on to Princeton or Yale or—

LK: So, at this time, did you realize, even at this young age, "I am doing acting because I can do it. But I want to do other things?"

MB: I studied for a while to be a dancer at Katherine Dunham's school of dance. And I formerly had been a trap drummer, a stick drummer. And I got—I was encapsulated in Puerto Rican music.

LK: Would you rather have been a musician?

MB: I don't know. If the dog hadn't stopped to pee, he might have caught the rabbit. How could I possibly know?

LK: Well, because you know if you love it—

MB: What? I'll do it right now.

LK: A few more things on acting, and then I want to touch other bases. But on acting—

MB: Acting is the most important thing in the world, because—

LK: We all do it.

MB: We all do it, and we do it for a reason. It serves a sociological purpose. And when you think of it, it's an absurd process, because I go, and I pretend that I've got a hole in my leg, and because I'm limping on one side, this girl won't fall in love with me. And her grandmother is trying to arrange—some crazy thing. And people go to a dark room and pay money to see somebody pretend that they've got a hole in their leg.

LK: Now you're making light of it. But in—

MB: I'm not making light of it.

LK: But in pretending you've got the hole in the leg—

MB: Because it is a fundamental process. It's older than whoring. It's older than being a whore, because if you examine the behavior of chimpanzees, or other related ape groups, even—well, you see it in many different animal species, but especially the gorilla. If you look the gorilla right in the face, a grayback—a silverback gorilla, he would most likely attack you, because—and that's not very far from the drunk, who is in—in a bar, when you look at him, he says, "Who the hell you think you're looking at, huh?" And so, either you take your legs off—either you take—

LK: No, but back to the point, though, if you can—

MB: This is precisely the point.

LK: If you can make me understand the man with the hole in the leg, and what that feels like, the pain of the loss of the wife or the grandmother—

MB: We all have related pain. For instance, if I'm sad, you don't know what I'm sad about, and you can say—you can say, in a play, "He's sad because his life is so full of emptiness," or, "He dreads getting cancer of the nose," or something like that. And—

LK: But the energy you bring.

MB: All I have to do is think about something that reminds me of a sadness that I've had in my life.

LK: Okay. And you'll bring that to whether it's a disappointment in *On the Waterfront*, an anger in *The Godfather*, right? Or a scene in *Viva Zapata*? You bring that emotion, that feeling, to whether you're on horseback or on a gangplank.

MB: Or—or, my dear—or, my dear friend, a reasonable facsimile thereof. Because you don't know whether I'm feeling it or not. As long as I can convince you that I am, I have done my job.

LK: Willing suspension of disbelief, right? That's what a good actor makes me do.

MB: No. A willing suspension to believe, not to disbelieve.

LK: To believe?

MB: A willing—I shouldn't say willing—

LK: Well, it's a willing—to disbelieve that that's Marlon Brando, but that is in fact—

MB: A willingness to believe.

LK: Yeah, to believe that you're not Brando. You're the Godfather.

MB: But, you see, it's part of the process, because you pay hard cash. You have to pay the babysitters, you have to pay for the popcorn, you have to pay for the tickets. You have to pay for a lot of things, besides getting robbed on the way to the movie. So—

LK So, you've got to willingly suspend and believe. All right, let me get a break. We'll come back with Marlon Brando. There's lots of other things to talk about.

MB: No, I'm leaving now. It doesn't matter what he says.

LK: No. And we're going to take phone calls. You love Don Rickles, right? Tell them, because—

MB: I love Don Rickles.

LK: He loves Don Rickles.

MB: I want to know how it is that you comb your hair with a washrag so successfully. . . .

[Commercial break]

LK: . . . Okay. Why Tahiti?

MB: Tahiti—one thing that has been very problematic about being an actor and getting some measure of celebrity is the fact that you lose your identity, and everybody calls you, instantly, "Mr. Brando," instead of "Hey, you." And then people make up notions. They want your autograph. And I used to shovel manure from horses and cows for a living. I milked cows, and I've dug ditches, real ditches for Malcolm Ball's father, in Libertyville, Illinois. I was an elevator boy at Best & Company. And I was a short-order cook for a while, and a sandwich man, a waiter.

LK: All right. And then you got famous and rich.

MB: And then your life changes. You don't change, but, suddenly, there's a lot more girls saying, "Hi, Mar."

LK: And that's good, ain't it?

MB: I used to think it was good, until—it took me a while to realize that it was just part of the game. And, I always wanted to be liked for myself, known to myself. So, anyway, long story short . . . I went to Tahiti, where they don't give a damn who you are. The Tahitians are marvelously free. First of all, it's a classless society, and if you put on airs, they just tease the life out of you.

LK: So, ego don't work there?

MB: Doesn't work there. Well, ego works, but not for long, because they tease you so much that you have to—you get rid of it pretty good. . . .

LK: What has fame done to you, if anything?

MB: It's made me feel kind of isolated and a little alone. The society I know and trust are the people I have known for a long time and loved.

LK: Are you happier now?

MB: I'm happy now. Most of the time, I'm happy. I may have a few blips now and then. But it took me a long time to hit my stride.

LK: Were you ever what might be termed depressed?

MB: No. I was never depressed. I was—

LK: Were you—were you ever—

MB: I had trouble—

LK: Mood swings?

MB: No. It wasn't mood swings. I was—I think that I was mostly an angry guy.

LK: At your childhood?

MB: A quick temper. Quick to fight. And I had a bad—bad bringing up.

LK: You had some childhood, right? You had a tough childhood?

MB: Well, it's all relative. There are some guys—one of my very closest friends was Jimmy Baldwin—and I met him when I was eighteen. And we were instant friends.

LK: He had it tougher than you.

MB: He—well, first of all, he was black, which is tough, to grow up in this country. Secondly, he was dominated by his father, who was not such a wonderful man, according to what he told me. And he wanted to be a writer, which at that time was a very—there weren't any black writers. He was one of the first black writers that we had that achieved popularity.

LK: So when you say it's relative, you can look at Baldwin and say, "I had it better than he did?"

MB: I can look at him and say, maybe he had a capacity to deal with life. I know people that have it worse than I have, and they pull through.

LK: All right, but does that make it easier for you, because they had it worse?

MB: It's all relative. It's very, very difficult to say when somebody is brave or when somebody is cowardly, because what might be a brave choice for you, for another person is just—they just simply don't experience fear. So it doesn't mean anything.

LK: Anger—did you use that anger ever in a pro sense? In other words, anger is not a very good thing to have. Did you ever use it, say, in your career, to your benefit?

MB: Well, I suppose acting, you have to be angry at something. You think of something that makes you—

LK: All right. What changed you? What diminished the anger?

MB: Pain. I knew I had to deal with it, and I had to find out why I was angry. We all do. And, as opposed to you, from what we said before, I believe that unless we look inward, we will not ever be able to clearly see outward.

LK: We were talking before we went on the air that I have a difficult time looking inward. Marlon was kind of analyzing this. You can look inward, right? . . . Most people can't.

MB: I have the sense that I can. In any event, the total result is that I have felt much calmer, and I've had moments of real tranquillity since I just put a brake on everything. I've done a lot of meditation, and—

LK: Professional help, too?

MB: I was uselessly psychoanalyzed and exploited by a psychoanalyst. Or maybe sometimes sincerely. I don't want to degrade their intentions. But they make a lot of money getting you, five days a week, to lie down, and say, "I understand that your mother used to like to pinch your blackheads. What does that mean to you?"

LK: Where's your Oscar?

MB: I don't know.

LK: You don't know where your Oscar is?

MB: I think my secretary has it.

LK: George C. Scott said—

MB: I know one guy that has it. But—

LK: George C. Scott said that he doesn't want to ever compete because he thinks competition among actors is wrong, unless all of them played the same part.

MB: I think it's foolish. Originally, I think that the Academy Awards was put together by some very cogent businessmen who thought that they would improve their product if they had a gala and all of that stuff. And that was when Hedda Hopper and—what's the other—

LK: Louella Parsons.

MB: —Louella Parsons were running the show. And it came out of that. And now people take it very seriously. And—

LK: Do you?

MB: No, I don't believe in any kind of award, no matter what it is.

LK: Because?

MB: And I don't believe in any kind of censure.

LK: No censure, no awards?

MB: No.

LK: No awards, why?

MB: Because I don't think that I'm any better than the camera operator, the boom man. I don't think that I'm any better than you are.

LK: But in your profession—

MB: And I don't think that they are better than I am. They all have their personal, intimate—

LK: So, in a Brando world there would be no Emmys or Tonys or award shows?

MB: In a Brando world? I don't know. That's hard to envision. Oh, I suppose, if I were king of the world—

LK: Okay. By the way, did you want good reviews?

MB: I never read reviews.

LK: You know, people say that. That's really true? You've never read—you wouldn't say—if I said to you, "Marlon—"

MB: I have read reviews.

LK: —the *Washington Post* tomorrow gives you a rave—

MB: Yes, I have read reviews. Generally, I don't. And I don't see the movie. Anybody can tell you.

LK: When a movie comes on of yours, like tonight, if it's playing on television, do you watch it?

MB: It all depends on the movie. Some of them bore the hell out of me.

LK: What movie would you definitely watch? What would you say, "This is—"

MB: Oh, there he is.

LK: The dog. What movie would you say, "This is good work?"

MB: Bring him in. I want to—I want you to—

LK: He's got a dog you wouldn't believe. . . . What movie would you say, "Yes, this is good work?"

MB: I tried hard in a movie called *Burn*. . . . It was a movie about slavery and slave rebellion. Come here, Tim. Tim, I want you to meet my friend. Tim, Tim, come here. Tim, over here, right here. Here. This is Tim. . . . Now, sit down, like a good boy. Now, shake hands with Larry. Shake hands. That a boy.

LK: Way to go, Tim.

MB: Good. Isn't that good?

LK: This is what kind of breed?

MB: This is a mastiff.

LK: How heavy is Tim?

MB: Tim is 180—here—

LK: I'm not going to eat Tim's food.

MB: No, I don't want you to eat it. I want you to just—

LK: Oh, feed him.

MB: —put it in your mouth, like this. Here. You're getting nearsighted. I have to get you glasses, like Larry. . . .

[*Commercial break*]

LK: Let's take some calls for Marlon Brando. Montreal, Quebec, Canada. Hello.

CALLER: [*Montreal, Quebec*] Hello, Mr. Brando? Hi. I just wanted to ask you, considering that you are—

MB: What is your name, please?

CALLER: [*Montreal, Quebec*] Natalia.

MB: Natalia.

CALLER: [*Montreal, Quebec*] Yes.

MB: Oh.

LK: Okay, calm down, Marlon. Go ahead, Natalia.

CALLER: [*Montreal, Quebec*] Okay. Considering that you are a very private person, why, after so many years of obscurity, of refusing to be in the spotlight, have you decided to publish your autobiography?

MB: I think that you have misunderstood something. I wouldn't be on that program, on this program—somebody in Louisiana, a woman, I don't know who she was, said anybody who shows his face in public is an ass. And perhaps that's true by some standards. In any event, fate has brought me to his moment.

LK: All right. Her question was, why did a private person write an autobiography?

MB: Oh. I was just explaining to Larry that the reason that I wrote it was, it was an exercise in freedom. I want to be able to say to you or to Larry or to myself anything that I believe to be true. And it's a very, very difficult thing to do, to go through life—and one of the things that, in this culture, money is everything. Money is God. Money is our religion. And, it determines everything we do.

LK: So they paid you to do this. They paid you to do the book.

MB: They paid me $5 million to write the story of my life, but I had decided to do it before.

LK: But you would also do things for nothing. You did a movie for nothing, right?

MB: I did the last—next to last movie I did for nothing.

LK: When I mentioned to you that, last night, Ted Turner and Robert Redford signed a big deal in New York to do movies about the Native Americans, you said you'd work for them.

MB: That's right. I said I'd work for nothing, too.

LK: Why?

MB: Because I believe that we must understand one another, and if we don't, we're going to be in an awful lot of trouble. And I don't think that is enough. I think that we have to alter ourselves in a fundamental sense. And the idea of being successful and having a lot of money and having all your dreams come true is completely crazy. I've had so much misery in my life, being famous and wealthy. And I know so many people—

LK: But how does that equate to the Native American?

MB: The Native Americans are an example of the kind of bifurcation of the Americans' sense of themselves. We committed genocide. We are, by the United Nations' definition, which we were a party to in forming, committing genocide on the American Indian. When all the other countries, France, England, Holland, Italy, all the countries of Europe, all the imperialistic countries, were giving up their possessions after World War II, we applauded softly with gloved hands. And although we say, "Oh, the Indians got a bad deal. They got a raw deal," we have never given one single postage stamp size of earth back to the American Indian.

LK: We've compensated them financially, though, and they now have gambling areas.

MB: That's nonsense, because of the—of the—well, I shouldn't say that. I don't mean to be—but I'm—I don't mind—I mean, we're all hypocrites, in one form or another. But, to have it institutionalized, historialized—what is that word, historialized?

LK: It's a word we just invented. Let me get in another call. I understand where we're going. Louisville, Kentucky, with Marlon Brando. Hello.

CALLER: [*Louisville, Kentucky*] Hello, gentlemen. I have two quick questions to Mr. Brando. What is your opinion of Martin Scorsese and his work? I think he's the greatest. And my brother, Malcolm, wanted me to ask you about *One Eyed Jacks*. He says it's the greatest western of all time.

LK: I loved *One Eyed Jacks*. You directed that movie. Was that fun doing?

MB: I directed it because they couldn't get anybody else to do it.

LK: You worked with your friend Karl Malden?

MB: Oh, I love Karl. We go back to *Truckline Cafe*. But in answer to your question, Martin Scorsese is an inordinately talented person. And he has extraordinary instincts. He's dynamic. He's vibrant. He's real. He has taken film and put it in a much higher and noticeably higher dimension, with Bobby DeNiro and—and—

LK: Your friend, Mr. Pacino.

MB: Well, Al is certainly an accomplished person, a highly developed actor. I forgot his name.

LK: You mean who works with Scorsese?

MB: He played in *Taxi Driver*. How could I forget his name?

LK: DeNiro.

MB: No. Yes, DeNiro, but then, the guy who played the pimp.

LK: Harvey Keitel.

MB: Harvey Keitel. Sorry, Harvey.

LK: How good an actor is Harvey Keitel?

MB: Harvey Keitel is an excellent actor. And he's an actor, like Jack Nicholson, who dares. And Bobby Duvall is another actor who gets out there, and let's say we all fall on our face. But he's willing to try. And he's very good. And the more he goes on, the better he gets.

[*Commercial break*]

LK: Atlanta. Hello.

CALLER: [*Atlanta, Georgia*] Hi. Thanks for taking my call. Mr. Brando, I hope it's not a frivolous question, but I understand you're a ham radio operator, or you were. And I wonder if you'd mind talking about that.

MB: I am a ham radio operator, and the thing I enjoyed about it is—is anonymity, because, when you call up and you say, "This is Marlon Brando calling," they give you the routine, or any famous person. . . . I still am a ham radio operator. As a matter of fact, I'm updating my license. And I think it's wonderful. And with the new international highway of communications that is now very quickly falling upon us, it's going to be tied up with computers. As a matter of fact, I'm on America Online. . . .

LK: What is this here that you wanted to show us?

MB: Oh. I wanted to show you—first of all, I want you to try one of these cookies.

LK: Are they fattening?

MB: It's not going to make you fat. It's not going to do anything. Just give me a reading of what it is.

LK: What it is?

MB: Yeah. You don't have to say it's delicious if it's not.

LK: Delicious. Very chewy and delicious. It's—

MB: I'm going to have one right now, too.

LK: Got sugar. It's a very tasty cookie.

MB: A *bissel* sugar.

LK: A *bissel* sugar. What is the point? Is there something—

MB: It comes from this plant.

LK: It comes from that plant?

MB: Yup. This plant is called salacornia. And this plant—they make paper out of this plant.

LK: The cookie is fantastic.

MB: Here's the paper. This is paper you can write on. Makes very interesting wallpaper. As a matter of fact, I'm going to have it all over my house. This is a picture— can you get a close-up of this? This plant is grown in seawater. It is irrigated in seawater. This—all this area here you see is desert.

LK: But may I ask what got you interested in this?

MB: CO_2. That's—CO_2 is carbon dioxide, which is wrecking our atmosphere; which is, by some scientific estimation, going to turn the world into a kind of heat trap that is going to melt the poles, which means New York goes underwater, London goes underwater, all the lowlands will be flooded, and the Mississippi Valley.

LK: How do you react to those people who say that's, like, wacko environmental poppycock?

MB: Yeah. That's what they used to say about tuberculosis and Pasteur. They said, "He's a nut. Get him out of here. He doesn't know what he's talking about." And everybody now has injections against—

LK: So you are very into the environment. Is this new, or has this—

MB: No, it's not that. It's your kids, and it's my kids. I'm going to live through it. But by the year—if we don't reverse the— Burning down the forests in Brazil has reduced the amount of oxygen that goes into the air. The use of burning fossil fuels, which we have to do for industry—nobody is going to stop that. Nobody is going to stop driving their car—is producing carbon dioxide, which is filling the earth's atmosphere. And if you want to know what the effect is, you get inside your car, you roll up the windows on a hot summer day, and you sit there. You'll be dead in about forty-eight minutes from—what do they call that? . . . You'll be boiled. And that's what's going to happen, because the—the ultraviolet—rather, the—the rays that come through the atmosphere . . .

LK: You're saying this is by the year 2050?

MB: I'm not saying. I'm not putting a date on anything. These are assumptions. Everybody knows that the Malthusian— Malthus was a man who said population is going to increase at this rate. He's right. We are now five billion people. By the year 2020, according to the way things are progressing, we are going to be—we're going to be 10 billion people in this world, 50 percent of which, if not more, are going to live on the sea coasts. Now, I want to make this all fast, and I can't. But these cookies are made from this plant, and this plant is raised and made—

LK: So, in other words, we could live off this plant?

MB: You can live off this plant. Not only this plant, but this plant can grow in any desert. There are 40,000 kilometers—

LK: Let me tell you another thing.

MB: What?

LK: This is one delicious cookie.

MB: It is a good cookie. Here—

LK: I'll have another one.

MB: Have another one. . . .

[*Commercial break*]

LK: We're going to have to do part two of this, because we'll never cover enough tonight. Also, we're going to do a show where I'm the guest. It will be *Marlon Brando Live*, right, and you'll ask questions?

MB: That's correct.

LK: Okay. Now we're going to show you a side of Brando you may not know since *Guys and Dolls*. We're going to do a tune, right? What tune you want to do?

MB: Let's see. What about "Limehouse Blues"?

LK: No, I don't know "Limehouse Blues." You could sing—you want to do "Limehouse Blues"? Do it.

MB: Well, what song do you know?

LK: Well, what's wrong with what we were just doing, "I've Flown Around the World in a Plane"?

MB: All right.

LK: Okay.

[*Both sing*]

LK: Let me take another call. Zurich, Switzerland. Hello.

CALLER: [*Zurich, Switzerland*] This is Sammy from Zurich. It's fascinating to talk to two legends at the same time. Larry, I'm sure that all the free thinkers in the world will agree with me that you deserve a Nobel Prize of your own.

MB: For what? . . .

LK: Do you have a question for Mr. B?

CALLER: [*Zurich, Switzerland*] Yes. Mr. Brando has a political and social agenda sometimes. You defended the American Indians, for example. Have you ever considered a political career in your life, like—

LK: Ever want to run for office?

MB: Yes. Larry has cut you off.

LK: Well, he got to his point. I'm moving him along.

MB: Yes. Okay.

LK: I didn't cut him off, I—

MB: I have been in support of the Jews who came out of the concentration camps, to
try to find a home for them. I was in support of the Indians in America. Four hundred treaties—read them—four hundred treaties have been broken by the
United States government. If one time Cuba said, "I'm sorry, we don't recognize
the treaty of Guantanamo," they'd have the Marines in there in eight seconds.
They'd bomb Havana flat. They'd make a parking lot out of it. Why is it that we
cannot give— One-third of America is owned by the U.S. government. The
blacks in this country have struggled, have fought, have died of misery and broken hearts, perfectly and wonderfully documented by the best writer of the
world, in my estimation, Toni Morrison, in her books. And I think they should be
read everywhere in the world, to have a sense— Don't look at your watch.

LK: I know. I've got to get a break. Hey, we're coming—we're going to do more of
this. We just touched the surface. . . . Have you ever wanted to run for office?

MB: I wanted to run *from* office, but never *for* office. Thank you.

[*Commercial break*]

LK: "Got a Date with an Angel." We're going to do "Got a Date with an Angel."

MB: Okay. Let's get together for this—

LK: All right.

MB: Okay.

[*Both sing*]

MB: You're off key. Darling, good-bye.

LK: Good-bye. Marlon Brando. [*They kiss*]

Oprah Winfrey

The number-one television talk show host in the world, Oprah Gail Winfrey was born, an illegitimate baby, in Kosciusko, Mississippi, on January 29, 1954. She is now one of the richest, most powerful, and most highly respected women in the world. She started on local radio in Nashville and became the youngest woman—— and first African American—to anchor TV news there. After a stint in Baltimore, she moved to Chicago in 1984 as host of A.M. Chicago, *which was nationally syndicated as* The Oprah Winfrey Show *in 1986.*

In 1985, Winfrey was featured in Steven Spielberg's The Color Purple, *for which she earned an Oscar nomination. Since then she has appeared in* The Women of Brewster Place *(1989) and* There Are No Children Here *(1993). The two most burning questions the public has about Oprah Winfrey is why she suddenly refused to release the autobiography she wrote in 1993 and why she doesn't marry Stedman Graham, her boyfriend of ten years.*

"I think you never go beyond color. I never forget that no matter how much money I have, how much so-called 'power,' how many people say I'm powerful, that when I walk into a supermarket, the first thing that they see is a black woman."

LARRY KING: Next year, the Oprah Winfrey show will celebrate its tenth anniversary. We've come to know a lot about its host in the years she's been on the national scene. We've seen her show catapult to the top of the daytime ratings, watched her excellent film work. We have witnessed her weight gains and her losses and seen her realize the dream of completing a marathon. We followed her romance with Stedman Graham, who was there when she finished her twenty-six mile run. Joining us now in Chicago on the set of *The Oprah Winfrey Show*, at her own Harpo Studios, is Oprah Winfrey. . . . Okay. We go back a long way. But Oprah Winfrey once hosted a show in Baltimore, and I had just started the first national radio talk show. It was kind of getting popular. . . . I was invited on, I'm sitting there, and Oprah said, "Who is your favorite person in the whole world?" And I said, "My daughter," and a screen opened—

OPRAH WINFREY: And there she was, Kyah.

LK: There was Kyah. You brought her out. Remember that moment?

OW: I can't believe you still remember that. I mean, it was just a nice thing we wanted to do.

LK: Yeah, but it was such—it was a great gimmick.

OW: I love the fact that you love your daughter so much. I really do love that. Every time I talk to you, and in any conversation, wherever we are, wherever we meet, you always bring her up. I hope my dad does that about me.

LK: Do you want to be a mother?

OW: No—we're in the interview now?

LK: Yeah.

OW: I don't think that I—gosh, I don't think that I am prepared to be a mother, Larry, I really don't.

LK: Why?

OW: I just think that what it takes to do it—I have such respect every day for the people who stay at home and take care of their children. And the older I get, the more respect I get. Now, when I first started in TV and I recognized that, you know, women at home watched our show, and those were the mothers, I used to say it all the time, but I didn't know it the way I know it now.

LK: In other words, you wouldn't do it because you wouldn't be at home. You wouldn't be a good mother?

OW: I don't think I would. I think that what it takes to be a good mother is not what this life that I am leading right now is. I mean, like, right now—you know, Stedman gave me a new puppy for Christmas, and you can bring the puppy to work.

LK: Beautiful puppy. Yeah, you bring him in. You send him upstairs.

OW: That's right, you send him upstairs.

LK: Can't do that with a kid.

OW: But you can't do that with a child. I think that our children are in such—such terrible trouble in this country and that the people who do it right, who can stay at home, if you can stay at home and you can be nurturing, that is the most important job in the world. And I think that the problem is we just pay lip service to that. So all the people who say, "Oh, you could bring the baby to work, and you could have the baby in your life." Well, that's sacrificing the baby, I think.

LK: Daytime television has become kind of like—it's a joke.

OW: It's diseased.

LK: You say daytime television, and you think: *My aunt slept with my sister's boyfriend while I was out with my own mother.* What happened?

OW: Well, I think it really is unfortunate. And I also think that perhaps maybe five, six, ten years ago, when we started, a lot of the subjects that were taboo, bringing up child abuse, affairs, alcoholism, codependency, I think it was necessary to bring some of those things kind of out of the closet. I really do think it's good that we got the country talking. I think it's unfortunate that it's gone to this extreme. I think that it is unnecessary to have shows that are base and that allow people to, you know, fight each other, that bring out just the lowest common denominator of people.

LK: Do you ever watch them?

OW: I really don't. I did over the holiday season, this past Thanksgiving, for the first time. Working out on vacation, I got to see some other people's stuff. And actually, I ended up turning it off, just actually turned it off. I won't name the name of the person, but I was watching a show where I think it—the show was something about one-night stands, people who had one-night stands. And for the first time, I thought, *Well, maybe I'm getting older*, because I'm thinking, *Well, what is the message to the children if you're just doing a show on nothing but one-night stands?* And during this particular show, somebody else's show, the person is brought out, the one-night stands, the reunited one-night stands, and one person didn't remember the other person. And the person was humiliated. And it was just—I just thought—

LK: Why don't the people know that they're props? Because they are props, right?

OW: Well, I think that there are some people who like it. I really do. And I will say that, in the early days of our talk show, I was probably not as sensitive, certainly not as evolved and know as much as I do. I never in my life wanted to exploit or sensationalize or use people. But I think that they are— Because of the way television has become, there are people who like it. You know, it's just—it's theater for them.

LK: So what's the rule for Oprah now? Where is the line drawn?

OW: Well, I've always had lines drawn. There are always things I wouldn't do. Earlier in my career, I was more concerned about not doing anything that would cause any harm. You know, I would say, "Well, we don't want to do this because we don't want that to send the wrong message, and you're speaking to millions of people every day, so let's make sure we don't do anything that causes any harm." I'm now more concerned about using my life and my show to really have a message of goodness. I think, you know, for myself, having evolved emotionally, physically, financially, spiritually, that the spiritual dynamic of life is really the most important thing to me.

LK: What about, though, when Phil Donahue says, as he said—that the name of this game is money. You have to play to that. You have to do that if you want to do daytime talk?

OW: I don't think so. And I don't know if Phil really did say that, because I don't think Phil really—because Phil—you know, there wouldn't have been an Oprah, I don't believe, without a Phil. And, when Phil started—

LK: He's the man.

OW: Yes, he's the man. And when Phil first started out, Phil was the first to understand that the woman at home was an intelligent, sensitive, knowledgeable person who wanted to know more than how to bake toll-house cookies. So, I mean, Phil, in the beginning, really set the standard. Of course, we all know that the standard has changed. But I will say that unless there are those of us who are willing to take a stand—and I think that, of course, everybody says this is the most powerful medium on earth, the vehicle of television—unless you're willing to stand for something, we're all going to fall together. And I do believe that Phil certainly is one of those people who also understands that with the airwaves comes a sense of responsibility.

LK: What do you feel about the competition, Oprah, the Ricki Lakes? Ricki Lake has made a move, they say, based on appealing to younger people watching talk. Do you like competition? Some people like it.

OW: I like it. I'm far more competitive than I ever thought I was. I mean, like, running on the track lots of times, I think I'm not competitive, but if I hear somebody behind me—like this morning there was a guy behind me. He doesn't know that he made me run faster.

LK: I know people like that. You're nuts. So you feel now—you're taking her on?

OW: No, I don't feel that at all. I will have to say that I think the whole— the issue of Ricki Lake and all the other competition has really been sort of created by the media, because I don't know if you really know the facts, but we outnumber our competition 2-to-1. Ricki Lake is not my competition. Really, the number-two talk show to us is *Regis & Kathie Lee*. Hi, Reg, Kathie! They're the number-two talk show. . . . But the truth of the matter is, this past November rating, I think we were down three-tenths of a point from last year. I consider that to be phenomenal, with over twenty talk shows.

LK: And more—there's going to be forty shows.

OW: Going to be forty shows. I think there are too many talk shows. . . .

LK: What drives you when you have it all? I mean, you could, let's be logical, retire.

OW: Yeah, that's why when you talk about money— I mean, I'm certainly not doing this for the money, and I never did it for the money. That's the great thing about this job.

LK: Nobody good at it ever did it for the money. . . . So what drives you here every day?

OW: What really is the driving force for me now are those moments when I know that I've reached somebody. When we did a show this past September, I think, on how to protect your children from strangers, I knew in the middle of that show that I was going to save some children. I *knew* it. There are days when you do shows where maybe you don't know you're going to save a child's life. And we did a show with sisters who were fighting each other and prayed on the air for the sisters. Marianne Williamson prayed on the air for the sisters and said, "If you want peace, you can have it." And we put out the message that you can choose to be right or you can choose to have peace in your life. I knew at the moment we said that that some people would get it and others would not.

LK: So you still want to keep on doing—there's no thought of burning out?

OW: I feel that for as long as I feel that I am being effective, that I'm reaching people's lives in a way that lifts them up—I think that really is one of my callings in life is to lift people up.

[*Commercial break*]

LK: All right, Oprah just mentioned, here's a show helping people who are obviously overweight live with that and get better at it, and all her mail comes in about the dress she was wearing, who designed it, the colors, et cetera. Fame.

OW: Fame.

LK: Look what's happened to you.

OW: It's a trip.

LK: No one has gotten it more than you.

OW: Yeah, actually, I think I get a lot of it. You know, Princess Di, yeah, I think she gets a lot of it, too.

LK: And you're probably the number-one tabloid person.

OW: Yeah, I am.

LK: How do you deal with that?

OW: It used to really bother me. It doesn't anymore. I had a great lesson from Maya Angelou, and at the time she was saying that to me, I couldn't understand. She'd say, "At the time that they sit down to write the tabloid story, you're not involved in that. You don't have anything to do with it. Your life goes on. Your life is going to continue regardless of what anybody says about you. You have to define your life from the inside out." And it took me a while. After a while, after so many stories, after so many rumors, after so many untruths, you just learn to live with it. You know, when I ran the marathon, one of the things that amused me the most was that I had two tabloid reporters running alongside me. They ran the whole way. They had trained to run the marathon, and they were there beside me. And I had—I had to pee from the fourteenth mile on, and I didn't because I didn't want a shot of it.

LK: Why you?

OW: I don't know.

LK: Why do you think?

OW: Why do I think? I think everybody has a calling. Mine just happens to be on television.

LK: There are other people on television who don't get it like you get. You get praised a lot, you get written about a lot, you get loved a lot, but you get rapped a lot.

OW: You know, for the longest time, I wanted to be a fourth-grade teacher, and my goal was, at the time, I was going to be the best fourth-grade teacher there was. And I wanted to, like—I thought I'd be teacher of the year. So I think in anybody's life, if you strive for excellence— I remember being, like, sixteen or seventeen years old, and I heard Jesse Jackson at an assembly program say once that excellence is the best deterrent to racism or sexism. I sort of took that on as my motto. So whatever I ever did, I always wanted to try to be the best at it, and my intention always in my life is I always try to do whatever is going to be the best for other people. For many years, I looked out for other people even more than I looked out for myself. So I think it's—it's intention. It's grace. It really is, a lot of it, just the grace of God.

LK: Do you think you have gone—it's terrible to say this, but it still exists in this country—beyond color?

OW: I think you never go beyond color. I never forget that no matter how much money I have, how much so-called "power," how many people say I'm powerful, that when I walk into a supermarket, the first thing that they see is a black woman.

LK: And you're aware of that, still?

OW: Yes, I'm aware of that. I mean, it just *is*. It's not something that makes me feel anything other than, yes, that *is*. That is a fact. That is a fact for this lifetime for me, that I was born black and female.

LK: Touch some other bases. Why did you say, "I'm going to do a book," then *not* do a book?

OW: Well, at the time I decided not to do the book after reviewing the book—and I thought Joan Bartel, who had worked with me for the past year, had done a terrific job of writing. But I did not feel that the book expressed a sense of empowerment for other people. I thought that it was really wonderfully written in terms of the details of my life and in terms of how I had grown up and what had happened in my career, but I really wanted to write something that I felt was going to leave people with a message of great hope for themselves, and I'm not really prepared to write that book now because I'm still doing that for myself.

LK: Why didn't you just add that, then?

OW: You know, the whole idea of an autobiography, as I looked through it, I thought, it seems so self-centered, so all about me. I'm thinking, really, what I would like for my legacy to be is not, you know, what I did, how many houses I had, how big was the studio, but what was my life able to do for other people. So when I'm able to write *that* book—and also, I felt that I was in the heart of a learning curve for myself. At the time, I was just starting to lose the weight and losing it for the right reason. And up until the time I started to write that book, I was thinking all those years that weight for me was just because I liked French fries, and not understanding that it really was all the years of my abuse, all the years of me not being willing to confront the truth, all the years of me wanting to be a pleaser. All of that should be involved in an autobiography about yourself.

LK: So there will be an autobiography?

OW: I think that there will be a book that will allow people to know and understand who I really am, yes.

LK: Soon?

OW: No, not soon, because I'm still writing my own book. I'm still—

LK: Why are we—the collective we—so involved in whether you get married or not? . . . Why do people ask—you know, people said to me, "Oprah tonight. Why doesn't she get married?"

OW: I really don't know. I really do consider that, like, to be an old issue. I don't really understand it. I think maybe it's because a lot of people are married, and they are happy, or—

LK: Do you have something against the institution?

OW: No, I really don't have anything against it. It's just that neither of us is ready to be. We just aren't. And the relationship works really well without being married right now. And it really bothers me that people think it's either he doesn't want me or I don't want him. And I was so pleased at the time to be asked, because I thought, at least people will know that I got asked. At least they'll know that. But, you know, I see marriage a lot differently than I think a lot of other people see it. I see it as the commitment to work on yourself with somebody and say, "Look, you're going to be there for me no matter what, and I'm going to be there for you no matter what."

LK: You're not ready to say that?

OW: Well, it's not that I'm not ready to say that. I'm saying it now in the relationship. I don't see it as the illusion of living happily ever after or needing it in my life to do anything other than what it really does . . .

[*Oprah* videotape excerpt]
OW: I just heard what you said. You just said, "I don't sit with monkeys." You think because she's black, because I'm black, we're monkeys?

SKINHEAD: That's a proven fact.

OW: That's a proven fact? It's a proven fact that I'm a monkey.

SKINHEAD: Could be.

OW: Go ahead. Go ahead.

SKINHEAD: First thing I want to get off my mind is—

OW: No, I want to talk about this monkey stuff. No, no, no. I want to talk about the monkey business. I want to talk—

LK: Okay, that is very typical of what is on daytime talk all over. That was how long ago?

OW: I don't know, somebody will get the exact year, but I would say at least five or six years ago. But I remember, after that show, it was during the commercial break— they all walked out on me at that show, the Skinheads did. And it was during that show that I thought, *I am never doing this again.* Now, at the time, though, I thought I was doing a service, because I thought exposing racism, hatred at its most vile level, was beneficial to the country, that people needed to know that. Like, the very first time I remember being a young reporter, interviewing the Grand Dragon of the Ku Klux Klan my first time, and being really nervous, because I felt the responsibility of every Jewish person, every black person, every Catholic— "I'm going to get him," thinking that this was my—this— "Now I'm going to make them feel responsible for what they've done to us all these years." Television is not the forum in which to do that. What I realized, doing shows like that, is what you're doing is giving this person a forum in order to spread their own hatred. And, so, let them do it someplace else.

LK: And you're also using him.

OW: Yes. And you're using—

LK: —know that that's exciting stuff to watch, and people like seeing it, right?

OW: That's right.

LK: So he's a prop to you, too.

OW: But, you know, at the time I really didn't think of it as a prop. But now, as I'm older, I say, yes, of course.

LK: So, are you embarrassed looking at it, or is it just like, that was yesterday?

OW: No. I'm not embarrassed looking at it. I say, that's what I needed to do to get to where I am right now. One of the things that I love is that you can look back at your life and say, you know, "I did in my twenties, I did in my thirties what I knew how to do. When I knew better, I did better."

LK: You may have been the first person to introduce—you and Phil [Donahue]— abuse to this country, right? Talking about abuse. . . .

OW: I was probably the first person—because I don't think Phil was abused—to discuss my own. . . . And I remember one day bringing it up, not because I thought— I certainly didn't know it was going to be, like, get the attention that it did. I didn't want the person who was on talking about it thinking that I was just trying to be a voyeur. I really just said, "Look, this happened to me, too." I remember in Baltimore, years ago, the first time I ever heard somebody talk about it on TV. I couldn't believe that it had happened to somebody else. And I was so tempted then—I was twenty-two years old the first time I heard it. And I hadn't told anybody about my own. And I—and I was like—I wanted to meet with the woman afterwards but didn't have the nerve to say, "This happened to me, too." So, years later, when I had the confidence on my own show to do it, I did it.

LK: Sometimes people look back and say, you know, "That bad thing that happened to me—" like, I had a heart attack, it made me stop smoking. That turned into a good heart attack.

OW: I think all things can turn into good things, if you let them.

LK: Is there anything good about abuse?

OW: Well, I think it's made me stronger now. I don't think that there's anything good about abuse when you're going through it. . . . I think it's a national shame, is what it is. . . .

LK: Why is it so around?

OW: I think it happens more than it doesn't happen.

LK: And it must have always happened. It's not a new phenomenon.

OW: And it has always happened. And I think that if my show or anybody's show has served any purpose in the world to bring that out of the closet, then that's really good. If we got kids talking about it or women who are battered talking about it, then I think that's really good. But, you know, I'm really at a place right now, both personally and professionally, I understand, yes, we have been abused, yes, we are dysfunctional. What in the hell are we going to do about it? We have to take responsibility for our own lives. And that's really where I am with myself and also with the show, trying to get people to see that, trying to get them to connect with that.

LK: You also give away a lot of money now, don't you?

OW: Well, yeah, but money is an easy thing to give away. You know what I did that I am the most proud of for myself? You didn't ask, but I'm going to tell you. I started a program called Families for a Better Life. . . . And you know, a lot of people talk about the money. And at this point, you can't give enough money, and if you give money, then they say, "Oh, well, it's easy for you to give money." But what I think I'm giving is a sense of a belief in themselves, for people to believe in themselves.

LK: You're giving the fishhook, not the fish.

OW: That's right. To take families out of the projects and get families jobs and get families working and work with them on a one-on-one basis so that you can break the cycle of poverty, that's the most important thing because you can take—you can *buy* anybody a house. I've done it—you know, I've done it in my own family. Buying a house doesn't mean anything. It is how you change the way people think. Breaking the cycle of victimization is what I'm trying to do . . .

LK: Okay. Before we start phone calls, this weight thing—

OW: What about it, Lar?

LK: What's with—what's with this gyration?

OW: I'm kind of over it. I'm over that.

LK: You're a skinny person now?

OW: Well, I wouldn't say I'm a skinny person now. I still work every day, very hard. I ran five miles this morning. Like I said, the guy on the track doesn't know he helped me out. And every day, I have to renew myself.

LK: So, this is a job every day?

OW: It's a job every day.

LK: Or you'd be fat?

OW: Or I would be fat.

LK: Okay. How much of a help has Rosie been?

OW: She's been terrific. She's in the kitchen.

LK: Rosie, the cook.

OW: Sold six million books already, but she's still in the kitchen. Made me lunch today.

LK: Okay. Do you want to run off and get that pizza?

OW: Oh, I have run off and gotten pizza. Are you kidding?

LK: But then, when you have it, do you think—

OW: No, then I just have to work harder. It's not like I'm just eating— I don't eat low-fat all the time. Matter of fact, I was on one of the tabloids—this is so interesting—I was on vacation in Hawaii, and the tabloids arrive. Usually it takes them a couple of days to arrive, so I know I got two days.

LK: You greet them?

OW: No, I never talk to them. I know they're there, though. I know when they get there, and they're in the bushes and everywhere taking pictures. Now, the worst thing is to see your picture on—so you never know when they're there. You're on the cover of a national tabloid, and you're eating, and nobody looks good eating. But, anyway, I remember thinking, *I won't have the pineapple upside-down pancakes*, and the first thing I think: *Damn it, I should have had those pineapple upside-down—*

LK: Might as well eat them.

OW: Might as well eat them. Everybody *thinks* I did. Yeah.

LK: Let's go to calls. Fort Bragg, California, for Oprah.

CALLER: [*Fort Bragg, California*] First of all, I want to thank you for all the work that you've been doing with domestic violence, and particularly the tape I saw about a month ago on the effects of children who live with domestic violence.

OW: Wasn't that good?

CALLER: [*Fort Bragg, California*] Yes, it was excellent. It touched me deeply. I have the honor of working with battered women and their children, and that particular tape deeply touched me.

OW: Thank you.

LK: Do you have a question?

CALLER: [*Fort Bragg, California*] Yes, my dream is to have some time with you by myself. Anyway, who has been one of the greatest influences of your life so far?

OW: That's a—that's a good—well, I would—Maya—Maya Angelou. You know, when I grew up and I first read *I Know Why the Caged Bird Sings*, I thought she was talking about my own life. So, I grew up reading and relating to books and authors and never imagined in my life—I have the most graced life, my God—that I would end up in a mother/daughter/sister/friend relationship with Maya Angelou. So she's had a tremendous impact on me.

My fourth-grade teacher, Mrs. Duncan, because for so many years, I wanted to be a fourth-grade teacher, because what she did was not just teach me long division, but really, that's where I learned to love learning, in the fourth grade. You know, throughout life I believe that all of us are brought to the light by people in our lives. Nobody gets to be anywhere in their life, of any note or success, without some other people who bring you along. . . .

LK: Dordrecht, the Netherlands. Hello.

CALLER: [*Dordrecht, Netherlands*] Hello, Oprah. First of all, I want to wish you a Happy New Year. . . . I think your show is great.

OW: You're watching in the Netherlands. That's always a thrill to me.

CALLER: [*Dordrecht, Netherlands*] I wanted to ask you how you got the energy to get through the whole marathon.

OW: It was the training. You know what, I think that's one of my great physical accomplishments. And that is not the actual running of the marathon in the rain in Washington, D.C., that day, but it is the twenty weeks prior to that, the discipline that it took to do that, is what I am most proud of. And it is the preparation. Just like in anything in life, it is how you prepare for it that allows you to be able to execute.

LK: Was there ever a moment when you wanted to stop?

OW: Yeah, there are moments when I would have wanted to stop, but I knew from the beginning that I would not be stopping. I didn't stop once, not once. Not even to Wee Willie Winkle did I stop. Yeah.

LK: Your show is now syndicated out of the country?

OW: Yes, we're in one hundred ten countries. Not—

LK: We're kind of used to that here.

OW: Not two hundred. Let me tell you this, we were in South Africa for Christmas, and we were at the Ingala Range Reserve, and we have the tracker, who is a black man, who is really one of the most powerful black men I have ever seen, because I thought, here in his own country, doing what he loves, tracking lions in front of the Jeep. I was asking him about Michael Jordan, and he didn't know who Michael Jordan was and was asking me to explain who Michael Jordan was. Of course, he didn't know who I was, either, so I wasn't going to bring *that* up. But he asked me if I knew Larry King. Larry King! I said, "Yeah, I kind of know him. But you don't know who Michael Jordan is." So I think the fact you—the fact that you are in a little village in Botswana, and the tracker who doesn't know who Michael Jordan is knows who you are, that just blows my mind.

LK: Blows mine, too. . . . Black girl, Jewish guy—sitting here, talking to the world.

OW: It's amazing. But we're in one hundred ten countries. . . .

LK: Something bugging me.

OW: What?

LK: How could you be as good an actress as you are—

OW: And not act.

LK: —and not act?

OW: That bugs me, too.

LK: Why not?

OW: Well, I have this day job.

LK: Yeah, but come on. . . . You have to do—don't you want to do more films?

OW: I really do want to do more films, and I'm doing something with Ted, with Ted Turner. I'm doing something this summer . . .

[*Commercial break*]

LK: Your fate, you talk about it a lot. Do you believe you're going on to something after this?

OW: I believe that we all are, whether you believe it or not.

LK: And it will be a conscious thing we're going to?

OW: When you go on? Yeah, I believe that. I believe that life is eternal. I believe that it takes on other forms. And I believe that there's so many different levels that the mind can't even hold it all. So I believe that, yes, life will continue.

LK: Minneapolis for Oprah. Hello.

CALLER: [*Minneapolis, Minnesota*] Hi, Larry. Hi, Oprah. How do you feel, Oprah—and did you know about being voted the fifth most admired woman in the world, as was reported by CNN recently? I think you're number one, by the way.

LK: When you hear something like that, what does it do?

OW: Well, that always makes me feel good, because it means that, I guess, I'm moving in the right direction. But, you know, Larry was talking earlier about this fame thing, and I just—you know, my theme for the show is "I'm Every Woman," because I think my life is more like other people's, in spite of all the fame that has come to me.

LK: You're kidding?

OW: I really do.

LK: More like other people?

OW: I really do.

LK: In what way?

OW: I think the external part of my life, I mean, where I live and, you know, what I drive, and what kind of panty hose I wear and can afford, and that kind of stuff—but I really do know that none of that stuff, in the end, means anything. The thing that I'm most proud of myself about is that I have acquired a lot of things, but not one of those things defines me. I feel that I am the same person I was when your daughter, Kyah, came out on the show twenty years ago. And I feel like I am that same person. All of the stuff I read—you know, I'll look at magazines or tabloids, and it's just—it feels like something outside of myself. It doesn't feel like me. It doesn't feel like the heart of who I am.

LK: Like you're looking at someone else. It's weird. Fame does that.

OW: Yes. This is weird, because you feel like you're the same person.

LK: Because you're still *you* inside. How old are you inside of you?

OW: Twenty-eight.

LK: That's old. . . . You are twenty-eight?

OW: I'm twenty-eight inside of me, yeah.

LK: You've matured. I mean, that's a lot—that's old. . . . Most people say nineteen.

OW: No, I'm twenty-eight because it was at about twenty-eight that I had one of those epiphanies, because I had, you know, been in television since I was seventeen, nineteen years old. And it was at about twenty-eight that I realized, oh, this just doesn't happen to everybody.

LK: Who do you want to have, Princess Di? Is she the one everyone—

OW: Well, you know, I'd love to do her. Wouldn't you like to do her?

LK: She wouldn't be number one, no.

OW: She would not?

LK: No. I'd like to do Al Pacino.

OW: Really?

LK: I'm fascinated.

OW: Do you want to do O. J.?

LK: Sure.

OW: Yeah, I do too. Sure.

LK: Why Princess Di? Other than you know it's going to get ratings through the roof, what fascinates you about her?

OW: Well, I think—what fascinates me about her, I think she's even more interesting now that she's now not married to—well not—you know, the situation is what it is. Because she is the classic example of the woman who had everything. She— the princess, the crown, the castle, and was still, with all of that external stuff, not able to attain happiness. She's a classic example of how you have to work from inside yourself.

LK: Because royalty can't interest you a great deal.

OW: Oh, please, no. But it just is a fascinating thing about how you have to work on yourself with all of that, a palace, everything.

LK: The slipper.

OW: The slipper. The slipper. She is Ms. Cinderella, and still had to come to terms with, *Who am I really? What does all of that mean?* I think she's a great example to women all over the world.

[Commercial break]

LK: It goes without saying of course, that we would love to have Princess Di on, in case she's calling to go with Oprah.

OW: She's probably watching you right now.

LK: I love her.

OW: Yeah. Everybody knows you all over the world.

LK: Okay. You're jealous, aren't you?

OW: Well, no. I think it's terrific. It's really—

LK: I love Princess Di. She's so pretty.

OW: Charming, too. Charming.

LK: Yeah.

OW: And also, what we were talking about during the break, when y'all weren't listening here is that my reason for wanting to interview her would be totally different than yours, because I think that I speak to the masses of women, because—women and men, but women more so because I am a woman and I identify with that. And I just think that so many women struggle with their own identity, and women believe that if they get that glass slipper, they get the prince, they get the house, everything is going to be okay. And she is proof that it isn't.

LK: Why don't you and I go over to London, do her together, you talk about your things, I talk about mine, right?

OW: And bring Al Pacino along.

LK: We'll bring Al Pacino along to close it.

OW: Yeah, to close it.

LK: Belfast, Northern Ireland. Hello.

CALLER: [*Belfast, Northern Ireland*] I just wanted to tell Oprah I really admire her. She's an inspiration. She's making me think of doing more things. I just wanted to know what her plans were for her program for the future. We just started getting it here in the U.K.

LK: They just started getting it in Northern Ireland.

OW: You just did?

LK: What are they going to see next week?

OW: So, am I blowed up or not?

LK: Is she fat or skinny?

CALLER: [*Northern Ireland*] Oh, you look gorgeous.

LK: Gorgeous.

OW: That could be fat or skinny.

CALLER: [*Northern Ireland*] No, no, you look good. You look terrific. You look—

LK: You're going to see her dog on Monday.

OW: Well, what are you asking? What do I plan to do for the show? I try to use this show as a voice for raising consciousness, for doing good, for letting people see themselves in a way that makes their lives better. So that's what I intend to continue to do with the show. You know, we're so thrilled to hear from you. We're just glad you're out there.

LK: Riverdale, New York, with Oprah. Hello.

CALLER: [*Riverdale, New York*] Hi, guys. How you doing? Oprah, I wish—I'd rather tell you this stuff off the air, because I'd rather do it that way. But I'll never get that chance. I'm a big fan of yours, but—and I think you're real well-intentioned and real nice—but I think there's two things you do that are really unfair to your audience and to the people who watch your show.

OW: That is?

CALLER: [*Riverdale, New York*] I think when you have Maya Angelou on and Marianne Williamson, and you never challenge them on anything. And I think there's like, some really bad things about them. Marianne Williamson, her stuff wouldn't apply to people who are dying in Somalia. You want—I think it leads people to inaction and not to take responsibility for their own lives. . . . And Maya Angelou is involved with all these black Republican conservatives, like—

LK: All right, that's a fair question. Do you think that you don't criticize guests enough, or is that not true?

OW: No, I don't think so. You know, I would really love to have this discussion with you on the air or off the air, and I wish we had more than three minutes in which to do it. I think you completely misunderstand Maya Angelou and Marianne Williamson if you think that what they're talking about is inactivity, because, more than anybody, I think those two people are saying the reason why there are starving children in Somalia is not because, you know, God said the children should starve. The children are starving in Somalia because the people of the world *allow* them to starve. Because nobody in this world has to starve. Nobody in the world has to starve.

LK: We're running close on time. . . . It's zero degrees outside.

OW: It's horrible here, isn't it?

LK: Why do you continue to want to live—I mean, Chicago is a great city.

OW: Well, because I built the studio here. I built it here, and I'm staying here. I feel committed to the city. And you know what—

LK: And you may be trapped here.

OW: You know what, if it wasn't twenty below zero wind-chill outside, everybody in the world would live here, because this is the greatest city in the world.

LK: So it's good that it's twenty below.

OW: Greatest city in the world, except for the weather.

LK: Thanks, Ope. . . .

OW: It's over?

LK: It's over.

OW: It's over. Thank you.

LK: Goodnight. Say goodnight.